T0176826

Practical Java®
Programming for IoT, AI,
and Blockchain

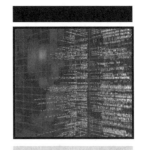

Practical Java®
Programming for IoT, AI,
and Blockchain

Dr. Perry Xiao

WILEY

Practical Java® Programming for IoT, AI, and Blockchain

Published by
John Wiley & Sons, Inc.
10475 Crosspoint Boulevard
Indianapolis, IN 46256
www.wiley.com

Copyright © 2019 by John Wiley & Sons, Inc., Indianapolis, Indiana

Published simultaneously in Canada

ISBN: 978-1-119-56001-2
ISBN: 978-1-119-56000-5 (ebk)
ISBN: 978-1-119-56003-6 (ebk)

Manufactured in the United States of America

C10011609_062419

No part of this publication may be reproduced, stored in a retrieval system or transmitted in any form or by any means, electronic, mechanical, photocopying, recording, scanning or otherwise, except as permitted under Sections 107 or 108 of the 1976 United States Copyright Act, without either the prior written permission of the Publisher, or authorization through payment of the appropriate per-copy fee to the Copyright Clearance Center, 222 Rosewood Drive, Danvers, MA 01923, (978) 750-8400, fax (978) 646-8600. Requests to the Publisher for permission should be addressed to the Permissions Department, John Wiley & Sons, Inc., 111 River Street, Hoboken, NJ 07030, (201) 748-6011, fax (201) 748-6008, or online at http://www.wiley.com/go/permissions.

Limit of Liability/Disclaimer of Warranty: The publisher and the author make no representations or warranties with respect to the accuracy or completeness of the contents of this work and specifically disclaim all warranties, including without limitation warranties of fitness for a particular purpose. No warranty may be created or extended by sales or promotional materials. The advice and strategies contained herein may not be suitable for every situation. This work is sold with the understanding that the publisher is not engaged in rendering legal, accounting, or other professional services. If professional assistance is required, the services of a competent professional person should be sought. Neither the publisher nor the author shall be liable for damages arising herefrom. The fact that an organization or Web site is referred to in this work as a citation and/or a potential source of further information does not mean that the author or the publisher endorses the information the organization or website may provide or recommendations it may make. Further, readers should be aware that Internet websites listed in this work may have changed or disappeared between when this work was written and when it is read.

For general information on our other products and services please contact our Customer Care Department within the United States at (877) 762-2974, outside the United States at (317) 572-3993 or fax (317) 572-4002.

Wiley publishes in a variety of print and electronic formats and by print-on-demand. Some material included with standard print versions of this book may not be included in e-books or in print-on-demand. If this book refers to media such as a CD or DVD that is not included in the version you purchased, you may download this material at http://booksupport.wiley.com. For more information about Wiley products, visit www.wiley.com.

Library of Congress Control Number: 2019942852

Trademarks: Wiley and the Wiley logo are trademarks or registered trademarks of John Wiley & Sons, Inc. and/or its affiliates, in the United States and other countries, and may not be used without written permission. Java is a registered trademark of Oracle America, Inc. All other trademarks are the property of their respective owners. John Wiley & Sons, Inc. is not associated with any product or vendor mentioned in this book.

This book is dedicated to my family. To my wife, May, my son, Zieger, and my daughter, Jessica, who make my life complete—without them, life would be meaningless. To my parents and my brother, who have shared their life and love with me that ultimately made me what I am today. To my friends and colleagues, who supported me throughout my career.

About the Author

Dr. Perry Xiao is an associate professor and course director at the School of Engineering, London South Bank University, London, United Kingdom. He got his BEng degree in Opto-Electronics, MSc degree in Solid State Physics, and PhD degree in Photophysics. He is a chartered engineer (CEng), a Fellow (FIET) of the Institution of Engineering and Technology (IET), and a Senior Fellow (SFHEA) of the Higher Education Academy (HEA). He has been teaching electronics, software, computer networks, and telecommunication subjects at both undergraduate and postgraduate levels for nearly two decades. He is also supervising BEng final project students and MSc project students every year. His main research interest is in developing novel infrared and electronic sensing technologies for skin bioengineering applications and industrial nondestructive testing (NDT). To date, he has finished seven PhD student supervisions, received two UK patent applications, published more than 100 scientific papers, been editorial reviewer for nine journals, and generated nearly £1 million in research grants.

He is also a director and cofounder of Biox Systems Ltd., United Kingdom, a university spin-off company that designs and manufactures state-of-the-art skin measurement instruments, AquaFlux and Epsilon, which have been used in more than 200 organizations worldwide, including leading cosmetic companies, universities, research institutes, and hospitals.

Acknowledgments

I would like to express my sincere gratitude to Wiley Publishing for giving me this opportunity. I would also like to thank Peter Mitchell, Devon Lewis, Pete Gaughan, Athiyappan Lalith Kumar, Evelyn Wellborn and Compton Editorial Services for their support. Without them, this book would be not possible.

Contents

Preface

I had my first programming experience when I was studying at Jilin University of Technology, China, in the 1990s. At that time, we were using mainframe computers, as personal computers (PCs) were not available in China. A mainframe computer is just one computer sitting somewhere in a room, and we connected to it through text-mode dumb terminals. As we connected to the mainframe computer using a shared account, a lot of strange things could happen. The program you created early on could be deleted or modified by someone else later. Printing was also a nightmare. For example, when you were printing your Fortran code, halfway through another student might send a printing request. The printer would immediately stop printing your code and start to print the other student's code. When finished, the printer would come back to resume printing the rest of your code. What kind of logic is that? So every time we wanted to print, we would shout "I am printing!" and hope others would not start to print their code at the same time. The programming language we used was Fortran, short for "formula translation." Fortran is primarily designed for scientific calculations, and it is a very powerful language, but the Go To statement drove me crazy. It makes the code very difficult to read.

Later, when IBM PCs started to become available, our university also bought some IBM PCs and built a dedicated two floor building to host these computers. Yes, you heard me, a whole building was dedicated to these IBM PCs. The building was designed like a clean room, with red carpeting, and reception.

You needed to take off your shoes, change into slippers, and wear a white lab coat to go in. The time for each student to use these computers was strictly limited.

Have you ever wondered why computer hard drives always start with Drive C, and not Drive A or Drive B? The reason is that in the beginning, IBM PCs did not have hard drives; instead, they had two 5¼ inch floppy drives. To use the computer, you needed two floppy disks—one floppy disk for the MS-DOS operating system, used to boot up the computer, and one floppy disk for saving your data. Each floppy disk could hold 512 KB of data. It could not fit even as much as a smart phone photo today. But that time, it was plenty. We started to learn the BASIC (Beginner's All-purpose Symbolic Instruction Code) programming language. BASIC is very simple to use, and we had endless fun with BASIC programming for both scientific calculations and drawing text based pictures.

I started to learn Java in 1997, just two years after it was first released by what was then Sun Microsystems, now part of Oracle Corporation. Since web pages at that time were pretty much just static text and static pictures, I was fascinated with Java's ability to create animations (Java Applets) inside a web page. But the time when I really fell in love with Java and fully appreciated its beauty was a few years later. I was preparing for an MSc module on Java network programming, and I was astonished by how simple it was to learn and use Java, especially for network programming. With just a few lines of Java code, you have a server!

I was also impressed with Java's memory garbage collection ability and the fact that Java has no pointers. C and C++ programmers, you'll be relieved to learn there are no pointers in Java! I had a tough time before Java, when I was using the C programming language for finite difference analysis and finite elements analysis. Pointers are variables to point to particular positions in memory, and they are essential for working with matrices. Ninety-nine percent of the time my programs crashed because of the mishandling of pointers. So I was over the moon when I heard there were no pointers in Java. Hallelujah! There is also no Go To statement in Java, which makes the Java code much easier to understand.

Java's exception handling is also worth mentioning. Java can "throw" exceptions. So when you run a program, if an exception/error occurs, for example, division by zero, reading a file that does not exist, or connecting to a remote computer that is not responding, instead of hanging the program or crashing the entire computer, Java will simply terminate the program and gracefully display an error message.

I have since developed many Java programs for teaching and researching. I have thoroughly enjoyed working with Java programming language, and I hope you will enjoy it too.

Dr. Perry Xiao
November 2018, London

Introduction

We are now living in an era of digital revolution. On the horizon, many emerging digital technologies, such as IoT (Internet of Things), AI (Artificial Intelligence), Cyber Security, Blockchain, and more are being developed at breathtaking speed. Whether we like it or not, whether we are ready or not, these digital technologies are going to penetrate deeper and deeper into every aspect of our lives. This is going to fundamentally change how we live, how we work, and how we socialize. Java, as a modern high-level programming language, is an excellent tool for helping us to learn these digital technologies, as well as to develop digital applications.

The aim of this book is to use Java as a tool to help readers to learn these new digital technologies, to demystify these digital technologies, and to be better prepared for the future.

How This Book Is Organized

This book is divided into three parts. Part I provides a basic introduction of Java programming language and gets readers started with Java programming. The chapters in Part II provide Java examples of conventional programming topics like console applications, Windows applications, network applications, and mobile applications. All of that is preparation for Part III. These chapters are the core of the book, providing an easy to read guide for the latest digital technologies (IoT, AI, Cyber Security, Blockchain, and Big Data), illustrated with Java programming examples.

Part I

Part II

Part III

Appendices

Downloading the Code Examples

All the example source code is available on the website that accompanies this book.

Who This Book Is For

This book is intended for university/college students, as well as software and electronic hobbyists, researchers, developers, and R&D engineers. It assumes that readers have a basic understanding of computers and a computer's main components such as CPU, RAM, hard drive, network interfaces, and so on. Readers should be able to use a computer competently, performing basic tasks such as switching on and off the computer, logging in and out, running some programs, and copying/moving/deleting files. It also assumes that readers have some basic programming experience, ideally in Java, but optionally also in other languages such as C/C++, Fortran, MatLAB, C#, BASIC, or Python, and that they know the basic syntax, the different types of variables, standard inputs and outputs, the conditional selections, and structures like loops and subroutines. Finally, it assumes that readers have a basic concept of computer networks and the Internet, and can use some of the most commonly used Internet services such as the World Wide Web, email, file download/upload, and online banking/shopping. This book can be used as a core textbook as well as a supplemental textbook.

What This Book Is *Not* For

This book is not for readers just want to learn Java programming language; there are already a lot of good Java programming books on the market. However, in order to make the information here accessible to as many programmers as possible, the first three chapters provide a basic introduction to Java and show how to get started with Java programming; so even if you have never programmed Java before, you can still use the book. If you want to learn all technical details of Java, please refer to the following suggested prerequisite reading list and to Appendix A for more books and resources.

Suggested Prerequisite Reading

The following sources will be helpful if you need more background to get up to speed on any of the topics covered in this book.

Computer Basics

Absolute Beginner's Guide to Computer Basics, 5th Edition, Michael Miller, QUE, 2009.
   Computers for Beginners (Wikibooks)

    https://en.wikibooks.org/wiki/Computers_for_Beginners

Java Programming

Head First Java, 2nd Edition, Kathy Sierra, Bert Bates, O'Reilly Media; 2005.
   Effective Java, 3rd Edition, Joshua Bloch, Addison-Wesley Professional, 2017
   Java: A Beginner's Guide, 6th Edition, Herbert Schildt, McGraw-Hill Education; 2014

Java: The Complete Reference, 9th Edition, Herbert Schildt, McGraw-Hill Education; 2014.

Java Programming (Wikibooks)

https://en.wikibooks.org/wiki/Java_Programming

Networking and the Internet

Computing Fundamentals: Digital Literacy Edition, Faithe Wempen with Rosemary Hattersley, Richard Millett, Kate Shoup, ISBN: 978-1-118-97474-2, 2014.

Understanding Data Communications: From Fundamentals to Networking, 3rd Edition, Gilbert Held, ISBN: 978-0-471-62745-6, 2000.

Communication Networks (Wikibooks)

https://en.wikibooks.org/wiki/Communication_Networks

The Raspberry Pi

Raspberry Pi For Dummies (For Dummies (Computers)), 3rd Edition, Sean McManus and Mike Cook, John Wiley & Sons, 2017.

What You Need

To work through the examples in this book, you will need the following:

- A standard personal computer with minimum 124MB hard drive, 128MB RAM, Pentium 2 266 MHz processor, running Windows operating systems (Vista/7/8/10 and Internet Explorer 9 and above) or Linux operating systems (Ubuntu Linux 12.04 and later, Oracle Linux 5.5 and later, Red Hat Linux 5.5 and later, etc.). You can also use a Mac computer (with Mac OS X 10.8.3 and later, administrator privileges for installation, 64-bit browser).

- Java JDK software (http://www.oracle.com/technetwork/java/javase/downloads/index.html)

- Text editors and Java IDEs (see Chapter 2)

- Raspberry Pi (https://www.raspberrypi.org/) (optional)

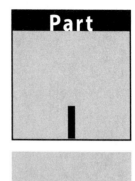

Part

I

In This Part:

Introduction to Java

"Experience is simply the name we give our mistakes."

—Oscar Wilde

1.1   What Is Java?

Java is a high-level, object-oriented, general-purpose programming language that was originally developed by James Gosling, a Canadian computer scientist, at what was then Sun Microsystems, in the U.S. state of California in 1991. Sun Microsystems was later acquired by Oracle Corporation, also in California, in 2010. Java was a byproduct of Sun's "Green" project, and it was originally designed as a platform-independent language for programming household electronic appliances. However, Java was too advanced for such applications. Gosling designed Java syntax based on the C and C++ languages, but with fewer low-level facilities. Java was named after the popular Indonesian Java coffee.

Java first appeared in 1995, through the HotJava and Netscape web browsers, as a plug-in called Java Applets, which could add dynamic content and interactions to static, pale web pages. Java soon became popular with all the major web browsers incorporating the ability to run Java applets. You've probably seen the famous Java logo, a cup of hot coffee, along with the Java mascot, Duke. Today, after decades of effect, Java has been developed into a fully functional, multi-purpose, and powerful language suitable for both individual and enterprise users. Java is different from JavaScript, which is a script language that runs only within a web browser.

The Java language has five main principles; it was designed to be all of the following:

- Simple, object-oriented, and familiar
- Robust and secure
- Architecture-neutral and portable
- High-performance
- Interpreted, threaded, and dynamic

The main advantage of Java is its platform independence; that is, programs written in the language can be "write once, run anywhere" (WORA). This independence is achieved through the concept of the Java Virtual Machine (JVM), illustrated in Figure 1.1. With conventional programming languages like C/C++, to run on different operating systems such as Windows, Mac, and Linux, the C/C++ source file needs to be compiled separately on each operating system. Because each executable file runs in its native operating system, the executable files compiled in one operating system cannot run in another operating system. Java works differently. The Java source code (a .java file) is compiled into Java *bytecode* (a .class file). The bytecode files are not executable files and cannot run directly in the operating system. Instead, they run in the JVM, which handles the differences between operating systems and presents an identical environment for Java programs to run in. JVM is a novel idea that makes Java platform-independent. The drawback of the JVM is that Java programs run much more slowly than the corresponding C programs; but for most applications, this difference is not noticeable.

Java is one of the most popular programming languages, especially for networking applications. According to Oracle, worldwide there are an estimated 9 million Java developers and about 3 billion devices that run Java.

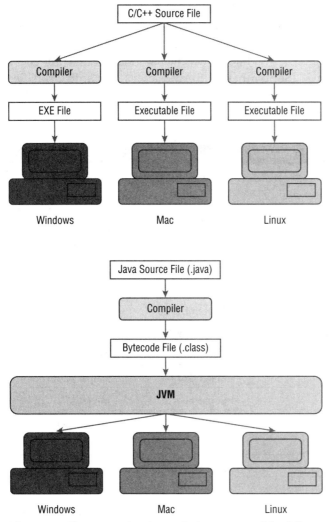

Figure 1.1: The conventional compilation process of the C/C++ programming language on different platforms (top) and the Java compilation process on different platforms (bottom)

1.2   Versions of Java

Java has had many versions; at the writing of this book, the current version is Java 11; by the time you read this, it will be Java 12. Alpha and Beta were the initial releases of the Java Development Kit (JDK) in 1995. JDK 1.0 was the first official version, released in 1996. Java JDK version 1.2 and newer are generally called Java 2. The collection of Java 2 languages, libraries, and tools is referred to as the Java 2 platform, or Java 2 Standard Edition (J2SE). Similarly, there are Java 5, Java 6, Java 7, and Java 8. The latest Java releases are Java 9 (July 2017), Java 10 (March 2018), Java 11 (September 2018), and Java 12 (March 2019). See Table 1.1 for details.

Table 1.1: Java Version History

VERSION	CODE NAME	RELEASE DATE	END OF LIFE
JDK Alpha and Beta		1995	Prior to 2008
JDK 1.0	Oak	January 1996	Prior to 2008
JDK 1.1		February 1997	Prior to 2008
J2SE 1.2	Playground	December 1998	Prior to 2008
J2SE 1.3	Kestrel	May 2000	Prior to 2008
J2SE 1.4	Merlin	February 2002	August 2008
J2SE 5.0	Tiger	September 2004	November 2009
Java SE 6	Mustang	December 2006	February 2013
Java SE 7	Dolphin	July 2011	April 2015
Java SE 8 (LTS)		March 2014	January 2019
Java SE 9		September 2017	March 2018
Java SE 10		March 2018	September 2018
Java SE 11 (LTS)		September 2018	
Java SE 12		March 2019	

For Java releases after Java SE 8, Oracle has designated a long-term-support (LTS) release every three years, and in between are non-LTS releases, also called *feature releases*, every six months. Java SE 9, Java SE 10, and Java 12 are all non-LTS releases, and Java SE 8 and Java SE 11 are LTS releases. Java end of life (EOL) occurs when the Java release is no longer publicly supported by Oracle. For the non-LTS releases, the EOL is the date of the next new release, and all the public support will be superseded. But for the LTS releases, the EOL is much longer, and customers will continue to get public support even after the new releases. That is why the widely used Java SE 8 has a much longer EOL than other releases. The next planned LTS release will be Java SE 17. This book is focused on the application of Java; the Java example codes used in this book will not be affected by the future Java releases.

For more information about Java releases and support road map, please visit the following:

```
https://www.oracle.com/technetwork/java/java-se-support-roadmap.html
https://en.wikipedia.org/wiki/Java_version_history
```

Each Java release is distributed as two different packages.

The **Java Runtime Environment (JRE)** is for running Java programs and is intended for end users. The JRE consists of the JVM and runtime libraries. You can use the JRE when you don't need to compile the Java program.

The **Java Development Kit (JDK)** is for software developers to compile, debug, and document Java programs. You will need to use the JDK in this book, as you will need to compile your Java programs.

1.3   Java Architecture

Figure 1.2 shows the relationship between the JDK, JRE, and JVM in the Java architecture. The JDK includes the JRE and Java development tools, and the JRE includes the JVM and library classes, as well as other files. Inside the JVM, there is a just-in-time (JIT) compiler, which compiles Java bytecode to native machine code during the execution of a Java program, that is, at run time. JIT improves the performance of Java applications.

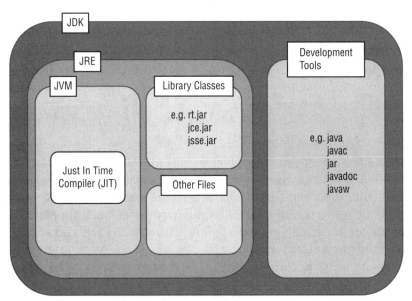

JDK = JRE + Development Tools
JRE = JVM + Library Classes + Other Files

Figure 1.2: The relationship between the JDK, JRE, and JVM in Java architecture

Figure 1.3 shows a more detailed version of Java architecture; this was re-created from the original Oracle Java architecture diagram found here:

`https://www.oracle.com/technetwork/java/javase/tech/index.html`

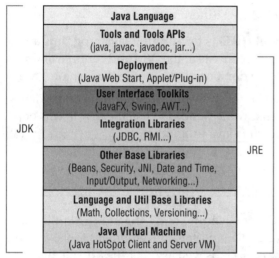

Figure 1.3: A conceptual diagram of the Java architecture

1.4   Editions of Java

There are four Java platform editions.

Java Card for smartcards

Java ME (Micro Edition) for mobile devices

Java SE (Standard Edition) for standard personal computers

Java EE (Enterprise Edition) for large distributed enterprise or Internet environments

Java SE is what most people use for Java programming. This edition comes with the complete Java Class Library, which includes the basic types and objects, networking, security, databases, and the classic Swing graphical user interface (GUI) toolkit. Most versions also include the modern JavaFX toolkit, which is intended to replace the Swing GUI toolkit; however, starting with Java SE 11, the JavaFX toolkit is no longer included in the Java SDK and is redesigned as a separate, stand-alone library. This book will be mainly focused on Java SE.

1.5   The Java Spring Framework

Java Spring is the most popular development framework for creating Java enterprise applications. Java Spring is an open source framework. Initially written by Rod Johnson, it was released under the Apache 2.0 license in June 2003. One of the main advantages of the Spring framework is its layered architecture, which allows developers to select which of its components to use. Figure 1.4 shows the home page of the Java Spring Framework (`https://spring.io/`). Figure 1.5 shows the Guides page for the Framework (`https://spring.io/guides`).

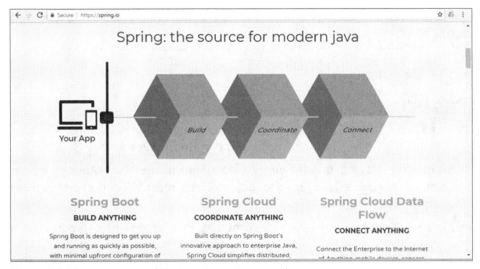

Figure 1.4: The home page of the Java Spring Framework

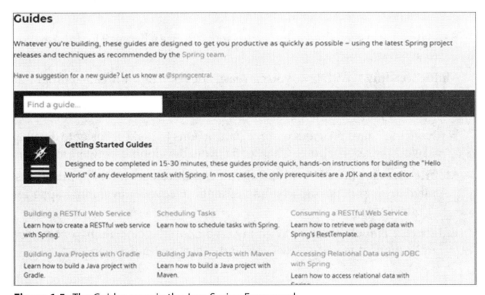

Figure 1.5: The Guides page in the Java Spring Framework

There are also several good Java Spring framework tutorials online.

```
https://www.tutorialspoint.com/spring/spring_overview.htm
https://howtodoinjava.com/spring-5-tutorial/
https://java2blog.com/introduction-to-spring-framework/
```

1.6   Advantages and Disadvantages of Java

I've already noted some of Java's advantages, but it also has a few disadvantages that may affect your choice of a development language. This section provides a quick summary of both. Many items are the topics of chapters or sections later in this book.

1.6.1   Advantages

These are the advantages:

Free Cost   Java is free to use, even for commercial applications, although you do need to pay for security and certain updates.

Simplicity   Java is much easier to learn and to use than other programming languages. Java also uses automatic memory allocation and garbage collection.

Platform Independence   Once compiled, Java programs can run on any operating system, thanks to the JVM.

Object Orientation   Java is a fully object-oriented programming language that allows you to create reusable Java modules (classes). Chapter 3 introduces Java's object orientation.

Security   Java is designed to be secure and safe. See Chapter 9 for information about security.

Multithreading   With Java, you can easily develop multithreaded programs that run several tasks simultaneously. Chapter 3 also introduces multithreaded programming.

Networking   Java provides a range of functions to make it easier to develop networking applications. Chapter 5 covers developing networking apps.

Mobile Development   With Java, you can develop mobile applications, called *apps*, on Android systems. Chapter 6 covers developing apps for mobile devices.

Enterprise Development   With Java, you can develop many enterprise applications, such as web servers and other application servers.

1.6.2   Disadvantages

These are the disadvantages:

Performance   Java is much slower than other natively compiled languages, such as C or C++, because of the use of the JVM. Java also takes more memory space and has limited options for latency critical tuning.

GUI Development   Generally speaking, it is not easy to develop GUI programs with Java, and the look and feel of the Java Swing toolkit is very different from native Windows, Mac, and Linux applications, although there are significant improvements in the JavaFX GUI toolkit. Chapter 4 shows how to overcome the difficulties and develop GUI apps using Java Swing and JavaFX.

1.7   Java Certification

Oracle offers a range of Java certificates, which can be generally divided into two levels, Associate and Professional, as shown in Figure 1.6 (`https://educa-tion.oracle.com/pls/web_prod-plq-dad/ou_product_category.getPageCert?p_cat_id=267`). You can start by applying for Java Foundations Certified Junior Associate, then move on to Oracle Certified Associate, and finally become an Oracle Certified Professional. Different Java versions require their own certificates. For example, there are separate certifications for Java SE 7 Programmer and Java SE 8 Programmer. Certificates for newer Java versions will continue to be introduced.

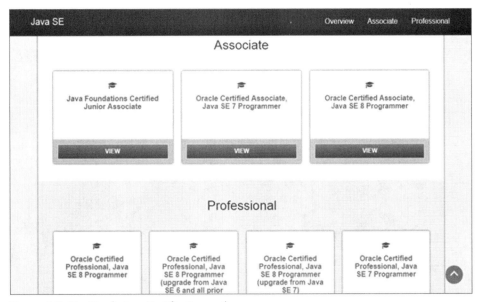

Figure 1.6: The Oracle Java Certification path

1.8   Summary

This chapter introduced the Java programming language, including its history, versions, and the four Java platform editions. It also introduced the popular Java Spring Framework for enterprise Java application development, summarized Java's advantages and disadvantages, and finally provided information about Java certification.

1.9   Chapter Review Questions

Q1.1.   What is Java? Explain the difference between a Java source file and Java bytecode.

Q1.2.   What is HotJava, and what is JavaScript?

Q1.3.   What is platform independence?

Q1.4.   Which Java versions are still supported?

Q1.5.   Use a diagram to describe the Java architecture.

Q1.6.   What are the JDK, JRE, JVM, and JIT?

Q1.7.   What are the four Java platform editions?

Q1.8.   What is the Java Spring Framework?

Q1.9.   What are the advantages and disadvantages of Java?

Q1.10.   What Java certifications are available?

CHAPTER 2

Getting Started with Java Programming

"If a craftsman wants to do good work, he must first sharpen his tools."
—Ancient Chinese proverb

2.1 Downloading and Installing Java

Let's get started with Java programming. First, you will need to download the latest Java software from the Oracle web site, as shown in Figure 2.1 (`www.oracle.com/technetwork/java/javase/downloads/index.html`). There are three download choices: JDK, Server JRE, and JRE. The server JRE and JRE are for running the Java programs only; since you will need to compile Java programs in this book, you need to download the JDK software package. Just follow the instructions on the web site to download and install the Java SE JDK on your computer.

Figure 2.1: The Java SE download web site

After installation, you will need to set up a few environmental variables, such as PATH and JAVA_HOME. Environment variables help programs know which folder to install files in, where to store temporary files, where to find user profile settings, and so on. To set up the environmental variables in Windows, go to Control Panel ⇨ Advanced System Settings ⇨ Environment Variables. In the section System Variables, find the PATH environment variable and double-click it to edit it. For example, if your Java JDK installation directory is C:\Program Files\Java\jdk-10.0.2\bin, then you just append a semicolon to the end, as in C:\Program Files\Java\jdk-10.0.2\bin;. The semicolon here is used to separate different PATH variables. Also in the section System Variables, find the JAVA _ HOME environment variable and double-click it to edit it. Change its value to C:\Program Files\Java\jdk-10.0.2, as shown in Figure 2.2.

For more details of setting up Java environment variables, please visit https://www.java.com/en/download/help/path.xml.

To set up Java environmental variables in Linux/Unix and macOS, you will need to edit your shell startup scripts. For example, if your Java JDK is installed in the /usr/local/jdk-10.0.2/ directory, in the Bash shell, you can edit the startup file (~/.bashrc) like this:

```
JAVA_HOME = /usr/local/jdk-10.0.2/
export JAVA_HOME
```

```
PATH=/usr/local/jdk-10.0.2/bin:$PATH
export PATH
```

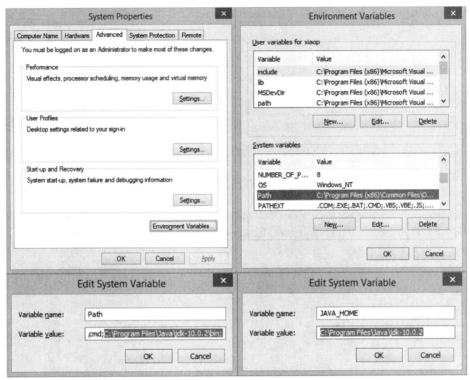

Figure 2.2: The Advanced tab of the System Properties window (top left); the Environmental Variables window (top right); and setting up the PATH (bottom, left) and JAVA_HOME (bottom right) variables

Save and close the file, and type in the following command to load the startup file:

```
./.profile
```

If you find Java installation difficult, Figure 2.3 shows an intuitive and simple Java installation guide from Nanyang Technological University in Singapore (www.ntu.edu.sg/home/ehchua/programming/howto/JDK _ HowTo.html).

Once the Java JDK has been installed properly, you can check the Java version from the Windows command prompt by typing **java -version**, as shown in Figure 2.4 (top). You can invoke the command prompt in Windows by choosing Start ➪ Run and typing **cmd**. You can also check the Java compiler by typing **javac**, as shown in Figure 2.4 (bottom).

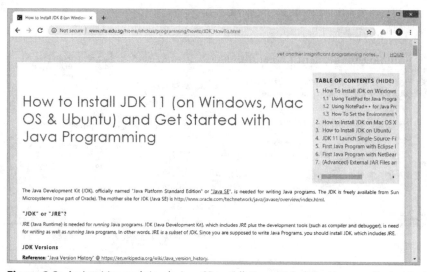

Figure 2.3: An intuitive and simple Java SE installation guide from Nanyang Technological University in Singapore

Figure 2.4: The commands to check the Java version (top) and to test the Java compiler (bottom)

2.2   Java IDEs

As you do with any programming language, to write a Java program you need a good integrated development environment (IDE), which can make programming much easier. There are many good options, and here I will introduce a few popular ones.

The first is Notepad++, shown in Figure 2.5. Notepad++ is an open source text editor that supports many programming languages, including Java. It supports opening multiple Java files, color-coding the Java keywords, and displaying line numbers. It also supports code folding. Text editors are lightweight IDEs and do not have all the functions of full IDEs. But they are much simpler to use.

The following is the download link for Notepad++:

`https://notepad-plus-plus.org/download/v7.5.8.html`

Other popular text editors include the following:

Textpad (`https://www.textpad.com/`), Windows operating systems

Sublime Text (`https://www.sublimetext.com/`), Windows and Linux operating systems

Another option is IntelliJ IDEA, which is a fully functional, powerful, dedicated Java IDE. IntelliJ IDEA is also relatively easy to use; see Figure 2.6. Compared to text editors, IntelliJ IDEA comes with many powerful features, such as smart completion, data flow analysis, language injection, inspections, and quick fixes. It also has many built-in developer tools, such as version control, a decompiler, an application server, and build tools such as Maven, Gradle, Ant, and others.

The following is the download link for IntelliJ IDEA:

`https://www.jetbrains.com/idea/`

Another option is Eclipse, which is a powerful IDE that supports Java and many other programming languages such as C and C++. But for beginners, Eclipse might look daunting, with its complex user interface and sophisticated configurations, as shown in Figure 2.7.

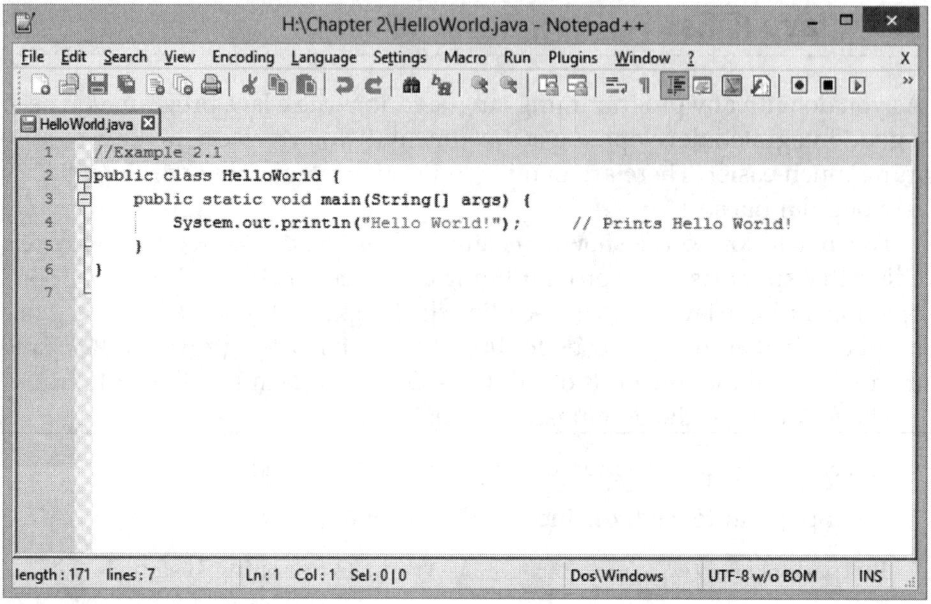

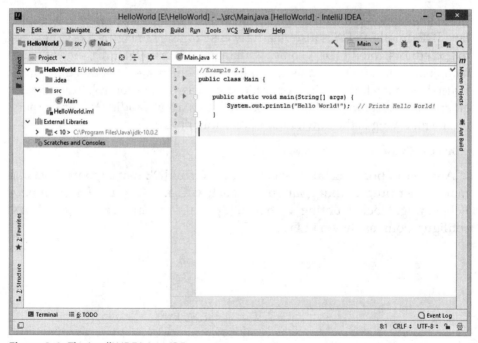

Figure 2.5: The Notepad++ text editor

Figure 2.6: The IntelliJ IDEA Java IDE

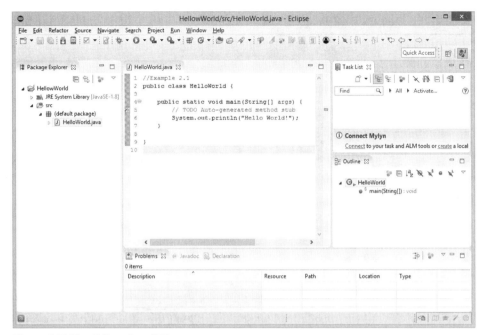

Figure 2.7: The Eclipse Java IDE

The following is the download link for Eclipse:

`www.eclipse.org/downloads/packages/release/mars/r/eclipse-ide-java-developers`

Last but not least, another option is NetBeans, which can be downloaded with the JDK as a bundle. So, you will not need to download the JDK software separately. NetBeans also supports drag-and-drop graphical user interface (GUI) components, which make it easier to develop Windows applications; see Figure 2.8.

The following is the download link for NetBeans:

`https://netbeans.apache.org/download/index.html`

For beginners, I recommend starting with a text editor, such as Notepad++, as you gain more and more experience and then moving on to a Java IDE.

Figure 2.8: The NetBeans Java IDE

2.3   Java Hello World Program

A computer program is essentially a collection of statements (instructions) that can be executed by a computer automatically. To create a Java program, first you need to create the Java source code, which is a text file with .java as the extension name. The source code contains statements, which are lines of code that perform some actions. Second, you need to compile the source code into bytecode, a machine-understandable binary file with .class as the extension name, which can then be executed within Java runtime environments (JREs). Java's platform independence is achieved by installing the JRE on every operating system. The JRE handles the differences of various operating systems and provides a common platform for the bytecode to run. Therefore, the same byte-code can run on all JREs and give you the same result, irrespective of what the underlying operating system is.

Example 2.1 shows a simple Java program named HelloWorld.java, which just prints Hello World! to your screen.

EXAMPLE 2.1 HELLOWORLD.JAVA

```
=====================================================================
//Example 2.1
public class HelloWorld {
```

```
        public static void main(String[] args) {
            System.out.println("Hello World!");
        }
    }
    ==========================================================================
```

In Java, every program consists of at least one class, and the source code file name (including the case) should be exactly the same as the class name, or it should be the name of the main class when there is more than one class.

Like C/C++, Java uses braces, { and }, to group blocks of codes, and it uses // to mark single-line comments and /* */ for multiple-line comments. Here's an example of a single-line comment:

```
//This is a single line comment
```

Here's an example of a multiple-line comment:

```
/*
   This is a multiple line comment
   Where you can write multiple lines
*/
```

Every Java application program (except for Java applets) has one, and only one, `public static void main(String [] args)` method. For the `main()` method, the keyword `public` means it is accessible to other Java classes, `static` means it can be invoked without using any object, `void` means it does not return any value, and `args` is a String type array variable, which saves all the parameters typed at the command line. The `main()` method should always be `static` and `public`. In Java, each line that ends with a semicolon (;) is called a *statement*; that is, it's an action that is asking the computer to do something. In this example, there is only one statement:

```
System.out.println();
```

This is a Java statement for printing messages on the screen. The `System.out.println()` statement is just an object-oriented way of saying call the `println()` method, which is a method (or function) of the `out` object in the `System` class. `System.out` is the standard output (your computer screen) object. Similarly, there is also `System.in`, the standard input (your keyboard) object; `System.err`, the standard error object; and so on.

Every Java method or class belongs to a package. The default package is `java.lang.*`, which does not need to be explicitly imported, as shown in the previous example. But if you are using any methods or classes that belong to other packages, they need to be imported at the beginning of the program. In the next chapter's examples, you will use the `java.text.*` and `java.util.*` packages. To run the `HelloWorld.java` program, first use your favorite text editor or IDE to type in the previous code and save it in a text file named `HelloWorld.java`. Figure 2.9 shows how to create the `HelloWorld.java` program using Notepad++

and save the file as a Java source file (*.java). Remember, the file name must be the same as the class name.

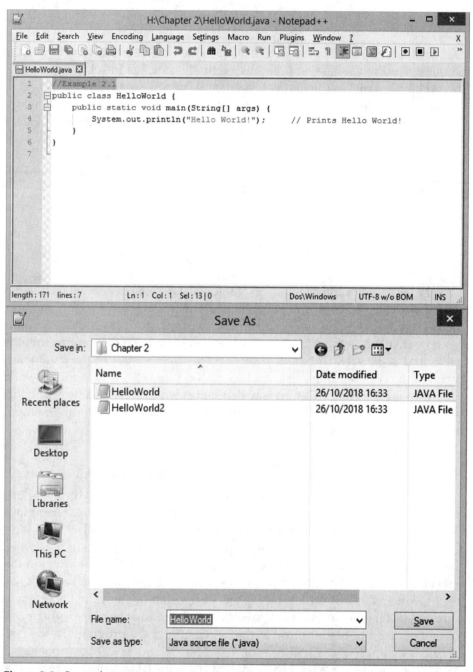

Figure 2.9: Create the `HelloWorld.java` program using Notepad++ and save the file as a Java source file. The file name must be the same as the class name.

Then open a Windows command prompt window in the directory where your file is saved and enter the following command to compile it to bytecode:

```
javac HelloWorld.java
```

A file named `HelloWorld.class` will be generated. Then use the following command to run the bytecode file, as shown in Figure 2.10:

```
java HelloWorld
```

Congratulations! You now have your first Java program running. In addition to Notepad++, you can use a Java IDE such as IntelliJ IDEA. In that case, you don't need the Windows command prompt. You can write, compile, and run the Java program within the IDE.

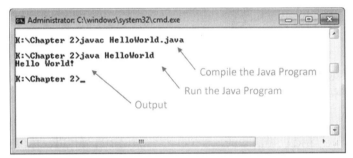

Figure 2.10: Commands to compile and run the `HelloWorld.java` program

EXERCISE 2.1   Modify the Example 2.1 Java program so that it prints your name and address.

Example 2.2 is an improved version of the previous Java program, named `HelloWorld2.java`. It will print `Hello xxx!` on your screen, where `xxx` is the first parameter that you type at the command line when you run the program. Figure 2.11 shows how to compile and run the `HelloWorld2.java` program. As explained, Java uses the `args` String array variable to store the command-line parameters, that is, the text you typed after **`java HelloWorld2`**. In this case, the command-line parameters are `Perry Xiao`; `args[0]` stores the value `Perry`, and `args[1]` stores the value `Xiao`. Therefore, `System.out.println("Hello " + args[0])` should print `Hello Perry!` on the screen. Here, Java uses the + sign to concatenate two strings.

```
==========================================================================
```

EXAMPLE 2.2

```
//Example 2.2
public class HelloWorld2 {
    public static void main(String[] args) {
```

```
        System.out.println("Hello " + args[0]);     // Prints Hello xxx!
    }
}
=========================================================================
```

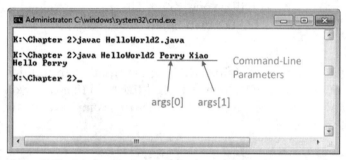

Figure 2.11: Commands to compile and run the `HelloWorldApplication2.java` program

EXERCISE 2.2   Modify the Example 2.2 Java program so that it prints both your first name and last name.

By default, the `javac` command uses the current directory (also called a *folder*) for Java source files and compiled class files. To use different directories or folders, you need to specify other options, such as **–classpath, –sourcepath, –d, –target**, and others. The **–classpath** (or **–cp**) option specifies where you can find the precompiled Java class files (such as libraries) when you are compiling or running a Java program. The **–sourcepath** option specifies where you can find the Java source files. The **–d** option specifies where you want to save the compiled Java class files. The **–target** option specifies which version of the Java runtime environment you want to target when compiling Java files.

For example, the following command compiles the `HelloWorld.java` program using the current directory (.), the `\examples` subdirectory, and the `\lib\funs.jar` file as the class path. In Windows, Java uses `;` to separate different directories, while in Linux, it uses `:` to separate different directories.

```
javac -classpath .;\examples;\lib\funs.jar  HelloWorld.java
```

The following command sets the `H:\examples` directory as the source path:

```
javac -sourcepath H:\examples  H:\examples\HelloWorld.java
```

The following command sets the `.\classes` subdirectory as the destination path for the compiled class files:

```
javac -d  .\classes  HelloWorld.java
```

For more details about the `javac` command options, type `javac -help` at the Windows command prompt.

2.4   Java Online Compilers

In addition to the text editors and IDEs introduced earlier, there are many online compilers, which means you don't need to download and install the Java JDK or an IDE onto your computer; you can simply write and run Java code from a web browser from your computers, tablets, and even phones.

Figure 2.12 shows a simple-to-use Java online compiler from Tutorialspoint (`https://www.tutorialspoint.com/compile_java_online.php`). On the left side you write the Java code, and you view the results on the right side. On the top-right side, there are also Fork, Project, Edit, Settings, and Login menus. You can create new projects and share projects. It supports compiling only a single file and supports only Java 8.

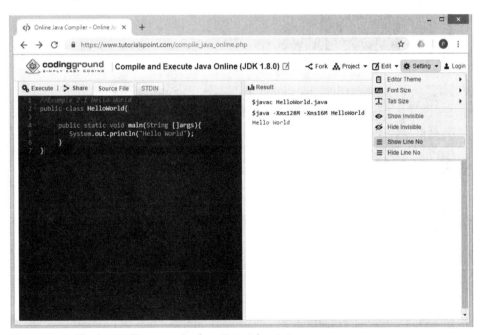

Figure 2.12: The Java online compiler from Tutorialspoint

Figure 2.13 shows the Codiva Java online compiler (`https://www.codiva.io/java#`). Codiva is a powerful online compiler. To use Codiva, you will need either to create an account (Figure 2.13A) or to try it without logging in (Figure 2.13B).

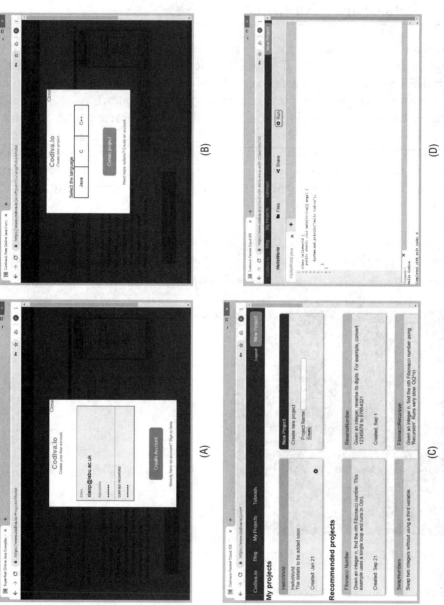

Figure 2.13: The Codiva Java online compiler: create a Codiva account (A); try Codiva without login (B); manage your project after login (C); and compile and run your project (D)

After login, you will be able to create more projects and see other people's projects (Figure 2.13C), as well as compile and run your project (Figure 2.13D). The best feature of Codiva is autocompilation, which mean that as you are typing, it automatically compiles the code and displays the results. It also has an autocompletion function, which makes writing code much easier and efficient. Codiva also supports multiple projects, files, packages, and Java 8 and 9 but not Java 10 or 11. Besides Java, Codiva supports the C and C++ languages but doesn't offer UI themes or different compiler settings.

Figure 2.14 shows the CompileJava.net online compiler (https://www.compilejava.net/). It is a simple compiler, supporting only one Java file, but it does allow you to select different IDE background schemes, as shown in the figure.

Figure 2.14: The CompileJava.net online compiler

Figure 2.15 shows JDoodle (https://www.jdoodle.com/online-java-compiler), a popular Java online compiler. Unlike other online compilers, JDoodle supports Java 8, 9, and 10, as shown in the figure. You can create an account or use your Google account to log in. After login, you can create new projects and manage all your projects. You can also collaborate with others; see the bottom menu in the figure. In addition to Java, JDoodle supports more than 70 other programming languages.

Figure 2.16 shows the Browxy Java online compiler (www.browxy.com/). Browxy used to be popular but is starting to lag behind as others catch up. It has almost no restrictions and supports multiple Java files and networking. As shown in the figure, you can run a Java networking program to get network information. You can learn more about Java networking programming in Chapter 5.

Browxy also offers several interesting Java example applications, such as Hello World, Animal Game, Thread Example, and so on. Browxy supports only Java 8.

Figure 2.15: The JDoodle Java online compiler

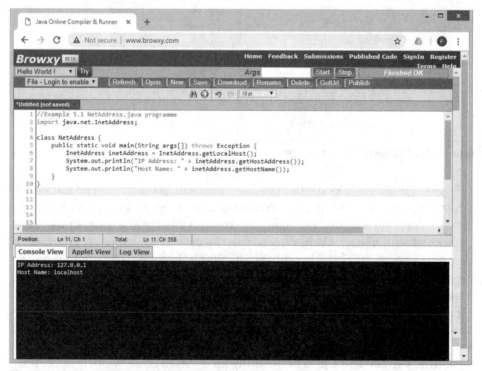

Figure 2.16: The Browxy Java online compiler

Figure 2.17 shows the OnlineGDB Java online compiler (`https://www.online-gdb.com/online_java_compiler`). OnlineGDB is another powerful online compiler. A distinctive feature is its online debugger, which allows you to set breakpoints in the code and run the code step-by-step. It also supports code folding and autocompletion, two more features that make writing a complex program easier. You can log in using your Google or Facebook account, and after login, you can create a new project and manage your projects.

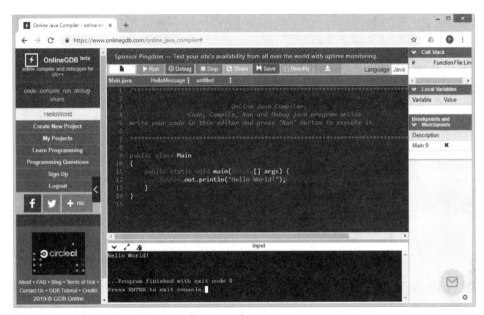

Figure 2.17: The OnlineGDB Java online compiler

Figure 2.18 shows the Rextester Java online compiler (`http://rextester.com/l/java_online_compiler`). Rextester stands for Regular Expression Tester. Rextester supports about 30 languages including Java, as shown in the figure (top), and is popular among C# users. Rextester has the best live collaboration support, which allows multiple users to edit the same file, as shown in the figure (bottom). Just click the Live Cooperation button in the page and give a name to your project. Rextester will then generate a unique URL, where multiple users can share and work on the same Java program. There is also a yellow chat box on the right, where users can exchange messages. But Rextester supports only a single Java file and only Java 8.

Figure 2.19 shows the IDEOne Java online compiler (`https://www.ideone.com/`). IDEOne claims to be one of the first online compilers. You can edit the code, fork the code (create new code), and download the code, as shown in the figure. It supports more than 60 programming languages, including Java.

IDEOne provides an API for compilation as a service, which means you can create your own online IDE using its API.

Figure 2.18: The Rextester Java online compiler

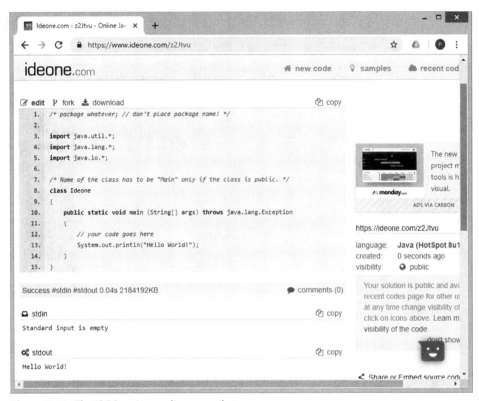

Figure 2.19: The IDEOne Java online compiler

2.5   Java Online Code Converters

Online code converters can translate an application's source code from one programming language into the source code of another programming language. Figure 2.20 shows the Carlosag online code translator (`https://www.carlosag.net/tools/codetranslator/`), which can translate Java code into C#, VB.NET, and TypeScript code, and vice versa.

Figure 2.21 shows the mtSystems C code to Java code translation (`https://www.mtsystems.com/`). You will need to contact them to convert your C code to Java code, but there is a free online demo, which demonstrates how to convert different types of C code to Java code.

2.6   Java Free Online Courses and Tutorials

Many free Java resources are available online. Figure 2.22 shows the Java tutorials from Oracle (`https://docs.oracle.com/javase/tutorial/index.html`). These comprehensive tutorials show you how to create applications in an easy and simple way. Topics include the basics, as well as more advanced topics such as object-oriented programming (OOP), GUIs, networking, and JavaBeans.

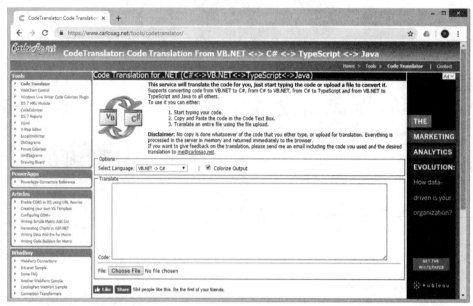

Figure 2.20: Carlosag online code translation

Figure 2.23 shows the Java courses from Coursera (`https://www.coursera.org/specializations/java-programming`), one of the best-known online course web sites. Course videos are available in English, Spanish, Russian, Chinese, and French languages, including subtitles. There are many Java courses there.

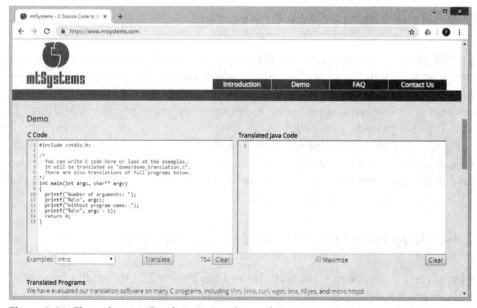

Figure 2.21: The mtSystems C code to Java code translation

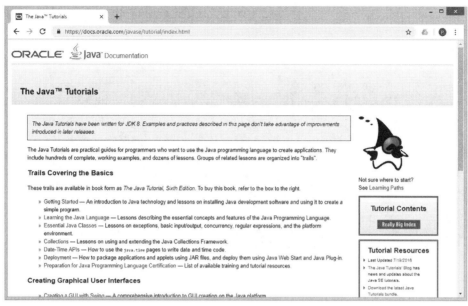

Figure 2.22: The Java tutorials from Oracle

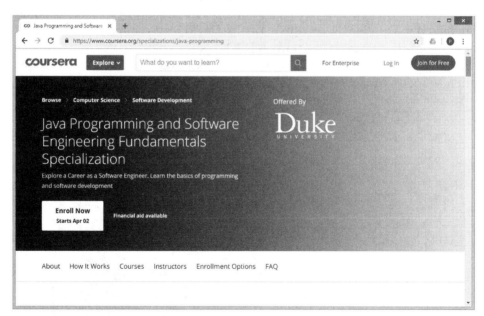

Figure 2.23: The Java courses from Coursera

Figure 2.24 shows the Java courses from Codecademy (https://www.codecademy.com/learn/learn-java), which is another popular place for online courses. Codecademy offers a free Java programming course for beginners. Students can learn the basics of the Java language and work on different projects.

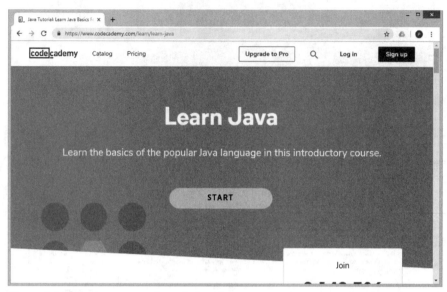

Figure 2.24: The Java courses from Codecademy

Figure 2.25 shows the Java courses from Udacity (https://eu.udacity.com/course/java-programming-basics--ud282), which is a for-profit educational organization founded by Sebastian Thrun, David Stavens, and Mike Sokolsky offering massive open online courses (MOOCs). Udacity's motto is "audacious for you, the student." It originally focused on offering university-style courses but now focuses more on vocational courses for professionals.

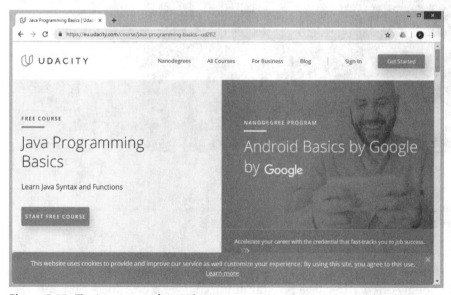

Figure 2.25: The Java courses from Udacity

Figure 2.26 shows the Java tutorial from LearnJavaOnline (`https://www.learn-javaonline.org/`), which also comes with a Java online compiler so that you can learn the Java programming and run the code all in the same web site. It offers both basic and advanced Java topics.

Figure 2.26: The Java tutorial from LearnJavaOnline

Figure 2.27 shows the Java course for complete beginners from CaveofProgramming (`https://courses.caveofprogramming.com/p/java-for-complete-beginners`), which was created by John Purcell, a software developer with 14+ years of experience. It is free, and you can choose your schedule for classes as each is self-paced.

Figure 2.28 shows a Java language basics tutorial from IBM (`https://www.ibm.com/developerworks/java/tutorials/j-introtojava1/index.html`). This is also a good tutorial that covers comprehensive Java language topics.

For more details about the Java language, please visit the Java API documentation web site.

```
https://docs.oracle.com/javase/10/docs/api/overview-summary.html
```

Figure 2.27: The Java course from CaveofProgramming

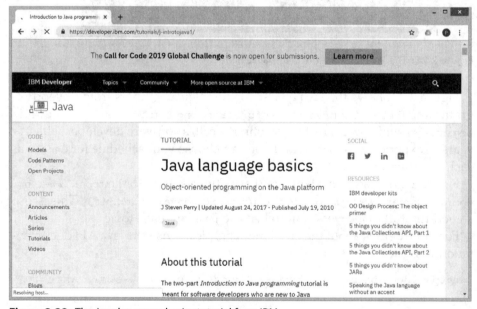

Figure 2.28: The Java language basics tutorial from IBM

2.7   Java Version Control

For software developers, version control means maintaining a history of the software development. Why do you need version control? Imagine the following scenario. You are working a big project, and you have just added a new function to your program when suddenly it stops compiling. How can you revert it to the previous working version? In another scenario, you are working on a group project with several other developers, and they are all using the same source directory. How do you know who has changed what? Or, how do you prevent the code you have just developed from being overwritten by someone else? The answer is to use version control software—a central storage hub where developers can check files in and out so that a file one user has checked out to work on can't be modified by anyone else until it is checked back in.

The software that handles this function is called a *version control system* (VCS). You can use either a centralized version control system (CVCS) or a distributed/decentralized version control system (DVCS). A CVCS uses a central server to store all files, but the drawback is that it suffers a single point of failure—when the server is down or the files on the server are corrupted, everything is down and no one can work. Therefore, the DVCS approach is more suitable, especially when the project developers are located in different cities or even different countries. A DVCS not only allows developers to check out the latest snapshot of the directory but also fully mirrors the repository. If the server goes down, then the repository from any developer can be copied to the server to restore it.

One of the most widely used distributed version control systems is Git, which has an emphasis on speed. Git was initially designed and developed by Linus Torvalds, the famous Finnish software engineer who developed the Linux operating system while he was studying at the University of Helsinki in 1991. Torvalds designed Git for Linux kernel development. GitHub is a web-based service for version control using Git. Compared to other version control software, Git has the advantages of being free to use, small and fast, and open source based. It also has implicit backup and good security, is easier to branch, and has no need of powerful hardware.

If you're doing collaborative development and need to implement a DVCS, see Appendix C for a complete tutorial on using Git and GitHub.

2.8   Summary

This chapter showed how to download and install the Java JDK software. It also introduced four popular Java text editors/IDEs and showed how they handle simple Java Hello World programs. Then you looked at some popular Java online compilers, Java online code converters, and some Java free online courses and tutorials. Finally, you learned about software version control and saw how to use Git and GitHub for that purpose.

2.9 Chapter Review Questions

Q2.1. Where can you download the latest Java JDK software? What is the latest version?

Q2.2. For what purpose should you download the Java JDK package, and for what purpose should you download the JRE package?

Q2.3. In the Java HelloWorld program, what do the keywords `public`, `static`, and `void` accomplish?

Q2.4. How do you invoke the Windows command prompt in Windows?

Q2.5. What is the command to compile a Java program?

Q2.6. What is the command to run a Java program?

Q2.7. What are command-line parameters?

Q2.8. Use a table to compare different Java online compilers, and indicate whether they support features such as single file, multiple files, create projects, different Java versions, debugging, and so on.

Q2.9. Find a piece of code written in another programming language, and use a code converter to convert it to Java.

Q2.10. Use a table to compare different Java online courses or tutorials, and indicate whether they are free, have videos, are self-paced or fixed date and time, and so on.

Q2.11. What is software version control, and why do you need it?

Q2.12. What are Git and GitHub?

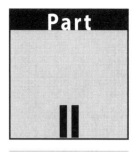
Part

II

In This Part:

Basic Java Programming

"If you think you can do a thing or think you can't do a thing, you're right."

—Henry Ford

3.1   Introduction

This chapter introduces the basic concepts of Java programming, intended for those who have some experience in coding and familiarity with programming concepts but are new to the Java language.

3.2   Variables

Java supports eight primitive types of variables: `byte`, `short`, `int`, `long`, `float`, `double`, `char`, and `boolean`. Variable names in Java are case-sensitive and must start with a letter, an underscore, or a dollar sign ($). They cannot start with a number. After the first character, a variable name can include any combination of letters and numbers. Spaces and special symbols, such as !, "", £, %, &, *, #, @, ~, and so on, are not allowed in variable names. In Java, all variables must be declared before they can be used. To declare a variable, you will need to specify the type, leave at least one space, and then specify the variable name and a semicolon (;).

```
type variablename;
```

The following code shows the declaration and initialization of an integer variable named x:

```
int x;        // Declares an integer type variable called x.
x = 10;       // Initialize x
```

or

```
int x = 10;  // Declaration and Initialization
```

You can also declare multiple variables of the same type all in one line.

```
int x, y, z;           // Declares three int variables, x, y, and z.
x = 10; y = 5; z=1;    // Initialize x, y, and z
```

or

```
int x = 10, y = 5, z=1;  // Declaration and Initialization
```

Example 3.1A shows a simple declaration and initialization of two integer variables. Here, as explained in Chapter 2, `System.out.println()` is used to display the text on the screen, and `println("x = " + x)` displays the text "x = " and the value of the variable x on the screen. The + sign means to concatenate the text and variable. You can find more details about input and output in section 3.5.

EXAMPLE 3.1A   DECLARING AND INITIALIZING JAVA VARIABLES

```
=============================================================================
//Example 3.1A Java variable example
public class VarExample {
    public static void main(String args[]) {
        int x = 10;    // declares and assigns integer variable
        int y = 5;     // declares and assigns integer variable
        int z;         // declares integer variable

        System.out.println("x = " + x );
        System.out.println("y = " + y);
        z = x + y;
        System.out.println("x + y = " + z);
    }
}
=============================================================================
```

If you want to declare the variables outside the main() method, you need to declare the variables as static, as only static variables or methods can be used in the main() method; see Example 3.1B.

EXAMPLE 3.1B   DECLARING A JAVA VARIABLE AS STATIC

```
=============================================================================
 //Example 3.1B Java variable example
public class VarExample2 {
    static int x = 10;    // declares and assigns integer variable
    static int y = 5;     // declares and assigns integer variable
    static int z;         // declares integer variable

    public static void main(String args[]) {
        System.out.println("x = " + x );
        System.out.println("y = " + y);
        z = x + y;
        System.out.println("x + y = " + z);
    }
}
=============================================================================
```

Example 3.1C shows an example of the declaration and initialization of different types of variables. Please note that you will need to put f at the end of the float number to indicate that it is a float number, not a double number. Similarly, you will need to put L at the end of a type long number to indicate that it is a long number.

EXAMPLE 3.1C   DECLARING JAVA VARIABLES OF DIFFERENT TYPES

```
===========================================================================
//Example 3.1C Java variable example
public class VarExample3 {
    public static void main(String args[]) {
        short x = 10, y = 5, z=1; // declares and assigns short variables
        byte B = 17;              // declares and assigns a byte variable
        long w = 234334000000L;   // declares and assigns a long variable
        double d = 5.01;          // declares and assigns a double variable
        float f = 5.01f;          // declares and assigns a float variable
        char ch = 'a';            // declares and assigns a char variable
        String s = "Hello World!";// declares and assigns a String variable
        boolean isDone = false;   // declares and assigns a Boolean variable

        System.out.println("ch = " + ch );
        System.out.println("isDone = " + isDone);
        System.out.println(s);
    }
}
===========================================================================
```

EXERCISE 3.1   Modify the Example 3.1A Java program so that it takes two integers from command-line parameters, `args[0]` and `args[1]`; performs the addition, subtraction, production, and division of the two integers; and displays the results on the screen. Comment the division result. (*Hint: use* `Integer.parseInt()` *to convert the* `args[0]` *or* `args[1]` *string to an integer number.*)

EXERCISE 3.2   Repeat the previous exercise, but perform the addition, subtraction, production, and division of two double numbers. Comment the division result. (*Hint: use* `Double.parseDouble()` *to convert the* `args[0]` *or* `args[1]` *string to a double number.*)

3.2.1   Constants

Constants are variables whose value does not change during program execution. You can define constants the same way as variables, but with the `static` and `final` keywords in the front. The `static` keyword means that the variable persists throughout the class, and only one copy of the value is maintained in memory. The `final` keyword means that the variable's value cannot be changed. Because their value cannot be changed, constants must be initialized at the time they are defined. Conventionally, constant names use all capital letters, as in these examples:

```
static final int TOTALNUMBER=120;
static final float PI=3.1415926F;
```

3.2.2   The String and StringBuffer Types

Java also supports two variable types, `String` and `StringBuffer`, in which you can store sequences of character values. The following code shows how to create a `String` variable that stores a student's class name:

```
String ClassName;
ClassName = new String();
ClassName = "Maple Tree Class";
```

Or you can simply merge those three steps into one.

```
String ClassName = "Maple Tree Class";
```

`String` variables are object variables, which come with many useful methods (Java's term for functions; see section 3.9 for details) for string operations, such as `length()`, `charAt()`, `equals()`, `concat()`, `trim()`, `compareTo()`, `toUpperCase()`, `toLowerCase()`, and `substring()`.

For example, if `t1` and `t2` are `String` type variables, the expression

```
t1.compareTo(t2)
```

returns 0 if `t1` and `t2` are equal in their American Standard Code for Information Interchange (ASCII) values, a negative number if `t1` is less than `t2`, or a positive number if `t1` is greater than `t2`. In ASCII, each alphabetic, numeric, or special character is represented with a 7-bit binary number. There are 128 possible characters.

The expression

```
t1 = t1.concat(t2)
```

appends (or concatenates) `t2` to the end of `t1`.

EXERCISE 3.3   Write a Java program that uses a `String` variable to store a sentence and then changes it to uppercase and displays it on the screen.

In Java, the `String` type is immutable. `String` immutability means that once a `String` object is created, it cannot be changed. This brings several benefits in caching, security, synchronization, and performance. For `String` caching, Java uses the concept of a `String` pool, a special memory place where all the `String` values are stored. Because `Strings` are immutable, Java can optimize the amount of memory usage by storing only one copy of each literal `String` in the pool. This enhances performance by saving memory.

For example, in the following code, both `s1` and `s2` are actually pointing to the same object `Hello` in the `String` pool:

```
String s1 = "Hello";
String s2 = "Hello";
```

But after the following concatenation, s2 points to a different object Hello World, while s1 is still pointing to the original object Hello:

```
s2 = s2 + " World";
```

For security, Java uses String variables to store usernames and passwords for remote database connections and other networking information. String immutability means that once these objects have been created, they cannot be hacked. Java also uses String variables to store the hashcode, which means that once the hashcode is cached at the time of creation, it doesn't need to be calculated again. All of these features make Java more secure. See Chapter 9 for more about hashcodes and Java security.

Also, because Strings are immutable, a single String instance can be shared across different threads. This avoids the usage of synchronization and makes multithreading safer.

The StringBuffer type provides functions similar to String but is a more powerful type that can handle dynamic string information. StringBuffer is used when there are many modifications to strings of characters. This is because StringBuffer is mutable.

For example, the following code appends text to the existing StringBuffer variable. This process is much faster than the previous String concatenation, such as t1 = t1.concat(t2) or s2 = s2 + " World", as String concatenation will end up creating a new String object each time.

```
StringBuffer sB = new StringBuffer("Hello");
sB.append(" World");
```

StringBuffer also has functions such as reverse(), delete(), replace(), and the like.

3.2.3   The VAR Variable Type

The VAR variable type has existed in many other languages, such as JavaScript and Visual Basic. VAR allows you to declare a variable without specifying its type. Java will automatically figure out the type, which makes programming simpler and also improves the readability of code. Java developers have long complained about the need to include boilerplate code and the resulting verbosity in code writing. Finally, beginning in Java 10, the VAR type variable is also available in Java. Here are some examples of how to use it:

```
//Java VAR type variable since Java 10
var str = "Java 10";                    // infers String
var list = new ArrayList<String>();     // infers ArrayList<String>
var stream = list.stream();             // infers Stream<String>s
```

3.3   Operators

Like many other languages, Java supports a full range of standard operators, such as arithmetic operators, comparison operators, logical operators, bitwise operators, and the assignment operator. Table 3.1 summarizes them.

Table 3.1: The Java Operators

OPERATOR TYPE	OPERATOR	COMMENTS
Arithmetic Operators	+	Addition and String concatenation
	–	Subtraction
	*	Multiplication
	/	Division
	%	Modulus (or remainder operator)
	++	Increment
	––	Decrement
Comparison Operators	<	Less than
	<=	Less than or equal to
	>	Greater than
	>=	Greater than or equal to
	==	Equal to *
	!=	Not equal to
Logical Operators	!	Logical not
	&&	Logical and
	||	Logical or
Bitwise Operators	~	Bitwise complement
	&	Bitwise and
	|	Bitwise or
	^	Bitwise xor
	<<	Left shift
	>>	Right shift
	>>>	Zero fill right shift
Assignment Operators	=	Assign a value
	+=	Add AND assign
	–=	Minus AND assign

Continues

Table 3.1 (*continued*)

OPERATOR TYPE	OPERATOR	COMMENTS
	*=	Multiply AND assign
	/=	Divide AND assign
	%=	Modulus AND assign
	>>=	Left shift AND assign
	<<=	Right shift AND assign
	&=	Bitwise and AND assign
	^=	Bitwise or AND assign
	|=	Bitwise xor AND assign

* Please note that == is for comparing numerical values. For comparing strings, use `equals ( )` instead.

3.4   Reserved Words

The following is a list of Java *reserved words*, or keywords that you cannot use for variable names, method names, or class names.

abstract	finally	short
assert	float	static
boolean	for	strictfp
break	goto	super
byte	if	switch
case	implements	synchronized
catch	import	this
char	instanceof	throw
class	int	throws
const	interface	transient
continue	long	true
default	native	try
do	new	var
double	null	void
else	package	volatile
enum	private	while
extends	protected	widefp
false	public	
final	return	

3.5   Input and Output

Input and output are important in almost all applications. In Java, `System.out` is used to print messages on the computer screen; this is called *standard output*. `System.in` and `System.console` are used to read text from the keyboard; this is called *standard input*.

Example 3.2 demonstrates Java input and output. `System.console.readline()` is used to read one line from the keyboard, and whatever the user types in will be stored in a `String` variable named x. Next, `System.out.print()` is used to display the text on-screen. Finally, `System.out.println()` works the same way as `System.out.print()`, except that after displaying the text, it moves the cursor to a new line. Figure 3.1 shows how to compile and run the example and its output.

EXAMPLE 3.2   JAVA STANDARD OUTPUT AND INPUT USING SYSTEM.CONSOLE

```
===========================================================================
//Example 3.2 Java standard output and input
public class InputOutputExample {
    public static void main(String[] args) {
        System.out.print("Enter something:");
        String x = System.console().readLine();
        System.out.println("You wrote: "+ x );
    }
}

===========================================================================
```

Figure 3.1: Commands to compile and run the `InputOutputExample.java` program

Example 3.3 demonstrates another form of Java input and output. In this code, `System.in` is used to read from the keyboard. Combined with the `Scanner` class, it can read one line at a time from the keyboard; it can also read an integer value from the keyboard. The line

```
import java.util.Scanner;
```

imports the `java.util.Scanner` library, which is needed by the `Scanner` class. This example first asks the user to enter a name, then reads the name from the keyboard, and finally displays the name on the screen. It also prompts for and displays the user's age. The name entered is stored in a `String` variable called name, and the age entered is stored in a variable named age.

EXAMPLE 3.3   JAVA STANDARD OUTPUT AND INPUT USING SYSTEM.IN

```
=========================================================================
//Example 3.3 Java standard output and input
import java.util.Scanner;

class InputOutputExample2 {
    public static void main(String[] args) {
        System.out.println("Enter your name: ");
        Scanner scanner = new Scanner(System.in);
        String name = scanner.nextLine();
        System.out.println("Your name is " + name);

        System.out.println("Enter your age: ");
        int age = scanner.nextInt();
        System.out.println("Your age is " + age);
    }
}
=========================================================================
```

In the Java input and output demonstrated in Example 3.4, System.in is used to feed into InputStreamReader and then into a BufferedReader. In Java all input and output sources are treated as streams, but the Stream type has limited functions, and it is often combined with BufferedReader. With BufferedReader, you can read one line each time from the keyboard. Integer.parseInt() is used to convert strings to integers. The throws IOException and try...catch blocks are used for handling exceptions. In Java it is mandatory to use exception handling for events such as input and output.

The try...catch block or try...catch...finally block is the classical approach to handling an exception in Java, as shown in the following pseudocode structure. The try block is used to enclose the code for doing something. One or more catch blocks are used to handle the exception. The finally block is used to enclose the code that is executed after the try block was successfully executed or a thrown exception was handled.

```
try {
    // do something
}
catch (one exception) {
    //display error message
}
catch (another exception) {
    //display error message
}
finally {
    //do something
}
```

The corresponding libraries, java.io.BufferedReader, java.io.IOException, java.io., and InputStreamReader, are also imported.

Can you guess what the program in Example 3.4 will do?

EXAMPLE 3.4   JAVA STANDARD OUTPUT AND INPUT USING
BUFFEREDREADER

```
============================================================================
//Example 3.4 Java standard output and input
import java.io.BufferedReader;
import java.io.IOException;
import java.io.InputStreamReader;

public class InputOutputExample3 {
    public static void main(String[] args) throws IOException {
        BufferedReader br = new BufferedReader(new
InputStreamReader(System.in));
        System.out.print("Enter String");
        String s = br.readLine();
        System.out.print("Enter Integer:");
        try{
            int i = Integer.parseInt(br.readLine());
        }catch(NumberFormatException nfe){
            System.err.println("Invalid Format!");
        }
    }
}
============================================================================
```

EXERCISE 3.4   Modify the Example 3.2 Java program so that it asks for your name and address and then displays them on the screen.

EXERCISE 3.5   Modify the Example 3.3 Java program so that it asks for your name, height, and weight and then displays them on the screen.

EXERCISE 3.6   Modify the Example 3.4 Java program so that it asks users to input two double numbers from the keyboard and then calculates the product of the two integers and displays the result on the screen. (*Hint: use* `Double.parseDouble()` *to convert string to double number.*)

3.6   Loops and Selections

There are three key ingredients that any programming language must have: sequences, loops, and selections. A *sequence* means statements executing sequentially, one after another. Loops and selections are control structures (or flow controls). Loops, also called *iterations* or *iterative statements*, are sets of statements that are executed repeatedly a number of times. Java supports for loops, while loops, and do loops. For example, the following for loop prints Hello World! five times:

```
for(i=0;i<5;i++){
    System.out.println("Hello World!");
}
```

Similarly, you can do the same thing using a while loop or a do loop. Both while and do loops need to define and initialize the counter variable before the loop (for example, int i=0;) and manually increase it during the loop (for example, i++). There is a subtle difference between the while loop and the do loop: the while loop checks the condition first before it runs the loop; the do loop runs the loop first and then checks the condition.

```
int i=0;
while(i<5){
    System.out.println("Hello World!");
    i++;
}

int i=0;
do{
    System.out.println("Hello World!");
    i++;
} while(i<5)
```

Example 3.5 uses a for loop to print all the command-line parameters. It uses args.length to get the total length of the parameters.

EXAMPLE 3.5   USING A FOR LOOP

```
==========================================================================
//Example 3.5 For Loops
class LoopExample {
    public static void main(String[] args) {
        int i;
        for(i=0;i<args.length;i++){
            System.out.println("Hello "+ args[i] + "!" );
        }
    }
}
==========================================================================
```

EXERCISE 3.7   Modify the Example 3.5 Java program so that it uses a while loop instead.

EXERCISE 3.8 Modify the Example 3.5 Java program so that it uses a do loop instead.

Selections, or *conditional statements,* allow your program to do different things under different conditions. Java supports the if...else conditional statement (a two-way choice), the switch conditional statement (multiple choices), and the ? operator (conditional assignment).

For example, if you want to do something when i==0 and do something else when it does not, you can write the following:

```
if (i==0){
...
}
else {
...
}
```

If you have more than two choices and want to do different things according to the value of i, you can use the switch conditional statement.

```
switch (i){
    case 1:
    ...
    break;
    case 2:
    ...
    break;
    case 3:
    ...
    break;
    default:
    ...
    break;
}
```

The ? symbol, often called the *ternary operator* because it takes three arguments, assigns either of two values to a variable depending on a condition. The following example assigns the value 3 to the variable y if i<0 and assigns the value 4 to y otherwise:

```
y=(i<0) ? 3:4;
```

Example 3.6 shows a simple Java program that demonstrates the use of the if...else conditional statement. Figure 3.2 shows how to compile and run the Hello1.java program and its output.

EXAMPLE 3.6   USING AN IF...ELSE STRUCTURE

```
========================================================================
//Example 3.6 If Else
class Hello1 {
    public static void main(String[] args) {
        if(args.length!=2){
            System.out.println("Usage: java Hello1 firstname surname!");
        }
        else{
            System.out.println("Hello "+ args[0] +" "+ args[1] + "!");
        }
    }
}
========================================================================
```

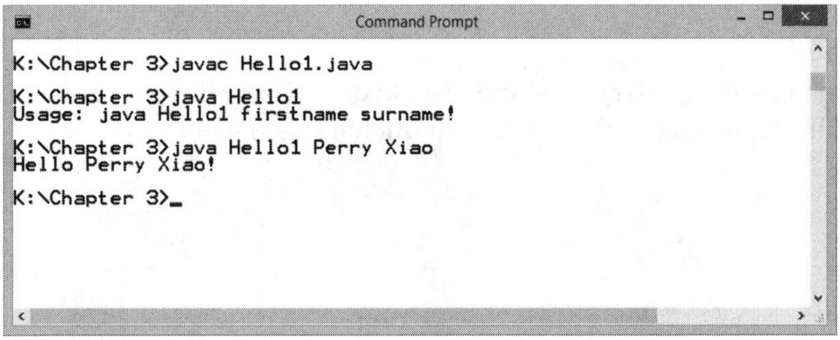

```
K:\Chapter 3>javac Hello1.java

K:\Chapter 3>java Hello1
Usage: java Hello1 firstname surname!

K:\Chapter 3>java Hello1 Perry Xiao
Hello Perry Xiao!

K:\Chapter 3>_
```

Figure 3.2: The compilation, execution, and output results of `Hello1.java`

3.7   Arrays, Matrices, and ArrayLists

Arrays are important in scientific and engineering programs. In Java, you can create one-dimensional arrays, two-dimensional arrays (matrices), multidimensional arrays, and dynamic arrays (lists), which can have a dynamic set of elements, growing and shrinking during the execution of the program.

The following examples show how to declare an `integer`-type one-dimensional array, a `float`-type two-dimensional array (a matrix), and a `double`-type multidimensional array, respectively:

```
int[] x=new int[10];

float[][] y=new float [2][5];

double[][][] z=new double [5][2][3];
```

Alternatively, you can declare and initialize them at the same time.

```
int[] x={1,2,3,4,5,6,7,8,9,0};

float[][] y={{1.0F,1.0F,1.0F,1.0F,1.0F},{2.0F,3.0F,4.0F,5.0F,6.0F}};

double[][][]
z={{{1,2,3},{4,5,6}},{{7,8,9},{10,11,12}},{{13,14,15},{16,
17,18}},{{19,20,21},{22,23,24}},{{25,26,27},{28,29,30}}};
```

You can also separate the array declaration into two steps. For example, the following:

```
int[] x;
x=new int[10];
```

is exactly the same as the previous one-line declaration, but the benefit of this approach is that it will allow you to decide on the size of the array later when you run the program.

Example 3.7 shows how to create an `integer`-type one-dimensional array called `x[]` and a double-type two-dimensional array called `y[][]`. Figure 3.3 shows the compilation, execution, and output results of `Array1.java`. (Please note that as the array `y[][]` is randomly generated, your final output may not be the same as in Figure 3.3.) In Java, you can refer to any element of an array using its index, such as `x[2]` or `y[0][1]`. All the elements of the array must be of the same type.

EXAMPLE 3.7   USING AN ARRAY

```
===============================================================================
//Example 3.7 Array example
import java.util.*;

class Array1 {
    public static void main(String[] args) {
        int[] x;
        double [][] y;
        int i, j, row, col;
        if(args.length!=2){
            System.out.println("Usage: java array1 row colume");
            System.exit(0);
        }
        //initialize the arrays
        row=Integer.parseInt(args[0]);
        col=Integer.parseInt(args[1]);
        x=new int[row];
        y=new double[row][col];
        for (i=0;i<row;i++){
            x[i]=i;
        }
        for (i=0;i<row;i++){
            for (j=0;j<col;j++){
```

```
                    y[i][j]=Math.random();
            }
        }
        //display the arrays
        System.out.print("x[]=");
        for (i=0;i<row;i++){
            System.out.print(x[i]+"\t");
        }
        System.out.println();
        System.out.println("y[][]=");
        for (i=0;i<row;i++){
            for (j=0;j<col;j++){
                System.out.print(y[i][j]+ "\t");
            }
            System.out.println();
        }
    }
}
```

===

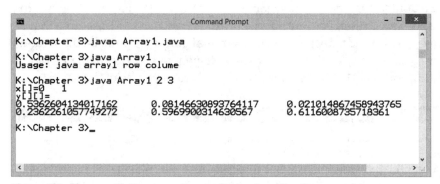

Figure 3.3: The compilation, execution, and output results of `Array1.java`

A drawback of arrays is that their size is fixed when they are defined. Sometimes you need an array whose size can be changed as the program executes. You can create such an array by using Java's `ArrayList` class, which implements a "growable" array of objects. The following examples show how to declare dynamic arrays of String, `integer`, and `double` types. Similarly, you can also create an `ArrayList` of any objects.

```
ArrayList<String> v=new ArrayList<String>();
ArrayList<Integer> v=new ArrayList<Integer>();
ArrayList<double> v=new ArrayList<double>();
```

The angular braces, < >, indicate that this is a generic `ArrayList`. Java generic programming was introduced in Java SE 5 with the aim of reducing bugs and dealing with type-safe objects. As illustrated next, the nongeneric `ArrayList` example code can be compiled without any errors, but when you try to run the code, it will give a runtime error, as you are trying convert a string into an integer. In the generic `ArrayList` example code, `<String>` forces the `ArrayList` to contain only string values; therefore, it will generate a compilation error. In this way, generics programming makes Java code more robust and less error prone.

Here's the nongeneric `ArrayList` example code:

```
ArrayList list=new ArrayList();
list.add("hello");
Integer i = (Integer)list.get(0);
```

Here's the generic `ArrayList` example code:

```
ArrayList<String> list = new ArrayList<String>();
list.add("hello");
Integer i = (Integer)list.get(0);
```

For more information about Java generic programming, please visit these sites:

https://docs.oracle.com/javase/tutorial/java/generics/index.html
https://en.wikipedia.org/wiki/Generics _ in _ Java
http://tutorials.jenkov.com/java-generics/index.html

Example 3.8 shows how to create a dynamic `ArrayList` named `list`, which can grow using an `add()` method, as well as shrink using a `remove()` method. Figure 3.4 shows the compilation, execution, and output results of `arraylist1.java`.

EXAMPLE 3.8   USING AN ARRAYLIST

```
==========================================================================
// Example 3.8  ArrayList example
import java.util.*;

class Arraylist1 {
    public static void main(String[] args) {
        ArrayList<Integer> list=new ArrayList<Integer>();
        int i, j;
        for (i=0;i<4;i++){
            list.add(i);
        }
        System.out.println("The total elements of ArrayList list
is:"+list.size());
        System.out.println(list);

        System.out.println("The second element is :");
                System.out.println(list.get(1));
        System.out.println("Now remove the second element:");
        list.remove(1);
        System.out.println(list);
    }
}
==========================================================================
```

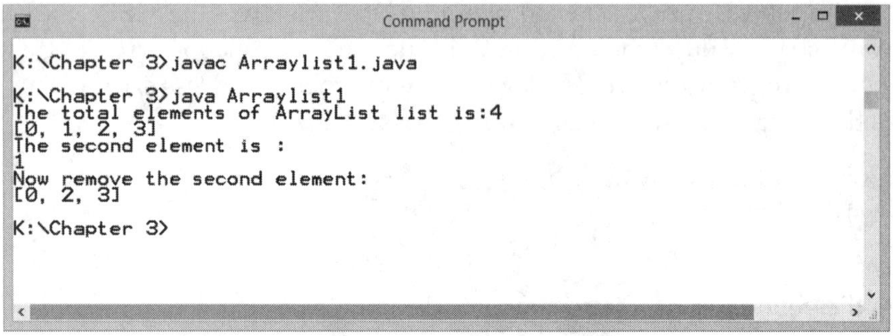

Figure 3.4: The compilation, execution, and output results of `Arraylist1.java`

3.8   Reading and Writing Files

Many applications need to read and write files. Java supports reading and writing both text and binary files, but I will cover only text files here. There are many ways in Java to read and write text files; the most basic one is by using the `FileReader` and `FileWriter` classes of the `java.io` package.

To use the `FileWriter` class to write to a text file, take the following steps:

1. Create a `FileWriter` object associated with the text file that you want to write.

2. Create a `BufferedWriter` object associated with the `FileWriter` object.

3. Write to the buffer.

4. Flush the buffer.

5. Close the file.

Using the `BufferedWriter` class for writing is optional; you can also write to a text file without using a buffer. But using a buffer, with the `BufferedWriter` and `BufferedReader` classes, can make the reading and writing process more efficient. The `BufferedWriter` class first bundles up several small write requests in its own internal buffer, and then when the buffer is full or the `flush()` method is called, it writes the whole buffer into the text file in one go. For file read and write, a `try...catch` block must be used to handle exceptions.

Example 3.9 shows how to write data to a text file using the `FileWriter` and `BufferedWriter` classes. It uses the `args[0]` parameter to get the name of the text file, which you will write data into. It will produce an error message and exit the program if no file name is provided.

EXAMPLE 3.9   TEXTWRITE1.JAVA TO WRITE DATA TO A TEXT FILE

```
===========================================================================
// Example 3.9 TextWrite1.java
import java.io.*;
class TextWrite1 {
    public static void main(String[] args) {
        String filename="";
        if (args.length==1){
            filename=args[0];
        }
        else {
            System.out.println("Usage: java TextWrite1 Filename.txt ");
            System.exit(0);
        }
        try {
            FileWriter file=new FileWriter(filename);
            BufferedWriter filebuff= new BufferedWriter(file);
            for (int i=0;i<3;i++){
                filebuff.write(i+"\t"+i*i+"\n");
            }
            filebuff.flush();
            file.close();
        }
        catch(IOException e) {
            System.err.println("Error -- " + e.toString() );
        }
    }
}
===========================================================================
```

To use the `FileReader` class to read from a text file, take the following steps:

1. Create a `FileReader` object associated with the text file that you want to read.

2. Create a `BufferedReader` object associated with the `FileReader` object.

3. Read from the buffer.

4. Flush the buffer.

5. Close the file.

Again, using the `BufferedReader` class is optional, but it does make text file reading more efficient.

Example 3.10 shows how to read data from a text file using the `FileReader` and `BufferedReader` classes.

EXAMPLE 3.10   TEXTREAD1.JAVA TO READ DATA FROM A TEXT FILE

```
=============================================================================
// Example 3.10 TextRead1.java
import java.io.*;
class TextRead1 {
    public static void main(String[] args) {
        String filename="";
        if (args.length==1){
            filename=args[0];
        }
        else {
            System.out.println("Usage: java TextRead1 Filename.txt ");
            System.exit(0);
        }
        try {
            FileReader file=new FileReader(filename);
            BufferedReader filebuff= new BufferedReader(file);
            boolean endof=false;
            String line;
            while (!endof) {
                line=filebuff.readLine();
                if (line == null){ endof=true; break;}
                System.out.println(line);
            }
            file.close();
        }
        catch(IOException e) {
            System.err.println("Error -- " + e.toString() );
        }
    }
}
=============================================================================
```

3.9   Methods

Methods, also called *functions, modules,* or *subroutines* in other languages, allow programmers to modularize their programs and hence reduce the complexity of their software and improve its reusability. Methods normally have some input parameters, which are also called *formal parameters* or *arguments,* to carry out their specific tasks. The variables defined within a method are called *local variables* because they can be used only within that method. Formal parameters are also local variables.

Example 3.11 demonstrates the use of methods. Instead of printing out the Hello message directly, this program calls a method called printhello() to do the job. printhello() has one String type input parameter, msg. The void keyword means that there is no returned parameter for printhello().

The static keyword means that printhello() exists within the entire class. It is compulsory here, as only the static methods can be called in the main() method. The private keyword means this method can be called only within the current class.

EXAMPLE 3.11   USING A METHOD

```
===========================================================================
// Example 3.11   Method example
class Method1 {
    public static void main(String[] args) {
       printhello(args[0]);
    }
    //printhello method
    private static void printhello(String msg){
       System.out.println("Hello "+ msg + "!" );
    }
}
===========================================================================
```

Example 3.12 shows another example of methods. In the main() method, a Method2 class object is created first, Test test = new Test();, and then the pupAge() method is called.

```
test.pupAge();
```

In this case, the pupAge() method is called through an object-oriented approach, and therefore it does not need to be static. See the next section for more details about object-oriented programming.

EXAMPLE 3.12   AN OBJECT-ORIENTED APPROACH TO USING METHODS

```
===========================================================================
// Example 3.12   Method example
public class Method2 {
    public void pupAge() {
       int age = 0;
       age = age + 7;
       System.out.println("Puppy age is : " + age);
    }

    public static void main(String args[]) {
       Method2 test = new Method2 ();//create an Method2 object
       test.pupAge();                //call the pupAge() method of Method2
class
    }
}
===========================================================================
```

In cases where you do need to return some value from a method, you need to specify what type of value will be returned. For example, the add() method shown in Example 3.13 takes in two double numbers, adds them, and returns the sum.

EXAMPLE 3.13   RETURNING A VALUE FROM A METHOD

```
// Example 3.13  Method example
class Method3 {
    public static void main(String[] args) {
        double x=3, y=5;
        double s = add (x, y);
        System.out.println("The sum of x and y is: " + s);
    }
    //add() method
    private static double add(double x, double y){
        return x+y;
    }
}
```

3.10   Object-Oriented Programming

When a problem is simple, you can just write one Java program, or one class, to solve it. But as the problems become more and more complicated, it is better to write the program using "separation of concerns" or "divide-and-conquer" approaches, that is, to write multiple classes in an object-oriented programming (OOP) fashion. OOP is a huge topic that itself can fill a whole book. But the benefits of OOP are obvious. Because it divides a big Java class into several smaller, self-contained, and reusable Java classes, it makes the code more understandable, more manageable, and less bug-prone.

In the simplest terms, OOP in Java means developing or using self-contained Java classes, which have specific attributes and certain behavior. The attributes are parameters (variables, or objects), and the behavior consists of methods (again, called *functions* in other languages). These parameters are used for exchanging input/output values with external programs, and the methods are for performing specific tasks. The following are the most important OOP concepts.

3.10.1   Classes and Objects

A *class* is a template that specifies the attributes and behavior of typical instances of that class. An *object* is an instance that is created based on a class. A real-life analogy can be tree (class) and oak, palm, pine (objects), or animal (class) and lion, tiger, dog (objects). In object-oriented programming, a problem is described as a collection of objects with various interactions between them. This will, in turn, reduce the complexity of the problem and improve the reusability of software code.

3.10.2   Instantiation

The process of creating an object from a class is called *instantiation*. The object is an *instance* of that class.

3.10.3   Encapsulation

In object-oriented programming, all objects are self-contained. This means that although the methods of objects can be called by external programs, their details are hidden from outside. This approach is called *encapsulation*, and it makes object-oriented programming easier and less error-prone. To use encapsulation in Java, you need to declare the variables of a class as private and provide public setter and getter methods to modify and view the variable values.

3.10.4   Inheritance

In object-oriented programming, not only can you create classes, but you can also create subclasses using the existing classes to enrich their functionalities. This is called *inheritance*. Unlike other OOP languages, Java supports only single inheritance, which means that a subclass can be derived from only a single parent class. This constraint is intended to make OOP simpler. In cases where multiple inheritance is needed, you must create it through the Java interface, which defines collections of parameters and methods. You can create a Java class that implements as many interfaces as you like.

3.10.5   Overriding and Overloading

In Java, when a child class inherits its parent class's methods, it can also redefine the content of the methods. This standard OOP technique is known as *method overriding*. Another similar approach is *method overloading*, which allows you to define two or more functions with exactly identical names but with different formal parameters.

3.10.6   Polymorphism

In object-oriented programming, when an overriding method is invoked, the method that is associated with the class (or subclass) of the object is always used. In this example, there is a `getLeafShape()` method in a class called `Tree`, which is overridden in its subclasses `Oak` and `Pine`.

```
Tree tree;
Oak oak=new Oak();
Pine pine=new Pine();
tree=oak;
tree.getLeafShape();
tree=pine;
tree.getLeafShape();
```

There are two identical `tree.getLeafShape()` statements. The first one calls the `Oak` class's `getLeafShape()` method, while the second one calls the `Pine` class's `getLeafShape()` method. This feature is known as *polymorphism*, and it improves software reusability and enhances information hiding.

3.10.7   Object Accessibility

When an object, a variable, or a method is defined in a class, it falls into one of the four categories that control its accessibility or scope: public, protected, package, and private. For example, a public variable can be accessed from anywhere, but a private variable can be accessed only within the same class. The default is package, and there is no keyword for package accessibility. Table 3.2 summarizes class object accessibility.

Table 3.2: Class Object Accessibility

CATEGORY	SAME CLASS	SUBCLASS	SAME PACKAGE	OTHER
Public	Yes	Yes	Yes	Yes
Protected	Yes	Yes	No	No
Package	Yes	Yes	Yes	No
Private	Yes	No	No	No

3.10.8   Anonymous Inner Classes

In Java, anonymous inner classes provide a way to create an object without a name and without having to actually subclass a class. An anonymous inner class can be useful when making an instance of an object with overloading methods of a class or interface.

Example 3.14A gives you a taste of OOP. It has two classes, `Math1` and `Oop1`. The class `Oop1` is the main class because it has the `main()` function in it. The `Oop1` class first creates an object (using the `new` keyword) named `m` using the `Math1` class and then calls the `setZ()` method and the `getZ()` method to set the value for the private variable `z` in the `Math1` class, which is hidden from outside the class; this is called *encapsulation*.

You can also separate the `Math1` class and the `Oop1` class into two files, one called `Math1.java` and one called `Oop1.java`. The program will run exactly the same way, but separation into different files will make the code much easier to manage and understand.

EXAMPLE 3.14A   BASIC OBJECT-ORIENTED PROGRAMMING

```
==========================================================================
// Example 3.14A Object oriented programming example
class Math1
    private int z;                             //encapsulation
    public void setZ(int x){                   //setter method
       z=x;
    }
    public int getZ(){                         //getter method
       return z;
    }
}

class Oop1 {
    public static void main(String[] args) {
       Math1 m = new Math1();                  //instantiation (Math1:
                                                 class  m:object)
       m.setZ(5);                              //call setter method
       System.out.println(m.getZ());           //call getter method
    }
}
==========================================================================
```

Example 3.14B is another example of OOP. It also has two classes, `Math2` and `Oop2`, where `Oop2` is the main class. The `Oop2` class first creates an object (using the `new` keyword) named `m` using the `Math2` class and then calls the public parameters and methods by using dot notation (for example, `m.add()`, `m.W`, and so on). This is different from other languages such as C++ that use `->` notation.

Note that there are two `add` functions in the `Math2` class. This is an example of *method overloading*. The `Math2()` method is a special type of method called a *constructor* method. The constructor method is called automatically each time an object is created, and it is mainly used for initializing parameters. In Java, there are many ways to access the public parameters in a class.

EXAMPLE 3.14B   METHOD OVERLOADING IN OBJECT-ORIENTED PROGRAMMING

```
==========================================================================
// Example 3.14B Object oriented programming example
class Math2
    public int W;                              //Public variable
```

```
        public Math2(){                              //constructor method
        }
        public double add(double x,double y){
            return x+y;
        }
        public int add(int x,int y){                 //method overloading
            return x+y;
        }
}

class Oop2 {
    public static void main(String[] args) {
        Math2 m = new Math2();
        System.out.println(m.add(3,2));          //call add method
        System.out.println(m.add(4.0,2.1));      //call add method
        System.out.println(m.W);                 //get public variable W
    }
}
========================================================================
```

Example 3.14C shows another example of OOP. It has three classes, the Math3 class, the Math3a class, and the Oop1 class, where Math3a is a subclass of Math3. When a child class is created from its parent class, it will not only inherit all the public and protected parameters and methods of the parent class but will also introduce its own new parameters and methods (toDegree()). In this example, the func() method has been redefined in the subclass, an example of method overriding.

You can also separate the Math3 class, Math3a class, and Oop3 class into three files, one called Math3.java, one called Math3a.java, and one called Oop3.java. They will still run in the same way.

EXAMPLE 3.14C   INHERITANCE IN OBJECT-ORIENTED PROGRAMMING

```
========================================================================
// Example 3.14C Object oriented programming example
class Math3{                                      //parent class
    public Math3(){
    }
    public double func(double x){
        return Math.cos(x);
    }
}
class Math3a extends Math3{                        //sub-class, inheritance
    public double func(double x){                 //method overriding
        return Math.sin(x);
    }
    public double toDegree(double x){             //create a new method in
                                                  //    sub-class
        return Math.toDegrees(x);
    }
}
```

```
class Oop3 {
    public static void main(String[] args) {
        Math3 m = new Math3();
        Math3a n = new Math3a();
        System.out.println(m.func(0.0));
        System.out.println(n.func(0.0));
        System.out.println(n.toDegree(3.14));
    }
}
=============================================================================
```

Example 3.15A shows an example of an interface in OOP. It has an interface called `Animal`, which has a method called `speak()`. The `Dog` class implements the `Animal` interface and creates a definition of the `speak()` method. Finally, in the `main()` method, an object named `p` is created, and the `speak()` method is called.

EXAMPLE 3.15A   USING AN INTERFACE IN OBJECT-ORIENTED PROGRAMMING

```
=============================================================================
// Example 3.15A Object oriented programming example
interface Animal{
  public void speak();
}
class Dog implements Animal{
    public void speak(){
        System.out.println("Woof! Woof!");
    }
    public static void main(String args[]){
        Dog p = new Dog();
        p.speak();
    }
}
=============================================================================
```

Example 3.15B shows an anonymous inner class version of the previous example. As you can see, it creates an object, overriding the `speak()` method, and calls the `speak()` method, without needing to give the object a name or implement the interface. This has greatly simplified the code.

EXAMPLE 3.15B   OBJECT-ORIENTED PROGRAMMING USING AN ANONYMOUS INNER CLASS

```
=============================================================================
// Example 3.15B Object oriented programming example
interface Animal{
  public void speak();
}
```

```
class Dog2 {
    public static void main(String args[]){
        //anonymous inner class
        new Animal(){
            public void speak(){
                System.out.println("Woof! Woof!");
            }
        }.speak();
    }
}
```

===

3.11   Multithreading

To thread or not to thread, that is the question—but not for Java programmers, fortunately.

Many applications need to perform several tasks at the same time. Multithreading is a powerful way of achieving that. In software programming, a thread is an independent path of executing a task within a program. Multithreading means to execute two or more tasks, or threads, concurrently within a single program. Unlike other traditional programming languages, Java supports multithreading natively. Threads are a standard part of the Java language.

Example 3.16A shows a simple multithreading program called `HelloThread0.java`. The `HelloThread0` class is a subclass of the Java `Thread` class. You need to override the `run()` method of the `Thread` class in order to specify what you want to execute in the thread. In this example, this is only one thread, which just prints a message. Once the thread object has been created, you can use the `start()`, `yield()`, `join()`, and `stop()` methods to start, hold (give other threads a chance to execute), wait until another thread completes, and stop the thread.

EXAMPLE 3.16A   BASIC MULTITHREADED PROGRAMMING

===
```
//Example 3.16A Multithreading programming example
public class HelloThread0 extends Thread{
    public void run(){
        System.out.println("This is a thread...");
    }
    public static void main(String[] args) {
        HelloThread0 ht1 = new HelloThread0();
        ht1.start();
    }
}
```
===

Example 3.16B shows a slightly more complicated version of the previous program. In this case, it has three threads, and each thread can print different messages so that you can differentiate them from each other. The message is passed into the thread through the thread constructor method. When you run the code, you will find that the threads might not appear in order. That is because they are executed independently.

EXAMPLE 3.16B   MULTITHREADED PROGRAMMING WITH THREE THREADS

```
==========================================================================
//Example 3.16B Multithread programming example
public class HelloThread1 extends Thread{
    String message;
    //pass message into thread
    HelloThread1 ( String message ) { this.message = message; }
    public void run(){
       System.out.println( message );
    }
    public static void main(String[] args) {
        HelloThread1 ht1 = new HelloThread1("Thread 1 ...");
        HelloThread1 ht2 = new HelloThread1("Thread 2 ...");
        HelloThread1 ht3 = new HelloThread1("Thread 3 ...");
        ht1.start();
        ht2.start();
        ht3.start();
    }
}
==========================================================================
```

Although Example 3.16A and Example 3.16B show a standard way of creating a multithreaded program, Java's single-inheritance limitation sometimes makes it much more desirable to implement the Runnable interface to achieve multithreaded programming. You also need to override the run() method in the class to specify what you want to execute in the thread. Example 3.16C shows the details.

EXAMPLE 3.16C   MULTITHREADED PROGRAMMING USING THE RUNNABLE INTERFACE

```
==========================================================================
//Example 3.16C Multithread programming example
public class HelloThread2 implements Runnable {
    String message;
    HelloThread2 ( String message ) { this.message = message; }
    public void run(){
       System.out.println( message );
    }
```

```
    public static void main(String[] args) {
        HelloThread2 ht1 = new HelloThread2("Thread 1 ...");
        HelloThread2 ht2 = new HelloThread2("Thread 2 ...");
        HelloThread2 ht3 = new HelloThread2("Thread 3 ...");
        Thread t1 = new Thread(ht1);
        Thread t2 = new Thread(ht2);
        Thread t3 = new Thread(ht3);
        t1.start();
        t2.start();
        t3.start();
    }
}
==========================================================================
```

Example 3.16D shows another simple, elegant way of implementing multi-threaded programming in Java by using a Java anonymous inner class, in which you create the thread object, define the `run()` method, and start the thread all in one go. See the previous OOP discussion for more details on Java anonymous inner classes.

EXAMPLE 3.16D   MULTITHREADED PROGRAMMING USING AN ANONYMOUS INNER CLASS

```
==========================================================================
//Example 3.16D Multithread programming example
public class HelloThread3{
    public static void main(String[] args) {
        new Thread(new Runnable() {
            public void run() {
                System.out.println("Thread  ...");
            }
        }).start();

    }
}
==========================================================================
```

Example 3.16E shows an object-oriented approach of implementing multi-threaded programming. Here a separated class called `Hello4` is created, which implements the `Runnable` interface.

EXAMPLE 3.16E   OBJECT-ORIENTED MULTITHREADED PROGRAMMING

```
==========================================================================
//Example 3.16E Multithread programming example
public class HelloThread4  {
    public static void main(String[] args) {
        Hello4 ht1 = new Hello4("Thread 1 ...");
        Hello4 ht2 = new Hello4("Thread 2 ...");
```

```
        Hello4 ht3 = new Hello4("Thread 3 ...");
        Thread t1 = new Thread(ht1);
        Thread t2 = new Thread(ht2);
        Thread t3 = new Thread(ht3);
        t1.start();
        t2.start();
        t3.start();
    }
}
class Hello4 implements Runnable {
    String message;
    Hello4 ( String message ) { this.message = message; }
    public void run(){
        System.out.println( message );
    }
}
```
===

Example 3.16F also shows an object-oriented approach to implementing multithreaded programming. Here a separate class named Hello5 is created, which is a subclass of the Thread class.

EXAMPLE 3.16F   MULTITHREADED PROGRAMMING EXAMPLE

===
```
//Example 3.16F Multithread programming example
public class HelloThread5{
    public static void main(String[] args) {
        Hello5 ht1 = new Hello5("Thread 1 ...");
        Hello5 ht2 = new Hello5("Thread 2 ...");
        Hello5 ht3 = new Hello5("Thread 3 ...");
        ht1.start();
        ht2.start();
        ht3.start();
    }
}
class Hello5 extends Thread{
    String message;
    Hello5 ( String message ) { this.message = message; }
    public void run(){
        System.out.println( message );
    }
}
```
===

Example 3.16G shows a more complicated multithreading program that does some calculations in the thread. It is based on the previous OOP multithreaded example. Figure 3.5 shows the compilation, execution, and output results.

EXAMPLE 3.16G   MULTITHREADED PROGRAMMING USING CALCULATIONS

```
========================================================================
//Example 3.16G Multithread programming example
public class Thread1 {
    public static void main( String args[] )
    {
        CalcThread thread1, thread2;
        thread1 = new CalcThread( "Calculation1" );
        thread2 = new CalcThread( "Calculation2" );
        thread1.start();
        thread2.start();
    }
}

class CalcThread extends Thread {
    private int num,sum=0;
    public CalcThread( String name )
    {
        super( name );
        // generate a random number between 0 and 100
        num = (int) ( Math.random() * 100 );
    }

    // execute the thread
    public void run(){
        System.err.println( getName() + " started!" );
        for (int i=0;i<num;i++){
            sum+=i;
        }
        System.err.println( getName() +": sum (0 to "+num+"): " + sum );
        System.err.println( getName() + " done!" );
    }
}
========================================================================
```

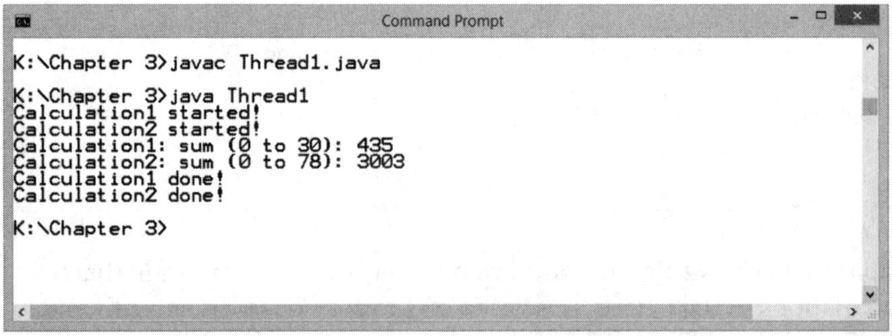

```
K:\Chapter 3>javac Thread1.java

K:\Chapter 3>java Thread1
Calculation1 started!
Calculation2 started!
Calculation1: sum (0 to 30): 435
Calculation2: sum (0 to 78): 3003
Calculation1 done!
Calculation2 done!

K:\Chapter 3>
```

Figure 3.5: The compilation, execution, and output results of Thread1.java. Please note that your result might be different from the screenshot, as the threads can be executed in random order.

Example 3.16H is a variation of Example 3.16A. Instead of inheriting from the Thread class, it implements the Runnable interface.

EXAMPLE 3.16H   MULTITHREADED PROGRAMMING USING THE RUNNABLE INTERFACE

```
=============================================================================
//Example 3.16H Multithread programming example
public class Thread2 {
    public static void main( String args[] )
    {
        Runnable calc= new CalcThread();
        Thread thread1 = new Thread( calc, "Calculation1" );
        thread1.start();
    }
}

class CalcThread implements Runnable {
    // execute the thread
    public void run(){
        int num,sum=0;
        System.err.println( "started!" );
        num = (int) ( Math.random() * 100 );
        for (int i=0;i<num;i++){
            sum+=i;
        }
        System.err.println( "sum (0 to "+num+"): " + sum );
        System.err.println( "done!" );
    }
}
=============================================================================
```

3.11.1   The Life Cycle of a Thread

A thread can be in one of several defined states. When a thread is created, it is in the born state. When the thread's start() method is called, the thread enters the ready state. When the thread begins executing, it enters a running state. A running thread can then enter a waiting state, sleeping state, or blocking state, and a dead state when it is terminated. You can use the getState() method to determine the state of a thread.

The Java thread states are as follows:

- New
- Runnable
- Running
- Nonrunnable (blocked)
- Terminated

Example 3.17A shows a simple example of how to use the `getState()` method to get the state of a thread. This is the same thread as shown in Example 3.16A, which simply prints a message. After creating the thread object, it displays the state of the thread before it starts and after it starts. It then waits for one second and displays the states again. The delay is achieved by using the `Thread.sleep()` method; please note that this method must be placed in a `try...catch` block. You can find more details about the `Thread.sleep()` method in the next section.

EXAMPLE 3.17A   MULTITHREADED PROGRAMMING USING THE GETSTATE() METHOD

```
=========================================================================
//Example 3.17A Multithread programming example
class StateThread1 extends Thread{
    public void run(){
        System.out.println( "This is a thread..." );
    }
    public static void main(String[] args) {
        StateThread1 st1 = new StateThread1 ();
        System.out.println("thread before start(): "+ st1.getState());
//states before start()
        st1.start();
        System.out.println("thread after start(): "+ st1.getState());
//states after start()

        try {
//sleep for 1000ms
            Thread.sleep(1000);
        } catch (InterruptedException e) {
            e.printStackTrace();
        }
        System.out.println("thread after 1s:  "+ st1.getState());
//states after 1s
    }
}
=========================================================================
```

The following is the output of Example 3.17A. You can see the different states of the thread, and after one second, the thread has been terminated.

```
thread before start(): NEW
This is a thread...
thread after start(): RUNNABLE
thread after 1s: TERMINATED
```

Example 3.17B is an improved version of the previous program. In this case, I added a five-second wait in the thread. Again, the wait is implemented by using the `Thread.sleep(1000)` method, placed in a `try...catch` block. After creating the thread object, it displays the state of the thread before it starts and then after it starts. It then waits for one second and displays the states again.

EXAMPLE 3.17B   MULTITHREADED PROGRAMMING USING A TRY... CATCH **BLOCK**

```
=============================================================================
//Example 3.17B Multithread programming example
public class StateThread2 extends Thread{
   public void run(){
     System.out.println( "This is a thread..." );
        try {
//sleep for 5s
            Thread.sleep(5000);
        } catch (InterruptedException e) {
            e.printStackTrace();
        }
    }
   public static void main(String[] args) {
        StateThread2 st = new StateThread2 ();
        System.out.println("thread before start(): "+ st.getState());
//states before start()
        st.start();
        System.out.println("thread after start(): "+ st.getState());
//states after start()

        try {
//sleep for 1s
            Thread.sleep(1000);
        } catch (InterruptedException e) {
            e.printStackTrace();
        }
        System.out.println("thread after 1s:  "+ st.getState());
//states after 1s
    }
}
=============================================================================
```

The following is the output of Example 3.17B. As you can see, because of the five-second delay in the thread, the thread is in the TIMED _ WAITING state after one second.

```
    thread before start(): NEW
    This is a thread...
    thread after start(): RUNNABLE
    thread after 1s:  TIMED_WAITING
```

3.11.2   Thread Priorities

Different threads can have different priorities. Use the `setPriority()` method to set a thread's priority, which can range from 1 to 10, where 1 is the `Thread.MIN_ PRIORITY`, 10 is the `Thread.MAX _ PRIORITY`, and 5 is the `Thread.NORM _ PRIORITY`.

Example 3.17C shows a simple thread priority example. It uses the `setPriority()` method to set the priority of each thread. If you run the code, you will find that the thread with higher priority tends to be executed first.

EXAMPLE 3.17C   SETTING THREAD PRIORITY

```
===========================================================================
//Example 3.17C Thread Priority example
public class ThreadPriority1 extends Thread{
    String message;
    ThreadPriority1 ( String message ) { this.message = message; }
    public void run(){
        System.out.println( message );
    }
    public static void main(String[] args) {
        ThreadPriority1 ht1 = new ThreadPriority1("Thread 1 ...");
        ThreadPriority1 ht2 = new ThreadPriority1("Thread 2 ...");
        ThreadPriority1 ht3 = new ThreadPriority1("Thread 3 ...");
        ThreadPriority1 ht4 = new ThreadPriority1("Thread 4 ...");
        ThreadPriority1 ht5 = new ThreadPriority1("Thread 5 ...");
        ht1.setPriority(2);
        ht2.setPriority(4);
        ht3.setPriority(6);
        ht4.setPriority(8);
        ht5.setPriority(10);

        ht1.start();
        ht2.start();
        ht3.start();
        ht4.start();
        ht5.start();
    }
}
===========================================================================
```

3.11.3   Thread Scheduling

Many Java platforms use *time slicing* to execute threads. With time slicing, the CPU time is divided into a series of small slots called *quanta*. Threads with equal priority will be executed in a round-robin fashion, one thread per quantum. Threads with higher priority will be executed ahead of those with lower priority.

3.11.4   Thread Synchronization

When several threads are operating on the same object and it has synchronized methods, the threads also need to be synchronized, which means that only one thread at a time is allowed to execute synchronized methods on the object. This requirement is implemented by locking the object when a synchronized method is invoked.

Example 3.17D demonstrates simple thread synchronization. In this example, the `Test()` class has a `printMessage()` method, which prints a message five times and waits for 500 ms each time. In the `main()` method, two threads were created, and both need to access the same `Test()` object. Without synchronization, you can see both threads can access the object.

Now uncomment the `//synchronized void printMessage(String txt)` line, and comment out the `void printMessage(String txt)` line. By adding the `synchronized` keyword in front of the `printMessage()` method, it becomes synchronized, which means that when the `Test()` object is accessed by one thread, it will be locked; the second thread cannot access it until the first thread has finished.

EXAMPLE 3.17D   THREAD SYNCHRONIZATION

```
=========================================================================
//Example 3.17D Thread Synchronization example
class Test{
  void printMessage(String txt){//method not synchronized
  //synchronized void printMessage(String txt){//method synchronized
    for(int i=1;i<=5;i++){
        System.out.println(txt);
        try{
            Thread.sleep(500);
        }catch(Exception e){System.out.println(e);}
    }
  }
}

class ThreadSyn1 extends Thread{
    String message;
        Test t;
    ThreadSyn1 ( Test t,  String message ) {
        this.t=t;
        this.message = message;
        }
    public void run(){
        t.printMessage( message );
    }
    public static void main(String args[]){
        Test m = new Test();
        ThreadSyn1 t1=new ThreadSyn1(m,"A");
```

```
        ThreadSyn1 t2=new ThreadSyn1(m,"B");
        t1.start();
        t2.start();
    }
}
```

==

3.12   Date, Time, Timer, and Sleep Methods

You'll often need dates, times, and accurate timers in your programs. In Java, you can use the new Date().toString() method to get the date and time string, you can use the System.currentTimeMillis() method, or you can use the new Date().getTime() method to get the current time in milliseconds past midnight, January 1, 1970, UTC. You can also use the System.nanoTime() method to get the most accurate system time in nanoseconds.

Example 3.18A is a simple program that illustrates how to use the Date() class to get date and time information. Figure 3.6 shows the output result.

EXAMPLE 3.18A   GETTING THE DATE AND TIME USING THE DATE() CLASS

```
====================================================================
//Example 3.18A Date and Time Example
import java.util.*;
public class DateExample {
    public static void main(String[] args) throws InterruptedException
    {
        //Get the current date and time
        Date date = new Date();
        System.out.println("The current Date and Time is: " + date.toString());
        //Get the current time in millis
        long tm = date.getTime();
        System.out.println("The current time in milliseconds : " + tm);
    }
}
====================================================================
```

Figure 3.6: The compilation, execution, and output results of DateExample.java

The `LocalDateTime()` class, which belongs to the `java.time.*` package, provides the most useful date and time functions, such as `getYear()`, `getMonth()`, `getDayofMonth()`, and `getDayofWeek()`. You can also display the date and time using a certain format.

Example 3.18B is a simple program that illustrates how to use the `Local-DateTime()` class to get date and time information. Figure 3.7 shows the output result.

EXAMPLE 3.18B   GETTING THE DATE AND TIME USING THE LOCALDATETIME() CLASS

```
===========================================================================
//Example 3.18B Date and Time
import java.time.LocalDateTime;              // Import the LocalDateTime
                                                class
import java.time.format.DateTimeFormatter;  // Import the
                                                DateTimeFormatter class

public class DateExample2 {
  public static void main(String[] args) {
    LocalDateTime dt = LocalDateTime.now();
    System.out.println("Year:             " + dt.getYear());
    System.out.println("Month:            " + dt.getMonth());
    System.out.println("Day:              " + dt.getDayOfMonth());
    System.out.println("Day of the week: " + dt.getDayOfWeek());
    System.out.println("Unformatted:      " + dt);

        DateTimeFormatter f = DateTimeFormatter.ofPattern("dd-MM-yyyy
HH:mm:ss");
    System.out.println("Formatted:        " + dt.format(f));
  }
}
===========================================================================
```

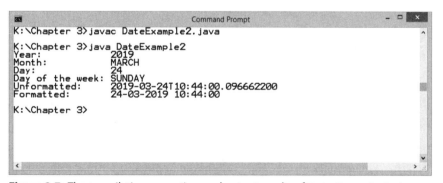

Figure 3.7: The compilation, execution, and output results of `DateExample2.java`

The `timer()` class, also from the `java.util` package, provides the most accurate timer function, which you can set up using the `schedule()` method. Any class that you want to run in the timer must be a subclass of `TimerEvent()`, and it must override the `run()` method.

Example 3.19A is a simple timer program, which runs every 1000 ms (one second). It uses the `System.currentTimeMillis()` class to get the current time in milliseconds. From the output in Figure 3.8, you can see that the timer is accurate, with about 1 ms to 2 ms error. This is comparable to other programming languages.

EXAMPLE 3.19A   A SIMPLE TIMER PROGRAM

```
============================================================================
//Example 3.19A Timer example
import java.util.*;
import java.awt.Toolkit;

public class Timer1 {
    long t1,t2;
    Toolkit toolkit;
    Timer timer;
    public Timer1() {
        t1=System.currentTimeMillis();
      toolkit = Toolkit.getDefaultToolkit();
        timer = new Timer();
        timer.schedule(new RemindTask(),
                    0,        //initial delay
                  1*1000);  //subsequent rate
    }
    class RemindTask extends TimerTask {
        int i=0;
        public void run() {
          if (i <5) {
              toolkit.beep();
                t2=System.currentTimeMillis();
            t2=(t2-t1);
                System.out.println(i+ ": "+t2*0.001+" s");
              i++;
              } else {
                    System.out.println(new GregorianCalendar().getTime());
                System.exit(0);
          }
        }
    }
    public static void main(String[] args) {
      new Timer1();
    }
}
============================================================================
```

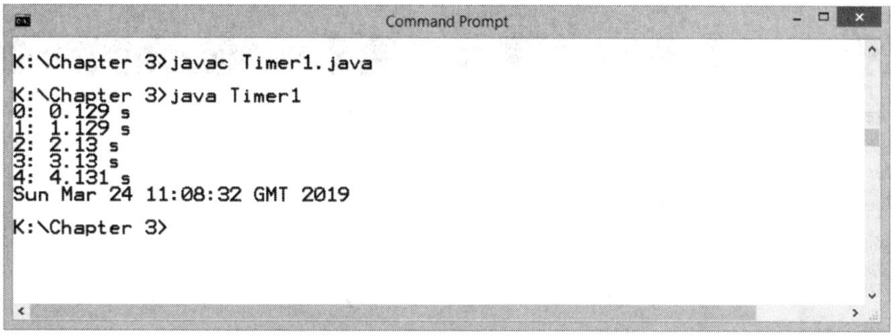

Figure 3.8: The compilation, execution, and output results of `Timer1.java`

However, many people prefer using `ScheduledExecutorService` instead of `Timer`, as it's much more flexible—you don't have to worry about the timer blocking the rest of your program, and it handles exceptions better. Example 3.19B shows a simple `ScheduledExecutorService` example, which repeatedly executes a printing task, starting at 0 seconds and repeating every 10 ms.

EXAMPLE 3.19B   USING A `SCHEDULEDEXECUTORSERVICE`

```
===========================================================================
//Example 3.19B ScheduledExecutorService example
import java.util.concurrent.*;
public class SEService {
    public static void main(String[] args) {
        ScheduledExecutorService ses
                    =   Executors.newScheduledThreadPool(5);
        ses.scheduleAtFixedRate((()->{
            //do the task repeatedly, start at 0s with a gap of 100ms
            System.out.println("Time: "+ new java.util.Date());
        }, 0, 100L, TimeUnit.MILLISECONDS);
    }
}
===========================================================================
```

Example 3.19C shows another version of the previous `ScheduledExecutor-Service` program. This time, the task is defined separately and uses a `count` variable to count how many times the task has been executed. It waits for five seconds first and then repeats the task every second. In addition to running the task repeatedly, you can run the task just once. To do so, just uncomment the last two lines, and comment out the `ses.scheduleAtFixedRate()` line.

EXAMPLE 3.19C   USING A SCHEDULEDEXECUTORSERVICE **WITH A** COUNT **VARIABLE**

```
//Example 3.19C ScheduledExecutorService example
import java.util.concurrent.*;
public class SEService2 {
    private static int count = 0;
    public static void main(String[] args) {
        ScheduledExecutorService ses = Executors.newScheduledThreadPool(1);
        //define the task
        Runnable task1 = () -> {
            System.out.println("Running task1 " + count);
            count++;
        };
        //run this task repeatedly after 5 seconds
        ses.scheduleAtFixedRate(task1, 5, 1, TimeUnit.SECONDS);

        //run this task once after 5 seconds
        //ses.schedule(task1, 5, TimeUnit.SECONDS);
        //ses.shutdown();
    }
}
```

Delay, or sleep, is also a useful function in many applications. In Java, you can use the Thread.sleep() class to implement a delay. Example 3.20 is a simple program that prints a message, delays for 5,000 milliseconds (5 seconds), and then prints another message. Figure 3.9 shows the output result.

EXAMPLE 3.20   IMPLEMENTING A SLEEP OR DELAY

```
//Example 3.20 Sleep or delay Example
public class SleepExample {
    public static void main(String[] args)throws InterruptedException
    {
        System.out.println("Start to sleep");
        Thread.sleep(5000);
        System.out.println("Finish");
    }
}
```

Example 3.21 is a variation of the previous program. By combining sleep() with the System.currentTimeMillis() class, you can display how many milliseconds the program has delayed or slept.

Figure 3.9: The compilation, execution, and output results of `SleepExample.java`

EXAMPLE 3.21   COMBINING `SLEEP()` **WITH THE** `SYSTEM.CURRENT-TIMEMILLIS()` **CLASS**

```
========================================================================
//Example 3.21 Sleep or delay Example
public class SleepExample2 {
   public static void main(String[] args) throws InterruptedException
   {
        long start = System.currentTimeMillis();
        Thread.sleep(2000);
        System.out.println("Sleep time in ms = "+(System.
currentTimeMillis()-start));
   }
}
========================================================================
```

3.13   Executing System Commands

In Java, it is possible to run other applications in your operating system. This allows you to run, or to call, system programs and command-line programs from your Java program.

Example 3.22 is a simple program that illustrates how to use the `Runtime.getRuntime().exec()` class to get and execute the Windows `Notepad.exe` program. Figure 3.10 shows the output result.

EXAMPLE 3.22   THE `EXECUTE1.JAVA` **PROGRAM, USING THE** `RUNTIME.GETRUNTIME().EXEC()` **CLASS**

```
========================================================================
//Example 3.22 Execute1.java program
import java.util.*;
import java.util.regex.*;

public class Execute1 {
    public static void main(String args[]) {
        try {
            String line;
```

```
        boolean more = false;
        String[] cmd = {"notepad.exe"};
        Process p = Runtime.getRuntime().exec(cmd);
    }
    catch (Exception e) {
        e.printStackTrace();
    }
    }
}
```

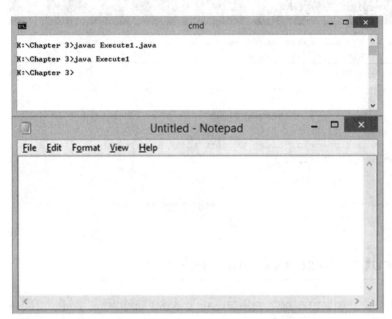

Figure 3.10: The compilation and execution of `Excute1.java` (top) and the `Notepad.exe` program that results (bottom)

Example 3.23 shows another program that uses the `Runtime.getRuntime()`
`.exec()` class to execute the Windows command-line command `dir C:\\`. The `cmd`
`.exe` program is the Windows console (or terminal) command, and `/c` is the flag
of `cmd.exe`, which says that the Windows console should carry out the command
specified by `String` and then terminate. Figure 3.11 shows the output result.

EXAMPLE 3.23   THE `EXECUTE2.JAVA` **PROGRAM, USING** `RUNTIME.`
`GETRUNTIME().EXEC()` **TO EXECUTE THE WINDOWS COMMAND LINE**

```
//Example 3.23 Execute2.java program
import java.util.*;
import java.util.regex.*;
import java.io.*;
```

```java
public class Execute2 {
    public static void main(String args[]) {
        try {
            String line;
            boolean more = false;
            String[] cmd = {"cmd.exe", "/c", "dir","c:\\"};
            Process p = Runtime.getRuntime().exec(cmd);
            BufferedReader input = new BufferedReader(new
                InputStreamReader(p.getInputStream()));
            while ((line = input.readLine()) != null) {
                System.out.println(line);
            }
            input.close();
        }
        catch (Exception e) {
            e.printStackTrace();
        }
    }
}
```

===

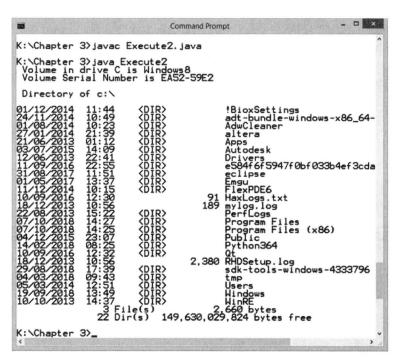

Figure 3.11: The compilation, execution, and output results of `Execute2.java`

3.14   Packages and Programming on a Large Scale

For simple, small-scale Java applications, you can just write a few Java programs and put them in the save directory without needing to worry about directory structures. But for large-scale applications, a key part is to create reusable software components; therefore, directory structures become important. Java packages provide such a mechanism for organizing reusable Java classes and interfaces into different directory structures.

Example 3.24A and Example 3.24B show how to create a reusable Java class in a Java package and how to call this class. The reusable Java class is called SpecialFunctions.java (Example 3.24A). The program to test this special function is called SFTest1.java (Example 3.24B). To create a reusable Java class in a package, you need these two steps:

1. Define a public class, like so:

        public class SpecialFunctions

2. Define a package name, like so:

        package biz.biox

The package name also specifies the subdirectory that this Java class must belong to. In this example, if the current directory is H:\ProjectA\, then SpecialFunctions.java must be in H:\ProjectA\biz\biox\, and the SFTest1 .java file must be in the H:\ProjectA\ directory, as shown here:

```
H:\ProjectA\
|----------- SFTest1.java
|---------->\biz\
|------------->\biox\
|------------------- SpecialFunctions.java
```

EXAMPLE 3.24A   SPECIALFUNCTIONS.JAVA, THE REUSABLE JAVA CLASS

```
===========================================================================
// Example 3.24A SpecialFunctions.java
package biz.biox;
import java.util.*;
public class SpecialFunctions{

    public double ExpErfc(double z){
        double w;
        if (z<0.0){
            w=2*Math.exp(-z*z)-(0.3480242*erf1(-z)-0.0958798*erf1
(-z)*erf1(-z)+0.7478556*erf1(-z)*erf1(-z)*erf1(-z));
        }
```

```
        else{
            w=(0.3480242*erf1(z)-0.0958798*erf1(z)*erf1(z)+0.7478556*erf1
(z)*erf1(z)*erf1(z));
        }
        return w;
    }

    public double erf(double z){
        return (1.0-erfc(z));
    }

    public double erfc(double z){
        double w;
        if (z<0.0){
            w=2.0-(0.3480242*erf1(-z)-0.0958798*erf1(-z)*erf1(-z)
+0.7478556*erf1(-z)*erf1(-z)*erf1(-z))*Math.exp(-z*z);
        }
        else{
            w=(0.3480242*erf1(z)-0.0958798*erf1(z)*erf1(z)+0.7478556*erf1(z)
*erf1(z)*erf1(z))*Math.exp(-z*z);
        }
        return w;
    }
    private double erf1(double z){
        return 1.0/(1.0+0.47047*z);
    }
}
```
===

EXAMPLE 3.24B   SFTEST1.JAVA, REUSABLE CLASS TEST PROGRAM

===
```
// Example 3.24B SFTest1.java Program
import java.text.*;
import biz.biox.SpecialFunctions;

class SFTest1{

    public static void main(String args[]){
        double x;
        SpecialFunctions sf=new SpecialFunctions();
        System.out.println("Number \t Erf \t Erfc \t ExpErfc");
        for (int i=0;i<10;i++){
            x=(i-5)/10.0;
            System.out.println(x+"\t "+sf.erf(x)+"\t "+sf.erfc(x)+"\t
"+sf.ExpErfc(x));
        }
    }
}
```
===

To compile the `SpecialFunctions.java` program from a current directory of `H:\ProjectA\`, enter the following command, as shown in Figure 3.12:

```
H:\ProjectA> javac .\biz\biox\SpecialFunctions.java
```

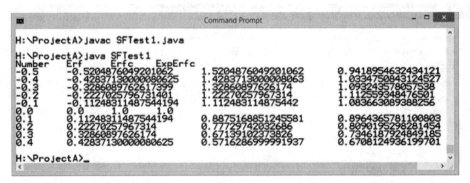

Figure 3.12: The compilation of `SpecialFunctions.java` in the `biz.biox` package

`SFTest1.java` in Example 3.24B shows how to use the `SpecialFunctions` `.java` class in the `biz.biox` package. Make sure to add the following line at the beginning of the file:

```
import biz.biox.SpecialFunctions;
```

Type in the following commands to compile and run the `SFTest1.java` program. Figure 3.13 shows the output results.

```
H:\ProjectA> javac SFTest1.java
H:\ProjectA> java   SFTest1
```

Figure 3.13: The output from `SFTest1.java`

3.15   Software Engineering

Writing software is like making commercial products—quality is absolutely paramount. But how can you guarantee software quality? The answer is through *software engineering*. This concept means you should develop your software using a systematic engineering approach and write your code in a good programming style.

Using a systematic engineering approach means you should *not* simply go to your computer and start typing in code whenever you want to write a program. Instead, you should always follow the software development cycle; that is, you should design first and then write the code.

Good programming style means the software source code should be well structured, with correct indentations and sufficient comments. You also need to give your classes, methods, and variables meaningful names. Writing programs in good programming style will make programs easy to manage, modify, and debug, as well as less error-prone.

3.15.1   The Software Development Cycle

To develop high-quality software, you must follow the standard development cycle, shown here:

Step 1: Specify.

Step 2: Design.

Step 3: Implement (or code).

Step 4: Test and debug.

Step 5: Document.

Step 6: Go back to step 1 for the next version of software.

I cannot emphasize enough the importance of the specification and design steps in software development. You should always do a proper software specification and design first, before you start coding. Specification defines what your software is going to do, and it should be simple, precise, complete, and unambiguous. Design specifies how your software is going to do what it is supposed to do. The most commonly used design tools are flowcharts and pseudocode (or structured language).

For example, the Java code in Example 3.24B can be expressed as the following pseudocode. Pseudocode doesn't need to have a predefined syntax but should be in plain English with common programming constructs. It should also be generic and not specific to any languages.

```
Begin
    Define double x
    Create a SpecialFunctions object sf
    Print the heading: "Number  Erf  Erfc ExpErfc"
    For each integer i in 1 to 10:
        x=(i-5)/10.0;
        Print x, sf.erf(x), sf.erfc(x), sf.ExpErfc(x)
    End of loop
End
```

For more details about flowcharts and pseudocode, please visit these web sites:

```
https://www.tutorialspoint.com/programming_methodologies/
programming_methodologies_flowchart_elements.htm
https://www.programiz.com/article/flowchart-programming
https://www.go4expert.com/articles/pseudocode-tutorial-basics-t25593/
```

Once the software has been developed, documentation—which is often ignored—is an important step toward making it understandable to others, as well as easy to maintain. Luckily, Java provides a useful tool called `javadoc`, which can generate Java documents directly from your Java code. The documents generated by `javadoc` are in HTML format, so they can be easily put on a web site. As mentioned earlier, the elements of good coding style you will look at next—indentation, commenting, and following standard naming conventions—are also forms of documentation that contribute to code readability and ease of maintenance.

3.15.2   Indentation

Although indentation has no effect on the compilation and execution of the program, it is an important way to make the source code understandable to both yourself and others. Example 3.25A shows a Java program (the same as `Hello1.java` in Example 3.6) with correct indentation, and Example 3.25B shows poor or no indentation. You can imagine a program with hundreds of lines and nested loops; it would be difficult to understand the structure without proper indentation. Therefore, I strongly recommend that when writing a program, big or small, you should always use indentation to show the logical structure of your code and use it consistently throughout the program.

EXAMPLE 3.25A   JAVA CODE WITH CORRECT INDENTATION

```
============================================================================
// Example 3.25a Java code with correct indentation
class Hello1a {
    //indentation inside the class
    public static void main(String[] args) {
        //indentation inside the main()
        if(args.length!=2){
            //indentation inside if else
            System.out.println("Usage: java Hello1a firstname surname!");
        }
        else{
            //indentation inside if else
            System.out.println("Hello "+ args[0] +" "+ args[1] + "!");
        }//end of if else
    }//end of main
}//end of class
============================================================================
```

EXAMPLE 3.25B   JAVA CODE WITH POOR OR NO INDENTATION

```
==========================================================================
// Example 3.25B Java code with poor or no indentation
class Hello1b {
public static void main(String[] args) {
if(args.length!=2){
System.out.println("Usage: java Hello3 firstname surname!");
}
else{
System.out.println("Hello "+ args[0] +" "+ args[1] + "!");
}
}
}
==========================================================================
```

3.15.3 Comments

Like indentation, comments are also important in source code even though they do not affect the compilation and execution of the program. Sufficient comments can make a program much more understandable, especially for others, which is essential in a team project. Like C/C++, Java supports both single-line comments (//) and multiple-line comments, grouped by (/*) and (*/). Example 3.26 shows the Hello1.java program again, but with comments.

Note that for multiple-line comments, there is no difference between

```
/*
 This is a multiple line
 comment
*/
```

and

```
/**
 * This is a multiple line
 * comment
 */
```

However, because the javadoc tool can recognize comments beginning with /**, we recommend using /** and */comments at least for classes and methods, as they will be automatically used to generate program documents by the javadoc tool. You can find more information about Java documentation and the javadoc tool in Appendix A.

EXAMPLE 3.26   JAVA CODE WITH COMMENTS

```
===========================================================================
//Example 3.26 Java code with comments

/**
 *   Program: Comment1.java
 *   Auther:  Perry Xiao
 *
 */
class Comment1 {
    /*
    This is the main method of the program
    */
    public static void main(String[] args) {
        //if argument length is not two, display usage information
        if(args.length!=2){
            System.out.println("Usage: java Hello3 firstname surname!");
        }
        //if argument length is two, display hello message
        else{
            System.out.println("Hello "+ args[0] +" "+ args[1] + "!");
        }
    }
}
===========================================================================
```

3.15.4   Naming Conventions

Giving sensible names to your classes, methods, and variables is important, especially when there are tens and hundreds of them. The most popular naming convention in many programming languages is *Hungarian notation*, which simply says that any variable name must have a prefix and suffix. The prefix should identify the type of the variable, and the suffix should provide its meaning. Normally the prefix is in lowercase, and the suffix is a string of words, without spaces, with only the first letter of each word capitalized. For example, a double-type variable that stored the ambient temperature could be named any of the following:

```
doubleAmbientTemperature
dblAmbientTemperature
dAmbientT
```

The following are some more examples of variable names:

```
strPlotTitle        //A String variable that stores the plot title
bolDeviceOn         //A boolean variable that stores a true or false
                       value for
                    //representing the on/off status of a device
intNumberOfPoints   //An integer variable that stores the total number of
                    //points
```

Although you probably do not need prefixes for class names and method names, you do need to make them meaningful; and it is better to follow the Java naming convention for classes and methods. According to this convention, the Java class name should be a collection of words without spaces, with the first letter of each word capitalized; the Java method name should also be a collection of words without spaces, with the first letter of each word except the first capitalized. Here's an example:

```
getCurrentDirectory()      //A method that returns the current directory
setCurrentDirectory()      //A method that sets the current directory
toString()                 //A method that returns a string representing
                             the object
FileReader()               //A class that reads character files
FileWriter()               //A class that writes character files
```

You do not need to follow Hungarian notation, as Java is already strongly typed. But whatever naming convention you use, you should be consistent throughout your programs.

For more details about Java code conventions, please visit these web sites:

https://www.oracle.com/technetwork/java/codeconventions-135099.html

http://gee.cs.oswego.edu/dl/html/javaCodingStd.html

https://google.github.io/styleguide/javaguide.html

3.16   Deploying Java Applications

For Linux/Unix users, there may seem nothing wrong with compiling and running Java programs through the text mode terminal or console, as you've done so far. But for Windows users, who have been used to graphical interfaces and a mouse, opening a text mode Windows command prompt to type in commands such as **java HelloWorld** to run a Java program is not very appealing. Therefore, in this section you will first look at several different ways of creating an executable Java program, which can be run with just a double mouse click. Then you will see how to deploy Java applications.

3.16.1   Using a Windows Batch File

The simplest way to compile and run Java code is to use a Windows batch file. You can use Notepad++ or any other text editor to create the batch file. Figure 3.14 shows an example of creating a Windows batch file called Oop1run.bat to compile and run the previous Oop1.java program. It has three lines of commands: the first line is to compile the code, the second line is to run the code, and the third line, the pause command, is to hold the screen so that you can observe the results. Once the batch file is created, all you need to do is double-click the file to compile and run the program, as shown in Figure 3.15. This approach is simple, quick, and efficient.

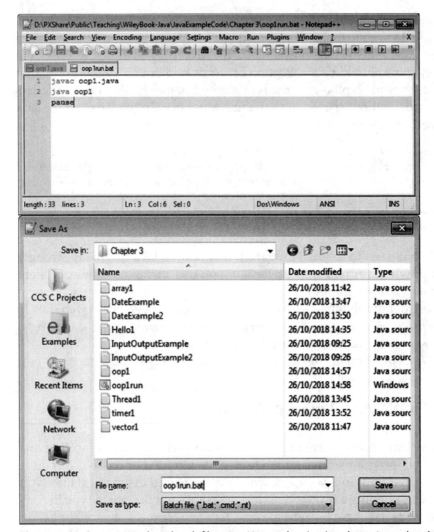

Figure 3.14: Create a Windows batch file using Notepad++ (top) and save it as a batch file called `Oop1run.bat` (bottom).

3.16.2   Using an Executable JAR File

Java technologies support the concept of executable JAR files, which means you can create a JAR (which is a Java archive, the equivalent of a zipped file) that can run when it's double-clicked.

To create an executable JAR file, you must first create a `mainClass` manifest file, which contains two lines specifying where `mainClass` is to be found in the JAR file. In this example, the `mainClass` file is named `Oop1.mf`, and the following is its content:

```
Main-Class: Oop1
Class-Path: Oop1.jar
```

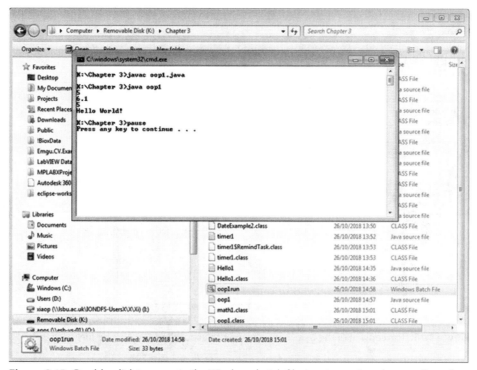

Figure 3.15: Double-click to execute the Windows batch file `Oop1run.bat` to compile and run the `Oop1.java` program.

Now you can create an executable JAR file by typing in the following command in a Windows command prompt window:

```
jar cmf Oop1.mf Oop1.jar *.class
```

This combines all the Java classes (`*.class`) to create an executable JAR file called `Oop1.jar`.

To run this JAR file, just type the following:

```
java -jar Oop1.jar
```

You can also double-click the `Oop1.jar` file to run it. Figure 3.16 shows the content of the `Oop1.mf` file and the corresponding `Oop1.jar` file.

3.16.3   Using Microsoft Visual Studio

You can also use Microsoft Visual Studio to write a simple Windows command prompt program to compile and run Java programs using system calls. Microsoft Visual Studio is a popular software development tool in the industry, and you can use it to create an installation package easily. Figure 3.17 shows an example of creating a Microsoft Visual Studio C# program to use the `System.Diagnostic .Process.Start()` class to execute the `javac Oop1.java` command to compile the Java program and to execute the `java Oop1` command to run the Java program.

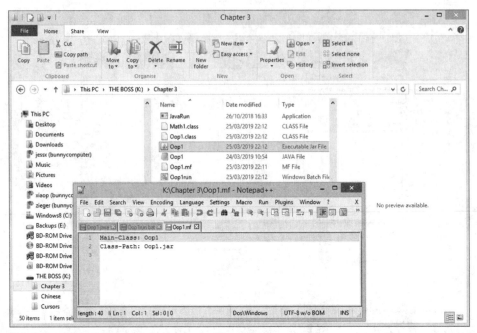

Figure 3.16: The content of the `Oop1.mf` file and corresponding `Oop1.jar` file

3.16.4   Java Application Installations

When you are developing commercial Java applications or you need to give your programs to others to use, you will need to use dedicated professional software to create an installation package to deploy your Java applications.

Install Creator 2 is a simple, user-friendly, and yet powerful professional software deployment and installation tool from ClickTeam. It offers a range of standard installation options, such as specifying the version to install, languages, software registration code, and installation directory, and it can produce a colorful installation process. With Install Creator 2, you can also specify a range of installation-related operations, such as configuring the main executable program; copying the DLL, EXE, and ActiveX files to system directories; registering the DLL and other elements to the Windows Registry; installing device drivers; and creating new entries in the Windows INI and Registry files. For more details, visit this site:

```
https://www.clickteam.com/install-creator-2
```

Advanced Installer is another Windows Installer authoring tool. It offers a friendly and easy-to-use graphical user interface for creating and maintaining installation packages (EXE, MSI, and so on) based on Windows Installer technology. For more details, visit this site:

```
https://www.advancedinstaller.com/
```

Figure 3.17: The C# program to execute the Java command for compilation and execution

Install4J is an application from EJ technologies. Install4J is a powerful multi-platform Java installer builder that generates native installers and application launchers for Java applications. For more detail, visit this site:

`https://www.ej-technologies.com/products/install4j/overview.html`

Oracle also has a tutorial on how to deploy Java; see the following for details:

`https://docs.oracle.com/javase/tutorial/deployment/selfContainedApps/index.html`

3.17   Summary

This chapter provided a basic introduction to Java programming. Topics included variables, operators, reserved words, input and output, loops and selections, arrays, matrices and vectors, file read and write, object-oriented programming, multithreading, methods, dates and times, system commands, software engineering, and deployment.

This chapter lays the foundation for the coming chapters; it is important especially when you are new to Java programming. The variables, operators, and control structures such as loops and selections are the fundamental building blocks of the Java programming language. You will see them used throughout the book. Arrays and lists are useful for storing complex user data. The file read and write tools allow programs to read information from a file and save information into a file. OOP is one of the main features of the Java language, and all the example programs in this book use OOP in one way or another. Multithreaded programming is also crucial for many networking applications, as different threads are needed to handle different connections. It is good practice to develop Java software programs using a systematic, engineering approach. If you want to distribute your Java program to others, it is best to package your program in an installation package.

3.18   Chapter Review Questions

Q3.1.   What are the standard input and output? Which Java classes deal with standard input, and which classes deal with standard output?

Q3.2.   Which eight primitive variable types does Java support?

Q3.3.   What is a constant? What is a VAR type variable?

Q3.4.   What is the difference between String and StringBuffer?

Q3.5.   What is ASCII?

Q3.6.   What operators does Java support?

Q3.7.   How many reserved words are there in Java?

Q3.8.   What are loops and selections?

Q3.9.   What is the difference between a Java array and a Java vector?

Q3.10. How do you read and write text files in Java?

Q3.11. What are the advantages of object-oriented programming?

Q3.12. What is the life cycle of a Java thread?

Q3.13. What is the software development cycle?

Q3.14. How do you create an executable Java program?

Java Programming for Windows Applications

"There are no shortcuts to any place worth going."

—Beverly Sills

4.1 Introduction
4.2 Java Swing Applications
4.3 JavaFX Applications
4.4 Deploying JavaFX Applications
4.5 Summary
4.6 Chapter Review Questions

4.1   Introduction

You have now explored basic Java programming as a console application—text-based applications with no graphics. But on many occasions you might prefer to have graphical user interface (GUI) applications. In Java, you can use the Java Abstract Window Toolkit (AWT), Java Swing, and JavaFX widget toolkits to develop GUI programs. GUI programming has always been Java's Achilles heel, meaning it was cumbersome and had no built-in charting functions. Thanks to the latest version of JavaFX, all this is going to change. Comparing with Java Swing, JavaFX has improved event handling, has special effects, allows skins to be created with Cascading Style Sheets (CSS), has more consistent controls, is easier for animation, and supports modern touchscreen devices. JavaFX claims to be the next-generation client application platform for desktop, mobile, and embedded systems built on Java. In this chapter, I will introduce first Java Swing applications and then JavaFX applications.

4.2   Java Swing Applications

Java Swing is a GUI widget toolkit that was developed to provide a more sophisticated set of GUI components than the earlier Java AWT widget toolkit. Example 4.1 shows a standard Java Swing GUI application, named `GUIApplication.java`. To create a Java Swing GUI program, you need to extend the `JFrame` class, which is in the `javax.swing.*` library. You also need to implement the `createAndShowGUI()` method, which creates and sets up the window. To display the window, you need to call the `createAndShowGUI()` method as a thread in the `main()` method. Figure 4.1 shows the output of the `SwingApplication1.java` program, which in this case is just a blank window.

EXAMPLE 4.1   A FIRST JAVA SWING APPLICATION

```
============================================================================
//Example 4.1 Java Swing example
import javax.swing.*;

public class SwingApplication1 extends JFrame{
    public SwingApplication1 () {
        super("Hello World Swing Application");
    }

    /**
     * Create the GUI and show it.  For thread safety,
     * this method should be invoked from the
     * event-dispatching thread.
     */
    private static void createAndShowGUI() {
        //Make sure we have nice window decorations.
        JFrame.setDefaultLookAndFeelDecorated(true);

        //Create and set up the window.
        JFrame frame = new SwingApplication1();
        frame.setDefaultCloseOperation(JFrame.EXIT_ON_CLOSE);
        //Set the window size and location
        frame.setSize(300, 300);
        frame.setLocationRelativeTo(null);          //Display the window.
        frame.pack();
        frame.setVisible(true);
    }
```

```
        public static void main(String[] args) {
            //Schedule a job for the event-dispatching thread:
            //creating and showing this application's GUI.
            javax.swing.SwingUtilities.invokeLater(new Runnable() {
                public void run() {
                    createAndShowGUI();
                }
            });
        }
    }
    =========================================================================
```

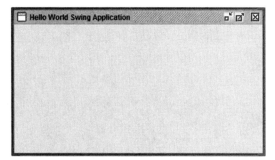

Figure 4.1: The output of the `SwingApplication1.java` program

EXERCISE 4.1   Modify the Example 4.1 Java program so that it uses green as the background color.

Next, you can add some components to the `SwingApplication1.java` program, such as a label and a text field, as shown in Example 4.2. The layout of the window is `FlowLayout`, which means you add the components to the window from left to right and from top to bottom. You can also add some actions to the text field so that each time the user types something in the text field and hits the Enter key, it is copied to the label. To do this, your code must extend from the `JFrame` class, and it also needs to implement `ActionListener` and import the `javax.swing.*`, `javax.awt.*`, and `javax.awt.event.*` libraries. Java `ActionListener` is a type of event handler that is triggered when an action happens, such as a button being pressed, a check box being ticked, and so on. Figure 4.2 shows the output of the `SwingApplication2.java` program.

EXAMPLE 4.2   JAVA SWING APPLICATION WITH LABEL AND TEXT FIELD

```
=========================================================================
//Example 4.2 Java Swing example with Label and text field
import java.awt.*;
import java.awt.event.*;
```

```java
import javax.swing.*;

public class SwingApplication2 extends JFrame implements ActionListener
{

    private JLabel label;
    private JTextField tf;

    public SwingApplication2 () {
        super("Java Swing with Label");
        setLayout(new FlowLayout());

        label=new JLabel("This is a swing label!");
        add(label);

        tf =new JTextField (20);
        tf.addActionListener(this);
        add(tf);
    }


    /**
     * Create the GUI and show it.  For thread safety,
     * this method should be invoked from the
     * event-dispatching thread.
     */
    private static void createAndShowGUI() {
        //Make sure we have nice window decorations.
        //JFrame.setDefaultLookAndFeelDecorated(true);

        //Create and set up the window.
        JFrame frame = new SwingApplication2 ();
        frame.setDefaultCloseOperation(JFrame.EXIT_ON_CLOSE);

        //Display the window.
        frame.pack();
        frame.setVisible(true);
    }

    public static void main(String[] args) {
        //Schedule a job for the event-dispatching thread:
        //creating and showing this application's GUI.
        javax.swing.SwingUtilities.invokeLater(new Runnable() {
            public void run() {
                createAndShowGUI();
            }
        });
    }
    public void actionPerformed (ActionEvent e){
        label.setText(tf.getText());
    }
}
```

===

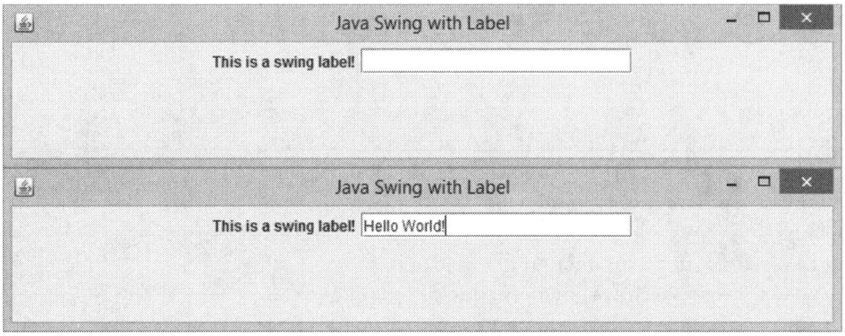

Figure 4.2: The output of the `SwingApplication2.java` program

EXERCISE 4.2 Modify the Example 4.2 Java program so that it copies the text in the text field into the label in uppercase.

Example 4.3 shows another Java Swing program with a text field, a button, and a label. It adds an action to the button so that each time you click the button, it calculates the square of the number typed in the text field and displays it in the label. Figure 4.3 shows the output.

EXAMPLE 4.3 JAVA SWING APPLICATION WITH LABEL AND TEXT FIELD

```
========================================================================
//Example 4.3 Java Swing example with label and text field
import java.awt.*;
import java.awt.event.*;
import javax.swing.*;

public class SwingApplication2 extends JFrame implements ActionListener
{

    private JLabel label;
    private JTextField tf;
    private JButton button;
    public SwingApplication2 () {
        super("Java Swing with Label");
        setLayout(new FlowLayout());

        tf =new JTextField (20);
        add(tf);

        button=new JButton ("Equals");
        button.addActionListener(this);
        add(button);

        label=new JLabel("This is a swing label!");
```

```
            add(label);
    }


    /**
     * Create the GUI and show it.  For thread safety,
     * this method should be invoked from the
     * event-dispatching thread.
     */
    private static void createAndShowGUI() {
        //Make sure we have nice window decorations.
        //JFrame.setDefaultLookAndFeelDecorated(true);

        //Create and set up the window.
        JFrame frame = new SwingApplication2 ();
        frame.setDefaultCloseOperation(JFrame.EXIT_ON_CLOSE);

        //Display the window.
        frame.pack();
        frame.setVisible(true);
    }

    public static void main(String[] args) {
        //Schedule a job for the event-dispatching thread:
        //creating and showing this application's GUI.
        javax.swing.SwingUtilities.invokeLater(new Runnable() {
            public void run() {
                createAndShowGUI();
            }
        });
    }
    public void actionPerformed (ActionEvent e){
        float s;
        if (e.getSource()==button){
            s=Float.parseFloat(tf.getText());
            s=s*s;
            label.setText("The square of "+ tf.getText() + " is " + s);
        }
    }
}
```

===

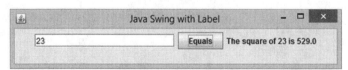

Figure 4.3: The output of the SwingApplication3.java program

When you have a lot of GUI components in your program, you need to use the Java Layout Manager, which is included in the standard Java JDK. The Java Layout Manager supports many layouts, such as `FlowLayout`, `BorderLayout`, `GridLayout`, `BoxLayout`, `CardLayout`, `GridBagLayout`, `GroupLayout`, and `Spring-Layout`. The default is `FlowLayout`.

> **EXERCISE 4.3** Modify the Example 4.3 Java program so that it uses `GridLayout`, with the text field on the top, button in the middle, and label at the bottom.

4.2.1   For More Information

For more information and tutorials on Java Swing, see the following links:

```
https://docs.oracle.com/javase/tutorial/uiswing/
https://docs.oracle.com/javase/tutorial/uiswing/layout/visual.html
https://docs.oracle.com/javase/8/docs/technotes/guides/swing/index.html
https://www.tutorialspoint.com/swing/
https://www.javatpoint.com/java-swing
https://netbeans.org/kb/docs/java/quickstart-gui.html
```

4.3   JavaFX Applications

JavaFX is a Java library designed for developing sophisticated Java GUI applications. JavaFX can be used to develop both standard desktop applications and rich Internet applications (RIAs), which are the web applications that provide features and an experience similar to those of desktop applications. Applications built in JavaFX can run on multiple platforms, including web, mobile, and desktops. RIAs do not require any additional software to run. The other two main RIA technologies are Adobe Flash and Microsoft Silverlight.

JavaFX was originally developed by Sun Microsystems, and JavaFX 1.0 was released on December 4, 2008. Since the release of JavaFX 8.0 in March 2014, JavaFX has been an integral part of Java. Oracle will continue to support it until March 2022. The latest version is JavaFX 11.0, released on September 18, 2018. It builds on top of Java 10 or preferably Java 11. It is now released as a stand-alone library and is no longer part of the standard Java SDK. In the future, JavaFX will be supported by the company Gluon as a downloadable module in addition to the JDK.

For more information about the latest JavaFX, its download, and the installation instructions, please visit this site:

```
https://openjfx.io/openjfx-docs/#introduction
```

The simplest way to create a JavaFX application is to use a Java IDE, such as IntelliJ IDEA, which comes with the JavaFX plugin enabled by default. Figure 4.4 shows how to create a JavaFX project using IntelliJ IDEA.

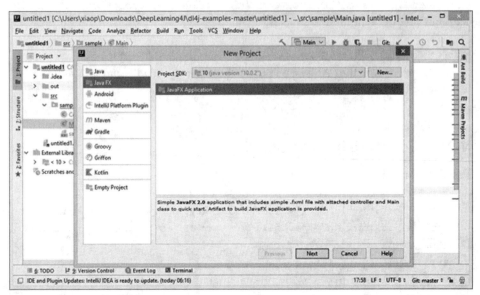

Figure 4.4: Creating a JavaFX project using the IntelliJ IDEA software

A typical JavaFX application will have three major components: stage, scene, and nodes. A *stage* is a window that contains all the GUI components of a JavaFX application. A stage has two parameters, `width` and `height`. It is divided as Content Area and Decorations (Title Bar and Borders).

There are five types of stages: Decorated, Undecorated, Transparent, Unified, and Utility.

A *scene* is a container in which all the components are presented, and the *nodes* are the GUI components that can be added to the scene. A node can be a 2D or 3D object (circle, rectangle, polygon, and so on), a GUI control (label, button, check box, choice box, text area, and so on), container (layout panes, such as border pane, grid pane, flow pane, and so on), or a media element (such as audio, video, or image).

4.3.1   JavaFX Window

Example 4.4 shows a simple JavaFX program, which merely creates an empty window program. To create a JavaFX program, your program needs to extend the `Application` class, which is part of the `javafx.application` package, and you also need to import a range of other JavaFX libraries. You will also need to implement the `start()` method to set up all your GUI components and use the `launch()` method to run your program. To run this example, just create a JavaFX project called `JavaFXApplication1` using IntelliJ IDEA and copy the following code into the `main.java` program (a procedure you'll follow for all of this chapter's JavaFX examples). Figure 4.5 shows the example code in IntelliJ IDEA and the running output window of the program.

EXAMPLE 4.4   A SIMPLE JAVAFX PROGRAM

```
==============================================================================
//Example 4.4 JavaFX example
package sample;

import javafx.application.Application;
import javafx.fxml.FXMLLoader;
import javafx.scene.*;
import javafx.stage.Stage;

import javafx.scene.control.*;
import javafx.scene.layout.*;
import javafx.event.*;


public class Main extends Application {

    @Override
    public void start(Stage primaryStage) throws Exception{
        primaryStage.setTitle("Hello World!");

        FlowPane root = new FlowPane();

        primaryStage.setScene(new Scene(root, 300, 250));
        primaryStage.show();
    }


    public static void main(String[] args) {
        launch(args);
    }
}
==============================================================================
```

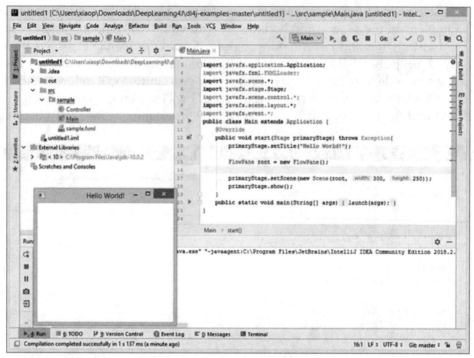

Figure 4.5: A simple JavaFX program and its running output window

EXERCISE 4.4   Modify the Example 4.4 Java program so that it uses red for the window's background color.

4.3.2   Creating a Label and Button in JavaFX

Example 4.5 shows an improved version of the previous JavaFX program, with a label and a button. It uses the `FlowPane` layout, in which the GUI objects can be added as in the flow layout. An action was also added to the button so that each time you click the button, it displays `Hello World!` on the label. To run this example, just create a JavaFX project called `JavaFXApplication2` using IntelliJ IDEA and copy the following code into the `main.java` program. Figure 4.6 shows the output.

EXAMPLE 4.5   JAVAFX PROGRAM WITH LABEL AND BUTTON

```
===========================================================================
//Example 4.5 JavaFX example with label and button
package sample;
```

```java
import javafx.application.Application;
import javafx.fxml.FXMLLoader;
import javafx.scene.*;
import javafx.stage.Stage;

import javafx.scene.control.*;
import javafx.scene.layout.*;
import javafx.event.*;


public class Main extends Application {

    @Override
    public void start(Stage primaryStage) throws Exception{
        primaryStage.setTitle("Hello World!");
        Label label = new Label("My Label");
        Button btn = new Button();
        btn.setText("Say 'Hello World'");
        btn.setOnAction(new EventHandler<ActionEvent>()

            @Override
            public void handle(ActionEvent event) {
                //System.out.println("Hello World!");
                label.setText("Hello World!");
            }
        });

        FlowPane root = new FlowPane();
        root.getChildren().add(label);
        root.getChildren().add(btn);
        primaryStage.setScene(new Scene(root, 300, 250));
        primaryStage.show();
    }


    public static void main(String[] args) {
        launch(args);
    }
}
```
==

Similar to Java Swing, JavaFX also supports many different layouts, called *layout panes*, such as FlowPane, BorderPane, GridPane, StackPane, HBox, VBox, TextFlow, AnchorPane, TitlePane, and so on.

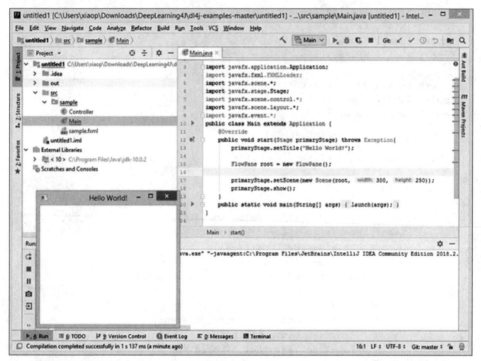

Figure 4.6: The JavaFX program with a label and button, and its running output window

EXERCISE 4.5   Add another button to the Example 4.5 Java program so that when you click the second button, it clears the text in the label.

4.3.3   JavaFX Charts

For many years, Java offered no built-in charting functions. Thanks to JavaFX, users can now easily create bar charts, pie charts, line charts, scatter charts, and so on, using the built-in JavaFX chart functions. Example 4.6 shows how to create a line chart in JavaFX using the `LineChart`, `NumberAxis`, and `XYChart` classes. To create a chart, you will first need to create `NumberAxis` objects for the x- and y-axes. Next, you'll create a `LineChart` object with `NumberAxis` objects added to it, then create an `XYChart.Series` object, and finally add the XY data to it as `XYChart.Data` objects. Next, add the `XYChart.Series` object to the `LineChart` object.

To run this example, just create a JavaFX project called `JavaFXApplication3` using IntelliJ IDEA, and copy the following code into the `main.java` program. Figure 4.7 shows the output window created by the code.

EXAMPLE 4.6   CREATING A LINE CHART WITH JAVAFX

```
=============================================================================
//Example 4.6 JavaFX Line chart example
package sample;

import javafx.application.Application;
import javafx.scene.Group;
import javafx.scene.Scene;
import javafx.stage.Stage;
import javafx.scene.chart.LineChart;
import javafx.scene.chart.NumberAxis;
import javafx.scene.chart.XYChart;

public class Main extends Application {
    @Override
    public void start(Stage stage) {
        //Defining the x axis
        NumberAxis xAxis = new NumberAxis(0, 50, 10);
        xAxis.setLabel("Time [s]");

        //Defining the y axis
        NumberAxis yAxis = new NumberAxis  (0, 20, 2);
        yAxis.setLabel("Voltage [V]");

        //Creating the line chart
        LineChart linechart = new LineChart(xAxis, yAxis);

        //Prepare XYChart.Series objects by setting data
        XYChart.Series series = new XYChart.Series();
        series.setName("Measurement Results");

        series.getData().add(new XYChart.Data(0, 15));
        series.getData().add(new XYChart.Data(10, 3));
        series.getData().add(new XYChart.Data(20, 6));
        series.getData().add(new XYChart.Data(30, 12));
        series.getData().add(new XYChart.Data(40, 2));
        series.getData().add(new XYChart.Data(50, 10));

        //Setting the data to Line chart
        linechart.getData().add(series);

        //Creating a Group object
        Group root = new Group(linechart);

        //Creating a scene object
        Scene scene = new Scene(root, 600, 400);
```

```
            //Setting title to the Stage
            stage.setTitle("Line Chart");

            //Adding scene to the stage
            stage.setScene(scene);

            //Displaying the contents of the stage
            stage.show();
        }
        public static void main(String args[]){
            launch(args);
        }
    }
```
==

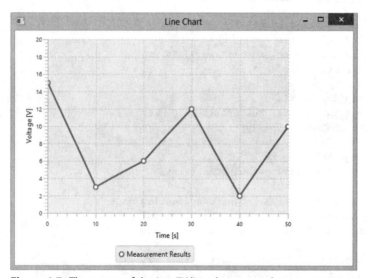

Figure 4.7: The output of the JavaFX line chart example program

EXERCISE 4.6   Modify the Example 4.6 Java program so that it displays the data in a bar chart.

4.3.4 Handling Logins in JavaFX

Handling user logins is a basic function of any GUI application. Example 4.7 shows a JavaFX login example using GUI components such as a label, a text field, and buttons. The GridPane layout is used, allowing the GUI objects to be added in the grid. To run this example, just create a JavaFX project called JavaFXApplication4 using IntelliJ IDEA, and copy the following code into the main.java program. Figure 4.8 shows the output from this example.

EXAMPLE 4.7   USING A JAVAFX GUI COMPONENT FOR LOGINS

```
==========================================================================
//Example 4.7 JavaFX GUI component Login example
package sample;

import javafx.application.Application;
import static javafx.application.Application.launch;
import javafx.geometry.Insets;
import javafx.geometry.Pos;

import javafx.scene.Scene;
import javafx.scene.control.Button;
import javafx.scene.control.PasswordField;
import javafx.scene.layout.GridPane;
import javafx.scene.text.Text;
import javafx.scene.control.TextField;
import javafx.stage.Stage;

public class Main extends Application {
    @Override
    public void start(Stage stage) {
        //creating label email
        Text text1 = new Text("Username");

        //creating label password
        Text text2 = new Text("Password");

        //Creating Text Filed for email
        TextField textField1 = new TextField();

        //Creating Text Filed for password
        PasswordField textField2 = new PasswordField();

        //Creating Buttons
        Button button1 = new Button("Login");

        //Creating a Grid Pane
        GridPane gridPane = new GridPane();

        //Setting size for the pane
        gridPane.setMinSize(400, 200);

        //Setting the Grid alignment
        gridPane.setAlignment(Pos.CENTER);

        //Arranging all the nodes in the grid
        gridPane.add(text1, 0, 0);
        gridPane.add(textField1, 1, 0);
        gridPane.add(text2, 0, 1);
```

```
        gridPane.add(textField2, 1, 1);
        gridPane.add(button1, 0, 2);

        //Creating a scene object
        Scene scene = new Scene(gridPane);

        //Setting title to the Stage
        stage.setTitle("Bank Login");

        //Adding scene to the stage
        stage.setScene(scene);

        //Displaying the contents of the stage
        stage.show();
    }
    public static void main(String args[]){
        launch(args);
    }
}
```

==

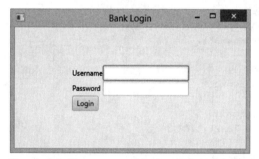

Figure 4.8: The output of the JavaFX login example program

In JavaFX, you can use the `Alert` class to display a pop-out message box to display an error message; here's an example:

```
new Alert(Alert.AlertType.ERROR, " An error occurred!").showAndWait();
```

Here's another example:

```
Alert alert = new Alert(Alert.AlertType.ERROR);
alert.setHeaderText("An error occurred!");
alert.showAndWait();
```

You can also use the `Alert` class to display a standard message box with OK and Cancel buttons, as in this example:

```
Alert alert = new Alert(Alert.AlertType.WARNING,
            "Are you sure to continue? ",
            ButtonType.OK,
            ButtonType.CANCEL);
```

```
alert.setTitle("Warning");
Optional<ButtonType> result = alert.showAndWait();

if (result.get() == ButtonType.OK) {
    //do something
}
else{
    //do something else
}
```

EXERCISE 4.7   Add an action to the Login button in the Example 4.7 Java program so that when you click the button, it checks the username and password and displays an alert message.

4.3.5   Creating an Image Viewer in JavaFX

A picture is worth a thousand words, especially online, and image viewers have become a common and convenient tool in today's computing environment. Example 4.8 shows a JavaFX image viewer example using the `Image` and `ImageView` classes. To view an image, first you need to create an `Image` object, which can load an image from a file using the `FileInputStream` class. The xxxx indicates the path of the image you want to view, such as C:\\bigbang.png. You also need to throw a `FileNotFoundException`. The next step is to create an `ImageView` object and add the `Image` object to it. To run this example, just create a JavaFX project called `JavaFXApplication5` using IntelliJ IDEA and copy the following code into the `main.java` program. Figure 4.9 shows the output of the example.

EXAMPLE 4.8   CREATING AN IMAGE VIEWER IN JAVAFX

```
===========================================================================
//Example 4.8 JavaFX image viewer example
package sample;

import java.io.FileInputStream;
import java.io.FileNotFoundException;
import javafx.application.Application;
import javafx.scene.Group;
import javafx.scene.Scene;
import javafx.scene.image.Image;
import javafx.scene.image.ImageView;
import javafx.stage.Stage;

public class Main extends Application {
    @Override
    public void start(Stage stage) throws FileNotFoundException {
```

```
        stage.setTitle("Image Viewer");

        Image image = new Image(new FileInputStream("xxxx"));
        ImageView imageView = new ImageView(image);

        //Creating a Group object
        Group root = new Group(imageView);

        Scene scene = new Scene(root, 900, 600);
        stage.setScene(scene);
        stage.show();
    }
    public static void main(String args[]) {
        launch(args);
    }
}
==============================================================================
```

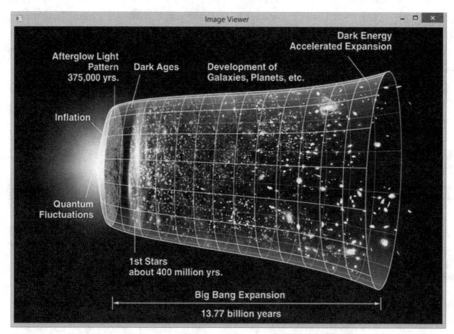

Figure 4.9: The output of the JavaFX image viewer example program

The source of the embedded image is `https://en.wikipedia.org/wiki/Big_Bang#/media/File:CMB_Timeline300_no_WMAP.jpg`.

4.3.6   Creating a JavaFX Web Viewer

You can also use JavaFX to connect to the Web and view its content. Example 4.9 shows a JavaFX web viewer created using the WebView class. To run this example, just create a JavaFX project called JavaFXApplication6 using IntelliJ IDEA, and copy the following code into the main.java program. Figure 4.10 shows the output from the example.

EXAMPLE 4.9   CREATING A WEB VIEWER IN JAVAFX

```java
==========================================================================
//Example 4.9 JavaFX Web viewer example
package sample;

import javafx.application.Application;
import javafx.stage.Stage;
import javafx.scene.Scene;
import javafx.scene.web.WebView;
import javafx.scene.Group;

public class Main extends Application {

    public static void main(String[] args) {
        launch(args);
    }

    public void start(Stage stage) {
        stage.setTitle("Web Viewer");

        WebView webView = new WebView();

        webView.getEngine().load("http://google.com");

        Group root = new Group(webView);
        Scene scene = new Scene(root, 800, 500);

        stage.setScene(scene);
        stage.show();

    }
}
==========================================================================
```

Figure 4.10: The output of the JavaFX web viewer example program

4.3.7 Creating a Menu in JavaFX

Menus are another common element of GUI applications. Example 4.10 shows a simple JavaFX menu created using the `Menu`, `MenuBar`, `MenuItem`, and `SeparatorMenuItem` classes. To create a menu, the program takes the following steps:

1. Create a `MenuBar` object.

2. Create a `Menu` object, along with some `MenuItem` objects; in this case, there is `Open`, `Separator`, and `Exit`. An action is added to the `Exit` object so that when the item is clicked, the program terminates: `Platform.exit()`.

3. Add `MenuItem` objects to the `Menu` object.

4. Add a `Menu` object to the `MenuBar` object.

5. Create a `BorderPane` layout, and add the `MenuBar` object to the north.

6. Add the `BorderPane` layout to the scene.

Here, for the menu object, `setOnAction()` is used to add actions to the object, and `Platform.exit()` will terminate the program. For example,

```
exitMenuItem.setOnAction(actionEvent -> Platform.exit())
```

will add program termination to the `exitMenuItem` object. To run this example, just create a JavaFX project called `JavaFXApplication7` using IntelliJ IDEA, and copy the following code into the `main.java` program. Figure 4.11 shows the output from the example.

EXAMPLE 4.10   CREATING A MENU WITH JAVAFX

```
========================================================================
//Example 4.10 JavaFX Menu example
package sample;

import javafx.application.Application;
import javafx.application.Platform;
import javafx.stage.Stage;
import javafx.scene.Scene;
import javafx.scene.layout.BorderPane;
import javafx.scene.control.Menu;
import javafx.scene.control.MenuBar;
import javafx.scene.control.MenuItem;
import javafx.scene.control.SeparatorMenuItem;
import javafx.scene.Group;

public class Main extends Application {
    public static void main(String[] args) {
        launch(args);
    }

    @Override
    public void start(Stage primaryStage) {
        primaryStage.setTitle("JavaFX Menu");
        MenuBar menuBar = new MenuBar();
        menuBar.prefWidthProperty().bind(primaryStage.widthProperty());

        // File menu - new, save, exit
        Menu fileMenu = new Menu("File");
        MenuItem newMenuItem = new MenuItem("Open");
        MenuItem exitMenuItem = new MenuItem("Exit");
        exitMenuItem.setOnAction(actionEvent -> Platform.exit());
        fileMenu.getItems().addAll(newMenuItem, new SeparatorMenuItem(),
exitMenuItem);
        menuBar.getMenus().add(fileMenu);

        BorderPane bp = new BorderPane();
        bp.setTop(menuBar);
        Scene scene = new Scene(bp, 400, 300);

        primaryStage.setScene(scene);
        primaryStage.show();
    }
}
========================================================================
```

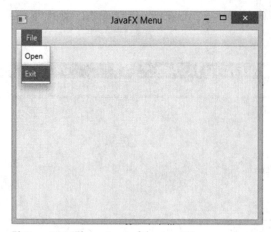

Figure 4.11: The output of the JavaFX menu example program

4.3.8   Creating a JavaFX File Chooser

In many applications, you need to read and write files. In JavaFX, you can use the FileChooser class to open a file chooser dialog where the user can select files for reading and writing. Example 4.11 shows a JavaFX menu application that uses the FileChooser class. This is an improved version of the previous image viewer example. Instead of loading the same image file, it presents a button that allows the user to select an image file to view. Again, a FileNotFoundException exception must be thrown or handled using a try...catch block.

To run this example, just create a JavaFX project called JavaFXApplication8 using IntelliJ IDEA, and copy the following code into the main.java program. Figure 4.12 shows the output from the example.

EXAMPLE 4.11   CREATING A JAVAFX MENU USING THE FILECHOOSER
CLASS

```
========================================================================
//Example 4.11 JavaFX Menu example
package sample;

import javafx.application.Application;
import javafx.application.Platform;
import javafx.stage.Stage;
import javafx.scene.Scene;
import javafx.scene.control.Button;
import javafx.scene.layout.BorderPane;
import javafx.stage.FileChooser;
import javafx.scene.image.Image;
```

```
import javafx.scene.image.ImageView;
import javafx.scene.Group;
import java.io.File;
import java.io.FileInputStream;
import java.io.FileNotFoundException;

public class Main extends Application {
    public static void main(String[] args) {
        launch(args);
    }

    @Override
    public void start(Stage primaryStage)throws FileNotFoundException  {
        primaryStage.setTitle("JavaFX File Chooser");
        ImageView imageView = new ImageView();
        FileChooser fileChooser = new FileChooser();
        Button button = new Button("Select a Image File");
        button.setOnAction(e -> {
            File file = fileChooser.showOpenDialog(primaryStage);
            if (file != null) {
                System.out.println("Selected file: " + file);
                try {
                    Image image = new Image(new FileInputStream(file));
                    imageView.setImage(image);
                }
                catch (FileNotFoundException ex){
                    //
                }
            }
        });

        BorderPane bp = new BorderPane();
        bp.setTop(button);
        bp.setCenter(imageView);
        Scene scene = new Scene(bp, 700, 500);

        primaryStage.setScene(scene);
        primaryStage.show();
    }
}
```

==

EXERCISE 4.8   Create a Java program that has a text field, a button, and a web
viewer. Use a `GridPane` layout to add a field and a button to the north and a web
viewer in the center. Add an action to the button so that when clicked, it displays the
web page of the URL typed in the text field.

Figure 4.12: The output of the JavaFX file chooser example program

EXERCISE 4.9   Modify the Java image viewer from Example 4.8 to have a File menu that contains Open, Save, and Exit menu items. Add actions so that when you click the Open menu item, it opens a file chooser dialog, where you can choose an image file to view; when you click Save, it saves the current image into a file, and when you click Exit, the program closes.

4.3.9   JavaFX Tutorials

There are many good JavaFX tutorials on the Internet. Figure 4.13 shows the official JavaFX tutorial from Oracle (`https://docs.oracle.com/javafx/2/get_started/jfxpub-get_started.htm`), which is comprehensive and includes all the JavaFX documentation.

Figure 4.14 shows a JavaFX tutorial from Tutorialspoint (`https://www.tutorialspoint.com/javafx/`). This is a well-presented tutorial that covers a lot of JavaFX topics with illustrative examples.

Figure 4.15 shows another JavaFX tutorial, this one from Jenkov Apps (`http://tutorials.jenkov.com/javafx/scatterchart.html`). This is an interesting tutorial, packed with different topics and examples of code.

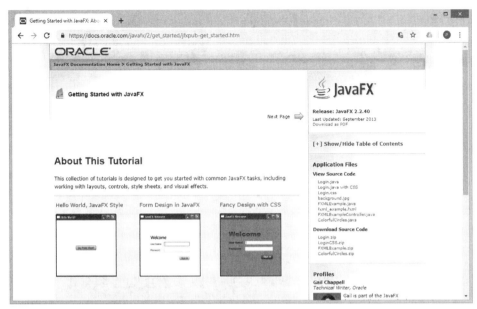

Figure 4.13: The official JavaFX tutorial from Oracle

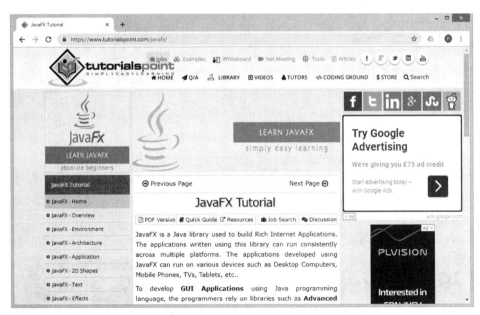

Figure 4.14: The JavaFX tutorial from Tutorialspoint

Figure 4.16 shows the JavaFX tutorial from Eclipse (`http://wiki.eclipse.org/Efxclipse/Tutorials`). This is mainly focused on how to develop JavaFX applications using the Eclipse IDE.

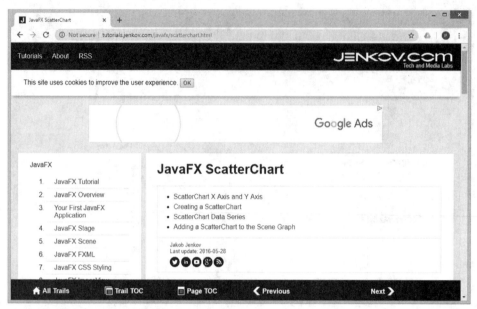

Figure 4.15: The JavaFX tutorial from Jenkov Apps

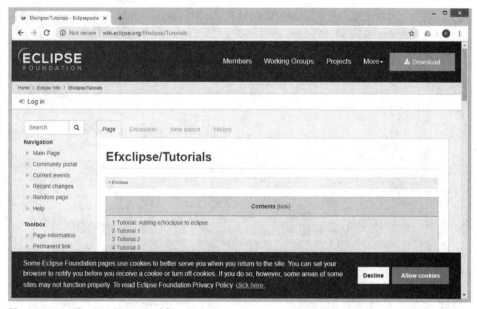

Figure 4.16: The JavaFX tutorial from Eclipse

Figure 4.17 shows the JavaFX official documentation web site from Oracle (`https://docs.oracle.com/javafx/2/`). Figure 4.18 shows the corresponding JavaFX API documentation web site from Oracle (`https://docs.oracle.com/javafx/2/api/index.html`).

Figure 4.17: The JavaFX documentation web site from Oracle

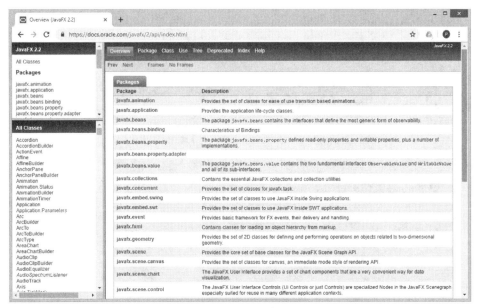

Figure 4.18: The JavaFX API documentation web site from Oracle

4.4   Deploying JavaFX Applications

The simplest way to deploy a JavaFX application is as a stand-alone executable JAR file, as described in section 3.13 of the previous chapter. Besides this, JavaFX applications can be deployed to run in a browser, to run on the Web, and as self-contained applications. Java IDEs such as Eclipse and NetBeans all provide JavaFX deployment functions.

Figure 4.19 shows a comprehensive JavaFX deployment guide from Oracle (`https://docs.oracle.com/javafx/2/get_started/basic_deployment.htm`). Figure 4.20 shows a JavaFX deployment guide from code.makery (`https://code.makery.ch/library/javafx-tutorial/part7/`).

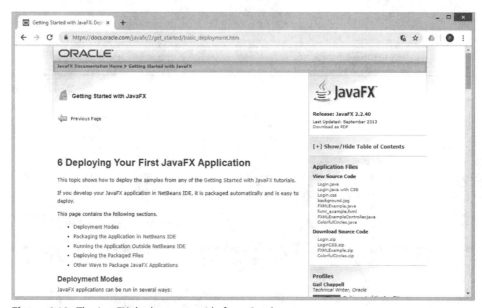

Figure 4.19: The JavaFX deployment guide from Oracle

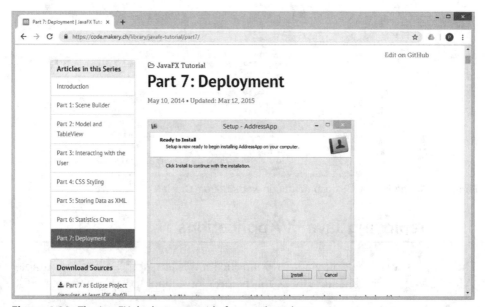

Figure 4.20: The JavaFX deployment guide from code.makery

4.5   Summary

This chapter introduced Java GUI programming. It first introduced Java GUI development using the Java Swing toolkit and then introduced Java GUI development using the latest JavaFX toolkit. It also provided resources including several interesting JavaFX tutorials and information about JavaFX deployment.

4.6   Chapter Review Questions

Q4.1.   What is the difference between a Java console application and a Java GUI application?

Q4.2.   What is Java AWT? What is Java Swing?

Q4.3.   What layouts does Java Swing support? What is the default layout?

Q4.4.   What is JavaFX?

Q4.5.   What is the relationship between the stage, scene, and nodes in JavaFX?

Q4.6.   What types of charts are supported in JavaFX?

Q4.7.   What layout panes are available in JavaFX?

Q4.8.   What is the relationship between `Menu`, `MenuBar`, and `MenuItem`?

Java Programming for Networking Applications

"Nothing is so embarrassing as watching someone do something that you said couldn't be done."

—Sam Ewing

5.1 Introduction

Computer networks have become an increasingly integrated part of our lives. With the Internet, the fast-growing, globalized computer network of networks, we are able to do shopping, banking, emailing, messaging, and booking flights or hotels online, all with just a few mouse clicks. The Internet has revolutionized our lives. According to the Internet Live Stats web site (`http://www.internetlives-tats.com/internet-users/`), there are more than 4 billion Internet users today.

The magic behind this Internet phenomenon is a technology known as TCP/IP, which was developed through the U.S. Advanced Research Projects Agency (ARPA)'s research project ARPANET in the 1960s. ARPA is a research arm of the United States Department of Defense, so TCP/IP has also been called the Department of Defense (DoD) model.

The TCP/IP model consists of a whole suite of protocols, built around two core protocols: Transmission Control Protocol (TCP) and Internet Protocol (IP). IP defines a scheme of devices addresses and delivers data from device to device based on those IP addresses, and TCP provides the control of the delivery. The TCP/IP model is divided into four layers: Application, Transport, Internet, and Link (see Figure 5.1).

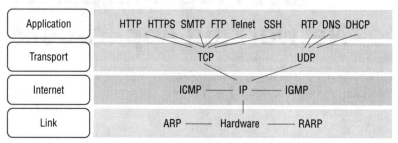

Figure 5.1: The TCP/IP model and its protocols

The Application layer provides an interface between users or user programs and the underneath communication protocols. The main protocols in this layer are Hypertext Transfer Protocol/ Hypertext Transfer Protocol Secure (HTTP/HTTPS) for web services, File Transfer Protocol (FTP) for file upload/download, Simple Mail Transfer Protocol (SMTP) for emails, Post Office Protocol (POP3) for retrieving email from an email server, Secure Shell (SSH) for remote login, Domain Name System (DNS) for translating domains to IP addresses and vice versa, and Dynamic Host Configuration Protocol (DHCP) for automatic host configuration.

The Transport layer manages the data transmission and provides services such as connection-oriented communication, reliability, flow control, and multiplexing. The main protocols in this layer are TCP for reliable transmission and User Datagram Protocol (UDP) for real-time transmission.

The Internet layer delivers the data, called *packets*, from source device to destination device, based on IP addresses. The main protocol in this layer is IP for delivering data. Also in the layer are Internet Control Message Protocol (ICMP) for error reporting and Internet Group Management Protocol (IGMP) for multicast.

The Link layer deals with the physical components of the networking devices, such as Ethernet, Token Ring, Fiber Optics, and WiFi connections. It is sometimes referred to as the Network Interface layer. The Link layer can also be subdivided into a Data Link layer and Physical layer. The main protocols in this layer are Address Resolution Protocol (ARP) for resolving IP addresses into hardware addresses or Medium Access Control (MAC) addresses, Reverse Address Resolution Protocol (RARP), and Neighbor Discovery Protocol (NDP) for gathering information about neighbor devices.

Any computers, phones, tablets, or other devices on the Internet must have TCP/IP suite software installed to function, as shown in Figure 5.2. Each device also needs its own IP address and port number to communicate with other devices on the network. The IP address is used to uniquely identify the device, a bit like a telephone number. There are two types of IP addresses: IP version 4 (IPv4) and IP version 6 (IPv6). IPv4 addresses are 32-bit binary addresses that are commonly expressed in dotted decimal format, such as 10.0.0.1, 136.148.1.27, or 192.168.0.1. IPv6 addresses are the new 128-bit binary addresses that are commonly expressed in hexadecimal format separated by colons, such as FE80:CD0 0:0000:0CDE:1257:0000:211E:729C, 2001:0DB8:85A3:0000:0000:8A2E:0370:7334, or FF01:0:0:0:0:0:0:1. The four billion IPv4 addresses have already been exhausted, so IPv6 addressing is going to be the future. There are 3.4×10^{38} IPv6 addresses in total, enough to assign an address to every single grain of sand on Earth. The port number is used to uniquely identify the programs you run on your device, such as web browsers, email agents, and chat programs. The port number is a 16-bit binary number, ranging from 0 to 65535. The port numbers 0–1023 are *well-known port numbers*, also called *system ports*. Here are some examples:

20: FTP (data transfer)
21: FTP (command control)
22: SSH
25: SMTP
53: DNS
67: DHCP Server
68: DHCP Client
80: HTTP
110: POP3
443: HTTPS

The port numbers 1024–49151 are called *registered ports*. The port numbers 49152–65535 are called *ephemeral ports*. When you are writing your Java programs, you should not use system ports; instead, you should use the registered ports or ephemeral ports.

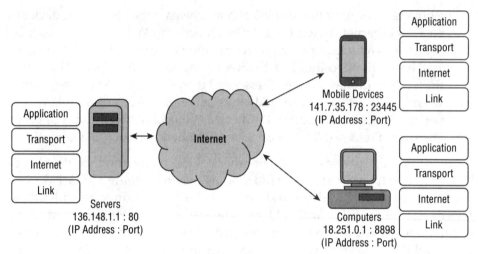

Figure 5.2: The TCP/IP model, IP address, and port number exchanged over the Internet

For more details about TCP/IP, please visit the following resources:

```
https://en.wikipedia.org/wiki/Internet_protocol_suite
http://www.pearsonitcertification.com/articles/article.aspx?p=1804869
https://docs.oracle.com/cd/E19683-01/806-4075/ipov-10/index.html
https://www.cisco.com/c/en/us/support/docs/ip/routing-information-
protocol-rip/13769-5.html
```

5.1.1   Local Area Network and Wide Area Network

A computer network can be physically classified as either a local area network (LAN) or a wide area network (WAN). A LAN is a group of interconnected computers within a building or a campus. A WAN is a collection of LANs that are spread out over a large area. A WAN within a city is also called a *metropolitan area network* (MAN). A LAN typically belongs to one organization and has high-speed connections, such as Fast Ethernet (100 Mbps) or Gigabit Ethernet (1000 Mbps). A MAN or WAN typically belongs to different organizations and has relatively low-speed connections. The Internet is an example of a worldwide public WAN.

5.1.2   The Cisco Three-Tier Enterprise Network Architecture

Large organizations with huge computer networks typically adopt Cisco's three-tiered enterprise network architecture, shown in Figure 5.3. From top to bottom, the tiers are Core, Distribution, and Access.

The Access layer provides the network access to end-user devices, such as computers, printers, or servers. The typical networking devices are switches, which connect all the devices in either a star network topology or a tree network topology (which consists of several star network topologies connected in a hierarchical structure).

The Distribution layer bridges the gap between the Access layer and the Core layer. The typical networking devices are routers, which connect all the switches in the Access layer to the Core layer. The Distribution layer also provides the network connection with redundancy by using mesh network topology.

The Core layer connects all the distribution routers together and provides the Internet access. The core layer is also known as the *backbone*. The typical networking device is a *gateway router*, also called the *default gateway*. Large organizations may have more than one gateway router to provide the Internet connection with more bandwidth and redundancy.

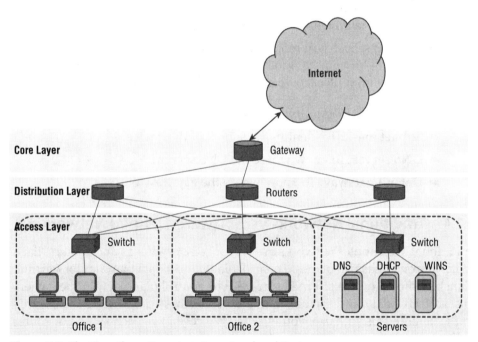

Figure 5.3: The Cisco three-tier enterprise network architecture

5.1.3   Key Network Components

Figure 5.3 shows the following key network components: switches, routers, a default gateway, and various servers such as DNS and DHCP servers. For a Windows computer network, you will also need a Windows Internet Name Service (WINS) server.

▪ A *switch* is a device used to connect users' client computers and usually has a large number of the same type of interface, called *ports*. A switch can have 8 ports, 16 ports, 64 ports, or even 128 ports.

- A *router* is a device to connect different networks, not users' computers, and usually has a few interfaces of different types, such as Ethernet, Fast Ethernet, Gigabit Ethernet, serial, Fiber Distributed Data Interface (FDDI), Asynchronous Transfer Mode (ATM), and Integrated Services Digital Network (ISDN). Routers are so called because they also perform routing functions to find the best route to a destination.

- The *gateway*, or *default gateway*, is where the local computer network connects to the Internet. The gateway is also the place where the network proxy server, network policy, and network firewall are commonly implemented.

- The *DNS* is another key component. The computers work based on IP addresses, but we humans are not good at remembering numbers, so we prefer names. DNS servers translate the human-understandable domain names into machine-understandable IP addresses, and vice versa.

- The *DHCP* server automatically provides the network configuration information for your computer. The following are four minimum pieces of information you need to configure your computer to access the Internet:

  - **IP address:** To identify the device
  - **Subnet mask:** To identify the subnet of the device
  - **DNS server:** To know where the DNS server is
  - **Default gateway:** To know where the gateway router is

5.1.4   Traditional Networks vs. Software-Defined Networking

Traditionally, computer networks are composed of switches and routers. Each switch or router has two planes, a control plane, and a data plane (or forwarding plane), as shown on the left in Figure 5.4. The control plane determines where to send traffic data, and the data plane executes these decisions and forwards traffic data. In this scenario, you will need to configure each switch or router individually. This approach is therefore time-consuming and error-prone, which makes it difficult to cope with the scalability problems of growing computer networks.

Software-defined networking (SDN) is an emerging technology that has become a new key buzzword in the computer networking/IT industry. With SDN, the control planes of switches and routers are taken away from individual devices and managed centrally using a dedicated server, as shown on the right in Figure 5.4. SDN is a software layer that sits on the top of existing computer networks. The server controls the traffic centrally by programming the switches and routers directly. This brings several benefits.

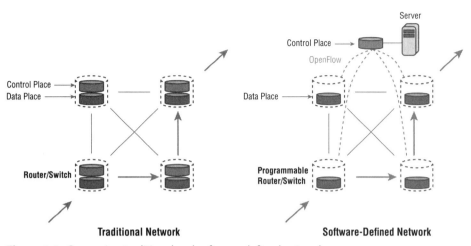

Figure 5.4: Comparing traditional and software-defined networks

Central management: You can configure, monitor, and troubleshoot the network all from the controller. You can also view the complete network topology from the controller.

Lighter-weight network devices: Because all the controls are performed centrally, you can use slimmed-down switches and routers to reduce network costs.

Network virtualization: SDN helps to virtualize the networks. Virtualization of networks has brought a revolution in the IT industry to virtualize storage and computing entities, which have played a key role in efficiently utilizing resources.

The most commonly used SDN communication protocol is OpenFlow, which is an open standard managed by the Open Networking Foundation. (You'll learn how to obtain and get started with it later in the chapter.) OpenFlow needs to be implemented in both switches/routers and the controller. OpenFlow carries messages between switches/routers and the controller. To control network switches/routers, the controller will use OpenFlow to push rules, such as forwarding rules and security rules, into switches/routers so that they can make decisions when network traffic hits them. Switches/routers need to maintain such rules in an OpenFlow table. Rules are also called *flows* and are stored in *flow tables*. To monitor switches/routers, the controller uses OpenFlow's various request and response messages to fetch the statistics information and events messages to update the controller about changes or failures that occur at switches/routers.

Floodlight is a popular SDN controller project. (You'll also learn how to obtain and get started with it later in the chapter.) It is a Java-based, Apache-licensed OpenFlow controller that you can use to help build a software-defined network. Floodlight is developed by an open community of developers, and it is simple to build and run. Floodlight supports a broad range of virtual and physical OpenFlow switches. Floodlight can handle mixed OpenFlow and non-OpenFlow networks. Floodlight is designed to be high-performance; it is multithreaded from the ground up, and it supports the OpenStack (link) cloud orchestration platform.

OpenDaylight is another Java-based open source SDN controller project. (You'll also learn how to obtain and get started with it later in the chapter.) It is a baseline project upon which many other controllers are built. The OpenDaylight project is conducted by the Linux Foundation. The goal of the project is to promote software-defined networking and network functions virtualization (NFV). NFV is another hot topic at the moment. SDN is closely related to NFV but is different. SDN focuses on separating the network's control plane from the forwarding plane and provides a centralized control of the network. NFV focuses on improving and virtualizing the network services themselves, such as DNS, caching, load balancing, firewalls, intrusion detection, and so on. Both SDN and NFV aim to advance a software-based approach to networking to make the network more scalable, more agile, and better supported.

In summary, SDN provides traffic programmability, agility, and the ability to create policy-driven network supervision and to implement network automation. It also allows the creation of a framework to support more data-intensive applications such as big data and virtualization. SDN can reduce both the capital expenses (CAPEX) of network equipment and the operational and maintenance expenses (OPEX) of a network. As a result, more and more companies are starting to adopt SDN.

For more details about SDN, please visit the following resources:

```
https://en.wikipedia.org/wiki/Software-defined_networking
https://en.wikipedia.org/wiki/OpenFlow
https://en.wikipedia.org/wiki/List_of_SDN_controller_software
https://www.cisco.com/c/en_uk/solutions/software-defined-networking/
overview.html
https://www.juniper.net/uk/en/products-services/sdn/
https://github.com/mininet/openflow-tutorial/wiki
http://www.projectfloodlight.org/floodlight/
https://www.opendaylight.org/
http://sdnhub.org/tutorials/
```

5.2   Java Network Information Programming

Java, with its rich networking capabilities, is suitable for developing applications that run in networked and distributed computer environments. This chapter will focus on how to develop networking-based applications using Java.

With Java, you can easily write a program to get network information. Example 5.1 shows how to get the IP address and hostname of your computer using the inetAddress class. Figure 5.5 shows the compilation and execution of the program.

EXAMPLE 5.1   THE NETADDRESS1.JAVA **PROGRAM**

```
//Example 5.1 NetAddress1.java program
import java.net.InetAddress;

class NetAddress1 {
    public static void main(String args[]) throws Exception {
        InetAddress inetAddress = InetAddress.getLocalHost();
        System.out.println("IP Address: " + inetAddress.
getHostAddress());
        System.out.println("Host Name: " + inetAddress.getHostName());
    }
}
```

Figure 5.5: The compilation and execution of the NetAddress.java program

Example 5.2 shows how to get the IP address and MAC address of your computer using the inetAddress and NetworkInterface classes. Figure 5.6 shows the compilation and execution of the program. The subnet 24 means 255.255.255.0.

EXAMPLE 5.2   THE NETINFO.JAVA **PROGRAM**

```
//Example 5.2 NetInfo.java program
import java.net.*;

class NetInfo {
    public static void main(String args[]) throws Exception {
        //Get IP address
        InetAddress ip;
        ip = InetAddress.getLocalHost();
        System.out.println("IP address : " + ip.getHostAddress());
        NetworkInterface network = NetworkInterface.getByInetAddress(ip);

        //Get subnet mask
        InetAddress localHost = Inet4Address.getLocalHost();
```

```
                NetworkInterface networkInterface = NetworkInterface.
getByInetAddress(localHost);
                System.out.println("Subnet Mask : "+networkInterface.
getInterfaceAddresses().get(0).getNetworkPrefixLength());

        //Get MAC address
        byte[] mac = network.getHardwareAddress();
        StringBuilder sb = new StringBuilder();
        for (int i = 0; i < mac.length; i++) {
                sb.append(String.format("%02X%s", mac[i], (i < mac.
length - 1) ? "-" : ""));
        }
        System.out.println("MAC address : " + sb.toString());
    }
}
```

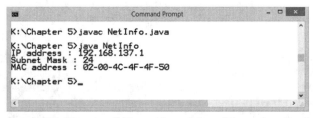

Figure 5.6: The compilation and execution of the Net Info.java program

EXERCISE 5.1   Based on the Java programs in Examples 5.1 and 5.2, do some research on the inetAddress class, and write a Java example program to use other functions of the class, such as getAllByName(String host), getLoopbackAddress(), hashCode(), or isLinkLocalAddress().

EXERCISE 5.2   Based on the Java programs in Examples 5.1 and 5.2, do some research on the NetworkInterface class, and write a Java example program to use other functions of the class, such as getDisplayName(), getSubInterfaces(), isPointToPoint(), or supportsMulticast().

Example 5.3 shows a longer version of the network information program using the inetAddress and NetworkInterface classes. Figure 5.7 shows the compilation and execution of the program.

EXAMPLE 5.3   THE NETADDRESS2.JAVA **PROGRAM**

```
//Example 5.3 NetAddress2.java program
import java.net.*;
import java.util.*;
```

```java
public class NetAddress2
{
    public static void main(String[] args)
    {
        try
        {
            System.out.println("getLocalHost: " + InetAddress.
getLocalHost().toString());

            System.out.println("All addresses for local host:");
            InetAddress[] addr = InetAddress.getAllByName(InetAddress.
getLocalHost().getHostName());
            for(InetAddress a : addr)
            {
              System.out.println(a.toString());
            }
        }
        catch(UnknownHostException _e)
        {
            _e.printStackTrace();
        }

        try
        {
            Enumeration<NetworkInterface> nicEnum = NetworkInterface.
getNetworkInterfaces();
            while(nicEnum.hasMoreElements())
            {
                NetworkInterface ni=nicEnum.nextElement();
                System.out.println("Name: " + ni.getDisplayName());
                System.out.println("Name: " + ni.getName());
                Enumeration<InetAddress>addrEnum =
ni.getInetAddresses();
                while(addrEnum.hasMoreElements())
                {
                    InetAddress ia= addrEnum.nextElement();
                    System.out.println(ia.getHostAddress());
                }
            }
        }
        catch(SocketException _e)
        {
            _e.printStackTrace();
        }
    }
}
```

Figure 5.7: The compilation and execution of the Net Address2.java program

In Windows operating systems, **ipconfig** is a powerful command to get network information. You can run **ipconfig** to get a summary of your computer network information, and you can run **ipconfig /all** to get more detailed network information. Example 5.4 shows how to execute the **ipconfig** command in Java to get network information using system calls, as illustrated in Chapter 3. Figure 5.8 shows the compilation and execution of the program.

EXAMPLE 5.4 THE IPCONFIG1.JAVA **PROGRAM**

```java
//Example 5.4 IPConfig1.java program
import java.io.*;

public class IPConfig1 {
    public static void main(String args[]) {
        try {
            String line;
            String[] cmd = {"cmd.exe", "/c", "ipconfig /all"};
            Process p = Runtime.getRuntime().exec(cmd);
            BufferedReader input = new BufferedReader(new
                InputStreamReader(p.getInputStream()));

            while ((line = input.readLine()) != null) {
                System.out.println(line);
            }
```

```
            input.close();
        }
        catch (Exception e) {
            e.printStackTrace();
        }
    }
}
```

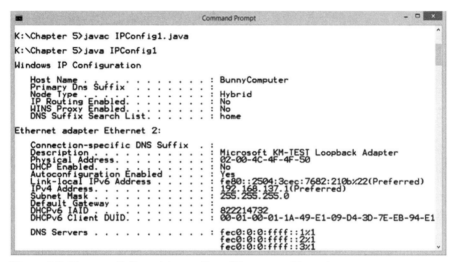

Figure 5.8: The compilation and execution of the IPConfig1.java program

Example 5.5 is an improved version of Example 5.4. This version searches for the DHCP server in the **ipconfig /all** command output using Java Pattern and Match classes. Java pattern matching is an efficient way of searching for a particular pattern within a given text. The following are the steps to use pattern matching:

```
Pattern pattern = Pattern.compile("DHCP Server");  //Create a pattern
Matcher matcher = pattern.matcher("");             //Create a text
matcher.reset(line);                               //Reset the text
matcher.find()                                     //Search the pattern
                                                   //  in the text
```

Figure 5.9 shows the compilation and execution of the program.

EXAMPLE 5.5   THE IPCONFIG2.JAVA **PROGRAM**

```
//Example 5.5 IPConfig2.java program
import java.util.*;
import java.util.regex.*;
import java.io.*;
```

```java
public class IPConfig2 {
    public static void main(String args[]) {
        try {
            String line;
            String[] cmd = {"cmd.exe", "/c", "ipconfig /all"};
            Process p = Runtime.getRuntime().exec(cmd);

            BufferedReader input = new BufferedReader(new
                InputStreamReader(p.getInputStream()));

            Pattern pattern = Pattern.compile("DHCP Server");
            Matcher matcher = pattern.matcher("");
            while ((line = input.readLine()) != null) {
                matcher.reset(line);
                if (matcher.find()) {
                    System.out.println(line);
                }
            }
            input.close();
        } catch (Exception e) {
            e.printStackTrace();
        }
    }
}
```

```
K:\Chapter 5>javac IPConfig2.java
K:\Chapter 5>java IPConfig2
      DHCP Server . . . . . . . . . . . . : 192.168.1.254
K:\Chapter 5>_
```

Figure 5.9: The compilation and execution of the `IPConfig2.java` program

EXERCISE 5.3   Modify the Example 5.5 Java program so that it can find and display other information from the `ipconfig /all` command output, such as the DNS servers, default gateway, IPv4 address, subnet mask, physical address, and hostname.

EXERCISE 5.4   After you complete Exercise 5.3, modify the Java program so that it can take the information such as DNS servers, default gateway, and so on, from the Java command-line arguments, to search for and display it from the `ipconfig /all` command output.

5.3   Java Socket Programming

In computer networks, a *socket* is an endpoint of a two-way communication channel between two computers over the Internet. A socket consists of an IP address and a port number. Java's Socket API supports two types of sockets: UDP sockets and TCP sockets. With a User Datagram Protocol socket, you can develop Java networking applications, such as audio or video chatting, which require simple, fast data transmission with minimum delays. With a Transport Control Protocol socket, you can develop Java networking applications, such as web, email, and file transfers, that require reliable data transmissions and have traffic flow control.

5.3.1   Java UDP Client-Server Programming

The User Datagram Protocol is a Transport layer protocol. UDP provides a connectionless, unreliable, but simple and fast service. Therefore, UDP is mostly used in time-critical applications such as Internet telephony, web broadcasts, or online video, where sending data without delay is more important than sending data without error.

Example 5.6 is a simple UDP client-server program. Example 5.6A, UDPServer1.java, is the server program, and Example 5.6B, UDPClient1.java, is the client program. In this example, the server program needs to run first, waiting for the client's connection, and the client program needs to run second so it can connect to server. In the client program, users need to type in a one-line sentence that will be sent to the server. When the server receives this data, it will echo it back to the client. Finally, the client will print out the server's response.

The following is the UDPServer1.java program's execution logic:

```
begin
    create a Server Datagram Socket on port 3301
    create a Datagram packet for receiving data
    receive data from a client
    print client's IP address and port number
    create another Datagram packet containing client's data
    send packet to client
    close Socket
end
```

EXAMPLE 5.6A THE UDPSERVER1.JAVA **PROGRAM**

```java
//Example 5.6A UDPServer1.java program
import java.net.*;

class UDPServer1 {
    public static void main(String argv[]) throws Exception{
        byte[] buf = new byte[256];
        String strData;
        int PORT = 3301;
        DatagramSocket serverSocket = new DatagramSocket(PORT);
        DatagramPacket packet = new DatagramPacket(buf, buf.length);

        serverSocket.receive(packet);
        strData = new String(packet.getData());
        InetAddress IPAddress = packet.getAddress();
        PORT = packet.getPort();
            System.out.println("Datagram received: "+IPAddress+":"+PORT);

        buf = strData.getBytes();
        packet = new DatagramPacket(buf, buf.length, IPAddress, PORT);
        serverSocket.send(packet);
        serverSocket.close();
    }
}
```

The following is the UDPClient1.java program's execution logic:

```
begin
    create a BufferReader associating with keyboard
    create a client Datagram Socket
    read in a line from keyboard
    create a Datagram packet containing that line
    send packet to server
    create another Datagram packet for receiving data from server
    receive data from server
    print server's response
    close Socket
end
```

EXAMPLE 5.6B THE UDPCLIENT1.JAVA **PROGRAM**

```java
// Example 5.6B UDPClient1.java program
import java.io.*;
import java.net.*;
class UDPClient1 {
    public static void main(String argv[]) throws Exception {
        int PORT = 3301;
```

```
        String HOST="localhost";
        String strData;

        System.out.println("Please enter your text:");
        BufferedReader inputLine =
        new BufferedReader(new InputStreamReader(System.in));

        DatagramSocket clientSocket = new DatagramSocket();
        InetAddress IPAddress = InetAddress.getByName(HOST);
        byte[] buf = new byte[256];
        strData = inputLine.readLine();
        buf = strData.getBytes();

        DatagramPacket packet =
        new DatagramPacket(buf, buf.length, IPAddress, PORT);
        clientSocket.send(packet);

        packet = new DatagramPacket(buf, buf.length);
        clientSocket.receive(packet);
        strData = new String(packet.getData());
        System.out.println("FROM SERVER:" + strData.toUpperCase());
        clientSocket.close();
    }
}
```

Figure 5.10 shows the compilation and execution of the `UDPServer1.java` program and the `UDPClient1.java` program. In this example, the server runs on localhost (127.0.0.1), port 3301; the client runs on localhost (127.0.0.1), port 3024. Please note that you will need two separate console windows to run the `UDPServer1.java` program and the `UDPClient1.java` program.

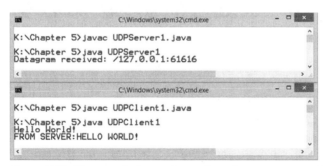

Figure 5.10: The compilation and execution of `UDPServer1.java` (top) and `UDPClient1.java` (bottom)

EXERCISE 5.5   Modify the UDP server Java program in Example 5.6A so that it receives the data from the client, changes it to uppercase, and echoes it back.

> **EXERCISE 5.6**   Modify the UDP client Java program in Example 5.6A so that
> it uses a `for` loop to send data to the server 10 times. Modify the UDP server Java
> program accordingly.

5.3.2   Java TCP Client-Server Programming

Transmission Control Protocol is also a Transport layer protocol. Unlike UDP,
TCP provides connection-oriented, reliable, streaming services. Because of TCP's
error detection, error correction, and traffic flow control, TCP has been widely
used in web, email, FTP download, and Telnet services, where the integrity of
the data has the highest priority.

Example 5.7 is a simple TCP echo program. `TCPServer1.java` is the server
program that provides an echo service. `TCPClient1.java` is the client program
that sends a line of data to the server and prints the server's echo reply on screen.

The following is the `TCPServer1.java` (Example 5.7A) program's execution logic:

```
begin
    create a server TCP Socket on port 3301
    create a client Socket waiting for client's connection
    print client's IP address and port number
    create a BufferReader for receiving data from client
    create a DataOutputStream for sending data to client
    send data to client
    close client Socket
    close server Socket
end
```

EXAMPLE 5.7A   THE `TCPSERVER1.JAVA` **PROGRAM**

```java
// Example 5.7A TCPServer1.java program
import java.io.*;
import java.net.*;

class TCPServer1 {
  public static void main(String argv[]) throws Exception {
      ServerSocket serverSocket = null;
      Socket clientSocket = null;
      //You can use any other port numbers (1024 - 65535), if 3301 is
not available
      int PORT = 3301;
      serverSocket = new ServerSocket(PORT);
      clientSocket = serverSocket.accept();
      System.out.println("Connected from:"
                      + clientSocket.getInetAddress() + ":"
                      + clientSocket.getPort());
```

```
        BufferedReader inputLine =
               new BufferedReader(new InputStreamReader(clientSocket.
getInputStream()));
        DataOutputStream  outputLine =
               new DataOutputStream(clientSocket.getOutputStream());
        outputLine.writeBytes(inputLine.readLine());

        clientSocket.close();
        serverSocket.close();
    }
}
```

The following is the TCPClient1.java (Example 5.7B) program's execution logic:

```
begin
    create a BufferReader associating with keyboard
    create a client TCP Socket associating with a TCP server
    print server's IP address and port number
    create a DataOutputStream for sending data to server
    create a BufferReader for receiving data from server
    read in a line from keyboard and send it to server
    create a Datagram packet containing that line
    receive data from server and print server's response
    close Socket
end
```

EXAMPLE 5.7B   THE TCPCLIENT1.JAVA PROGRAM

```
// Example 5.7B TCPClient1.java program
import java.io.*;
import java.net.*;
class TCPClient1 {
    public static void main(String argv[]) throws Exception {
        Socket clientSocket = null;
        int PORT = 3301;
        String HOST = "localhost";

        BufferedReader inputLine =
          new BufferedReader(new InputStreamReader(System.in));

        clientSocket = new Socket(HOST, PORT);
        System.out.println("Connected to: " + clientSocket.
getInetAddress() + ":" +
                          clientSocket.getPort());

        DataOutputStream outputLine =
          new DataOutputStream(clientSocket.getOutputStream());
```

```
        BufferedReader replyLine =
            new BufferedReader(new InputStreamReader(clientSocket.
getInputStream()));

        outputLine.writeBytes(inputLine.readLine() + '\n');
        System.out.println("FROM SERVER: " + replyLine.readLine().
toUpperCase());

        clientSocket.close();
    }
}
```

Figure 5.11 shows the compilation and execution of the TCPServer1.java and TCPClient1.java programs. Again, you need to run TCPServer1.java first in a console window and then run TCPClient1.java in another console window. In this example, the TCP server runs on localhost (127.0.0.1) and on port 3301, and the TCP client runs on localhost (127.0.0.1) and on port 3020.

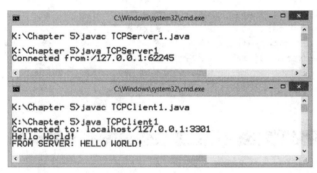

Figure 5.11: The compilation and execution of TCPServer1.java (top) and TCPClient1.java (bottom)

EXERCISE 5.7   Modify the TCPServer1.java program in Example 5.7A so that it runs in an endless loop. If it receives the word *date*, it will send the date information to the client. If it receives the word *time*, it will send the time information to the client. If it receives the word *bye*, it will send a good-bye message to the client and then terminate the loop.

EXERCISE 5.8   Modify the TCPClient1.java program in Example 5.7B so that it also runs in an endless loop that can send text such as *date*, *time*, and *bye* to the server.

5.3.3   Java Multithreaded EchoServer Programming

The echo server in the previous section runs on a single thread and therefore can accept only one client at a time. Example 5.8A shows a multithreaded echo server, which allows the echo server to accept multiple clients simultaneously and echo back the message from each client separately.

EXAMPLE 5.8A A MULTITHREADED ECHO SERVER

```java
//Example 5.8A Multithreaded Echo Server
import java.io.*;
import java.net.*;

public class EchoServer2 {

    public static void main(String [] args){
        ServerSocket echoServer;
        int id=0;
        try{
            echoServer=new ServerSocket(9999);
            while(true){
                Socket clientSocket = echoServer.accept();

                ChatThread cliThread = new ChatThread(clientSocket,id++);
                cliThread.start();
            }
        }
        catch (IOException e)
        {
            System.out.println(e);
        }
    }
}
class ChatThread extends Thread{
    Socket clientSocket;
    int id;

    BufferedReader br;
    PrintWriter os;
    String line;

    ChatThread ( Socket clientSocket, int id ) {
        this.clientSocket=clientSocket;
        this.id=id;
    }
    public void run(){
        try{
            br=new BufferedReader(new InputStreamReader(clientSocket
.getInputStream()));
            os = new PrintWriter(clientSocket.getOutputStream(),true);

            while ((line = br.readLine())!=null){
                System.out.println(id+"-Received: "+line);
```

```
                os.println(line);
            }
    }
    catch (IOException e){
        System.out.println(e);
    }
    finally{
        try{
          br.close();
          os.close();
          clientSocket.close();
          System.out.println(id+"...Stopped");
        }
        catch(Exception e){
            e.printStackTrace();
        }
    }
    //System.out.println( message );
  }
}
```

Example 5.8B shows the corresponding echo client.

EXAMPLE 5.8B   THE ECHO CLIENT   o

```
//Example 5.8B Echo Client
import java.io.*;
import java.net.*;

public class EchoClient{

    public static void main(String[] args){
        Socket echoSocket;
        PrintWriter out;
        BufferedReader in;
        try
        {
            echoSocket = new Socket("localhost", 9999);
            out = new PrintWriter(echoSocket.getOutputStream(),true);
            in = new BufferedReader(new InputStreamReader(
                echoSocket.getInputStream()));
            BufferedReader stdIn = new BufferedReader(
                new InputStreamReader(System.in));

            String userInput;
            while ((userInput = stdIn.readLine()) != null)
            {
                out.println(userInput);
                System.out.println("echo: " + in.readLine());
            }
```

```
            out.close();
            in.close();
            stdIn.close();
            echoSocket.close();
        }
        catch(Exception e)
        {
            System.out.println("Error: "+e.toString());
            System.exit(-1);
        }
    }
}
```

EXERCISE 5.9   Modify the multithreaded echo server Java program in
Example 5.8A so that it takes the port number from the command-line parameter, that
is, by using `args`.

EXERCISE 5.10   Modify the echo client Java program in Example 5.8B so that it
takes the server IP address and port number from the command-line parameter, that
is, by using `args`.

For more information on Java socket programming, see the following resources:

https://docs.oracle.com/javase/tutorial/networking/sockets/index.html
https://www.javaworld.com/article/2077322/core-java/core-java-sockets-
programming-in-java-a-tutorial.html
https://o7planning.org/en/10393/java-socket-programming-tutorial

5.4   Java HTTP Programming

HTTP stands for Hypertext Transfer Protocol; it is the protocol for communicating between web clients and servers. HTTP works on the basis of requests
and responses, in which a web client (web browser) sends a request to the web
server, and the web server responds with the result (a web page). HTTP is the
magic behind the World Wide Web, which is no doubt the most popular service on the Internet today. With Java, you can easily develop web applications
with HTTP.

5.4.1   A Java HTTP/HTTPS Client

Example 5.9 shows a series of Java HTTP clients—web clients. First, Example 5.9A
is a simple client using the URL and URLConnection classes. In this example, it
opens the web page specified by its uniform resource locator (URL), in this case
www.google.com/. Figure 5.12 shows the compilation and execution of the program.

EXAMPLE 5.9A   AN HTTP CLIENT

```java
//Example 5.9A HTTP Client
import java.net.*;
import java.io.*;

public class HTTPClient {
    public static void main(String[] args) throws Exception {
        URL u = new URL("http://www.google.com/");
        URLConnection uc = u.openConnection();
        BufferedReader in = new BufferedReader(new InputStreamReader(
                                 uc.getInputStream()));
        String inputLine;
        while ((inputLine = in.readLine()) != null)
            System.out.println(inputLine);
        in.close();
    }
}
```

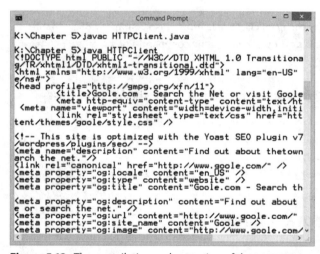

Figure 5.12: The compilation and execution of the `HTTPClient.java` program

EXERCISE 5.11   Modify the Example 5.9A Java program so that it takes the URL of a web site from the command-line parameter, that is, by using `args`.

Example 5.9B is a variation of the previous Java program, which uses `Http-sURLConnection()` to connect to a secure web site, using the HTTPS protocol.

EXAMPLE 5.9B   AN HTTPS CLIENT

```java
//Example 5.9B: HTTPS Client
import java.net.*;
import java.io.*;
```

```
import javax.net.ssl.HttpsURLConnection;

public class HTTPSClient {
    public static void main(String[] args) throws Exception {
        URL u = new URL("https://www.google.com/");
        HttpsURLConnection uc = (HttpsURLConnection) u.openConnection();
        BufferedReader in = new BufferedReader(new InputStreamReader(
                                uc.getInputStream()));
        String inputLine;
        while ((inputLine = in.readLine()) != null)
            System.out.println(inputLine);
        in.close();
    }
```

Example 5.9C is a version of the same program, but it also prints the digital certificate information from the HTTPS server.

EXAMPLE 5.9C   ANOTHER HTTPS CLIENT

```
//Example 5.9c HTTP Client 2
import java.net.*;
import java.io.*;
import java.security.cert.Certificate;
import javax.net.ssl.HttpsURLConnection;
public class HTTPSClient2 {
    public static void main(String[] args) throws Exception {
        String urltxt = "https://www.google.com/";
        URL u = new URL(urltxt);
        HttpsURLConnection uc = (HttpsURLConnection) u.openConnection();
        try {
            System.out.println("Response Code : " +
uc.getResponseCode());
            System.out.println("Cipher Suite : " + uc.getCipherSuite());
            System.out.println("\n");

            Certificate[] certs = uc.getServerCertificates();
            for(Certificate cert : certs){
                System.out.println("Cert Type : " + cert.getType());
                System.out.println("Cert Hash Code : " + cert.
hashCode());
                System.out.println("Cert Public Key Algorithm : "
                                    + cert.getPublicKey().
getAlgorithm());
                System.out.println("Cert Public Key Format : "
                                    + cert.getPublicKey().getFormat());
                System.out.println("\n");
            }
        } catch (IOException e){
            e.printStackTrace();
```

```
        }

        BufferedReader in = new BufferedReader(new InputStreamReader(
                                    uc.getInputStream()));
        String inputLine;
        while ((inputLine = in.readLine()) != null)
            System.out.println(inputLine);
        in.close();
    }
```

HTTP/HTTPS clients can use either the GET or POST method to talk to HTTP/HTTPS servers. The default is the GET method, which is used to retrieve information from the server. The POST method is for sending information to the server, such as sending login details, submitting forms, searching keywords, and similar tasks. Example 5.10 shows a simple Java HTTP/HTTPS client using the GET method to get information from the server, similar to the previous example. This version of the program opens the web page specified by its URL, in this case https://docs.oracle.com/javase/tutorial/. Figure 5.13 shows the compilation and execution of the program.

EXAMPLE 5.10   THE HTTPGET1.JAVA **PROGRAM**

```
//Example 5.10 The HTTPGet1.java program
import java.io.*;
import java.net.*;

public class HTTPGet1 {
    // HTTP GET request
    public static void getHTML(String website) throws Exception {
        URL url = new URL(website);
        HttpURLConnection conn = (HttpURLConnection) url.
openConnection();
        conn.setRequestMethod("GET");
        conn.setRequestProperty("User-Agent", "Chrome/51.0.2704.63");
        conn.setRequestProperty("Accept-Language", "en-US,en");
        int responseCode = conn.getResponseCode();
        System.out.println("\nSending 'GET' request to URL : " +
website);
        System.out.println("Response Code : " + responseCode);

        BufferedReader br = new BufferedReader(
                new InputStreamReader(conn.getInputStream()));
        StringBuilder response = new StringBuilder();
        String line;
        while ((line = br.readLine()) != null) {
            response.append(line);
        }
```

```
        br.close();
        System.out.println( response.toString());
    }
    public static void main(String[] args) throws Exception
    {
        getHTML("https://docs.oracle.com/javase/tutorial/");
    }
}
```

Figure 5.13: The compilation and execution of the `HTTPGet1.java` program

EXERCISE 5.12   Modify the Example 5.10 Java program so that it takes the URL of a web site from the command-line parameter, using `args`.

EXERCISE 5.13   Based on the previous Java programs, do some research on the `Certificate` class and write a Java example program to use other functions of the class, such as `verify(PublicKey key)`, `hashCode()`, or `toString()`.

Example 5.11 shows a simple Java HTTP client using the POST method to send search results to the server. In this example, it opens the web page `https://www.amazon.co.uk/s/ref=nb _ sb _ noss _ 2?` and searches for the keyword *java*. Figure 5.14 shows the compilation and execution of the program. Because of the output length, only the first 1,000 characters are printed. You can also search in another web site, such as Google; just uncomment the following two lines in the code:

```
//String website="https://www.google.co.uk/search?";
//String urlParameters="q=java";
```

EXAMPLE 5.11   THE HTTPPOST1.JAVA **PROGRAM**

```java
//Example 5.11 HTTPPost1.java program
import java.io.*;
import java.net.*;
import javax.net.ssl.HttpsURLConnection;

public class HTTPPost1 {
    // HTTP POST request
    private static void postHTML(String website, String urlParameters)
throws Exception {
        URL url = new URL(website);
        HttpsURLConnection conn = (HttpsURLConnection) url.
openConnection();
        conn.setRequestMethod("POST");
        conn.setRequestProperty("User-Agent", "Chrome/51.0.2704.63");
        conn.setRequestProperty("Accept-Language", "en-US,en");
        // Send post request
        conn.setDoOutput(true);
        DataOutputStream wr = new DataOutputStream(conn.
getOutputStream());
        wr.writeBytes(urlParameters);
        wr.flush();
        wr.close();

        int responseCode = conn.getResponseCode();
        System.out.println("\nSending 'POST' request to URL : " +
website);
        System.out.println("Post parameters : " + urlParameters);
        System.out.println("Response Code : " + responseCode);

        BufferedReader in = new BufferedReader(
                new InputStreamReader(conn.getInputStream()));
        String inputLine;
        StringBuffer response = new StringBuffer();

        while ((inputLine = in.readLine()) != null) {
            response.append(inputLine);
        }
        in.close();

        //print result (first 1000 characters)
        System.out.println(response.toString().substring(0,1000));

    }
    public static void main(String[] args) throws Exception
    {
        //Search java in Amazon
        String website="https://www.amazon.co.uk/s/ref=nb_sb_noss_2?";
```

```
        String urlParameters="url=search-alias%3Daps&field-
keywords=java";
        //Search java in Google
        //String website="https://www.google.co.uk/search?";
        //String urlParameters="q=java";

        postHTML(website, urlParameters);
    }
}
```

Figure 5.14: The compilation and execution of the `HTTPPost1.java` program

EXERCISE 5.14   Modify the Example 5.11 Java program so that it takes the URL of a web site and URL parameters from the command-line parameter by using `args`.

Example 5.12 shows another Java HTTP example using URL class. It parses the URL of a web page and shows the corresponding information such as the protocol, host, port, path, and query. Figure 5.15 shows the compilation and execution of the program.

EXAMPLE 5.12   URL PARSING

```
//Example 5.12 URL Parsing
import java.net.*;
public class URLExample1{
    public static void main(String[] args) {
        try {
            URL url = new URL("http://www.google.come:80/
search?q=java");
            System.out.println("URL created: " + url);
            System.out.println("protocol: " + url.getProtocol());
            System.out.println("host: " + url.getHost());
            System.out.println("port: " + url.getPort());
            System.out.println("path: " + url.getPath());
```

```
                    System.out.println("query: " + url.getQuery());
                }
                catch (MalformedURLException e) {
                    System.out.println("Malformed URL: " + e.getMessage());
                }


        }
```

```
┌──────────────────────────────────────────────────────────────────┐
│ ▣                        Command Prompt                 – □ ✕      │
├──────────────────────────────────────────────────────────────────┤
│ K:\Chapter 5>javac URLExample1.java                            ▲  │
│                                                                   │
│ K:\Chapter 5>java URLExample1                                     │
│ URL created: http://www.google.come:80/search?q=java              │
│ protocol: http                                                    │
│ host: www.google.come                                             │
│ port: 80                                                          │
│ path: /search                                                     │
│ query: q=java                                                     │
│                                                                   │
│ K:\Chapter 5>                                                  ▼  │
│ <                                                              >  │
└──────────────────────────────────────────────────────────────────┘
```

Figure 5.15: The compilation and execution of the URLExample1.java program

5.4.2   A Java HTTP Server

Example 5.13 shows a simple Java HTTP server program, using ServerSocket classes. It runs on port 8088, and when a web browser client is connected, it displays Hello World! in the browser. Figure 5.16 shows the compilation and execution of the program. To view the web page, open a web browser and type the IP address of your computer and port 8088, as shown in the figure.

EXAMPLE 5.13   AN HTTP SERVER

```java
//Example 5.13 HTTP Server
import java.io.*;
import java.net.*;

public class HTTPServer {
  protected void start() {
    ServerSocket s;

    System.out.println("Starting up HTTP Server...");
    try {
      s = new ServerSocket(8088);
    } catch (Exception e) {
      System.out.println("Error: " + e);
      return;
    }

    System.out.println("Waiting... ");
```

```
  for (;;) {
    try {
      Socket remote = s.accept();
      System.out.println("Connected....");
      BufferedReader in = new BufferedReader(new InputStreamReader(
          remote.getInputStream()));
      PrintWriter out = new PrintWriter(remote.getOutputStream());

      String str = ".";
      while (!str.equals("")){
        str = in.readLine();
        System.out.println(str);
      }

      out.println("HTTP/1.1 200 OK");
      out.println("Content-Type: text/html");
      out.println("Server: Java HTTP Server");
      out.println("");
      // Send the HTML page
      out.println("<H1>Hello World!</H1>");
      out.flush();
      remote.close();
    } catch (Exception e) {
      System.out.println("Error: " + e);
    }
  }
}

public static void main(String args[]) {
  HTTPServer sr = new HTTPServer();
  sr.start();
}
}
```

EXERCISE 5.15   Modify the Example 5.13 Java program so that it also prints the date and time information, as well as the client's IP address, on the web page.

5.4.3   Java Multithreaded HTTP Server

Example 5.14A is a multithreaded version of the previous HTTP server. In this version, it first creates a `ServerSocket` object on port 8088 and then uses a `while` loop to listen to client requests. Each time it accepts a client connection, it generates a separate thread dealing with that connection. Inside the thread, within the `run()` method, it reads all the lines of the HTTP request message from the client and sends back a `Hello Multithreaded HTTP Server!` message.

Figure 5.16: The compilation and execution of the `HTTPServer.java program` (top) and testing the server using a web browser (bottom)

EXAMPLE 5.14A   A MULTITHREADED HTTP SERVER

```java
//Example 5.14A Multithreaded HTTP Server
import java.io.*;
import java.net.*;

public class HTTPServer2 {
    public static void main(String args[]) {
        int port =8088;
        ServerSocket web;
        try {
            web = new ServerSocket(port);
        } catch (Exception e) {
```

```java
                System.out.println("Error: " + e);
                return;
            }

        while(true){
            System.out.println("MultiThreaded Web Server Running on
port: "+ port);
                try{
                    Socket client = web.accept();
                    System.out.println("Accepted Client : " + client);
                    HTTPServer2Thread s = new HTTPServer2Thread(client);
                    s.start();
                }
                catch(Exception e){
                    System.out.println("Error: " + e);
                    return;
                }
            }
        }
}
class HTTPServer2Thread extends Thread{
    Socket client;
    HTTPServer2Thread(Socket client){
        this.client = client;
    }
    public void run(){
        try {
            BufferedReader in = new BufferedReader(new
InputStreamReader(
                client.getInputStream()));
            PrintWriter out = new PrintWriter(client.getOutputStream());

            String str = ".";
            while (!str.equals("")){
                str = in.readLine();
                System.out.println(str);
            }
            out.println("HTTP/1.1 200 OK");
            out.println("Content-Type: text/html");
            out.println("Server: Java HTTP Server");
            out.println("");
            // Send the HTML page
            out.println("<H1>Hello Multithreaded HTTP Server!</H1>");
            out.flush();
            out.close();
            client.close();
        } catch (Exception e) {
            System.out.println("Error: " + e);
        }
    }
}
```

EXERCISE 5.16   Modify the Example 5.14A Java program so that instead of using a separate thread class, it uses the main class to inherit from the `Thread` class.

Example 5.14B is another multithreaded version of the earlier HTTP server. In this version, it finds out what file does the client request, finds and opens the file, reads line by line until finished, and also sends each line to the client accordingly. To test the HTTP server, just open a web browser and type the IP address of your computer and port 8088, exactly the same as in the previous figure.

EXAMPLE 5.14B   MULTITHREADED HTTP FILE SERVER

```java
//Example 5.14B Multithreaded HTTP File Server
import java.io.*;
import java.net.*;

public class HTTPServer3 {
    public static void main(String args[]) {
        int port =8088;
        ServerSocket web;
        try {
            web = new ServerSocket(port);
        } catch (Exception e) {
            System.out.println("Error: " + e);
            return;
        }

        while(true){
            System.out.println("MultiThreaded Web Server Running on
port: "+ port);
            try{
                Socket client = web.accept();
                System.out.println("Accepted Client : " + client);
                HTTPServer3Thread s = new HTTPServer3Thread(client);
                s.start();
            }
            catch(Exception e){
                System.out.println("Error: " + e);
                return;
            }
        }
    }
}
class HTTPServer3Thread extends Thread{
    Socket client;
    HTTPServer3Thread(Socket client){
        this.client = client;
    }
```

```java
    public void run(){
        try {
            BufferedReader in = new BufferedReader(new
InputStreamReader(
                    client.getInputStream())));
            PrintWriter out = new PrintWriter(client.getOutputStream());
            String reqMeth = "";
            String reqURL = "";
            String reqProto = "";
            String str = ".";
            int i=0;
            while (!str.equals("")){
                str = in.readLine();
                System.out.println(i+": " +str);
                if (i==0){
                    reqMeth = str.substring(0, 3);
                    reqURL = str.substring(5, (str.
lastIndexOf("HTTP/1.")));
                    reqProto = str.substring(str.indexOf("HTTP/1."));
                }
                i++;
            }
            //Send HTTP header
            out.println("HTTP/1.1 200 OK");
            out.println("Content-Type: text/html");
            out.println("Server: Java HTTP Server");
            out.println("");
            // Open the file and send out line by line
            FileReader file=new FileReader(reqURL.trim());
            BufferedReader filebuff= new BufferedReader(file);
            boolean endof=false;
            String line;
            while (!endof) {
                line=filebuff.readLine();
                if (line == null){ endof=true; break;}
                out.println(line);
            }
            file.close();

            //Close all the streams
            out.flush();
            out.close();
            client.close();
        } catch (Exception e) {
            System.out.println("Error: " + e);
        }
    }
}
```

EXERCISE 5.17 Modify the Example 5.14B Java program so that instead of using a separate thread class, it uses the main class to inherit from the `Thread` class.

5.5   Java Email SMTP Programming

Simple Mail Transfer Protocol is used to transfer email messages over the Internet. Example 5.15 shows a Java SMTP example. It connects to the email server at port 25, where SMTP is running, and uses HELO, MAIL, RCPT TO, DATA, and QUIT to send an email to a receiver.

EXAMPLE 5.15   AN SMTP APPLICATION

```
//Example 5.15 SMTP Example
import java.io.*;
import java.net.*;

public class smtpClient {
    public static void main(String[] args) {
        Socket smtpSocket = null;
        DataOutputStream os = null;

        BufferedReader br = null;
        //Please use your own email settings for the following
parameters
        String client = "Your Name";
        String server = " yourmailserver.com";
        String sender = "youremail@yourmailserver.com";
        String receiver = "receiver@receiverserver.com";

        try {
            smtpSocket = new Socket(server, 25);
            os = new DataOutputStream(smtpSocket.getOutputStream());

            br = new BufferedReader(new InputStreamReader(smtpSocket.
getInputStream()));
        } catch (UnknownHostException e) {
            System.err.println("Don't know about host: "+server);
        } catch (IOException e) {
            System.err.println("Couldn't get I/O for the connection to:
hostname");
        }

        if (smtpSocket != null && os != null && br != null) {
            try {
```

```
            os.writeBytes("HELO "+ client +"\n");
            os.writeBytes("MAIL From: "+ sender +"\n");
            os.writeBytes("RCPT To: "+ receiver +"\n");
            os.writeBytes("DATA\n");
            os.writeBytes("From: "+ sender +"\n");
            os.writeBytes("Subject: testing\n");
            os.writeBytes("Hi there 1\n"); // message body
            os.writeBytes("\n.\n");
            os.writeBytes("QUIT\n");

            String responseLine;
            while ((responseLine = br.readLine()) != null) {
                System.out.println("Server: " + responseLine);
                if (responseLine.indexOf("Ok") != -1) {
                  break;
                }
            }

            os.close();
            smtpSocket.close();
        } catch (UnknownHostException e) {
            System.err.println("Trying to connect to unknown host: "
  + e);
        } catch (IOException e) {
            System.err.println("IOException: " + e);
        }
      }
    }
}
```

A much more elegant and sophisticated way of sending and checking email is to use the JavaMail API. To use this API, you need to download two JAR files. For JavaMail, you need a file named `javax.mail.jar`, which you can get here:

`https://javaee.github.io/javamail/`

For the JavaBeans Activation Framework (JAF), you need a file named `activation.jar`, which you can get here:

`https://www.oracle.com/technetwork/java/javase/downloads/index-135046.html`

Find the `javax.mail.jar` and `activation.jar` files from the download, and copy them to your current Java directory. Example 5.16A shows a simple Java program for sending email through Transport Layer Security (TLS) using the JavaMail API. Please amend your SMTP server name, your username, your password, your email address, and recipient's email address accordingly. Please note that this code will not work if you have set up your email using two-factor or multifactor authentication, which requires you to present two or more pieces of evidence to log in.

EXAMPLE 5.16A   JAVAMAIL API EXAMPLE

```java
//Example 5.16A JavaMail API Example
import java.util.*;
import javax.mail.*;
import javax.mail.internet.*;

public class JavaMail1 {
    public static void main(String[] args) {
        final String username = "youremail@gmail.com";
        final String password = "yourpassword";
        Properties props = new Properties();
        props.put("mail.smtp.auth", "true");
        props.put("mail.smtp.starttls.enable", "true");
        props.put("mail.smtp.host", "smtp.gmail.com");
        props.put("mail.smtp.port", "587");  //SSL/TLS port :587 normal:
465

        Session session = Session.getInstance(props,
          new javax.mail.Authenticator() {
            protected PasswordAuthentication getPasswordAuthentication()
{
                return new PasswordAuthentication(username, password);
            }
          });

        try {
            Message message = new MimeMessage(session);
            message.setFrom(new InternetAddress("youremail@gmail.com"));
            message.setRecipients(Message.RecipientType.TO,
                InternetAddress.parse("someone@somewhere.com"));
            message.setSubject("Your Research Paper");
            message.setText("Dear Perry,"
                + "\n\n Could please send me your GLCM paper?"
                + "\n\n Cheers!"
                + "\n\n Tom");

            Transport.send(message);

            System.out.println("Done");

        } catch (MessagingException e) {
            throw new RuntimeException(e);
        }
    }
}
```

To compile and run the Java program in Example 5.14A, you need to include the `javax.mail.jar` and `activation.jar` files in your classpath, as shown here:

```
javac -classpath .;javax.mail.jar;activation.jar  JavaMail1.java
java -classpath .;javax.mail.jar;activation.jar  JavaMail1
```

Example 5.16B shows another simple Java application for checking email using Post Office Protocol 3 (POP3). Again, it makes the connection through TLS using the JavaMail API. Please also amend the POP3 hostname, your username, and your password accordingly.

EXAMPLE 5.16B   JAVAMAIL API POP3 EXAMPLE

```java
//Example 5.16B JavaMail API POP3 Example
import java.util.*;
import javax.mail.*;

public class JavaMail2 {
    public static void main(String[] args) {

        String host = "pop.gmail.com";
        String username = "yourname@gmail.com";
        String password = "yourpassword";

        try {
            //create properties field
            Properties properties = new Properties();
            properties.put("mail.pop3.host", host);
            properties.put("mail.pop3.port", "995");
            properties.put("mail.pop3.starttls.enable", "true");
            Session emailSession = Session.getDefaultInstance(propert
ies);

            //create the POP3 store object and connect with the pop
server
            Store store = emailSession.getStore("pop3s");
            store.connect(host, username, password);

            //create the folder object and open it
            Folder emailFolder = store.getFolder("INBOX");
            emailFolder.open(Folder.READ_ONLY);

            // retrieve the messages from the folder in an array and
print it
            Message[] messages = emailFolder.getMessages();
```

```
                    for (int i = 0, n = messages.length; i < n; i++) {
                        Message message = messages[i];
                        System.out.println("--------------------------------");
                        System.out.println("Email Number " + (i + 1));
                        System.out.println("Subject: " + message.getSubject());
                        System.out.println("From: " + message.getFrom()[0]);
                        System.out.println("Text: " + message.getContent().
toString());

                    }
                    //close the store and folder objects
                    emailFolder.close(false);
                    store.close();
            } catch (Exception e) {
                e.printStackTrace();
            }
        }
    }
```

To compile and run the previous Java program, just type the following:

```
javac -classpath .;javax.mail.jar;activation.jar  JavaMail2.java
java -classpath .;javax.mail.jar;activation.jar  JavaMail2
```

For more information on SMTP and JavaMail, see the following resources:

```
https://en.wikipedia.org/wiki/Simple_Mail_Transfer_Protocol
https://www.oracle.com/technetwork/java/javamail/index.html
https://www.tutorialspoint.com/javamail_api/index.htm
https://www.journaldev.com/2532/javamail-example-send-mail-in-java-smtp
https://www.javatpoint.com/java-mail-api-tutorial
```

5.6   Java RMI Client-Server Programming

Remote method invocation (RMI) is a distributed systems technology that allows one Java virtual machine (JVM) to invoke object methods that will run on another JVM located elsewhere on a network. It is similar to remote procedure calls (RPCs), which were developed in the 1980s and allow a procedural program written in any language to call functions residing on another computer. But RPC supports only a limited set of simple data types, and it does not support objects. Although RMI currently supports only the Java language, it allows the passing and returning of Java objects, which makes it more powerful than RPC. RMI is useful for the development of large-scale systems, as it makes it possible to distribute resources and processing load across more than one machine.

RMI applications are divided into two kinds of programs: servers and clients. RMI servers create remote objects and register them with a lookup service to allow clients to find them. Clients use a remote reference to one or more remote objects in the server and then invoke methods on them.

To develop an RMI application, you need to create four programs.

- The remote interface program
- The remote interface implementation program
- The RMI server program
- The RMI client program

The remote interface program is a Java interface that defines the methods that can be called by clients. The remote interface implementation program implements the methods defined in the remote interface program. The RMI server program provides the service. Finally, the RMI client program uses the service. The remote interface, remote interface implementation, and RMI server programs run on the server computer, while the RMI client program runs on client computers.

Example 5.17 is a simple RMI application that can calculate the average of a series of double precision numbers. It contains four files, `Analysor1.java`, `Analysor1Impl.java`, `Analysor1Server.java`, and `Analysor1Client.java`. The file `Analysor1.java` is the interface program that defines only one method, called `Average()`. `Analysor1Impl.java` implements the `Average()` method. `Analysor1Server.java` provides an RMI service called `AnalysorService`, which contains the `Average()` method. By default, an RMI service runs on port 1099. The following are the two key statements of the server program:

```
Analysor1 c = new Analysor1Impl();
Naming.rebind("rmi://localhost:1099/AnalysorService", c);
```

`Analysor1Client.java` is the client program that will look for the `AnalysorService` service and call the `Average()` method. The following are the two key statements of the client program:

```
Analysor1 c = (Analysor1) Naming.lookup("rmi://localhost:1099/
AnalysorService");
System.out.println( "The average of array d: "+ c.Average(d));
```

Example 5.17A is the `Analysor1.java` program.

EXAMPLE 5.17A   ANALYSOR1.JAVA RMI INTERFACE PROGRAM

```
// Example 5.17a Analysor1.java RMI interface program
public interface Analysor1 extends java.rmi.Remote {
    public double Average(double d[])
        throws java.rmi.RemoteException;

}
```

Example 5.17B is the `Analysor1Impl.java` program.

EXAMPLE 5.17B   ANALYSOR1IMPL.JAVA RMI INTERFACE IMPLEMENTATION PROGRAM

```java
// Example 5.17B Analysor1Impl.java RMI interface implementation program
public class Analysor1Impl
    extends java.rmi.server.UnicastRemoteObject implements Analysor1 {
    public Analysor1Impl() throws java.rmi.RemoteException {
        super();
    }

    public double Average(double d[])
        throws java.rmi.RemoteException {
        double r=0.0;
        for (int i=0;i<d.length;i++){
            r+=d[i];
        }
        r/=d.length;
        return r;
    }
}
```

Example 5.17C is the `Analysor1Server.java` program.

EXAMPLE 5.17C   ANALYSOR1SERVER.JAVA RMI SERVER PROGRAM

```java
// Example 5.17c Analysor1Server.java RMI server program
import java.rmi.Naming;

public class Analysor1Server {

    public Analysor1Server() {
        try {
            Analysor1 c = new Analysor1Impl();
            Naming.rebind("rmi://localhost:1099/AnalysorService", c);
        } catch (Exception e) {
            System.out.println("Trouble: " + e);
        }
    }

    public static void main(String args[]) {
        new Analysor1Server();
    }
}
```

Example 5.17D is the `Analysor1Client.java` program.

EXAMPLE 5.17D ANALYSOR1CLIENT.JAVA RMI CLIENT PROGRAM

```java
// Example 5.17d Analysor1Client.java RMI client program
import java.rmi.Naming;
import java.rmi.RemoteException;
import java.net.MalformedURLException;
import java.rmi.NotBoundException;

public class Analysor1Client {

    public static void main(String[] args) {

        double d[]=new double[10];
        for (int i=0;i<d.length;i++){
            d[i]=i;
        }

        try {
            Analysor1 c = (Analysor1) Naming.lookup("rmi://
localhost:1099/AnalysorService");
            System.out.println( "The average of array d: "+
c.Average(d));
        }
        catch (MalformedURLException murle) {
            System.out.println();
            System.out.println("MalformedURLException");
            System.out.println(murle);
        }
        catch (RemoteException re) {
            System.out.println();
            System.out.println("RemoteException");
            System.out.println(re);
        }
        catch (NotBoundException nbe) {
            System.out.println();
            System.out.println("NotBoundException");
            System.out.println(nbe);
        }
        catch (java.lang.ArithmeticException ae) {
            System.out.println();
            System.out.println("java.lang.ArithmeticException");
            System.out.println(ae);
        }
    }
}
```

To run an RMI application, follow these steps:

1. Start the RMI registry so that RMI servers can register their services.

2. Start the RMI servers.

3. Start the RMI clients.

Figure 5.17 shows the details.

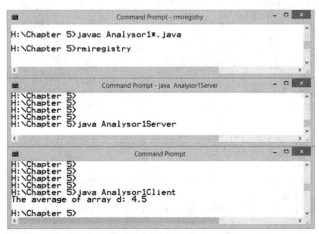

Figure 5.17: The compilation of all the RMI Java programs and start of the RMI registry (top); the start of the `Analysor1Server.java` RMI server (middle); and the start of the `Analysor1Client.java` RMI client (bottom)

5.7   Getting Started with SDN

Earlier in the chapter you explored the concept of software-defined networking. This approach has shown huge potential and is definitely the future of computer networks. If you want to get started with SDN, the following are a few good places to begin. These tutorials will get you started with the most important SDN tools introduced earlier: OpenFlow, Floodlight, and OpenDaylight.

5.7.1   Getting Started with OpenFlow

The simplest way to get started with OpenFlow is to use Mininet. Figure 5.18 shows an interesting GitHub site (`https://github.com/mininet/openflow-tutorial/wiki`) on the OpenFlow tutorial. It shows how to download and set up the relevant software and shows examples such as Learn Development Tools, Create A Learning Switch, Control A Slice Of A Real Network, Router Exercise, Advanced Topology, and Create Firewall.

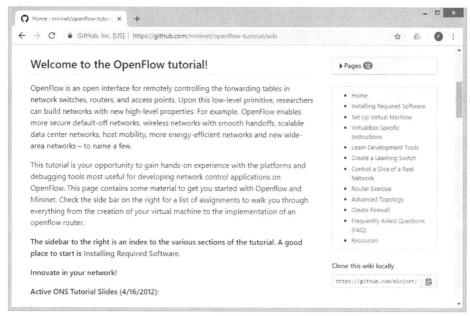

Figure 5.18: The GitHub site on the OpenFlow tutorial

To get started, you first need to download the following software:

- Mininet VM Images

https://github.com/mininet/mininet/wiki/Mininet-VM-Images

- VirtualBox

https://www.virtualbox.org/wiki/Downloads

- Xming

https://sourceforge.net/projects/xming/files/Xming/6.9.0.31/Xming-6-9-0-31-setup.exe/download

- Putty.exe

http://the.earth.li/~sgtatham/putty/latest/x86/putty.exe

Then follow the instructions at the following sites to import the Mininet virtual machine file into the VirtualBox software:

https://github.com/mininet/openflow-tutorial/wiki/Set-up-Virtual-Machine
http://mininet.org/vm-setup-notes/

Figure 5.19 shows the Mininet virtual machine in VirtualBox. Start the Mininet virtual machine, and use mininet for the username and mininet for the password to log in. The Mininet virtual machine is based on the Ubuntu Linux operating system.

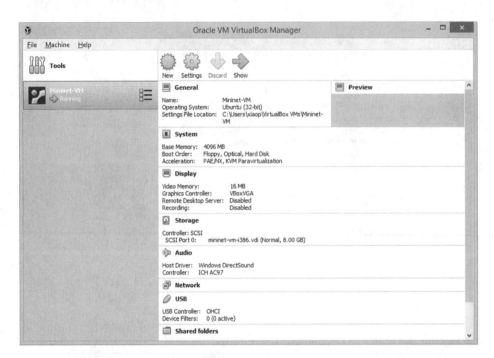

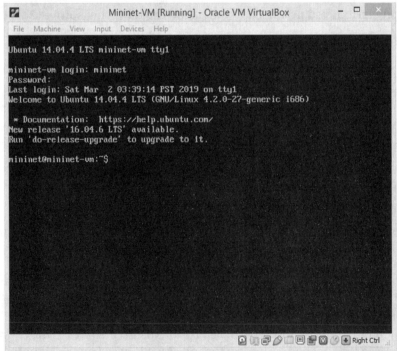

Figure 5.19: The Mininet virtual machine in VirtualBox (top) and the Mininet login (bottom)

After login, at the Linux shell prompt ($), you can type the following command to start Mininet and enter its command-line interface (CLI) mode. The `sudo` command means you run the Mininet as a superuser, or administrator.

```
$ sudo mn
```

This will start a simulated network with minimal topology, which includes a controller (`c0`), a switch (`s1`), and two hosts (`h1` and `h2`), as shown in Figure 5.20.

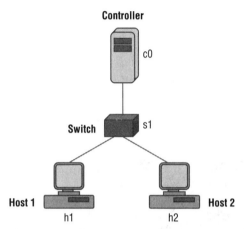

Figure 5.20: The Mininet simulated network with minimal topology

You can also start with other topologies by using the `--topo` option. For example, the following command starts a simulated network with single switch and four hosts:

```
$ sudo mn --topo single,4
```

The following command starts a simulated network with three switches connected in a line, and each has one host:

```
$ sudo mn --topo linear,3
```

You can use the following command to show more options of starting Mininet:

```
$ sudo mn -h
```

After starting Mininet CLI, at the **mininet>** prompt, type the following command to show all the nodes on the simulated network:

```
mininet> nodes
```

The following command shows network information on the simulated network:

```
mininet> net
```

The following command shows the information of all the links on the simulated network:

```
mininet> links
```

The following command shows more detailed information of all the nodes on the simulated network, including the IP address of each node:

```
mininet> dump
```

The following command shows the help information of all the Mininet CLI commands:

```
mininet> help
```

Figure 5.21 shows the output of some of the preceding commands in the Mininet virtual machine.

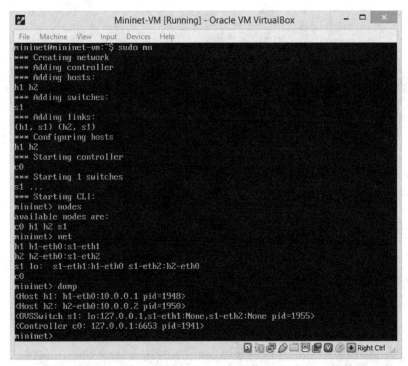

Figure 5.21: The Mininet commands to display information of the simulated network with minimal topology

The **ifconfig** command is a useful Linux command to display network information and to configure a network interface. It is similar to the Windows **ipconfig** command you used earlier. You can run the **ifconfig** command on the h1 node by typing the following command to display the network information for the h1 node:

```
mininet> h1 ifconfig
```

In this case, all the nodes use `10.0.0.0` IP addresses. Your simulated network might use different IP addresses, such as `192.168.0.0`, depending on your computer network settings.

EXERCISE 5.16   Modify the preceding command to display the network information for the `h2` node. Then do the same for the `s1` and `c0` nodes.

Similarly, the **ps** Linux command displays information about the processes running on the system. The **ps -a** command displays all the processes. You can run the **ps -a** command on the `h1` node by typing the following command:

```
mininet> h1 ps -a
```

EXERCISE 5.17   Modify the preceding command to display all the processes on the `h2` node. Then do the same for the `s1` node and the `c0` node.

The `ping` Linux command can check the connections between two nodes. You can ping from host 1 to host 2 by typing the following command. The **ping -c 10** command means to ping 10 times. Figure 5.22 shows the ping results.

```
mininet> h1 ping -c 10 h2
```

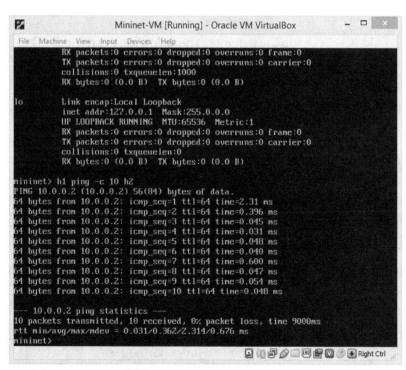

Figure 5.22: The Mininet ping command to ping from host 1 to host 2 for 10 times

You can also ping all nodes by typing the following command:

```
mininet> pingall
```

You can test the TCP bandwidth between the h1 node and the h2 node by typing the following command:

```
mininet> iperf
```

You can start the x terminal on the h1 node by typing the following command:

```
mininet> xterm h1
```

You can start a simple Python web server on the h1 node by typing the following command. The 80 means run the server on port 80, and & means to run the server in the background.

```
mininet> h1 python -m SimpleHTTPServer 80 &
```

You can view the web server content in text mode on the h2 node by typing the following command:

```
mininet> h2 wget -O - h1
```

You stop the Python web server on the h1 node by typing the following command:

```
mininet> h1 kill %python
```

You can also add new nodes to the network. The following are the steps. Type the following command to add a node called h3 to the network.

```
mininet> py net.addHost('h3')
```

Type the following command to add a new link between the s1 node and the h3 node:

```
mininet> py net.addLink(s1, net.get('h3'))
```

Type the following command to attach a new Ethernet interface on the s1 node:

```
mininet> py net.attach('s1-eth3')
```

Type the following command to configure the IP address for the h3 node:

```
mininet> py net.get('h3').cmd('ifconfig h3-eth0 10.0.0.3')
```

Type the following command to display the network information on the h3 node:

```
mininet> h3 ifconfig
```

Figure 5.23 shows the output of the preceding commands. As you can see, you should also be able to ping the h3 node from other nodes.

You can visualize the Mininet topology by using the online Mininet Topology Visualizer tool at the following web site:

```
http://demo.spear.narmox.com/app/?apiurl=demo#!/mininet
```

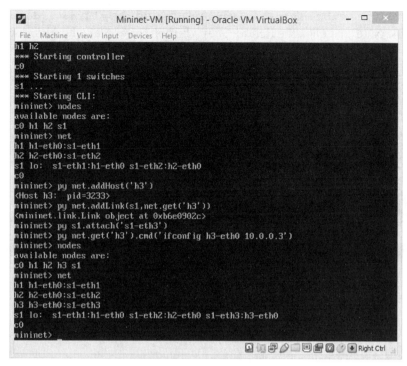

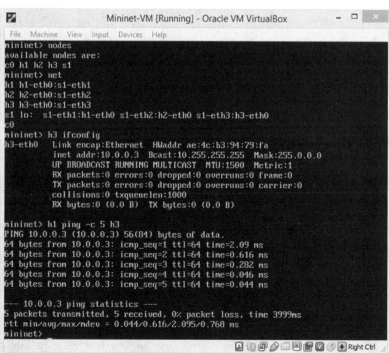

Figure 5.23: The commands to add and to configure a new node called h3 to the network

Just copy and paste the `mininet> links` results and the `mininet> dump` results into the page, and click the Render Graph button to generate the network topology, as shown in Figure 5.24.

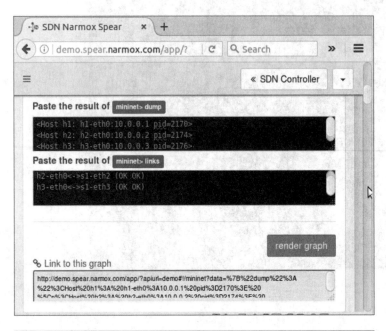

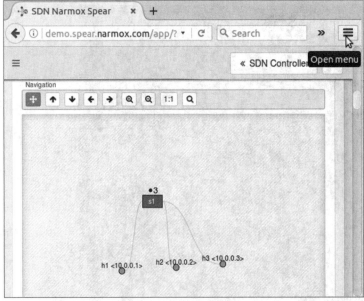

Figure 5.24: The Mininet Topology Visualizer web site (top) and the generated topology graph (bottom)

Finally, you can exit the Mininet simulation by typing the following command:

```
mininet> exit
```

You can clean up the Mininet simulation by typing the following command:

```
$ sudo mn -c
```

For more information and advanced usage about Mininet OpenFlow, such as configuring the routers and switches, as well as using an Xming server, `Putty. exe`, and more, please visit the following resources:

```
https://github.com/mininet/openflow-tutorial/wiki
http://mininet.org/
https://github.com/mininet/mininet/wiki/Introduction-to-Mininet
https://academy.gns3.com/p/sdn-and-openflow-introduction
https://www.cisco.com/c/en _ uk/solutions/software-defined-networking/
overview.html
```

5.7.2   Getting Started with Floodlight

The following is the Project Floodlight web site. It has a detailed "get started" guide for instructions on how to download and install Floodlight.

```
http://www.projectfloodlight.org/getting-started/
```

5.7.3   Getting Started with OpenDaylight

The following is the wiki site of OpenDaylight. It shows how to download the OpenDaylight software and shows how to get started by setting up the development environment and getting the code.

```
https://wiki.opendaylight.org/view/Main _ Page
```

5.8   Java Network Programming Resources

The following are a few interesting Java networking tutorials:

- Tutorialspoint
```
https://www.tutorialspoint.com/java/java _ networking.htm
```
- Java2S
```
www.java2s.com/Tutorial/Java/0320 _ _ Network/javanetSocket.htm
```
- GeeksforGeeks
```
https://www.geeksforgeeks.org/socket-programming-in-java/
```

5.9 Summary

This chapter introduced the basic concepts of computer networks, including the latest software-defined networking. It also provided some simple examples of using Java for network information, UDP sockets, TCP sockets, HTTP and HTTPS clients, HTTP servers, an SMTP client, a Java RMI client and server, and, finally, how to get started with SDN. More complicated Java examples based on the REST design model and the recent MQTT protocol are available in Chapter 7.

5.10 Chapter Review Questions

Q5.1.   What is the Internet, and what is TCP/IP?

Q5.2.   What are LANs and WANs?

Q5.3.   What is Cisco's three-tier network architecture?

Q5.4.   What is the difference between a switch and a router?

Q5.5.   What are DNS and DHCP?

Q5.6.   What is SDN? What are OpenFlow, Floodlight, and OpenDaylight?

Q5.7.   What are IP addresses, port numbers, and MAC addresses?

Q5.8.   What is the difference between IPv4 addresses and IPv6 addresses?

Q5.9.   What is a socket?

Q5.10.   What are the differences between UDP and TCP?

Q5.11.   What is HTTP? How many versions does HTTP have? What is the difference between HTTP and HTTPS?

Q5.12.   What is RMI, and how does RMI work?

Java Programming for Mobile Applications

"It is what you learn after you know it all that counts."

—John Wooden

6.1   Introduction

Ever since 2007, when Apple first introduced its iPhone, our passion for smartphones has become stronger and deeper. Smartphone sales have rocketed. There are around 2.5 billion smartphones worldwide in 2019, according to Statista (https://www.statista.com/). Smartphones are an excellent example of a modern technology that has fundamentally revolutionized our lives. With smartphones, you can search the Internet, book flights and hotels, and order food and taxies all with just a few finger swipes. With mobile payment, in many places, you can

183

survive with just a phone, without needing cash or credit card in your wallet! Smartphones have truly gone from luxury items to daily necessities in the span of about 10 years' time.

There are generally two main types of smartphones on the market, Google's Android phones and Apple's iPhones. There are an estimated five billion mobile users in the world. The largest market share is held by phones using Google's Android operating system, which occupies more than 80 percent of the market. The top Android phone makers are Samsung, Huawei, Google, HTC, LG, ZTE, Xiaomi, Oppo, Vivo, and so on. However, the largest single phone company is still Apple, with about 15 percent market share. The traditional mobile phone companies such as Nokia, Ericsson, Motorola, and the once-most-popular-with-business-customers BlackBerry, have all fallen out of favor and become nonexistent.

This chapter first introduces how to use Android Studio to develop mobile phone applications—*apps*—for Android phones and then introduces MIT App Inventor, another popular way of developing Java Android applications. MIT App Inventor is a web-based, visual programming tool, which allows users to build Java Android applications using visual objects. MIT App Inventor is particularly popular among beginners. Finally, this chapter introduces 5G, the most talked about and most researched next-generation mobile technology. 5G is going to significantly change the way we communicate, and therefore it is beneficial to understand what 5G is and how it works.

6.2   Android Studio

Android is an open source and Linux-based operating system for mobile devices, developed by Google. Android Studio is the official IDE for developing Android programs. Android Studio actually works based on IntelliJ IDEA, so instead of using Android Studio, you can also use IntelliJ IDEA to develop Android mobile applications.

To develop Android mobile applications, you will need the following:

- Java JDK (5 or later)
- Android Studio (or IntelliJ IDEA)

Because you installed the Java JDK in Chapter 2, here you just need to install Android Studio. Figure 6.1 shows the Android developer web site (`https://developer.android.com/studio/`) where you can download and install Android Studio. During the Android Studio installation, it will also install Android SDK for compiling your programs and Android Virtual Device (AVD) for running simulations of your programs.

Unfortunately, installing and configuring Android Studio is not a completely painless process; there are several tricky places, so you might need to try more than once. Figure 6.2 shows an excellent Android Studio installation tutorial from Tutorialspoint (`https://www.tutorialspoint.com/android/android_studio .htm`). There is also an excellent seven-part YouTube tutorial series (`https://www .youtube.com/watch?v=LN8fBh7LH9k&list=PLt72zDbwBnAW5TU96UHUbLtnivjviIKks`) called *Android App Development for Beginners (2018 Edition),* shown in Figure 6.3.

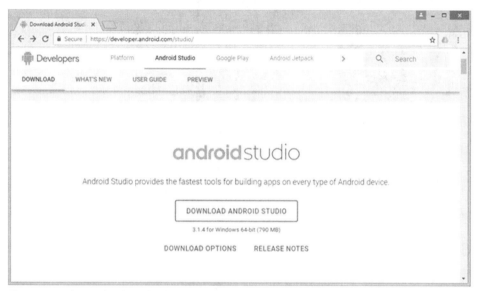

Figure 6.1: The Android Studio download web site

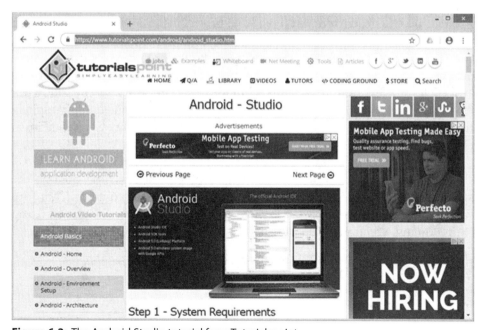

Figure 6.2: The Android Studio tutorial from Tutorialspoint

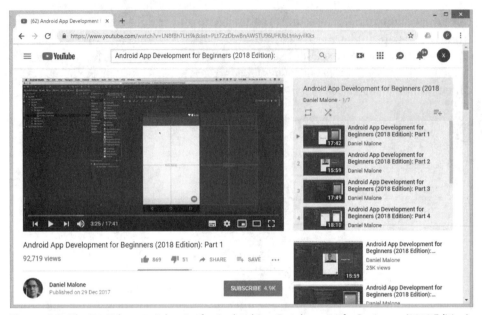

Figure 6.3: The YouTube tutorial series for *Android App Development for Beginners (2018 Edition)*

6.3 The Hello World App

Once you have successfully installed Android Studio, you can start to develop your own Android applications. In our first example, we will create a simple Android app that will display `Hello World!` on-screen.

First, you will need to create an Android project using Android Studio. When you first run Android Studio, a welcome window will appear, from which you can click Start A New Android Project, as shown in Figure 6.4 (top). A new project window will appear. Choose your project with the default empty activity and click the Next button, as shown in Figure 6.4 (middle). On the following Configure Your Project screen, choose your project name; the default application name is My Application, as shown in Figure 6.4 (bottom). Click the Finish button to finish creating the project.

Once the project is created, your screen will look as shown in Figures 6.5–6.8. This is a blank Android project. The left panel of the Android Studio shows the structure of your project, and the right panel shows the file contents. There are several key files in the project, which you can find from the left panel, using the following selection sequences:

- app ➪ java ➪ com.example.myfirstapp ➪ `MainActivity.java`

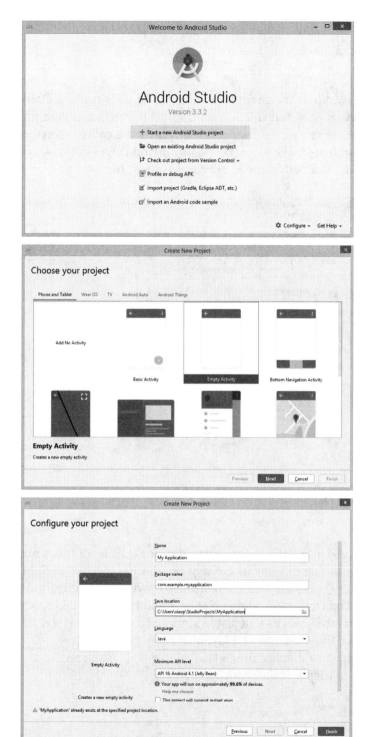

Figure 6.4: The Android Studio welcome window (top), the Choose Your Project window (middle), and Configure Your Project window (bottom)

- app ➪ res ➪ layout ➪ `activity_main.xml`
- app ➪ manifest ➪ `AndroidManifest.xml`
- Gradle Scripts files

The `MainActivity.java` file is the main Java program of your project. Double-click the file to view its content in a tab on the right panel, as shown in Figure 6.5. Inside the `MainActivity` class, the `onCreate()` method is called when the `MainActivity` class is first created. The `setContentView()` method gives information about the layout resource, defined in the `activity_main.xml` file.

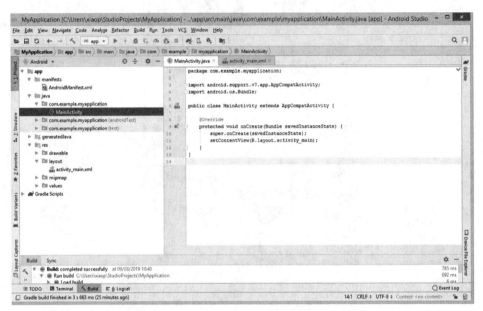

Figure 6.5: The Android project My Application in Android Studio, with the `MainActivity` `.java` tab

The `activity_main.xml` file defines the user interface (UI) layout of your Java app. Double-click the file to view its content on another tab in the right panel. Inside the `activity_main.xml` tab, there are also two subtabs at the bottom, Design and Text. The Design tab shows the look and feel of the UI layout (Figure 6.6), and the Text tab shows its Extensible Markup Language (XML) code (Figure 6.7). In this case, the program's UI layout contains only one `TextView` component, which is used to display the `Hello World!` text. You can simply modify this XML code to display other text.

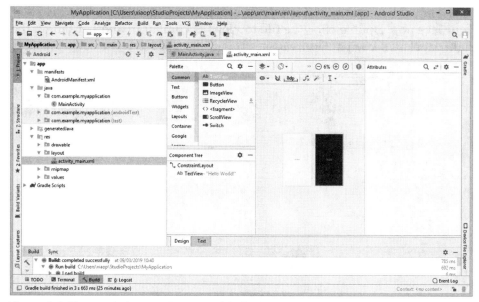

Figure 6.6: The `activity_main.xml` tab in Design view

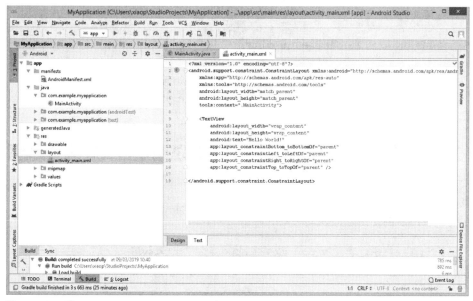

Figure 6.7: The `activity_main.xml` tab in Text view

The `AndroidManifest.xml` file describes the fundamental characteristics of your Java app. Double-click the file to view its content in another tab on the right panel, as shown in Figure 6.8.

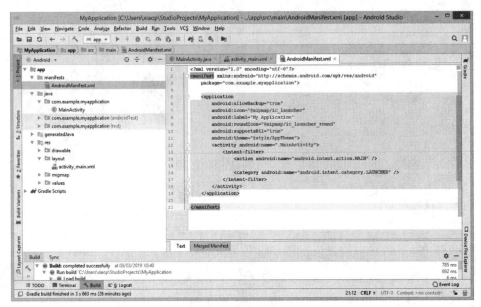

Figure 6.8: The `AndroidManifest.xml` tab

The Gradle Scripts files are used to build the project.

Example 6.1A shows the corresponding code of `MainActivity.java`, and Example 6.1B shows the `activity_main.xml` file.

EXAMPLE 6.1A   THE `MAINACTIVITY.JAVA` **CODE**

```java
package com.example.myapplication;

import android.support.v7.app.AppCompatActivity;
import android.os.Bundle;

public class MainActivity extends AppCompatActivity {

    @Override
    protected void onCreate(Bundle savedInstanceState) {
        super.onCreate(savedInstanceState);
        setContentView(R.layout.activity_main);
    }
}
```

EXAMPLE 6.1B   THE ACTIVITY_MAIN.XML **CODE**

```xml
<?xml version="1.0" encoding="utf-8"?>
<android.support.constraint.ConstraintLayout xmlns:android="http://
schemas.android.com/apk/res/android"
    xmlns:app="http://schemas.android.com/apk/res-auto"
    xmlns:tools="http://schemas.android.com/tools"
    android:layout_width="match_parent"
    android:layout_height="match_parent"
    tools:context=".MainActivity">

    <TextView
        android:layout_width="wrap_content"
        android:layout_height="wrap_content"
        android:text="Hello World!"
        app:layout_constraintBottom_toBottomOf="parent"
        app:layout_constraintLeft_toLeftOf="parent"
        app:layout_constraintRight_toRightOf="parent"
        app:layout_constraintTop_toTopOf="parent"/>

</android.support.constraint.ConstraintLayout>
```

To run the program, just click the green triangle Run button in Android Studio, or press Shift+F10, and your program will run in the Android Virtual Device (AVD), which is an emulator of Android phones. Please note that Android Studio requires you to download a disk image of the relevant AVD as well, on first setup. The program will show a blank screen with Hello World! in the middle, as in Figure 6.9. When you run your program for the first time, the AVD will take a while, as it mimics the bootup process of the phone.

Congratulations! You have successfully developed your first Android app!

EXERCISE 6.1   Modify the XML code of the My Application Java program so that it can display Hello XXX!, where XXX is your name.

EXERCISE 6.2   Modify the XML code of the My Application Java program so that it can display the date and time.

You can also run the program directly on your smartphone. Doing so allows you to test and debug your Android program on your smartphone directly over an Android Debug Bridge (ADB) connection. In this case, first you will need to change your phone's settings and run the program using ADB. The following are the steps:

1. From your phone, open the Settings menu, select Developer Options, and then enable USB Debugging.

2. Plug your phone into the computer using a USB cable.

3. Click the Run button in Android Studio to build and run your program on your phone.

For more information on developing Android Apps, see the following web sites:

`https://developer.android.com/training/basics/firstapp/`

`https://www.youtube.com/playlist?list=PLS1QulWo1RIbb1cYyzZpLFCKvdYV_yJ-E`

`https://www.javatpoint.com/android-tutorial`

Figure 6.9: The output of the Android project My Application in the AVD emulator

6.4 The Button and TextView Apps

In this example, you will create an Android app that contains a Button component and a TextView component in the UI. You will also add some action to the Button component, so that when clicked, it checks the text in the TextView.

Create another blank Android project in Android Studio, exactly the same way as in section 6.2, and change the application name to My Application 2. From the `activity_main.xml` tab, select the Design subtab at the bottom and drag a

Button component into the screen so there are two components in the screen, a TextView component and a Button component, as shown in Figure 6.10 (top). Select the Text subtab, and notice that the corresponding XML code has also been automatically generated for the Button components. Set the TextView component ID name to `textview`, and set the Button component ID name to `button`, as shown in Figure 6.10 (middle).

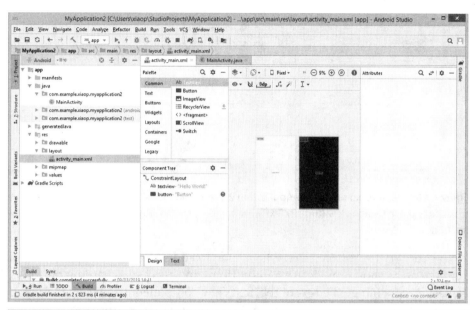

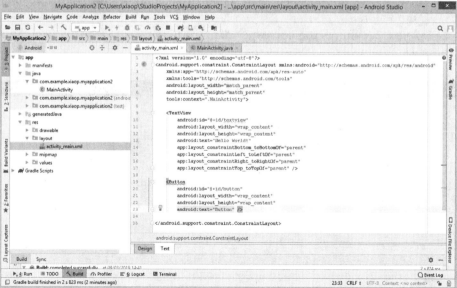

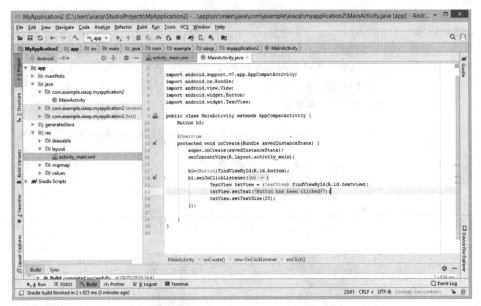

Figure 6.10: The Android project My Application 2 in Android Studio, with the `activity_main.xml` tab in Design view (top), in Text view (middle), and the `MainActivity.java` tab (bottom)

Now modify the `MainActivity.java` code to add some actions to the Button component, as shown in Figure 6.10 (bottom). In this case, when the button is clicked, it will change the text of the TextView component to `Button has been clicked!` and change the font size to 25. Figure 6.11 shows the output results in AVD emulator.

Example 6.2A shows the corresponding code of `MainActivity.java`, and Example 6.2B shows the `activity_main.xml` file.

EXAMPLE 6.2A   THE MAINACTIVITY.JAVA **CODE**

```
import android.support.v7.app.AppCompatActivity;
import android.os.Bundle;
import android.view.View;
import android.widget.Button;
import android.widget.TextView;

public class MainActivity extends AppCompatActivity {
    Button b1;

    @Override
    protected void onCreate(Bundle savedInstanceState) {
        super.onCreate(savedInstanceState);
        setContentView(R.layout.activity_main);
```

```
        b1=(Button)findViewById(R.id.button);
        b1.setOnClickListener(new View.OnClickListener() {

            @Override
            public void onClick(View v) {
                TextView txtView = (TextView) findViewById(R
.id.textview);
                txtView.setText("Button has been clicked!");
                txtView.setTextSize(25);
            }
        });

    }
}
```

Figure 6.11: The output of the Android project My Application 2 in AVD emulator

EXAMPLE 6.2B   THE ACTIVITY_MAIN.XML **CODE**

```
<?xml version="1.0" encoding="utf-8"?>
<android.support.constraint.ConstraintLayout xmlns:android="http://
schemas.android.com/apk/res/android"
    xmlns:app="http://schemas.android.com/apk/res-auto"
    xmlns:tools="http://schemas.android.com/tools"
    android:layout_width="match_parent"
    android:layout_height="match_parent"
```

```
tools:context=".MainActivity">

<TextView
    android:id="@+id/textview"
    android:layout_width="wrap_content"
    android:layout_height="wrap_content"
    android:text="Hello World!"
    app:layout_constraintBottom_toBottomOf="parent"
    app:layout_constraintLeft_toLeftOf="parent"
    app:layout_constraintRight_toRightOf="parent"
    app:layout_constraintTop_toTopOf="parent"/>

<Button
    android:id="@+id/button"
    android:layout_width="wrap_content"
    android:layout_height="wrap_content"
    android:text="Button"/>

</android.support.constraint.ConstraintLayout>
```

EXERCISE 6.3   Based on the My Application 2 Java program, add an EditText component, modifying the code so that each time you click the button, it copies the text contents of the EditText component to the TextView component.

6.5   The Sensor App

In this example, you will create an Android app that will display information from a sensor on the screen.

Create another blank Android project in Android Studio, exactly the same way as in section 6.2, and change the application name to My Application 3. From the `activity_main.xml` tab, select the Text subtab, and set the TextView component ID name to `textview`, as in Figure 6.12 (top right).

Now modify the `MainActivity.java` code to add some actions to get all the sensor information; see Figure 6.12 (bottom). In this case, the `SensorManager` class is used to handle the sensor service, the `List` class is used to store all the sensors, and the `TextView` component is used to display the information. A `for` loop is used to go through all the sensors and get their name, their vendor, and their version, and then display that information on the TextView component. Figure 6.13 shows the output results in the AVD emulator.

Example 6.3A shows the corresponding code of the `MainActivity.java` file, and Example 6.3B shows `activity_main.xml`.

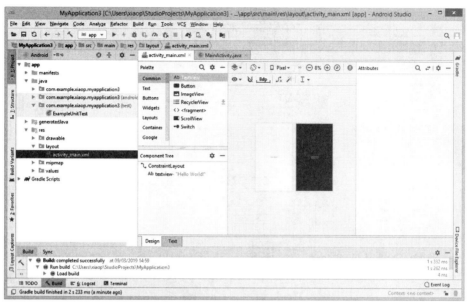

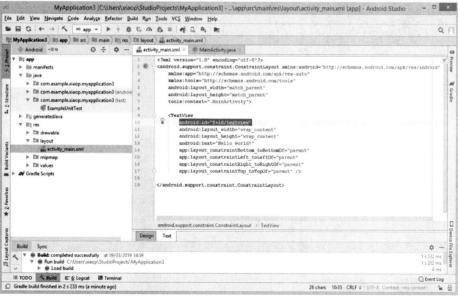

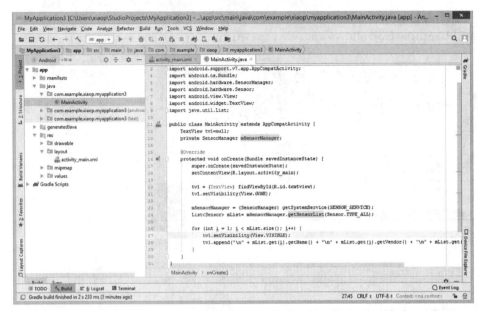

Figure 6.12: The Android project My Application 3 in Android Studio (top), with the activity_
main.xml tab (middle), and the MainActivity.java tab (bottom)

Figure 6.13: The output of the Android project My Application 3 in AVD emulator

EXAMPLE 6.3A   THE MAINACTIVITY.JAVA **CODE**

```java
package com.example.xiaop.myapplication3;

import android.support.v7.app.AppCompatActivity;
import android.os.Bundle;
import android.hardware.SensorManager;
import android.hardware.Sensor;
import android.view.View;
import android.widget.TextView;
import java.util.List;

public class MainActivity extends AppCompatActivity {
    TextView tv1=null;
    private SensorManager mSensorManager;

    @Override
    protected void onCreate(Bundle savedInstanceState) {
        super.onCreate(savedInstanceState);
        setContentView(R.layout.activity_main);

        tv1 = (TextView) findViewById(R.id.textview);
        tv1.setVisibility(View.GONE);

        mSensorManager = (SensorManager) getSystemService(SENSOR_SERVICE);
        List<Sensor> mList= mSensorManager.getSensorList(Sensor.TYPE_ALL);

        for (int i = 1; i < mList.size(); i++) {
            tv1.setVisibility(View.VISIBLE);
            tv1.append("\n" + mList.get(i).getName() + "\n" + mList
.get(i).getVendor() + "\n" + mList.get(i).getVersion());
        }
    }
}
```

EXAMPLE 6.3B   THE ACTIVITY_MAIN.XML **CODE**

```xml
<?xml version="1.0" encoding="utf-8"?>
<android.support.constraint.ConstraintLayout xmlns:android="http://
schemas.android.com/apk/res/android"
    xmlns:app="http://schemas.android.com/apk/res-auto"
    xmlns:tools="http://schemas.android.com/tools"
    android:layout_width="match_parent"
    android:layout_height="match_parent"
    tools:context=".MainActivity">

    <TextView
        android:id="@+id/textview"
```

```
        android:layout_width="wrap_content"
        android:layout_height="wrap_content"
        android:text="Hello World!"
        app:layout_constraintBottom_toBottomOf="parent"
        app:layout_constraintLeft_toLeftOf="parent"
        app:layout_constraintRight_toRightOf="parent"
        app:layout_constraintTop_toTopOf="parent"/>
```

```
</android.support.constraint.ConstraintLayout>
```

EXERCISE 6.4   Based on the My Application 3 Java program, add two Button components, modifying the code so that when you click the first button, it displays all the sensor information in the TextView component, and when you click the second button, it clears all the information in the TextView component.

EXERCISE 6.5   Based on the My Application 3 Java program, add two Button components, modifying the code so that when you click the first button, it retrieves the value of the temperature sensor and displays the temperature in the TextView component, and when you click the second button, it clears all the information in the TextView component.

6.6   Deploying Android Apps

Once you have finished developing your Android app and are ready to distribute it to others or publish it in the Google Play Store, you need to build a signed Android Package Kit (APK) file using Android Studio. APK is the package file format used by the Android operating system for distributing and installing mobile apps. It is similar to Windows EXE files. An APK file typically contains a compiled program's code, resources, certificates, and the manifest file. To sign your app, you need to generate an upload key and key store. In Java, a *key store* is used to store authorization certificates or public key certificates and is protected by a key store password. Key stores are often used by Java-based applications for encryption and authentication. More details about security, encryption, and authentication are available in Chapter 7.

As an example, you will build an APK file for the MyApplication3 project. To begin, from the Android Studio menu choose Build ➪ Generate Signed Bundle/ APK. The Generate Signed Bundle or APK window will appear, in which you can choose to generate a signed bundle or APK. Select APK and then click Next, as shown in Figure 6.14 (top). In the window that follows, for the Key Store Path field choose Create New, as shown in Figure 6.14 (middle).

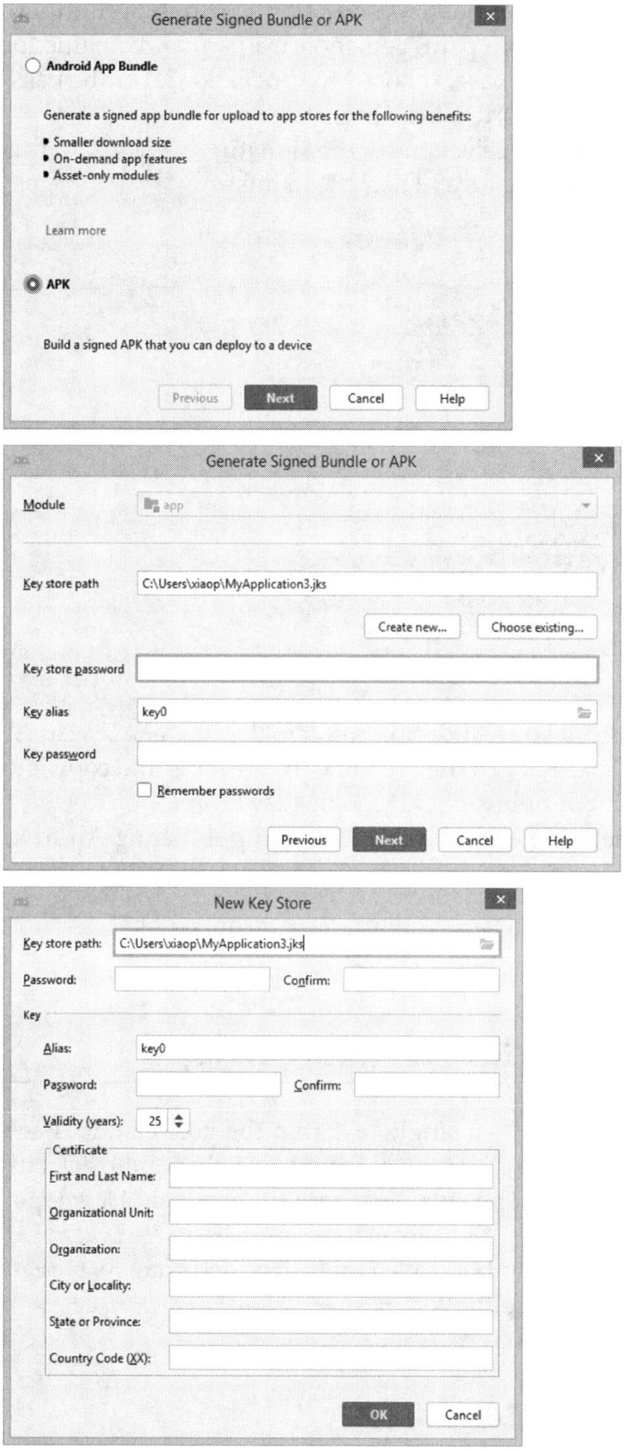

Figure 6.14: The Generate Signed Bundle or APK window to choose to generate signed bundle or APK (top), to select key store path and password (middle), and the New Key Store window (bottom)

A New Key Store window will appear, as shown in Figure 6.14 (bottom). Complete the fields. For the key store path, you choose a path and a name for your Java KeyStore (JKS) file. In this case, I chose MyApplication3. For the password, you choose your own password. Click OK.

In the next window (Figure 6.15), select one of the signature versions. In this example, I chose V2 (Full APK Signature). Then click Finish.

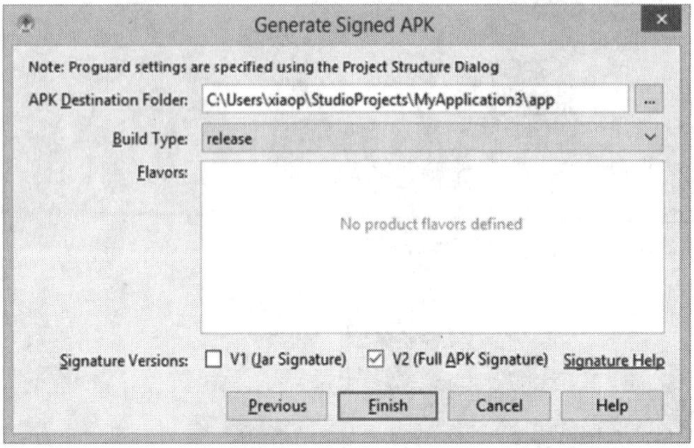

Figure 6.15: The Generate Signed APK window

You can find your APK file in your Android project folder, \MyApplication3\ app\release\app-release.apk. You can then rename the APK file and copy it to your smartphone to install it or publish it on Google Play Store.

For more details on generating a signed APK file and publishing Android apps, see the following resources:

```
http://www.androiddocs.com/tools/publishing/app-signing.html
https://developer.android.com/studio/publish/
```

6.7   The Activity Life Cycle of an Android App

In the Android system, an *activity* is a single task that the user can do. Each Android app can have one or more activities. Figure 6.16 shows the activity life-cycle diagram of an Android app, adapted from the Android Developer web site (https://developer.android.com/guide/components/activities/ activity-lifecycle). This activity life cycle can be divided into six stages, which can be invoked by different callbacks: onCreate(), onStart(), onResume(), onPause(), onStop(), onRestart(), and onDestroy().

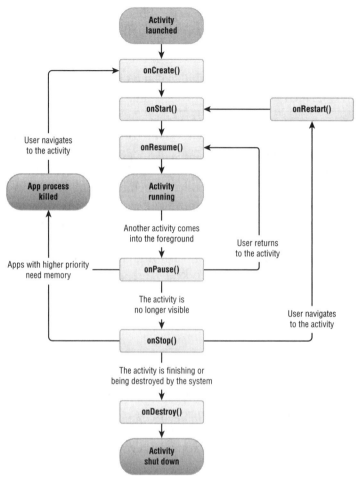

Figure 6.16: The activity life-cycle diagram of Android apps, from the Android Developer web site

The onCreate() callback is called when the activity is first created, similar to the main() method in standard Java programs. The opposite is the onDestroy() callback, which is called just before the activity is destroyed by the system. The onStart() callback is called when the activity is visible to users. The onResume() callback is called when the activity is interacting with users. This is the state in which the user is using the app. The app stays in this state until the user is doing something else to take focus away from the app. The onPause() call-back is called when the current activity is being paused, for example during multiscreen operations or while using transparent apps on top. After a pause, onResume() callback is called again. The onStop() callback is called when the activity is no longer visible. The onRestart() callback is called when the activity restarts after being stopped.

6.8　MIT App Inventor

In addition to Android Studio or similar IDEs, there are other ways to develop Android applications, such as MIT App Inventor.

MIT App Inventor is an open source, web-based, online Android development environment, developed by Massachusetts Institute of Technology (MIT) and Google. It is aimed at teaching young children, or newcomers, to develop Android apps using Open Blocks visual programming, without the need of writing Java code. There are two versions; the current version is App Inventor 2. My first encounter with MIT App Inventor was through one of Google's code camps. Within just a few hours, starting from knowing absolutely nothing, I had managed to develop several apps, including a speech recognition app and Chinese–English translation app. I was impressed with its simplicity and ease of use. Here are a few examples:

Speech Recognition App

In this example, you will build an app that includes a screen with a label and a button. When you click the button, a speech recognition engine will start. You can then speak an action, such as "open Google Map," "open BBC weather," "open YouTube," or "open Facebook," and the app will recognize it and run the corresponding apps on your phone.

To use the App Inventor 2, go to http://ai2.appinventor.mit.edu/, and log in using your Google account. Create a new project called PerryAsk; Figure 6.17 shows what it looks like when the project is created. In the top-right corner, there are two buttons, Designer and Blocks. The Designer button displays the front end of your app, or how your app looks. It is the default view. The Blocks button displays the backend of your app, the block editor. Here you write your program using the function blocks. App Inventor development is based on this front-end and backend concept, the same as LabVIEW, another popular visual programming tool.

In the Designer view, you have one or more screens (the default is one screen). To see how screens work, from the left palette drag a label and a button into the screen, and then drag five more invisible components: TextToSpeech, SpeechRecognizer, OrientationSensor, LocationSensor, and ActivityStarter. These components will not appear on the screen; instead, they will appear in the space below the screen, as shown in Figure 6.17 (top). Next, click the Blocks button, and edit the block code as shown in Figure 6.17 (bottom).

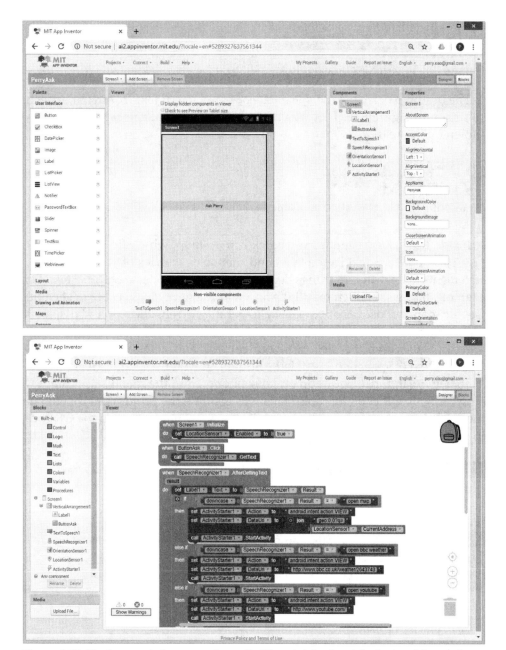

Figure 6.17: The front end of a new project called PerryAsk (top) and the backend (bottom), from the MIT App Inventor 2 web site

The full source code of the project, zipped in a file named `PerryAsk.aia`, is available on the web site accompanying this book.

The screen initialization block enables the `LocationSensor`, as shown in Figure 6.18. This block can also be used to initialize other variables used in the program.

Figure 6.18: The screen initialization block

The button block calls the SpeechRecognizer to get text from your speech, as shown in Figure 6.19. This will trigger the SpeechRecognizer block to run, shown in Figure 6.20.

Figure 6.19: The ButtonAsk Click **block**

Inside the SpeechRecognizer block is a do loop, which first displays the SpeechRecognizer text in the label and then uses a series of if ... else if statements to do different things depending on the SpeechRecognizer text. For example, if you say "open map," the app will use ActivityStarter to start the Google map and use LocationSensor to get the current address and display it on the map.

It can also search the Web, run your camera, and when you say "hello," it will use **TextToSpeech** to say "Hello, human" to you using an artificial voice.

To deploy and run your app on your phone, from the menu select Build ⇨ App (provide QR code for .apk). This will compile the program and generate the 2D QR code, as shown in Figure 6.21. Use your phone to scan the QR code to download and install the app.

EXERCISE 6.6   Modify the MIT App Inventor program so that if you say "text message," it will send a "hello" text message to one of your contacts.

EXERCISE 6.7   Modify the App Inventor program so that it can conduct some simple conversations, such as:

You: Hello!

App: Hello, Human!

You: What is your name?

App: My name is Android.

You: Where do you live?

App: Inside this silly phone case.

You: Bye!

App: Bye!

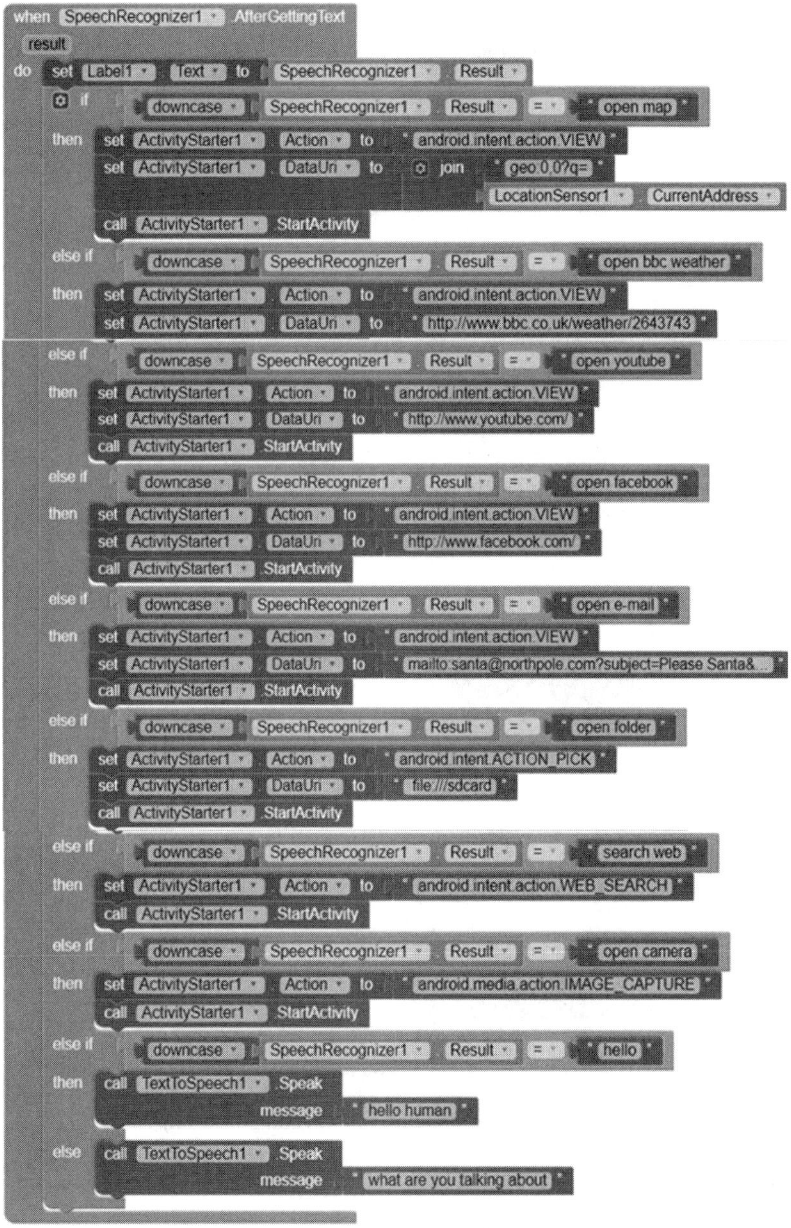

Figure 6.20: The `SpeechRecognizer` **block**

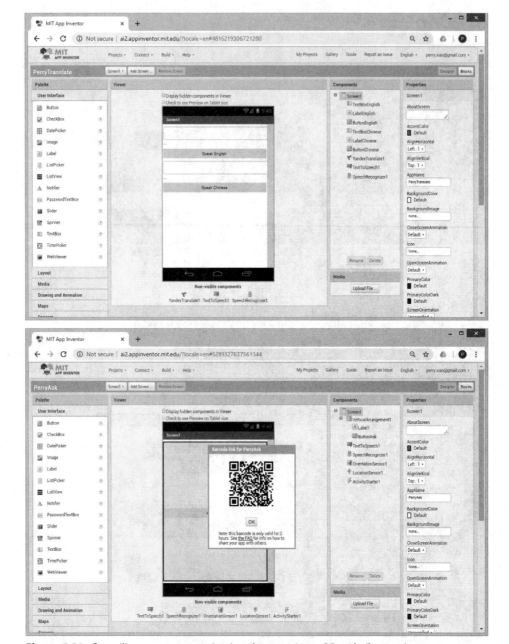

Figure 6.21: Compiling your program (top) and generating a QR code (bottom)

Translation App

App Inventor 2 also comes with an impressive language translation engine called YandexTranslate. In this example, you will build an app that does speech recognition and language translation at the same time. You press one button and then say something in English, and the app will recognize your speech in English, translate it to Chinese, and speak Chinese back to you. You press another button and say something in Chinese, and the app can recognize your speech in Chinese, translate it to English and speak English back to you. Cool!

Again, from the App Inventor 2 web site, create a new project called Perry-Translate, as shown in Figure 6.22. From the Designer view, drag the following visible components into the screen: TextBox for English, a Label for English, a Button for English, a TextBox for Chinese, a Label for Chinese, and a Button for Chinese. Also drag three invisible components into the screen: TextToSpeech, SpeechRecognizer, and YandexTranslate. Again, the full source code of the project, zipped in a file called `PerryTranslate.aia`, is available on the web site accompanying this book.

Now click the Blocks button to display the block editor. The screen initialization block enables the `Language` variable value to zero. In this case, zero presents English, and one presents Chinese. The `ButtonEnglish` block resets the `Language` variable value to zero. If the `TextBoxEnglish` is empty, it will start `SpeechRecognizer` to get text from your speech in English. This will trigger the `SpeechRecognizer` block to run. If the `TextBoxEnglish` is not empty, it will copy the text into `LabelEnglish`, as shown in Figure 6.23.

The `ButtonChinese` block resets the `Language` variable value to one. If the `TextBoxChinese` is empty, it will start `SpeechRecognizer` to get text from your speech in Chinese. This will trigger the `SpeechRecognizer` block to run. If the `TextBoxChinese` is not empty, it will copy the text into `LabelChinese`, as shown in Figure 6.24.

The `SpeechRecognizer` block contains a do loop, shown in Figure 6.25. Inside the do loop, if the `Language` variable is zero, it will set `LabelEnglish` to the text of `SpeechRecognizer` and then call the YandexTranslate engine to translate the `LabelEnglish` text to Chinese. After the YandexTranslate engine has produced the translated text, it will trigger the YandexTranslate `GotTranslation` block, which will set the `LabelChinese` text to the translated text, call the `TextSpeech` to speak the Chinese text, and then set the `TextBoxChinese` text to the `LabelChinese` text.

Inside the do loop, if the `Language` variable has a value of 1, it will do the same process but from Chinese to English. Simple!

Again, to run your app on your phone, select Build ➪ App (provide QR code for .apk) from the menu to compile the program and generate a QR code, as shown in Figure 6.26. Then use your phone to scan the QR code to download and install the app.

EXERCISE 6.8 Modify the MIT App Inventor program so that it can translate English into another language, such as Spanish, French, or German.

Figure 6.22: The PerryTranslate project's front end (top) and the backend (bottom), from MIT App Inventor 2 web site

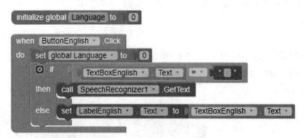

Figure 6.23: The screen initialization block and the `ButtonEnglish Click` block

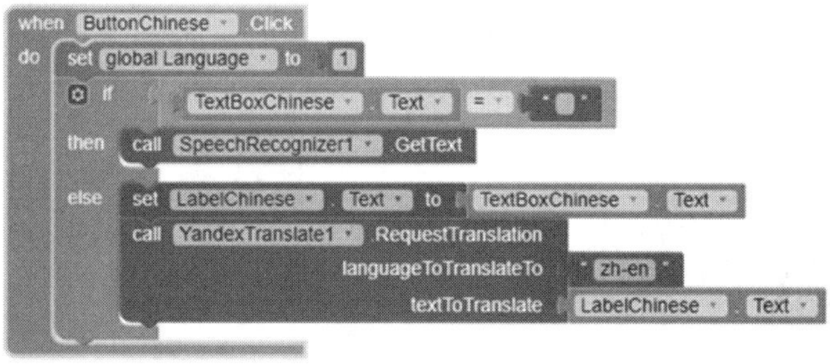

Figure 6.24: The ButtonChinese Click block

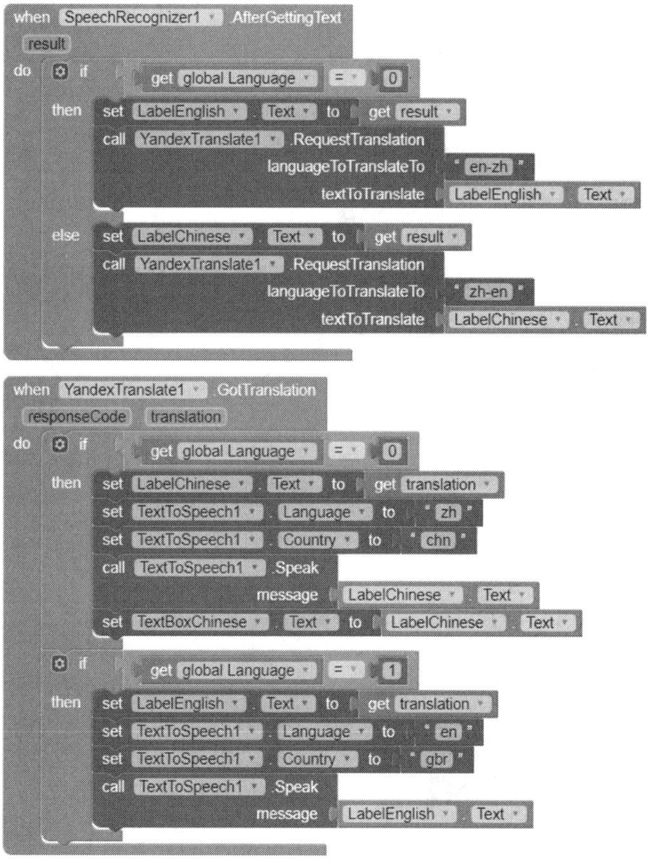

Figure 6.25: The SpeechRecognizer AfterGettingText block (top) and the YandexTranslate GotTranslation block (bottom)

EXERCISE 6.9   Modify the MIT App Inventor program, add a multiple-choice Combobox component to contain a few languages. When you click the button, it will listen to you speaking in English, convert your speaking to text, and then translate it to another language, specified by the Combobox component.

Figure 6.26: To compile your program (top) and to generate a QR code (bottom)

EXERCISE 6.10   Modify the MIT App Inventor program by adding two multiple-choice Combobox components that each contain a few languages. The first Combobox component should specify the language you are speaking, and the second should specify the language you are translating to. When you click the button, it will listen to you speaking in one language, convert your speech to text, and then translate it to another language, all specified by the two Combobox components.

For more information about App Inventor and tutorials, see the following resources:

```
http://appinventor.mit.edu/explore/ai2/tutorials.html
http://www.appinventor.org/book2
```

6.9 5G

When we talk about mobile applications, we have to talk about 5G, as it is no doubt one of the most talked about and heavily researched technologies. With all the biggest smartphone companies starting to launch their own 5G-ready smartphones, it will be an interesting way to conclude this chapter by looking at what exactly 5G is and what it means to us.

5G refers to the fifth generation of mobile technology. It is continued from 1G, 2G, 3G, and 4G technologies. The main difference is frequency spectrum, as all the wireless mobile technologies rely on electromagnetic waves to send and receive signals. Unlike previous generations, 5G uses a much higher frequency range, typically ranging from 3 to 86 GHz. Mobile networks work based on the concept of cells, where the mobile phones in each cell are connected to a base station (BS). Each base station is connected to a mobile switch center (MSC), which is then connected to a wired network. Mobile networks are therefore also called *cellular networks*. Figure 6.27 shows the cellular network architecture and how the mobile users communicate with each other. 1G has the largest cell size, 2G/3G/4G has a much small cell size, and 5G will have an even smaller cell size. Figure 6.28 shows the frequency range and cell size of different generations of mobile technology.

The main benefits of 5G are fast speed, low latency, and better connectivity. This makes 5G a key technology for the future driverless cars, virtual reality, augmented reality, Internet gaming, and Internet of Things (IoT) applications.

Fast Speed   5G networks are going to be significantly faster than previous networks. Table 6.1 shows a comparison of download times for a two-hour high-definition (HD) movie. While on a 3G network this takes 24 hours and on a 4G network it takes 7 minutes, on a 5G network it may take as little as a few seconds. Even if most users experience speeds that are a fraction of the potential maximum, it will still be impressive.

Table 6.1: Comparison of Download Speed of Different Networks for a Two-Hour HD Movie

NETWORK	MAXIMUM DOWNLOAD SPEED	MINIMUM TIME
3G network	384 Kbps	24 hours
4G network	100 Mbps	7 minutes
5G network	1-10 Gbps or faster	A few seconds

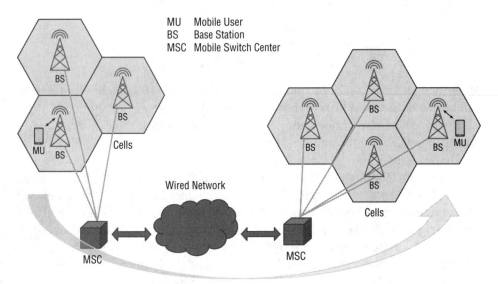

Figure 6.27: The cellular network architecture and how mobile users communicate with each other

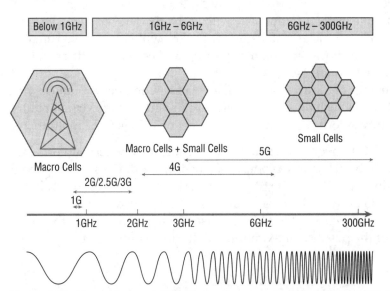

Figure 6.28: The electromagnetic frequency spectrum and the cell size of 1G, 2G, 3G, 4G, and 5G technologies

Low Latency *Latency time* is the time from when you've sent data to the Internet until it's received. The 5G network will have very low latency time compared to previous generations of networks, as shown in Table 6.2. (Note that a latency time of 1 ms is a goal; current latencies are said to be in the low to mid single digits.)

Table 6.2: Typical Latency Time of Different Network Generations

NETWORK GENERATION	MILLISECONDS (MS)
3G	100 ms
4G	50 ms
5G	1 ms

Better Connectivity 5G will not only connect more people and more devices but also provide more reliable connections, with very low downtime. 5G is claimed to have the always-on connectivity. Table 6.3 shows a comparison of 1G, 2G, 2.5G, 3G, 4G, and 5G technologies.

Table 6.3: Comparison of 1G, 2G/2.5G/2.75G, 3G, 4G, and 5G

	1G	2G / 2.5G / 2.75G	3G	4G	5G
Period	1970–1990	1990–2000	2000–2010	2010– 2020	2020–2030
Bandwidth	30 KHz	200 KHz	20 MHz	20 MHz	100 MHz
Frequency	800 MHz (Analog)	800 MHz to 1.8 GHz (digital)	1.6–2.1 GHz	2–8 GHz	3–300 GHz
Data Rate	2 Kbps	9.6 Kbps (2G) 64–114 Kbps (2.5G) 384 Kbps (2.75G)	384 Kbps (moving), 2 Mbps (stationary)	100 Mbps	>1 Gbps
Standard	MTS, AMTS, IMTS	2G: GSM 2.5G: GPRS 2.75G: EDGE	IMT-2000 3.5G-HSDPA 3.75G-HSUPA	Single unified standard	Single unified standard
Services	Analog voice, No data	Digital voice, SMS, MMS Web browsing (2.5G)	Audio, video streaming, web browsing, IPTV	Enhanced audio, video streaming, web browsing, HD TV	Dynamic information access, wearable devices with AI capability

(continued)

Table 6-3 (*continued*)

	1G	2G / 2.5G / 2.75G	3G	4G	5G
Multiplexing	FDMA	TDMA, CDMA	CDMA	CDMA	CDMA
Core Network	PSTN	PSTN	Packet network	Internet	Internet
Switching	Circuit	Circuit, Packet	Packet	All Packet	All Packet
Characteristic	First wireless communication	Digital	Digital broadband	Digital broadband, high speed, all IP	Digital broadband, ultra-high speed
Technology	Analog cellular	Digital cellular	CDMA, UMTS, EDGE	LTE, WiFi, WiMAX	WWWW Unified IP

1G refers to the first generation of mobile technology. It was first introduced in the late 1970s. It is an analog technology, for voice communication only. It was operating on the 800 MHz band, with 30 KHz bandwidth, and 2 kilobits per second (kbps) data rate. 1G typically has a cell size greater than 20 km, with each cell allowing up to 395 channels. Because 1G mobile phones need to transmit long distances, they tend to be bulky. 1G also suffers poor voice quality and no security.

2G refers to the second generation of mobile technology, also known as the global system for mobile communication (GSM). It was introduced in the 1990s and is a digital communication technology. It can be used for both voice and text, known as Short Message Service (SMS). It works initially on the 900 MHz band and later the 1800 MHz band. It has a bandwidth of 200 KHz and a data rate of 64 kbps. 2.5G is a transition from 2G to 3G, based on General Packet Radio Service (GPRS) technology. It has a slightly higher data rate of 114 kbps, and supports email, web browsing, and Multimedia Messaging Service (MMS), such as video and photo messages. 2.75G is similar to 2.5G. Based on Enhanced Data rates for GSM Evolution (EDGE) technology, it can have a data rate up to 384 kbps. 2G uses much smaller cells than 1G, which brings several benefits. First, it improves the frequency spectrum reusability, which means it can support more mobile users. Second, because the mobile phone does not need a lot of power to transmit signals to long distances, mobile phone size is also getting smaller. 2G mobile phones also start to have mobile phone cameras. 2G network typically has a cell size of several kilometers.

3G refers to the third generation of mobile technology and was introduced in the early 2000s. It mainly uses the 2.1 GHz frequency band with a bandwidth of 20MHz, but different countries have different frequency bands and slightly different bandwidths. It can have a data rate up to 3Mbps and supports video calls, chats, navigational maps, mobile gaming, music, movies, and mobile TV. Since the introduction of the iPhone in 2007, 3G mobile phones with touchscreen have been also called *smartphones*. 3G also introduced significantly greater security features such as network access, domain security, and application security.

4G refers to the fourth generation of mobile technology and was introduced in 2010. Again, different countries operate at different frequency bands, but mainly at 800 MHz, 1800 MHz, 2.1 GHz, and 2.6 GHz with a bandwidth of 20 MHz. It is based on Long Term Evolution (LTE) and can have a data rate up to 100 Mbps.

5G is the latest generation of mobile technology. It uses a much higher-frequency band than the previous generations and can support a data rate up to 1 Gbps. The following are the key technologies used in 5G.

6.9.1   Millimeter Waves

5G uses two frequency ranges, frequency range 1 (< 6 GHz) and frequency range 2 (24–86 GHz). The bandwidth of frequency range 1 is 100 MHz, and the bandwidth of frequency range 2 is 400 MHz. In physics, the electromagnetic waves with a frequency between 30 and 300 GHz are called *millimeter waves* because they have a wavelength ranging from 1 to 10 mm. This is different from electromagnetic waves below 6 GHz that were used for previous generations of mobile technologies in the past, which have wavelengths measured in tens of centimeters. Millimeter waves do not travel well; they can be easily blocked by buildings or obstacles, or absorbed by foliage and rain. That's why 5G networks use smaller cells. Also, because of the frequency differences, 5G cells cannot use existing 4G/3G/2G base stations' antennas for transmitting and receiving signals. 5G needs its own antennas and therefore its own infrastructure. All these factors lead to 5G's small-cell technology.

6.9.2   Small Cells

5G's small cells typically have a size of a few hundred meters, compared with several kilometers of 4G/3G/2G cells. 5G antennas on small cells are also smaller than traditional antennas if they are transmitting tiny millimeter waves. So, 5G antennas are typically miniaturized and use much less power to operate, which makes it easier to be installed on lamp posts and the tops of buildings. This new cell structure should provide more targeted and efficient use of spectrum. However, this also means it is hard to set up in rural areas.

6.9.3   Massive MIMO

The term *Multiple-Input, Multiple-Output* (MIMO) describes wireless systems that use two or more transmitters and receivers to send and receive more data at once. MIMO is already used in today's 4G network, in which base stations typically have a dozen ports for antennas, eight for transmitters, and four for receivers. 5G base stations can support about 100 ports, a capability called *massive MIMO*. Massive MIMO could significantly increase the capacity of mobile networks by allowing send and receive signals from many more users at once.

6.9.4 Beamforming

The biggest issue for massive MIMO is how to reduce interference while transmitting more information from many more antennas at once. Beamforming is designed for base stations to identify the most efficient data-delivery route to a particular user and to reduce interference for nearby users in the process. Beamforming allows base stations to send individual data packets in many different directions in a precisely coordinated pattern, which allows many users and antennas on a massive MIMO array to exchange much more information at once. Beamforming can also focus a signal in a concentrated beam that points only in the direction of a user to avoid obstacles and reduce interference for everyone else.

6.9.5 Full Duplex

In the current mobile network, a transceiver (transmitter and receiver) of a base station and a mobile phone must take turns transmitting and receiving information over the same frequency or use different frequencies for transmitting and receiving signals at the same time. With 5G, a transceiver will be able to transmit and receive data at the same time, on the same frequency. This is known as *full duplex* technology and could double the capacity of wireless networks. The main challenge of full duplex is to design a circuit that can route incoming and outgoing signals to avoid collision while an antenna is transmitting and receiving data at the same time. Full duplex also creates more signal interference.

6.9.6 Future 6G and 7G

Believe it or not, even though 5G is still yet to arrive, there is already research on the future 6G and 7G technologies. 6G is not going to replace 5G; instead, it will integrate 5G with the existing satellite network for global coverage. 6G will provide ultra-fast Internet access and will be used in smart homes and smart cities.

7G will go even further, integrating 6G and 5G, providing space roaming, and making the world completely wireless.

For more information about 5G, please visit the following resources:

```
https://spectrum.ieee.org/video/telecom/wireless/everything-you-need-
to-know-about-5g
```
```
https://5g.co.uk/guides/how-fast-is-5g/
```

```
https://5g.co.uk/guides/5g-frequencies-in-theuk-what-you-need-toknow/
https://www.qorvo.com/design-hub/blog/small-cell-networks-and-the-
evolution-of-5g
http://www.emfexplained.info/?ID=25916
https://www.digitaltrends.com/mobile/what-is-5g/
```

6.10   Summary

This chapter introduced Java programming for mobile applications. It first introduced the mobile software development tool Android Studio, then provided three mobile example programs, and finally introduced the deployment of mobile application programs. It also introduced MIT App Inventor, another popular way of developing Android applications. Finally, it introduced the next-generation mobile network technology, 5G, and briefly outlined how 5G works and what it can be used for.

6.11   Chapter Review Questions

Q6.1.   What is Android?

Q6.2.   Compare the market share of Android phones, Apple's iPhones, and other phones.

Q6.3.   What are Android SDK and Android AVD?

Q6.4.   Write down the steps for downloading and installing Android Studio.

Q6.5.   Write down the steps for creating an Android project using Android Studio.

Q6.6.   What is an Android Package Kit (APK) file?

Q6.7.   What is a Java KeyStore (JKS) file?

Q6.8.   Write down the steps for deploying an Android app.

Q6.9.   What is the activity life cycle of an Android app?

Q6.10.   What is MIT App Inventor? What is the current version?

Q6.11.   What is the difference between Designer view and Block view in MIT App Inventor?

Q6.12.   What is 5G? What are main benefits of 5G?

Q6.13.   What are the key technologies used in 5G?

Q6.14.   What are 6G and 7G?

Part

III

In This Part:

Java Programming for IoT Applications

Simplicity is prerequisite for reliability.

—Edsger Dijkstra

7.1   What Is the Internet of Things?

Internet of Things (IoT) is no doubt one of the hottest buzzwords at the moment. If you read technical magazines, it is everywhere. Related to IoT is the concept of Industry 4.0. So, what exactly is IoT, and what is Industry 4.0?

In the broadest sense, Internet of Things (IoT) refers to the global network of interconnected devices or "things." This is going to be the future of the Internet, which is currently a global network of interconnected computers, including smartphones and tablets. The *things* in IoT refer to the everyday physical devices that are not primarily computers but have embedded computing hardware (microcontrollers), such as TVs, fridges, cookers, kettles, lights, cars, doors, chairs, and so on. Figure 7.1 shows an illustrative IoT diagram.

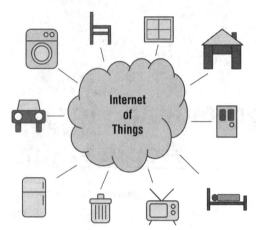

Figure 7.1: The Internet of Things

To connect these everyday devices to the Internet, you need several technologies.

Addressing   Each device on the IoT needs to have a unique address so that it can be uniquely identified. So, a lot of addresses are needed. Internet Protocol version 6 (IPv6) could be a candidate; it allows up to 2^{128} different addresses, which is enough to assign a different address to every single grain of sand on the planet.

Communication Protocols   Each device on the IoT needs to communicate with other devices. They do this communication using different protocols than the computers on the Internet.

Sensors and Actuators   Each device on the IoT needs to have sensors, which can provide you with information, such as whether the TV is on or off, the fridge is full or empty, the chair is free or occupied, the window is open or shut, and so on. Each device on the IoT might also need to have actuators, such as motors or piezoelectric devices. With actuators, you would be able to open the door, shut the window, and so on.

Microcontroller   Each device on the IoT needs to have a microcontroller to read data from the sensors, communicate with other devices, and perform certain tasks. Embedding this device is possible only when the microcontroller is small enough, is cheap enough, and has low enough power consumption.

Cloud Computing   With billions and billions of devices connected to the IoT, IoT will generate an enormous amount of data, which cannot be stored and analyzed by conventional methods. This is exactly why cloud computing is needed to store the data, to analyze the data, and to display the data.

An IoT system can generally be divided into four building blocks according to Farnell Ltd, a global distributor for electronic products. (`https://uk.farnell.com/internet-of-things`), as shown in Figure 7.2.

- **Collect:** Edge devices (sensors and actuators)
- **Connectivity block:** Wireless
- **Control:** Gateways
- **Cloud:** Data center

Figure 7.2: The building blocks of an IoT system

The Collect block is where you will find the edge devices, which are integrated with sensors and actuators. The sensors are for taking measurements; they include temperature sensors, humidity sensors, smoke sensors, flame sensors, poisonous gas sensors, distance sensors, water level sensors, motion sensors, light sensors, magnetic sensors, and more. The actuators are for doing something, such as opening and closing a valve or a door, moving a component, and so on. The Collect block is the front end of an IoT system.

The Connectivity block is where communication occurs between devices and devices and between devices and users. The communications can be done either wirelessly or through a wired connection. For wireless communication there are a range of technologies, such as Near Field Communication (NFC), Radio Frequency Identification (RFID), Bluetooth, Zigbee, Z-Wave (WPAN), WiFi, LoRa (LPWAN), Sigfox (LPWAN), and the most talked-about cellular technology, 5G. Later in the chapter, you'll see an example using WiFi.

The Control block is where you will find gateway devices that bridge the gap between the Edge block and the Cloud block. The gateway devices receive the data from IoT device sensors or other equipment in a system and send that data to the cloud. The gateway devices are a crucial part of any IoT system, as they also perform protocol translation, data processing, data storage, data filtering, and data security.

The Cloud block is where the data is stored, analyzed, and displayed. The IoT will generate an enormous amount of data, which cannot be stored and analyzed by conventional personal computers, or even local servers, which have limited storage space and computational power. The best way to store and analyze these enormous amounts of data is in the cloud, which is basically a computing service over the Internet. With the cloud, or *cloud computing*, you can have services such as servers, storage, databases, networking, software, analytics, intelligence, and more. Many technical giants, such as IBM, Google, Microsoft, and Amazon, provide their own cloud computing services. For example, with IBM's Watson Internet of Things (IoT) cloud, you can easily connect your IoT devices, store the data, analyze the data, and display the results on the Web, on computers, and on your mobile devices. Watson provides many sophisticated analysis software, including artificial intelligence, to get the most out of your data. The Cloud block is the brain of an IoT system.

With IoT, business and industry can improve their efficiency and productivity, improve customer engagement, enhance data collection and data analysis, and reduce waste. But with IoT, there will also be some issues, such as security, privacy, complexity, and compliance. Security is always the top priority. More details on security are available later in this chapter and in Chapter 9.

To date, IoT development is already well underway. The number of devices connected to the IoT has increased by 30 percent every year, and there were already about 8.4 billion IoT devices in 2017. By 2020, there will be estimated 30 billion IoT devices and a global market value of $7 trillion. The IoT is largely seen as the Next Big Thing, with many companies spending billions on IoT research and development.

The industrial version of IoT is called Industry 4.0, that is, the fourth industrial revolution. The first industrial revolution happened in the eighteenth century, when the steam engine revolutionized industrial production. The second industrial revolution happened in the nineteenth century, when electric power and the assembly line made mass production possible. The third industrial revolution, also called the *digital revolution*, happened at the twentieth century, when electronics and computers made automated production possible. The first three industrial revolutions all have significantly improved productivity.

The next industrial revolution, Industry 4.0, is on the horizon. In this revolution, suppliers, logistics, factories, and customers will be tightly integrated together. This will even more significantly improve productivity. Robotics and artificial intelligence will be widely used. All the data will be stored in the cloud, and artificial intelligence will be used to analyze the data, to predict trends, and to identify faults. Virtual production will also allow manufacturers to design, create, and test products in a virtual environment. Customers will be able to view and customize products online, and there will be increasing focus on customized and smart products. This trend is also referred to as *intelligent manufacturing*, with its products described as *smart-made*. Industry 4.0 will require a smaller and highly skilled workforce. Figure 7.3 illustrates the concept.

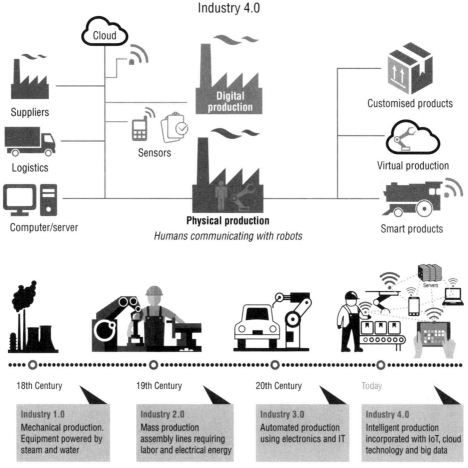

Figure 7.3: The fourth industrial revolution, or Industry 4.0 (top) and the previous industrial revolutions (bottom)

(Source: Adapted from `https://thingtrax.com/2017/10/05/` `industry-4-0-increases-machine-efficiency/`)

7.2   IoT Communication Protocols

The devices on the IoT communicate differently than computers communicating on the Internet, which tend to use a lot of bandwidth to transmit a large amount of data, for which timing is not always important. The most commonly used Internet protocol is the Hypertext Transfer Protocol (HTTP), which is the magic behind the World Wide Web (WWW). Devices on the IoT tend to have limited power supply, limited computing power, and limited bandwidth. They typically need to transmit a small amount data intermittently, but timing is often important. There are several communication protocols specifically designed for such communications. The following are some of the most important IoT protocols.

7.2.1   MQTT

Message Queuing Telemetry Transport (MQTT), developed by IBM in 1999, is a publish-subscribe messaging protocol. At the heart of MQTT is the MQTT broker, which accepts and publishes the messages. Figure 7.4 shows how MQTT works. In this example, a topic called *temperature* is first created on the MQTT broker. Then the temperature sensor, the laptop, and the mobile device all subscribe to the topic. The temperature sensor will make a measurement from time to time and publish the data to the topic on the MQTT broker. The MQTT broker will then relay the data to the laptop, which is the mobile device. Compared with HTTP protocols, MQTT requires much less computing power, less bandwidth, and less power consumption. You will explore an MQTT example later in the chapter.

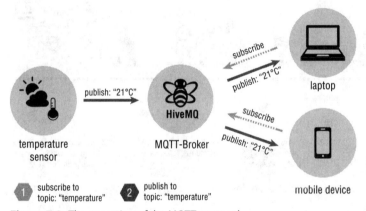

Figure 7.4: The operation of the MQTT protocol

(Source: Adapted from `https://www.hivemq.com/blog/how-to-get-started-with-mqtt`)

MQTT offers three levels of quality of service (QoS).

0: At most once. The message is sent only once.

1: At least once. The message is sent multiple times until acknowledgment is received.

2: Exactly once. Only one copy of the message is sent (guaranteed by a two-level handshake).

For more information about MQTT, see the following resources:

`http://mqtt.org/`

`https://www.hivemq.com/blog/how-to-get-started-with-mqtt`

7.2.2   CoAP

Constrained Application Protocol (CoAP) is a specialized web transfer protocol for use with constrained IoT devices (with limited computing power and limited power consumption) and constrained IoT networks (with limited bandwidth). The protocol is designed for machine-to-machine (M2M) applications such as smart energy and building automation. CoAP is based on request and response messages, similar to HTTP, but instead of running on Transmission Control Protocol (TCP), it uses User Datagram Protocol (UDP). CoAP hence has much smaller headers and is much faster.

For more information about CoAP, see the following resource:

```
http://coap.technology/
```

7.2.3   XMPP

Extensible Messaging and Presence Protocol (XMPP) is an open standard communication protocol based on the Extensible Markup Language (XML). XMPP enables real-time communication between IoT devices using structured, extensible messages. It provides a wide range of applications including instant messaging, presence, and collaboration.

For more information about XMPP, see the following resource:

```
https://xmpp.org/about/
```

7.2.4   SOAP

Simple Object Access Protocol (SOAP) is another XML-based messaging protocol, designed by Microsoft, for exchanging information among computers via the Internet. With XML messages, SOAP is highly extensible and can be used for web services.

For more information about SOAP, see the following resource:

```
https://www.w3schools.com/xml/xml_soap.asp
```

7.2.5   REST

Representational State Transfer (REST) is a lightweight architectural style for web services. REST is based on Uniform Resource Identifier (URIs) and Hypertext Transfer Protocol (HTTP), and it uses JavaScript Object Notation (JSON) for a data format. REST is fully browser compatible. We will explore a REST example later in the chapter.

For more information about REST, see the following resource:

```
http://rest.elkstein.org/
```

7.3   IoT Platforms

IoT platforms are software run on the Internet (the cloud) that connects sensors and user devices using IoT protocols such as MQTT, CoAP, XMPP, and so on. IoT platforms are also used for storing data, analyzing data, and displaying data. Artificial intelligence is often implemented in the IoT platforms to provide complex analysis.

The following is a list of popular IoT platforms.

Eclipse IoT: https://iot.eclipse.org/

Oracle IoT Cloud: https://cloud.oracle.com/iot

IBM Watson: https://www.ibm.com/watson/

Amazon AWS: https://aws.amazon.com/

Microsoft Azure: https://azure.microsoft.com/en-us/

Google Cloud: https://cloud.google.com/

Salesforce: https://www.salesforce.com/uk/products/iot-cloud/overview/

7.4   IoT Security

Security is fundamentally important for the IoT. With more and more devices connected to the IoT, there is an increasing risk of attacks, hacking, intrusions, and data theft. For many businesses, IoT security is the top priority when adopting IoT technologies.

To protect IoT systems and devices, IoT manufacturers should make hardware secure from the beginning, make it tamper-proof, ensure secure upgrades, and provide firmware updates/patches. IoT software developers should focus on secure software development and secure software integration. For those deploying IoT systems, the focus should be on hardware security and authentication. Finally, IoT operators should keep systems up-to-date and prevent system security from being compromised by mitigating malware, performing auditing, protecting infrastructure, and safeguarding credentials.

7.5   Why Java?

Java, with its rich networking functionality and high level of security, can be used in many IoT applications. According to Oracle, Java can be used in machine-to-machine (M2M) devices, wireless modules, industrial control, smart meters/sensors, and ehealth/telehealth. For example, Java can be used on many small, embedded systems, such as the Raspberry Pi, to read sensor data, transmit the data to the cloud, and perform controls.

With Java, devices can become more integrated and more efficient in exchanging information, which provides an enhanced experience. The devices can also have the ability to upgrade themselves and manage themselves, which enhances the life cycle of the products and reduces the product support cost. Java is an easy language to learn and to use. According to Oracle, there are more than nine million Java developers in the world. Market reach can also be increased with reusable modules and platform independence. Finally, the use of Java makes the devices secure and reliable.

7.6   Java IoT with Raspberry Pi

To compile Java programs in embedded devices, you will need a full operating system. The following are the three most popular devices—single-board computers—that run on the full Linux operating system and fully support Java. (For all of these devices, the specifications shown are based on models currently available at the time of writing and may have been upgraded by the time you read this.)

Raspberry Pi   Quad-core ARM Cortex CPU, Broadcom GPU, RAM, four USB ports, 10/100 M Ethernet, 802.11n Wireless LAN, Bluetooth 4.0, HDMI port, and GPIO pins. Price: $35. `https://www.raspberrypi.org/`

BeagleBone   ARM Cortex CPU, Graphics Engine, RAM, 4 GB onboard flash, two PRU 32-bit microcontrollers, two USB ports, 10/100M Ethernet, HDMI and LCD interfaces, serial port, ADC, I2C, SPI, PWM pins. Price: $67.99. `https://beagleboard.org/`

Odroid   Samsung Cortex CPUs, Mali GPU, RAM, eMMC flash storage, two USB 3.0, one USB 2.0, Gigabit Ethernet, HDMI port, and GPIO pins. Price: $59. `https://www.hardkernel.com/`

Here we are focused only on the Raspberry Pi, as it is the most popular embedded device. The Raspberry Pi is a credit-card-size single-board computer developed to promote the teaching of computer science in schools. The popularity of the Raspberry Pi has grown steadily since its introduction in 2005. By March 2018, 19 million Raspberry Pi devices had been sold worldwide. There have been several versions of it; the latest is Raspberry Pi 3, which has built-in WiFi and Bluetooth. Figure 7.5 shows the Raspberry Pi 3 Model B board and its key components. Figure 7.6 shows the Raspberry Pi 3 Model B 40 GPIO pinout diagram (`https://pi4j.com/1.2/pins/model-3b-rev1.html`).

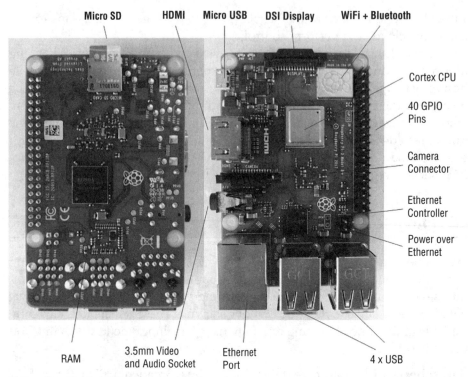

Figure 7.5: The Raspberry Pi 3 Model B board

7.6.1   Raspberry Pi Setup

To run Java on the Raspberry Pi, you will first need to have the Raspberry Pi hardware. You can visit the Raspberry Pi web site to find the nearest distributor or simply get it from Amazon or eBay. All the instructions here are based on the Raspberry Pi 3 Model B board.

Along with the Raspberry Pi board, you will also need a microSD card of 8GB or more to store the operating system called Raspbian, a GNU Debian Linux operating system. You can get a pre-installed Raspbian microSD card from either of the following:

RS (search for *raspberry pi microSD*):

`https://uk.rs-online.com/`

The Pi Hut: `https://thepihut.com/products/raspbian-preinstalled-sd-card`

Or you can download the operating image from `https://www.raspberrypi.org/downloads/`.

Figure 7.7 shows the Raspberry Pi Software Guide web site (`https://www.raspberrypi.org/learning/software-guide/quickstart/`), which provides a comprehensive guide to Raspbian software download and installation, as well as setting up the Raspberry Pi board and getting it running.

Raspberry Pi 3 Model B (J8 Header)					
GPIO#	*NAME*			*NAME*	GPIO#
	3.3 VDC Power	1	2	5.0 VDC Power	
8	GPIO 8 SDA1 (I2C)	3	4	5.0 VDC Power	
9	GPIO 9 SCL1 (I2C)	5	6	Ground	
7	GPIO 7 GPCLK0	7	8	GPIO 15 TxD (UART)	15
	Ground	9	10	GPIO 16 RxD (UART)	16
0	GPIO 0	11	12	GPIO 1 PCM_CLK/PWM0	1
2	GPIO 2	13	14	Ground	
3	GPIO 3	15	16	GPIO 4	4
	3.3 VDC Power	17	18	GPIO 5	5
12	GPIO 12 MOSI (SPI)	19	20	Ground	
13	GPIO 13 MISO (SPI)	21	22	GPIO 6	6
14	GPIO 14 SCLK (SPI)	23	24	GPIO 10 CE0 (SPI)	10
	Ground	25	26	GPIO 11 CE1 (SPI)	11
30	SDAD (I2C ID EEPROM)	27	28	SCLO (I2C ID EEPROM)	31
21	GPIO 21 GPCLK1	29	30	Ground	
22	GPIO 22 GPCLK2	31	32	GPIO 26 PWM0	26
23	GPIO 23 PWM1	33	34	Ground	
24	GPIO 24 PCM_FS/PWM1	35	36	GPIO 27	27
25	GPIO 25	37	38	GPIO 28 PCM_DIN	28
	Ground	39	40	GPIO 29 PCM_DOUT	29

Figure 7.6: The Raspberry Pi 3 Model B 40 GPIO pinout diagram

Figure 7.7: The Raspberry Pi Software Guide web site

To interact with the Raspberry Pi board, you will need a USB keyboard, a USB mouse, and either a TV with an HDMI port or a standard computer monitor through an HDMI-to-VGA converter.

Alternatively, you can connect the Raspberry Pi remotely using secure shell (SSH) or the Windows Remote Desktop Connection. To use SSH, you need to enable the SSH service on the Raspberry Pi first. You can enable the SSH service in one of three ways.

- From Raspberry Pi Desktop, launch Raspberry Pi Configuration from the Preferences menu, navigate to the Interfaces tab, select Enabled next to SSH, and click OK.

- From a Raspberry Pi terminal, type `sudo raspi-config`. From the configuration menu, select Interfacing Options, navigate to and select SSH, choose Yes, select OK, and choose Finish. Here `sudo` means execute the command as a superuser, that is, as an administrator.

- From a Rasbperry Pi terminal, type the following commands to enable and start SSH service:

```
$ sudo systemctl enable ssh
$ sudo systemctl start ssh
```

My favorite approach is to connect Raspberry Pi using the Windows Remote Desktop Connection, as SSH only provides a text mode connection. To do this, you will need to install the `xrdp` and `tightvncserver` packages on your Raspberry Pi first, using the following commands:

```
$ sudo apt-get remove xrdp vnc4server tightvncserver
$ sudo apt-get install tightvncserver
$ sudo apt-get install xrdp
```

Next connect your Raspberry Pi to the Internet using Ethernet cable or WiFi. To use the Windows Remote Desktop Connection to connect to Raspberry Pi, you will need to know the Raspberry Pi's IP address. If you don't have a TV with HDMI port or an HDMI-to-VGA converter, you can use a free program called the Advanced IP Scanner (https://www.advanced-ip-scanner.com/) to scan the Raspberry Pi's IP address, as shown in Figure 7.8.

Figure 7.8: The Advanced IP Scanner (top), the Windows Remote Desktop Connection (middle), and the Raspberry Pi desktop (bottom)

After you find the IP address, you can then use Windows Remote Desktop Connection to remotely log in to the Raspberry Pi. After typing in the username and password (the default is *pi* and *raspberry*), you should see the Raspberry Pi desktop, as shown in Figure 7.8.

Once the Raspberry Pi is up and running, you will need the Java JDK software, which should be included with the standard Raspbian operating system, including BlueJ Java IDE. If it is not or you want to install a different version of Java JDK software, you can simply run the following commands in a Raspbian terminal:

```
$ sudo apt-get update
$ sudo apt-get install oracle-java8-jdk
```

These commands install Java 8 on the Raspberry Pi, because Java 9 and later versions are not easily available. To read and write Raspberry Pi general-purpose input-output (GPIO) pins, you will also need to download and install the Pi4J library (http://pi4j.com/), as shown in Figure 7.9. There are different ways of downloading and installing the Pi4J library; I prefer to download the entire source from GitHub.

```
https://github.com/Pi4J/pi4j
```

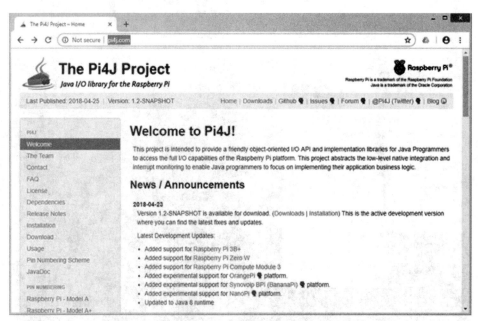

Figure 7.9: The Pi4J Project software web site

7.6.2   Java GPIO Examples

With setup completed, you can begin building your first Raspberry Pi Java application, using the GPIO pins first to control a blinking LED. Your code will be based on an example from the Pi4J library.

To start, create a dedicated folder for your Java programs. In my case, I created a folder called IoT Java under the standard Documents folder, as shown in Figure 7.10. From the Pi4J library download folder, find the file called pi4j-core. jar and copy it to the IoT Java folder. Also, find an example file called Control- GpioExample.java and copy it to the IoT Java folder. Then, from the Terminal window, use the cd command to navigate to the IoT Java folder. You can use the command nano ControlGpioExample.java to view and modify the code.

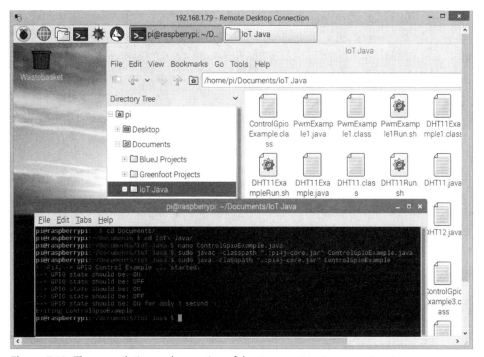

Figure 7.10: The compilation and execution of the ControlGpioExample.java program

The following is the full code, which basically uses GpioFactory.getInstance() to create a GPIO object and provisionDigitalOutputPin() to set the GPIO pin as digital output. In this case, it selects GPIO pin 01 as the digital output and then switches it to high, waits for 5000ms, switches it to low, waits for another 5000ms, and finally toggles it on and off. If you connect an LED to that pin, it will set the LED on and off accordingly.

```java
import com.pi4j.io.gpio.GpioController;
import com.pi4j.io.gpio.GpioFactory;
import com.pi4j.io.gpio.GpioPinDigitalOutput;
import com.pi4j.io.gpio.PinState;
import com.pi4j.io.gpio.RaspiPin;

/**
 * This example code demonstrates how to perform simple state
 * control of a GPIO pin on the Raspberry Pi.
 *
 * @author Robert Savage
 */
public class ControlGpioExample {
    public static void main(String[] args) throws InterruptedException {
        System.out.println("<--Pi4J--> GPIO Control Example ... started.");
        // create gpio controller
        final GpioController gpio = GpioFactory.getInstance();
        // provision gpio pin #01 as an output pin and turn on
        final GpioPinDigitalOutput pin = gpio.provisionDigitalOutputPin(R
aspiPin.GPIO_01, "MyLED", PinState.HIGH);
        // set shutdown state for this pin
        pin.setShutdownOptions(true, PinState.LOW);
        System.out.println("--> GPIO state should be: ON");
        Thread.sleep(5000);

        // turn off gpio pin #01
        pin.low();
        System.out.println("--> GPIO state should be: OFF");
        Thread.sleep(5000);

        // toggle the current state of gpio pin #01 (should turn on)
        pin.toggle();
        System.out.println("--> GPIO state should be: ON");
        Thread.sleep(5000);

        // toggle the current state of gpio pin #01  (should turn off)
        pin.toggle();
        System.out.println("--> GPIO state should be: OFF");
        Thread.sleep(5000);

        // turn on gpio pin #01 for 1 second and then off
        System.out.println("--> GPIO state should be: ON for only 1
second");
        pin.pulse(1000, true); // set second argument to 'true' use a
blocking call
        // stop all GPIO activity/threads by shutting down the GPIO
controller
        // (this method will forcefully shutdown all GPIO monitoring
threads and scheduled tasks)
        gpio.shutdown();
        System.out.println("Exiting ControlGpioExample");
    }
}
```

To compile and run the program, enter the following commands. It is important to include the `pi4j-core.jar` file in the classpath when compiling and running the program. It is also important to run the program as a superuser.

```
$ javac -classpath ".:pi4j-core.jar" ControlGpioExample.java
$ sudo java -classpath ".:pi4j-core.jar" ControlGpioExample
```

If you don't want to retype all the lengthy classpath details each time you compile and run the program, you can also create a shell script that does this automatically; see Figure 7.11. In this case, I created a Bash shell script file called `ControlGpioExample.sh`, which has the following content:

```
#!/bin/Bash
javac -classpath ".:pi4j-core.jar" ControlGpioExample.java
sudo java -classpath ".:pi4j-core.jar" ControlGpioExample
```

The hash exclamation mark (#!) is referred to as the *shebang*, followed by the path to the shell program. Here I'm using the Bash shell, but there are many other types of shell programs. The shebang must appear on the first line of the script file, and there must also be no spaces before the # or between the ! and the path to the shell program. To run the shell script, simply type the following:

```
$ bash ControlGpioExample.sh
```

Figure 7.11: The Linux Shell script for compilation and execution of the `ControlGpioExample.java` program

Based on the `ControlGpioExample.java` program, you can create a simple GPIO blinking LED demo program, as shown in Example 7.1. This application will use pin `GPIO_01` as the digital output pin and set the pin voltage high and low every 500ms. If you connect an LED to the pin, as illustrated in Figure 7.12, the LED will flash on and off accordingly.

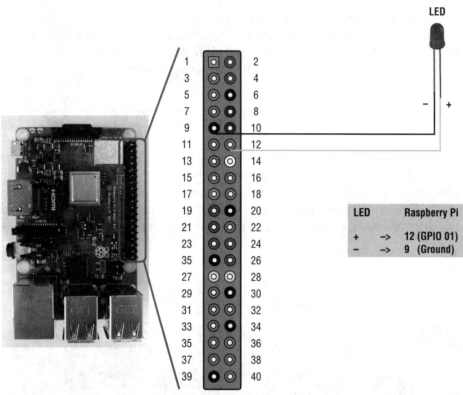

LED	Raspberry Pi
+ →	12 (GPIO 01)
− →	9 (Ground)

Figure 7.12: The circuit diagram of Raspberry Pi and LED

EXAMPLE 7.1 `CONTROLGPIOEXAMPLE1.JAVA`, **A SIMPLE GPIO BLINKING LED DEMO PROGRAM**

```java
// Example 7.1 ControlGpioExample1.java
import com.pi4j.io.gpio.GpioController;
import com.pi4j.io.gpio.GpioFactory;
import com.pi4j.io.gpio.GpioPinDigitalOutput;
import com.pi4j.io.gpio.PinState;
import com.pi4j.io.gpio.RaspiPin;

public class ControlGpioExample1 {
    // create gpio controller
    final static GpioController gpio = GpioFactory.getInstance();
    // provision gpio pin #01 as an output pin and turn on
```

```
        final static GpioPinDigitalOutput pin = gpio.provisionDigitalOutputP
in(RaspiPin.GPIO_01, "MyLED", PinState.HIGH);

    public static void main(String[] args) throws InterruptedException {
        // set shutdown state for this pin
        pin.setShutdownOptions(true, PinState.LOW);

        pin.high();
        Thread.sleep(500);
        pin.low();
        Thread.sleep(500);
        pin.high();
        Thread.sleep(500);

        gpio.shutdown();
    }
}
```

EXERCISE 7.1　Modify the Example 7.1 Java program so that it sets the pin voltage high and low in an indefinite loop.

EXERCISE 7.2　Modify the Example 7.1 Java program so that it sets the pin voltage high and low in a for loop with `Thread.sleep()` ranging from 0 to 1000 in steps of 100.

You can also create a simple Morse code demo program, as shown in Example 7.2. This program uses pin GPIO_01 as the digital output pin and sets the pin voltage high and low, according to the Morse code for the letter *A*, which is dot, dash, short space. Again, if you connect an LED to the pin, it will flash the Morse code accordingly.

EXAMPLE 7.2　A SIMPLE MORSE CODE DEMO PROGRAM

```
// Example 7.2 Morse Code demo program – MorseExample1.java
import com.pi4j.io.gpio.GpioController;
import com.pi4j.io.gpio.GpioFactory;
import com.pi4j.io.gpio.GpioPinDigitalOutput;
import com.pi4j.io.gpio.PinState;
import com.pi4j.io.gpio.RaspiPin;

public class MorseExample1 {
    // create gpio controller
    final static GpioController gpio = GpioFactory.getInstance();
    // provision gpio pin #01 as an output pin and turn on
    final static GpioPinDigitalOutput pin = gpio.provisionDigitalOutputP
in(RaspiPin.GPIO_01, "MyLED", PinState.HIGH);
```

```java
    public static void main(String[] args) throws InterruptedException {
        // set shutdown state for this pin
        pin.setShutdownOptions(true, PinState.LOW);

        System.out.println("Morse Code 'A' - dot, dash, shortspace");
        dot();
        dash();
        shortspace();
        gpio.shutdown();
    }
    static void dot() throws InterruptedException {
        pin.high();
        Thread.sleep(300);
        pin.low();
        Thread.sleep(300);
    }
    static void dash() throws InterruptedException {
        pin.high();
        Thread.sleep(900);
        pin.low();
        Thread.sleep(300);
    }
    static void shortspace() throws InterruptedException {
        Thread.sleep(600);
    }
}
```

EXERCISE 7.3   Modify the Example 7.2 Java program so that it displays *SOS* on the LED. In Morse code, the letter *S* is dot, dot, dot, short space; and the letter *O* is dash, dash, dash, short space.

Example 7.3 shows another GPIO example; it uses pin GPIO _ 01 as the digital output pin and toggles it high and low every 1000 milliseconds using the toggle() class in a for loop ten times.

EXAMPLE 7.3   A THIRD GPIO PROGRAM

```java
//Example 7.3
import com.pi4j.io.gpio.*;

public class ControlGpioExample2 {
    // create gpio controller
    final static GpioController gpio = GpioFactory.getInstance();
    // provision gpio pin #01 as an output pin and turn on
    final static GpioPinDigitalOutput pin = gpio.provisionDigitalOutputP
in(RaspiPin.GPIO_01, "MyLED", PinState.HIGH);
```

```
public static void main(String[] args) throws InterruptedException {
    // set shutdown state for this pin
    pin.setShutdownOptions(true, PinState.LOW);

    // toggle the current state of gpio pin #01
    for (int i=0; i<10; i++){
        pin.toggle();
        Thread.sleep(1000);
    }
    gpio.shutdown();
}
}
```

The GPIO pins can also be set as digital inputs. Example 7.4 shows how to set up GPIO pin 29 as the digital input and display its state using the getState() class in a for loop for ten times. You can attach a push button to GPIO pin 29, as illustrated in Figure 7.13. The resistors are simply used to protect the board. When you run the program, if you push down the button, the state of GPIO pin 29 will be shown as low; otherwise, it will be shown as high.

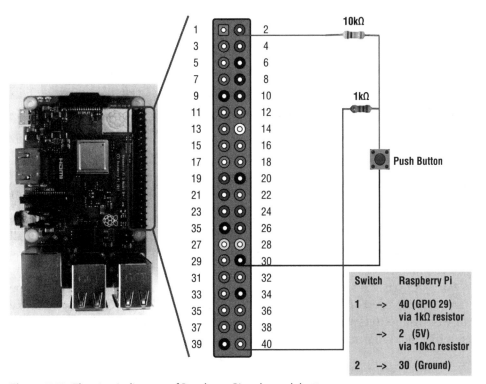

Figure 7.13: The circuit diagram of Raspberry Pi and a push button

EXAMPLE 7.4   USING THE GPIO PINS FOR INPUT

```
//Example 7.4
import com.pi4j.io.gpio.*;
public class ControlGpioExample3 {

    public static void main(String[] args) throws InterruptedException {

        // create gpio controller
        final GpioController gpio = GpioFactory.getInstance();

        // provision gpio pin #29 as an input pin
        final GpioPinDigitalInput Inp = gpio.provisionDigitalInputPin(Ra
spiPin.GPIO_29, PinPullResistance.PULL_DOWN);

        for (int i =0; i<10; i++){
            //Get the state of the pin, High or Low
            System.out.println(Inp.getState());
            Thread.sleep(1000);
        }

        // (this method will forcefully shutdown all GPIO monitoring
threads and scheduled tasks)
        gpio.shutdown();

    }
}
```

EXERCISE 7.4   Modify the Example 7.4 Java program so that it uses different GPIO pins as digital input.

7.6.3   Running Python Programs from Java

As you saw in Chapter 3, Java can also run system programs and commands. In the Raspberry Pi, Python is the default programming language that has all the natively supported functions. So if there is something you cannot do in Java, you can also call Python programs from within your Java program.

For example, the following is a simple Python GPIO program that turns the GPIO_01 pin on and off every half a second. It uses the Python GPIO Zero library for working with GPIO pins. Let's assume this program is called led.py, and it is in the /home/pi/ folder. Python uses # as comments.

```
#Example 7.4 Python GPIO example - led.py
#Modified from https://gpiozero.readthedocs.io/en/stable/
```

```
from gpiozero import LED      #import the GPIO Zero library
from time import sleep

led = LED(18) #GPIO_01 is 18 in GPIO Zero

while True:
    led.on()
    sleep(0.5)
    led.off()
    sleep(0.5)
```

For more information about the Python GPIO Zero library and its pin numbering, please visit the following resources:

https://gpiozero.readthedocs.io/en/stable/
https://gpiozero.readthedocs.io/en/stable/recipes.html

Example 7.5 is a demonstration program that makes a system call to run led.py within the Java program. Since led.py runs on an infinite loop, you need to press Ctrl+C on the keyboard to stop the program.

EXAMPLE 7.5   CALLING A PYTHON PROGRAM FROM WITHIN A JAVA PROGRAM

```
//Example 7.5 Java example to call Python program
import java.io.BufferedReader;
import java.io.InputStreamReader;

public class PythonExample {

    public static void main(String[] args) throws Exception {
        System.out.println("Running led.py, press CTRL + C to stop... ");
        Runtime rt= Runtime.getRuntime();
        Process p=rt.exec("python led.py"); [


    }
}
```

EXERCISE 7.5   Modify the Example 7.5 Java program so that it can run any Python program by getting the name of the Python program and its path from the command-line parameters.

EXERCISE 7.6   Modify the Example 7.5 Java program so that it can run any program by prompting the user to type in the name of the program to run.

7.6.4 Java PWM Example

Pulse Width Modulation (PWM) is a useful technique for many embedded systems. PWM can be used to control the brightness of an LED or to control a motor. In the Pi4J library, there is also a PWM example program, named `PwmExample.java`. Based on the previous example, you can create a simple Java PWM example program, listed in Example 7.6. This program uses the `CommandArgumentParser.getPin()` class to set the default parameters such as PWM pin, in this case `GPIO_01`, and uses the `provisionPwmOutputPin()` class to create a `PWM` object. It uses `pwmSetMode()` to set the PWM mode (`PWM_MODE_BAL` or `PWM_MODE_MS`), and it uses `pwmSetRange()` to set the PWM range (the default is 1024; here I'm setting it at 1000). It also uses `pwmSetClock()` to set the divisor for the PWM clock, which specifies the frequency of the PWM signal, as follows:

DIVISOR	FREQUENCY	NOTES
2048	9.375 kHz	
1024	18.75 kHz	
512	37.5 kHz	
256	75 kHz	
128	150 kHz	
64	300 kHz	
32	600.0 kHz	
16	1.2 MHz	
8	2.4 MHz	
4	4.8 MHz	
2	9.6 MHz	Fastest available
1	4.6875 kHz	Same as divisor 4096

Finally, it uses `setPwm()` to set the PWM rate, here we set it at 500, that is 500 out of 1000, so this is 50 percent PWM duty cycle. In PWM, duty cycle is the percentage of time the PWM pin is on over an interval or period of time. So 50 percent means half of the time the PWM pin is on and half of the time is off.

EXAMPLE 7.6 A SIMPLE JAVA PWM PROGRAM

```
//Example 7.6
import com.pi4j.io.gpio.*;
import com.pi4j.util.CommandArgumentParser;
public class PwmExample1
    public static void main(String[] args) throws InterruptedException {
```

```
         // create GPIO controller instance
         GpioController gpio = GpioFactory.getInstance();

         Pin pin = CommandArgumentParser.getPin(
                 RaspiPin.class,      // pin provider class to obtain pin
instance from
                 RaspiPin.GPIO_01,   // default pin if no pin argument found
                 args);              // argument array to search in

         GpioPinPwmOutput pwm = gpio.provisionPwmOutputPin(pin);

         com.pi4j.wiringpi.Gpio.pwmSetMode(com.pi4j.wiringpi.Gpio.PWM_
MODE_MS);
         com.pi4j.wiringpi.Gpio.pwmSetRange(1000);
         com.pi4j.wiringpi.Gpio.pwmSetClock(500);

         // set the PWM rate to 500
         pwm.setPwm(500);
         System.out.println("PWM rate is: " + pwm.getPwm());

         Thread.sleep(10000);  //wait for 10 seconds
         pwm.setPwm(0);
         System.out.println("PWM rate is: " + pwm.getPwm());
         // stop all GPIO activity/threads
         gpio.shutdown();
     }
}
```

The following commands show how to compile and run the program. Again, it is important to run the program as a superuser.

```
$ javac -classpath ".:pi4j-core.jar" PwmExample1.java
$ sudo java -classpath ".:pi4j-core.jar" PwmExample1
```

EXERCISE 7.7   Modify the Example 7.6 Java program, and change the `set-Pwm()` values from 100, 200, 300, and so on, to 1000. Attach an LED to the `GPIO _ 01` pin and observe the effects.

EXERCISE 7.8   Modify the Example 7.6 Java program, and change the `pwmSet-Clock()` values to different values, such as 1, 2, 4, 8, 16, 32, 64, 128, 256, 512, 1024, 2048, and 4096. Attach a digital oscilloscope to the `GPIO _ 01` pin and observe the effects of different values.

Example 7.6A shows another way of running PWM, using the Pi4J library's `wiringPi.SoftPwm` class. It uses `Gpio.wiringPiSetup()` to initialize the `wiringPi` library and uses SoftPwm.softPwmCreate() to set the PWM pin and the PWM range. In this case, it is the GPIO_01 pin, and the range is from 0 to 100. The code then uses SoftPwm.softPwmWrite() to write a value to the PWM pin, 50 out of 100, which means 50 percent PWM duty cycle.

EXAMPLE 7.6A   RUNNING PWM USING THE WIRINGPI.SOFTPWM **CLASS**

```java
//Example 7.6A
import com.pi4j.wiringpi.Gpio;
import com.pi4j.wiringpi.SoftPwm;
public class SoftPWM {
    private static int PIN_NUMBER = 1;
    public static void main(String[] args) throws InterruptedException {
        // initialize wiringPi library, this is needed for PWM
        Gpio.wiringPiSetup();

        // the range is set like (min=0 ; max=100)
        SoftPwm.softPwmCreate(PIN_NUMBER, 0, 100);
        int counter = 0;
        while (counter<10) {
            // softPwmWrite(int pin, int value)
            SoftPwm.softPwmWrite(PIN_NUMBER, 50);
            Thread.sleep(500);
            counter++;
        }
    }
}
```

7.6.5   Java PIR and LED Example

Based on the preceding examples, you can create a simple Raspberry Pi and Java smart lighting system using a passive infrared sensor (PIR) sensor and an LED; Figure 7.14 shows the circuit diagram. In this case, it uses the PIR sensor to detect the presence of people and switch on and off the light (LED) accordingly. Example 7.7 shows the Java code.

EXAMPLE 7.7   A SIMPLE RASPBERRY PI AND JAVA SMART LIGHTING SYSTEM

```java
//Example 7.7
import com.pi4j.io.gpio.*;

public class PIRGpioExample {
```

```
public static void main(String[] args) throws InterruptedException {

    // create gpio controller
    final GpioController gpio = GpioFactory.getInstance();

    // provision gpio pin #01 (GPIO_01) as an output pin and turn on
    final GpioPinDigitalOutput LEDpin = gpio.provisionDigitalOutputP
in(RaspiPin.GPIO_01, "MyLED", PinState.HIGH);

    // set shutdown state for this pin
    LEDpin.setShutdownOptions(true, PinState.LOW);

    // provision gpio pin #40 (GPIO_29) as an PIR input pin
    final GpioPinDigitalInput PIRpin = gpio.provisionDigitalInputPin
(RaspiPin.GPIO_29, PinPullResistance.PULL_DOWN);

    for (int i =0; i<10; i++){
        //Get the state of the pin, High or Low
        System.out.println(PIRpin.getState());

        if (PIRpin.getState()==PinState.HIGH){
            LEDpin.high();
        }
        else{
            LEDpin.low();
        }
        Thread.sleep(1000);
    }

    // (this method will forcefully shutdown all GPIO monitoring
threads and scheduled tasks)
    gpio.shutdown();

    }
}
```

EXERCISE 7.9   Modify the Example 7.7 Java program, and use another GPIO pin as digital input. When that GPIO pin is on, the LED should be always on, and when that GPIO pin is off, the LED should be on or off according to the state of the PIR pin. Attach a push button or an on/off switch to the corresponding GPIO pin and observe the effects.

Example 7.8 is a variation of the previous Java PIR program, which uses Gpio. pinMode() to set the GPIO pin as either input or output.

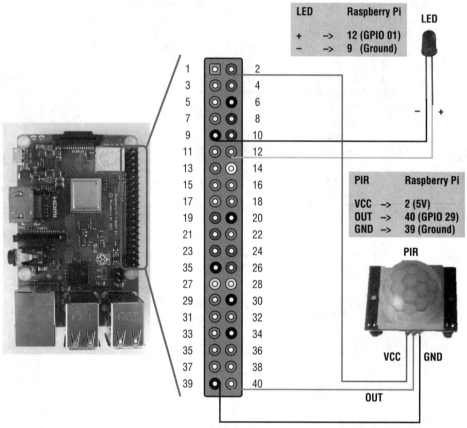

Figure 7.14: The circuit diagram of Raspberry Pi and Java based smart lighting system using PIR sensor and LED

EXAMPLE 7.8 **USING** `GPIO.PINMODE()` **TO SET THE GPIO PIN**

```
//Example 7.8
import com.pi4j.io.gpio.*;
import com.pi4j.wiringpi.Gpio;
import com.pi4j.wiringpi.GpioUtil;

public class PIRGpioExample2 {
    public static void main(String[] args) throws InterruptedException {
        // create gpio controller
        final GpioController gpio = GpioFactory.getInstance();

        // provision gpio pin #01(GPIO_01) as an output pin and turn on
        final GpioPinDigitalOutput LEDpin = gpio.provisionDigitalOutputP
in(RaspiPin.GPIO_01, "MyLED", PinState.HIGH);
```

```
        // set shutdown state for this pin
        LEDpin.setShutdownOptions(true, PinState.LOW);

        // provision gpio pin #40 (GPIO_29) as an PIR input pin
        Gpio.pinMode(40, Gpio.INPUT);

        for (int i =0; i<10; i++){

            if (Gpio.digitalRead(30)==1){
                LEDpin.high();
                System.out.println("High");
            }
            else{
                LEDpin.low();
                System.out.println("Low");
            }
            Thread.sleep(1000);
        }
        // (this method will forcefully shutdown all GPIO monitoring
threads and scheduled tasks)
        gpio.shutdown();
    }
}
```

7.6.6   Java I2C Example

Inter-Integrated Circuit (I2C, pronounced "I-squared-C") is a popular serial communication bus and protocol invented in 1982 by Philips Semiconductor (now NXP Semiconductors). I2C is a two-wire interface to connect low-speed devices such as microcontrollers, digital sensors, EEPROMs, A/D and D/A converters, and similar peripherals in embedded systems. Raspberry Pi comes with I2C support and has two default I2C pins, pin 3 for I2C SDA, and pin 5 for I2C SCL. To use I2C with the Raspberry Pi, you first need to enable it using Raspberry Pi configuration software by typing the following:

```
$ sudo raspi-config
```

The raspi-config interface differs slightly among Raspbian versions. Figure 7.15 shows the interface of Raspbian GNU/Linux 8 (Jessie). You can use the following command to find the version of your Raspbian operating system:

```
$ cat /etc/os-release
```

You can use the following commands to upgrade your Raspbian operating system:

```
$ sudo apt-get update
$ sudo apt-get dist-upgrade
```

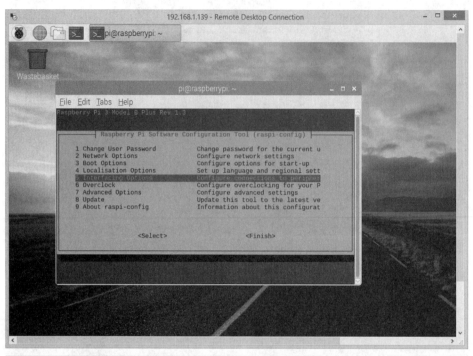

Figure 7.15: The configuration of I2C in Raspberry Pi

From the `raspi-config` interface, use the down arrow to select Interfacing Options. Then choose P5 I2C, press the Enter key, select Yes to enable it, finish the `raspi-config` program, and reboot the Raspberry Pi.

MAX30205 is a popular, accurate, I2C-based digital body temperature sensor. Figure 7.16 shows a simple Raspberry Pi I2C circuit with the MAX30205 body temperature sensor. Example 7.9 shows the corresponding I2C Java application code. It uses `I2CFactory.getInstance()` to create an I2C object and uses `i2c.getDevice()` to get the device at a particular address. It then uses `write()` to write a byte to the device and `read()` to read a byte from the device.

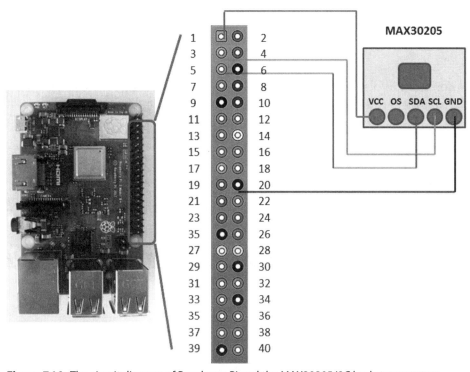

Figure 7.16: The circuit diagram of Raspberry Pi and the MAX30205 I2C body temperature sensor

EXAMPLE 7.9   A SIMPLE I2C JAVA APPLICATION

```
//Example 7.9
import java.io.IOException;
import com.pi4j.io.i2c.I2CBus;
import com.pi4j.io.i2c.I2CDevice;
import com.pi4j.io.i2c.I2CFactory;
import com.pi4j.io.i2c.I2CFactory.UnsupportedBusNumberException;
```

```java
public class I2CExample {
    public static void main(String args[]) throws InterruptedException,
UnsupportedBusNumberException, IOException {
        int addr = 0x48; // MAX30205 I2C address
        System.out.println("I2C Example");
        I2CBus i2c = I2CFactory.getInstance(I2CBus.BUS_1);
        I2CDevice device = i2c.getDevice(addr);

        while(true){
            device.write(addr, (byte) 0x00);
            System.out.println(device.read(addr));
            Thread.sleep(2000);
        }

    }
}
```

For more information about the MAX30205 body temperature sensor, visit the following resources:

https://www.maximintegrated.com/en/products/sensors/MAX30205.html

https://www.tindie.com/products/closedcube/max30205-01degc-human-body-temperature-sensor/

https://github.com/closedcube/ClosedCube_MAX30205_Arduino

Example 7.10 shows another I2C Java example, which scans all the addresses from 1 to 128 to see whether there are any I2C devices attached.

EXAMPLE 7.10   A SECOND I2C JAVA APPLICATION

```java
//Example 7.10
import java.util.*;
import com.pi4j.io.i2c.*;

public class I2CScan {

    public static void main(String[] args) throws Exception {
        final I2CBus bus = I2CFactory.getInstance(I2CBus.BUS_1);
        for (int i = 1; i < 128; i++) {
            try {
                I2CDevice device = bus.getDevice(i);
                device.write((byte)0);
                System.out.println("Found Address: " + Integer.
toHexString(i));
            } catch (Exception ignore) { }
        }
    }
}
```

For more I2C examples, see the following resources:

https://learn.sparkfun.com/tutorials/raspberry-pi-spi-and-i2c-tutorial/all

https://github.com/Pi4J/pi4j/blob/master/pi4j-example/src/main/java/bananapro/I2CExample.java

https://github.com/oksbwn/MCP23017-_Raspberry-Pi

7.6.7   Java ADC Examples

The Raspberry Pi does not have analog-to-digital converter (ADC) pins, so it cannot read directly from analog sensors. However, because Raspberry Pi supports I2C, you can use an I2C-based ADC module, such as the ADS1115 16-bit ADC (https://www.adafruit.com/product/1085), for connecting analog sensors.

Figure 7.17 shows an example circuit diagram of Raspberry Pi, ADS1115 16-bit ADC module board, and the LM35 analog temperature sensor. Raspberry Pi uses I2C to communicate with ADS1115, and ADS1115 reads the LM35 sensor value through channel A0.

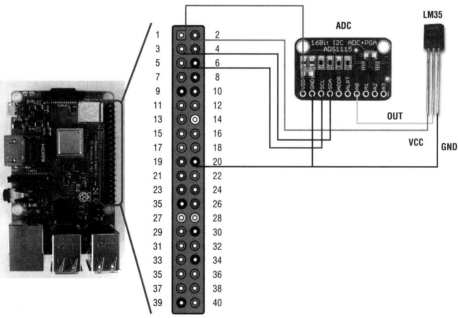

Figure 7.17: The circuit diagram of Raspberry Pi, ADS1115 16-bit ADC module, and LM35 analog temperature sensor

Figure 7.18 shows an example circuit diagram of Raspberry Pi, ADS1115 16-bit ADC module, and the light-dependent resistor (LDR) analog light sensor.

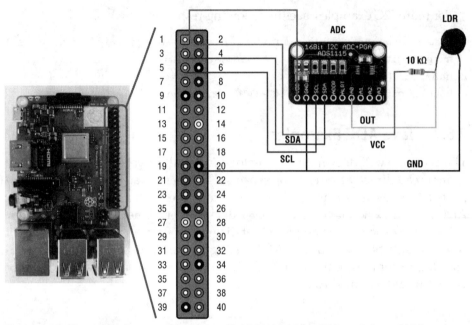

Figure 7.18: The circuit diagram of Raspberry Pi, ADS1115 16-bit ADC module, and LDR analog light sensor

In the Pi4j library, there is an ADS1115 code example, named ADS1115GpioExample.java, that can read four channel values from the ADS1115 module. The following is the full code:

```
/*
 * #%L
 * **********************************************************************
 * ORGANIZATION  :  Pi4J
 * PROJECT       :  Pi4J :: Java Examples
 * FILENAME      :  ADS1115GpioExample.java
 *
 * This file is part of the Pi4J project. More information about
 * this project can be found here:  http://www.pi4j.com/
 * **********************************************************************
 * %%
 * Copyright (C) 2012 - 2018 Pi4J
 * %%
 * This program is free software: you can redistribute it and/or modify
 * it under the terms of the GNU Lesser General Public License as
 * published by the Free Software Foundation, either version 3 of the
 * License, or (at your option) any later version.
 *
 * This program is distributed in the hope that it will be useful,
```

```
 * but WITHOUT ANY WARRANTY; without even the implied warranty of
 * MERCHANTABILITY or FITNESS FOR A PARTICULAR PURPOSE.  See the
 * GNU General Lesser Public License for more details.
 *
 * You should have received a copy of the GNU General Lesser Public
 * License along with this program.  If not, see
 * <http://www.gnu.org/licenses/lgpl-3.0.html>.
 * #L%
 */


import java.io.IOException;
import java.text.DecimalFormat;

import com.pi4j.gpio.extension.ads.ADS1115GpioProvider;
import com.pi4j.gpio.extension.ads.ADS1115Pin;
import com.pi4j.gpio.extension.ads.ADS1x15GpioProvider.
ProgrammableGainAmplifierValue;
import com.pi4j.io.gpio.GpioController;
import com.pi4j.io.gpio.GpioFactory;
import com.pi4j.io.gpio.GpioPinAnalogInput;
import com.pi4j.io.gpio.event.GpioPinAnalogValueChangeEvent;
import com.pi4j.io.gpio.event.GpioPinListenerAnalog;
import com.pi4j.io.i2c.I2CBus;
import com.pi4j.io.i2c.I2CFactory.UnsupportedBusNumberException;

/**
 * <p>
 * This example code demonstrates how to use the ADS1115 Pi4J GPIO
interface
 * for analog input pins.
 * </p>
 *
 * @author Robert Savage
 */
public class ADS1115GpioExample {


    public static void main(String args[]) throws InterruptedException,
UnsupportedBusNumberException, IOException {

        System.out.println("<--Pi4J--> ADS1115 GPIO Example ... started.");

        // number formatters
        final DecimalFormat df = new DecimalFormat("#.##");
        final DecimalFormat pdf = new DecimalFormat("###.#");

        // create gpio controller
        final GpioController gpio = GpioFactory.getInstance();
```

```
        // create custom ADS1115 GPIO provider
        final ADS1115GpioProvider gpioProvider = new
ADS1115GpioProvider(I2CBus.BUS_1, ADS1115GpioProvider.ADS1115_
ADDRESS_0x48);

        // provision gpio analog input pins from ADS1115
        GpioPinAnalogInput myInputs[] = {
                gpio.provisionAnalogInputPin(gpioProvider, ADS1115Pin.
INPUT_A0, "MyAnalogInput-A0"),
                gpio.provisionAnalogInputPin(gpioProvider, ADS1115Pin.
INPUT_A1, "MyAnalogInput-A1"),
                gpio.provisionAnalogInputPin(gpioProvider, ADS1115Pin.
INPUT_A2, "MyAnalogInput-A2"),
                gpio.provisionAnalogInputPin(gpioProvider, ADS1115Pin.
INPUT_A3, "MyAnalogInput-A3"),
                };

        // ATTENTION !!
        // It is important to set the PGA (Programmable Gain Amplifier)
for all analog input pins.
        // (You can optionally set each input to a different value)
        // You measured input voltage should never exceed this value!
        //
        // In my testing, I am using a Sharp IR Distance Sensor
(GP2Y0A21YK0F) whose voltage never exceeds 3.3 VDC
        // (http://www.adafruit.com/products/164)
        //
        // PGA value PGA_4_096V is a 1:1 scaled input,
        // so the output values are in direct proportion to the detected
voltage on the input pins
        gpioProvider.setProgrammableGainAmplifier(ProgrammableGainAmplif
ierValue.PGA_4_096V, ADS1115Pin.ALL);


        // Define a threshold value for each pin for analog value change
events to be raised.
        // It is important to set this threshold high enough so that
you don't overwhelm your program with change events for insignificant
changes
        gpioProvider.setEventThreshold(500, ADS1115Pin.ALL);


        // Define the monitoring thread refresh interval (in
milliseconds).
        // This governs the rate at which the monitoring thread will
read input values from the ADC chip
        // (a value less than 50 ms is not permitted)
        gpioProvider.setMonitorInterval(100);
```

```
        // create analog pin value change listener
        GpioPinListenerAnalog listener = new GpioPinListenerAnalog()
        {
            @Override
            public void handleGpioPinAnalogValueChangeEvent(GpioPinAnalo
gValueChangeEvent event)
            {
                // RAW value
                double value = event.getValue();

                // percentage
                double percent =  ((value * 100) / ADS1115GpioProvider.
ADS1115_RANGE_MAX_VALUE);

                // approximate voltage ( *scaled based on PGA setting )
                double voltage = gpioProvider.getProgrammableGainAmplifi
er(event.getPin()).getVoltage() * (percent/100);

                // display output
                System.out.println(" (" + event.getPin().getName() +") :
VOLTS=" + df.format(voltage) + "  | PERCENT=" + pdf.format(percent) + "%
 | RAW=" + value + "          ");
            }
        };

        myInputs[0].addListener(listener);
        myInputs[1].addListener(listener);
        myInputs[2].addListener(listener);
        myInputs[3].addListener(listener);

        // keep program running for 10 minutes
        Thread.sleep(600000);

        // stop all GPIO activity/threads by shutting down the GPIO
controller
        // (this method will forcefully shutdown all GPIO monitoring
threads and scheduled tasks)
        gpio.shutdown();

        System.out.println("Exiting ADS1115GpioExample");
    }
}
```

7.6.8   Java Digital Sensor Examples

The Raspberry Pi can connect to a digital sensor directly. Figure 7.19 shows an example circuit diagram of the Raspberry Pi with the DHT11 digital temperature and humidity sensor. The data pin of the DHT11 sensor is connected to the Raspberry Pi pin 40 (GPIO_29).

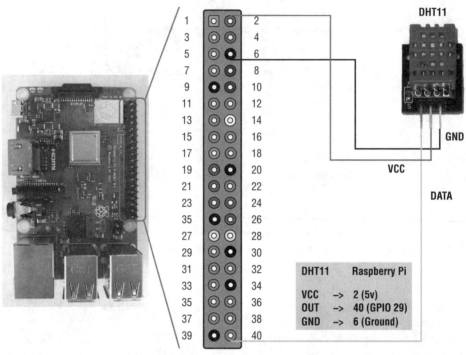

Figure 7.19: The circuit diagram of the Raspberry Pi and DHT11 digital temperature sensor

Example 7.11 shows a Java program that can read the temperature and humidity values from the DHT11 digital sensor and check the parity in order to validate the received data.

EXAMPLE 7.11   JAVA PROGRAM TO READ FROM THE DHT11 DIGITAL SENSOR

```
//Example 7.11
import com.pi4j.wiringpi.Gpio;
import com.pi4j.wiringpi.GpioUtil;

public class DHT11Example1 {
    private static final int    MAXTIMINGS  = 85;
    private final int[]         dht11_dat   = { 0, 0, 0, 0, 0 };
    private int pin = 29; //the default sensor data pin GPIO 29.
    public DHT11Example1(int pin) {

        // setup wiringPi
        if (Gpio.wiringPiSetup() == -1) {
            System.out.println(" ==>> GPIO SETUP FAILED");
            return;
        }

        GpioUtil.export(3, GpioUtil.DIRECTION_OUT);
        this.pin = pin;
    }
```

```
    public String readTemp() {
        String result = "";
        int laststate = Gpio.HIGH;
        int j = 0;
        dht11_dat[0] = dht11_dat[1] = dht11_dat[2] = dht11_dat[3] = dht11_
dat[4] = 0;

        Gpio.pinMode(pin, Gpio.OUTPUT);
        Gpio.digitalWrite(pin, Gpio.LOW);
        Gpio.delay(18);

        Gpio.digitalWrite(pin, Gpio.HIGH);
        Gpio.pinMode(pin, Gpio.INPUT);

        for (int i = 0; i < MAXTIMINGS; i++) {
            int counter = 0;
            while (Gpio.digitalRead(pin) == laststate) {
                counter++;
                Gpio.delayMicroseconds(1);
                if (counter == 255) {
                    break;
                }
            }

            laststate = Gpio.digitalRead(pin);

            if (counter == 255) {
                break;
            }

            /* ignore first 3 transitions */
            if (i >= 4 && i % 2 == 0) {
                /* shove each bit into the storage bytes */
                dht11_dat[j / 8] <<= 1;
                if (counter > 16) {
                    dht11_dat[j / 8] |= 1;
                }
                j++;
            }
        }
        // check we read 40 bits (8bit x 5 ) + verify checksum in the last
        // byte
        if (j >= 40 && checkParity()) {
            float h = (float) ((dht11_dat[0] << 8) + dht11_dat[1]) / 10;
            if (h > 100) {
                h = dht11_dat[0]; // for DHT11
            }
```

```
            float c = (float) (((dht11_dat[2] & 0x7F) << 8) + dht11_
dat[3]) / 10;
            if (c > 125) {
                c = dht11_dat[2]; // for DHT11
            }
            if ((dht11_dat[2] & 0x80) != 0) {
                c = -c;
            }
            result = "Humidity = " + h + "% Temperature = " + c + "C";
        } else {
            result = "";
        }
        return result;
    }

    private boolean checkParity() {
        return dht11_dat[4] == (dht11_dat[0] + dht11_dat[1] + dht11_dat[2]
+ dht11_dat[3] & 0xFF);
    }

    public static void main(String ars[]) throws Exception {
        int DHTpin =29;
        DHT11Example1 dht = new DHT11Example1(DHTpin );

        for (int i = 0; i < 10; i++) {
            System.out.println(dht.readTemp());
            Thread.sleep(1000);
        }
    }
}
```

To compile and execute the program, enter the following commands (or put them into a Linux Shell script):

```
$ javac -classpath ".:pi4j-core.jar" DHT11Example1.java
$ sudo java -classpath ".:pi4j-core.jar" DHT11Example1
```

Figure 7.20 shows the output results of the DHT11Example1.java program, which can read the temperature and humidity from the DHT11 digital sensor.

For more information about the Raspberry Pi and the DHT11 sensor, see the following resources:

http://www.circuitbasics.com/how-to-set-up-the-dht11-humidity-sensor-on-the-raspberry-pi/

https://tutorials-raspberrypi.com/raspberry-pi-measure-humidity-temperature-dht11-dht22/

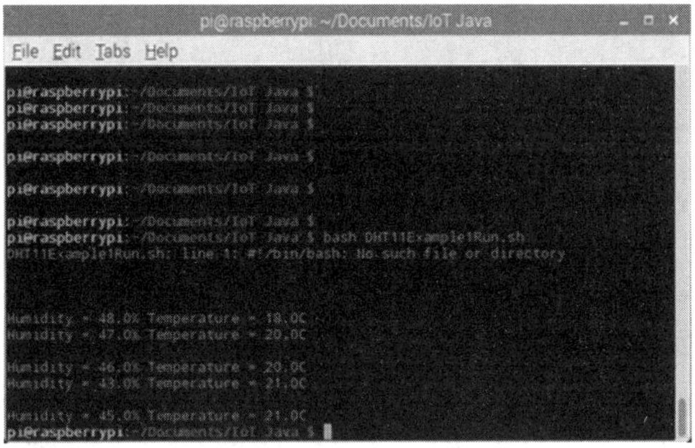

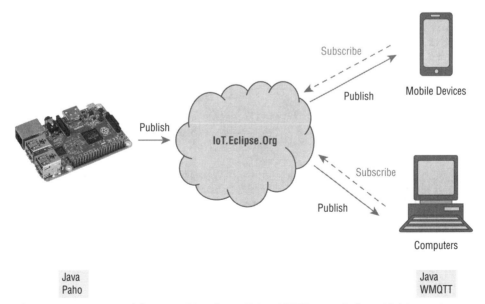

Figure 7.20: The results of the `DHT11Example1.java` program to read the temperature and humidity from a DHT11 digital sensor

7.6.9   Java MQTT Example

Message Queuing Telemetry Transport (MQTT) is an IoT protocol that allows IoT devices to publish messages on a topic through a broker, which in turn forwards the messages to all subscribers. In this example, we are going to create a Java MQTT program on the Raspberry Pi. We will use `iop.eclipse.org` as the MQTT broker to publish some temperature and humidity information to a topic called `PX Temperature and Humidity`, and we will use a computer (or other mobile devices) to subscribe to the topic and receive the messages using the IBM WMQTT A92 program. Figure 7.21 shows a conceptual diagram of the example.

Figure 7.21: Conceptual diagram of Raspberry Pi Java MQTT example for publishing and viewing MQTT messages

To implement this example, you will need to download two pieces of software:

- Eclipse Paho Java Client (on Raspberry Pi) `https://www.eclipse.org/paho/clients/java/`

- IBM's WMQTT IA92 Java utility (on computer) `https://github.com/mqtt/mqtt.github.io/wiki/ia92`

For the Eclipse Paho Java Client there are different versions, and you can choose the version you prefer. Here, you will use MQTT V3, version 1.0.2, which you can download directly from this link:

`https://repo.eclipse.org/content/repositories/paho/org/eclipse/paho/org.eclipse.paho.client.mqttv3/1.0.2/org.eclipse.paho.client.mqttv3-1.0.2.jar`

For IBM's WMQTT IA92, just go to the GitHub web site and follow the instructions to download and install it. The simplest way is to download it as a zipped file and just unzip it to your computer.

Example 7.12 is a simple Java MQTT program, modified from the `MqttPublishSample` Java example on the Eclipse Paho Java Client web site. The program uses `iot.eclipse.org:1883` as the broker, the topic is `Temperature and Humidity`, and message content is `T=30C` and `RH=40%`. The QoS is level 2, which means exactly once.

EXAMPLE 7.12   A SIMPLE JAVA MQTT PROGRAM

```
//Example 7.12 Modified from MqttPublishSample program in
//https://www.eclipse.org/paho/clients/java/
import org.eclipse.paho.client.mqttv3.MqttClient;
import org.eclipse.paho.client.mqttv3.MqttConnectOptions;
import org.eclipse.paho.client.mqttv3.MqttException;
import org.eclipse.paho.client.mqttv3.MqttMessage;
import org.eclipse.paho.client.mqttv3.persist.MemoryPersistence;

public class MqttExample {
    public static void main(String[] args) {
        String topic       = "PX Temperature and Humidity";
        String content     = "T=30C and RH=40%";
        int qos            = 2;
        String broker      = "tcp://iot.eclipse.org:1883";
        String clientId    = "JavaMQTTExmple";
        MemoryPersistence persistence = new MemoryPersistence();

        try {
            MqttClient sampleClient = new MqttClient(broker, clientId,
persistence);
            MqttConnectOptions connOpts = new MqttConnectOptions();
            connOpts.setCleanSession(true);
            System.out.println("Connecting to broker: "+broker);
```

```
            sampleClient.connect(connOpts);
            System.out.println("Connected");
            System.out.println("Publishing message: "+content);
            MqttMessage message = new MqttMessage(content.getBytes());
            message.setQos(qos);
            sampleClient.publish(topic, message);
            System.out.println("Message published");
            sampleClient.disconnect();
            System.out.println("Disconnected");
            System.exit(0);
        } catch(MqttException me) {
            me.printStackTrace();
        }
    }
}
```

Put the MQTT JAR file and the Java program in the same folder and then compile and execute the program using the following commands. Here it is important to include the MQTT JAR file in the classpath for both compilation and execution.

```
$ javac -classpath ".:org.eclipse.paho.client.mqttv3-1.0.2.jar"
MqttExample.java
$ sudo java -classpath ".:org.eclipse.paho.client.mqttv3-1.0.2.jar"
MqttExample
```

Figure 7.22 shows the compilation and execution of the MQTTExample.java program.

Figure 7.22: The compilation and execution of the `MQTTExample.java` program

To view the MQTT messages, go into IBM's WMQTT IA92 unzipped folder called `ia92`, and from the `J2SE` subdirectory find the `wmqttSample.jar` file and double-click it to run it. In case it does not run, you can also run it by typing `java -jar wmqttSample.jar` in the Windows command window. Make sure you connect to the `iot.eclipse.org` at `port 1883` first, and subscribe to the PX Temperature and Humidity topic. Then you will be able to receive the message every time the Java program sends output from Raspberry Pi. Figure 7.23 shows the program and the messages it receives.

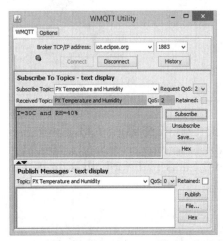

Figure 7.23: The WMQTT IA92 Java utility

7.6.10   Java REST Example

Representational State Transfer (REST) is another popular IoT communication protocol, similar to MQTT. But unlike MQTT, REST is web-based. So, you can just use a web browser to view the messages, with no extra software needed. In this example, you'll see how to create a Java REST program on the Raspberry Pi. It will send messages to a REST server, `Thingspeak`, and use a web browser to view the messages on a computer.

To do this example, you will need to do two things.

1. Download the Unirest Java library from `http://unirest.io/java.html`.

2. Register on the Thingspeak web site at `https://thingspeak.com/`.

For the Unirest Java library, there are many ways of downloading and using it. Here I'm downloading the Unirest Java JAR 1.4.9 file with all dependencies as a zipped file called `jar_files.zip` from the following link:

`https://jar-download.com/artifacts/com.mashape.unirest/unirest-java/ 1.4.9/source-code`

Then just unzip the `jar_files.zip` file to a folder, for example, `/home/pi` `/Downloads/unirest-1.4.9/`. It should contain the Unirest `unirest-java-1.4.9.jar` file and eight other JAR files; see Figure 7.24.

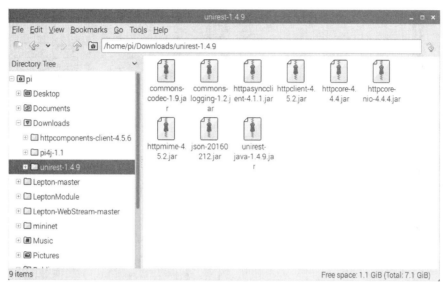

Figure 7.24: The Unirest Java JAR file `unirest-java-1.4.9.jar` file and all dependencies

For the REST server, you will use Thingspeak (`https://thingspeak.com/`), which is an open IoT platform with MATLAB analytics. You will need to sign up first, if you do not have an account already. After signing up, you will be able to log in and create a channel. In this case, I create a channel called PX Sensor, whose channel ID is 599274. Figure 7.25 shows the Thingspeak web page of my account. The different tabs show different views. The Private View tab and Public View tab show how the web page looks for private and public users, respectively. The Channel Settings tab shows the channel statistics and the fields. There can be many fields for many sensor values. Here I use only one field, Field 1, named Temperature. The API Keys tab shows the security keys used for writing to and reading from the Thingspeak REST server. The Data Import/Export tab shows how to update and retrieve data from the REST server using API requests.

Example 7.13 shows a Java demonstration of how to send dumb temperature sensor data using the REST protocol to the Thinkspeak REST server web site.

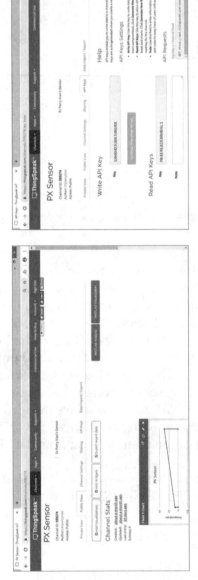

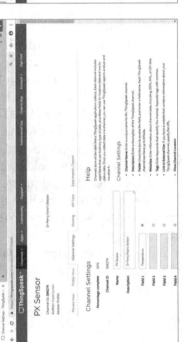

Figure 7.25: The Thinkspeak web page and the different tabs: Public View (top, left), Channel Settings (top, right), API keys (bottom, left), and Data Import/Export (bottom, right)

EXAMPLE 7.13   SEND DUMB TEMPERATURE SENSOR DATA USING THE REST PROTOCOL

```java
//Example 7.13
import java.io.InputStream;
import com.mashape.unirest.http.*;
import com.mashape.unirest.http.async.Callback;
import com.mashape.unirest.http.exceptions.UnirestException;


public class RESTCall implements Callback<JsonNode>{

    public void sendDataOverRest(double temp) {

        Unirest.post("https://api.thingspeak.com/update.json")
           .header("accept", "application/json")
           .field("api_key", "S0HXHD3UBNJUN6RX")
           .field("field1",temp)
           .asJsonAsync(this);
    }

    @Override
    public void cancelled() {
            System.out.println("The request has been cancelled");
    }

    @Override
    public void completed(HttpResponse<JsonNode> response) {
        int code = response.getStatus();

            JsonNode body =response.getBody();
            InputStream rawBody = response.getRawBody();

            System.out.println(code);
            System.out.println(body);
            System.out.println(rawBody);
    }

    @Override
    public void failed(UnirestException arg0) {
        System.out.println("The request has failed");
    }

        public static void main(String[] args) throws InterruptedException {
        RESTCall http = new RESTCall();

        double temp=30.0;
        http.sendDataOverRest(temp);


    }
}
```

Enter the following lines to compile and execute the program, making sure to include the Unirest library JAR file with all dependencies directory /home /pi/Downloads/unirest-1.4.9/ in the classpath.

```
$ javac -classpath ".:/home/pi/Downloads/unirest-1.4.9/*" RESTCall.java
$ sudo java -classpath ".:/home/pi/Downloads/unirest-1.4.9/*" RESTCall
```

Open a web browser, and log in to your Thinkspeak account, from either the Private View or the Public View tab, and you should be able to see the temperature values you are sending out from your Java REST program, as shown in Figure 7.25.

For more information on Java and the Raspberry Pi, see the following resources:

http://www.oracle.com/technetwork/articles/java/raspberrypi-1704896. html#Java%20,

http://www.oracle.com/technetwork/articles/java/cruz-gpio-2295970.html

http://www.oracle.com/webfolder/technetwork/tutorials/obe/java/Rasp-berryPi_GPIO/RaspberryPi_GPIO.html

https://iot.eclipse.org/java/tutorial/

http://agilerule.blogspot.com/2016/06/java-raspberry-pi-pi4j-pir-motion-sensor.html

http://www.robo4j.io/2017/05/be-ready-and-prepare-raspberry-pi-for.html

7.7   An Oracle Java ME Embedded Client

In addition to the Java Standard Edition, there is also Java Micro Edition, or Java ME (https://www.oracle.com/technetwork/java/embedded/javame/index .html). Java ME provides a robust, flexible environment for applications running on embedded and mobile devices in the IoT, such as microcontrollers, smart meters/sensors, gateways, mobile phones, TVs, and printers. Java ME Embedded is a Java runtime that leverages the core Java ME technologies and can run on many embedded devices, such as Freescale FRDM K64F, STM32429I-EVAL (Cortex-M4/RTX), STM 32F746GDISCOVERY (Cortex-M7/RTX), Intel Galileo Gen. 2, and Raspberry Pi (ARM 11/Linux).

For more information, see the following resources:

https://www.oracle.com/technetwork/java/embedded/javame/embedded-client/overview/meembeddedclientgetstarted-2177401.html

https://docs.oracle.com/javame/8.1/get-started-freescale-k64/install.htm

http://thomasweldon.com/tpw/courses/eegr6114/javambed/dspJavaMbed-Netbeans.html

7.8   Other Java IoT Uses

Besides running Java on embedded systems, you can also use Java to communicate with a range of IoT platforms.

7.8.1   Eclipse Open IoT Stack for Java

The Eclipse Open IoT Stack for Java is a set of open source technologies that will make it easier for Java developers to build IoT solutions. The focus of the technology is to enable developers to connect and manage the devices, sensors, and actuators that are part of their IoT solution. The Open IoT Stack for Java includes support for a number of popular IoT standards, such as MQTT, CoAP, Lightweight M2M (LWM2M), and a set of services for building IoT Gateways. All the information is available at the Eclipse Open IoT Stack for Java web site (`https://iot.eclipse.org/java/`). Eclipse simplifies the development of IoT solutions with Open IoT Stack for Java. There are several interesting Eclipse tutorials, such as to build a smart greenhouse (`https://iot.eclipse.org/java/tutorial/`) and to build a smart home (`https://www.eclipse.org/smarthome/getting-started.html`).

7.8.2   IBM Watson IoT for Java

IBM Watson IoT is another popular IoT platform (`https://internetofthings.ibmcloud.com/#/`). Figure 7.26 shows the IBM Watson IoT demonstration web site (`http://discover-iot.eu-gb.mybluemix.net/#/play`), where you can connect any of your embedded systems to the IBM IoT cloud and display the sensor readings there, without registration.

There are several interesting web sites, such as the IBM Watson IoT Java client library web site (`https://github.com/ibm-watson-iot/iot-java`) and the IBM Watson IoT recipes with Raspberry Pi (`https://developer.ibm.com/recipes/tutorials/?s=Raspberry`), as well as the IBM Watson IoT tutorial to use a Raspberry Pi camera and Watson Visual Recognition to determine whether an object of interest is in the image (`https://developer.ibm.com/recipes/tutorials/use-a-raspberry-pi-camera-and-watson-visual-recognition-to-determine-if-object-of-interest-is-in-the-image/`).

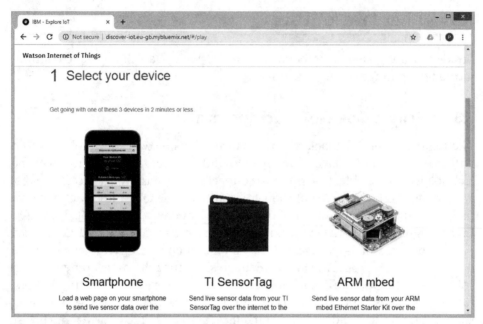

Figure 7.26: The IBM Watson IoT demonstration web site

7.8.3   Amazon IoT for Java

Amazon Web Services (AWS) offers reliable, scalable, and inexpensive cloud computing services. It's free to join; you pay only for what you use. You can find all the documents on Amazon AWS SDK for Java web site (https://aws.amazon.com/sdk-for-java/). You can find the example programs available for the Amazon AWS IoT SDK for Java from its GitHub web site (https://github.com/o-can/aws-java-iot-example).

For more information on the AWS IoT SDK for Java, see the following resources:

https://docs.aws.amazon.com/iot/latest/developerguide/iot-sdks.html#iot-java-sdk

https://aws.amazon.com/blogs/iot/introducing-aws-iot-device-sdks-for-java-and-python/

7.8.4   Microsoft Azure IoT for Java

Microsoft Azure is an open, flexible, enterprise-grade cloud computing platform that provides infrastructure as a service (IaaS), platform as a service (PaaS), and software as a service (SaaS). It supports many different programming languages including Java. IaaS allows users to launch general-purpose Microsoft Windows and Linux virtual machines. PaaS allows developers to easily publish and manage web sites. SaaS allows users to connect to and use cloud-based software over the Internet, such as email, calendaring, and office tools (Microsoft Office 365). Microsoft Azure IoT services allow users—without writing code—to connect, monitor, and control IoT devices; to run analytics on real-time data streams; to store the IoT data; and to automate data access and use data across clouds.

With Microsoft Azure Java SDK, you can develop Java applications to access Microsoft Azure Cloud Services such as Storage, Media Services, Queue Services, Service Bus Queues, and SQL Database. The best place to start with Java on Azure is its Java Developer Center (`https://azure.microsoft.com/en-us/develop/java/`), where you can get started with $200 credit and 12 months of popular services at no cost.

In the Microsoft Azure Java documentation hub for Java developers (`https://docs.microsoft.com/en-us/java/azure/`), you can find a Get Started guide and more in-depth information. Microsoft Azure SDK for Java is open source software, so you can modify it or change it whatever way you like. You can get the full source code from its GitHub site (`https://github.com/Azure/azure-sdk-for-java`).

7.9 Summary

This chapter introduced the concept of the Internet of Things (IoT), explained how the IoT works, and IoT technologies. It also introduced Java IoT applications with Raspberry Pi and Java for different IoT platforms such as Eclipse Open IoT Stack for Java, IBM Watson IoT, Amazon AWS IoT, and Microsoft Azure IoT.

7.10 Chapter Review Questions

Q7.1. What is the Internet of Things (IoT)?

Q7.2. How does the IoT works?

Q7.3. What are potential IoT applications?

Q7.4. What is Industry 4.0?

Q7.5. What are IoT communication protocols?

Q7.6. What are IoT platforms? Give a few examples.

Q7.7. What is the Raspberry Pi? What are other similar embedded computers on the market?

Q7.8.   What are Raspberry Pi's GPIO pins?

Q7.9.   What is PWM? Which is the Raspberry Pi's default PWM pin?

Q7.10.   What is I2C? Which are the Raspberry Pi's default I2C pins?

Q7.11.   What is MQTT?

Q7.12.   What is REST? Compare it with HTTP.

Q7.13.   What is IaaS, PaaS, and SaaS?

Q7.14.   Compare the different IoT platforms and list the features.

CHAPTER 8

Java Programming for AI Applications

"Life is like riding a bicycle. To keep your balance you must keep moving."

—Albert Einstein

8.1 What Is Artificial Intelligence?

Artificial intelligence (AI) is another hot buzzword at the moment. Just listen to the news—we have AI in this, AI in that, AI everywhere! So, what exactly is artificial intelligence? How is AI going to affect our lives? Is AI going to put all of us out of work one day?

Artificial intelligence is an area of computer science to create machines to do intelligent things, such as learning, planning, problem-solving, prediction, face and speech recognition, and so on. The beginning of artificial intelligence dates back to the 1950s, when Alan Turing, an English computer scientist, proposed the imitation game test to see if a computer could think and behave indistinguishably from a human. This is the famous Turing test. No computer has passed the Turing test so far.

Artificial intelligence as a research discipline was established in a workshop in 1956. The term *artificial intelligence* was coined by John McCarthy, a legendary computer scientist at Stanford University, who was also one of the most influential founders and leaders of AI research.

Artificial intelligence can be divided into narrow AI, general AI, and super AI.

Narrow AI, or weak AI, is the intelligence to perform one single task. Examples of narrow AI include weather forecasts, making purchase suggestions, sales predictions, computer vision, natural language processing, speech recognition, playing chess, and Google Translate. Narrow AI is what we have achieved so far. Narrow AI is where we are, and general AI is where we are going.

General AI, or strong AI, is the intelligence that can deal with more complex, more general tasks. General AI would possess the cognitive abilities and would be able to understand its environments. General AI would be able to observe, think, analyze, learn, invent, and have feelings, like humans. According to Ray Kurzweil, a well-known futurist and Google's director of engineering, by 2029 AI will pass the Turing test and by 2045, the technological singularity will occur. The singularity is the time when artificial intelligence starts to overtake human beings; Figure 8.1 illustrates the concept.

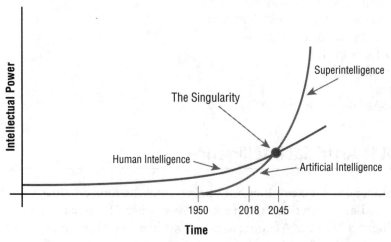

Figure 8.1: The technological singularity and the timeline of artificial intelligence compared with human intelligence

Super AI, or superintelligence, is AI after the singularity point. There are different views on what will happen with super AI. Some people have expressed worries and fears; for example, Elon Musk, SpaceX founder and CEO of Tesla Motors, has famously called AI the biggest existential threat. Stephen Hawking, the English theoretical physicist, has warned that AI is going to end humanity one day. Many others, such as Bill Gates (founder of Microsoft) and Mark Zuckerberg (founder of Facebook), believe that AI will benefit the human race. Just like many earlier technological revolutions, it will destroy some jobs but will create more new jobs. So ready or not, like it or not, AI is coming. Therefore, we will need to be prepared, to make sure that we will benefit from AI, and, even more importantly, to make sure that the doomsday scenario depicted in Hollywood movies such as *The Terminator* (with Arnold Schwarzenegger) never happen.

8.1.1   History of AI

The history of artificial intelligence research can be roughly divided into three stages, focusing on different techniques: neural networks (1950s–1970s), machine learning (1980s–2010s), and deep learning (the present day), as illustrated in Figure 8.2 (`https://www.sas.com/en_gb/insights/analytics/what-is-artificial-intelligence.html`).

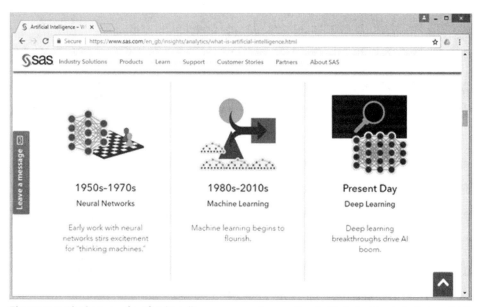

Figure 8.2: The history of artificial intelligence research according to Statistical Analysis System (SAS)

Neural Networks   Neural networks were developed based on human biological neural networks. Neural networks typically consist of three distinct layers: one input layer, one hidden layer, and one output layer. Once a neural network has been trained with a large amount of given data, it can be used to predict the output for unseen data. Neural networks attracted a lot of attention from the 1950s through the 1970s and stimulated much enthusiasm and optimism. But since the 1980s, following many disappointments and much criticism, funding and interest in artificial intelligence research were significantly reduced. This period is also called *AI winter*.

Machine Learning   Machine learning (ML) is a set of mathematical algorithms for automatic data analysis. ML started to flourish during the 1980s through the 2010s and includes popular algorithms such as support vector machine (SVM), K-mean clustering, linear regression, and native Bayes, to name a few.

Deep Learning   Deep learning uses neural networks with multiple hidden layers. This approach has been possible only since the 2010s, with the increase in available computing power, particular graphics processing units (GPUs), and improved algorithms. Today, with ever-increasing massive labeled data sets and ever-increasing GPU computing power, deep learning has shown huge potential in many application areas.

Figure 8.3 shows the timeline as well as the differences between artificial intelligence, machine learning, and deep learning, from the Nvidia site (`https://blogs.nvidia.com/blog/2016/07/29/whats-difference-artificial-intelligence-machine-learning-deep-learning-ai/`).

Figure 8.3: The timeline and differences between artificial intelligence, machine learning, and deep learning from Nvidia

8.1.2 Cloud AI vs. Edge AI

Many AI applications require large training data sets and enormous computing power. For these purposes, it is beneficial to run AI on the cloud. Many technology giants, such as Google, IBM, Microsoft, Amazon, Alibaba, and Baidu, all provide cloud-based AI services. There are many advantages for customers using cloud-based AI services. You don't need to purchase expensive hardware, you pay for what you use, and there is no need to worry about software installation, configuration, or troubleshooting and upgrading. The disadvantages of cloud-based AI are in latency, bandwidth requirements, and security. Because you need to send the data to the cloud and get the results back, there is latency in cloud-based AI. Sending a large amount of data to the cloud also requires a lot of bandwidth. Finally, if the cloud service is hacked, your data or information might be lost or stolen. For many IoT or other real-time applications, latency, bandwidth, and security could be problems. This is where Edge AI could be useful.

Edge AI means running AI software on the edge devices, such as microcontrollers, smart phones, or other devices. It is also called *on-device AI*. The advantages of Edge AI are that it operates in real time, can work offline, and is secure. Applications such as voice recognition, face recognition, object detection, driverless cars, and so on, can all use Edge AI. Cloud AI and Edge AI will be largely complementary to each other, and you can choose to use whichever is the best for your applications.

The following are some examples of Edge AI devices and applications.

OpenMV: Computer vision on a microcontroller (http://docs.openmv.io/)

JeVois: TensorFlow-enabled camera module (http://jevois.org/)

Google Edge TPU: TensorFlow Processing Unit (https://cloud.google.com/edge-tpu/)

Movidius: Intel's vision processing unit (https://www.movidius.com/)

NVidia JETSON: GPU-based AI (https://www.nvidia.com/en-us/autonomous-machines/embedded-systems-dev-kits-modules/)

UP AI Edge: AI boards powered by Intel's CPU, GPU, VPU, FPGA (https://up-shop.org/25-up-ai-edge)

Ultra96: Xilinx FPGA (https://www.96boards.ai/products/ultra96/)

TensorFlow Lite: Lightweighted TensorFlow for mobile and embedded devices (https://www.tensorflow.org/lite/)

uTensor: An extremely lightweight machine learning inference framework built on Mbed and TensorFlow (https://github.com/uTensor/uTensor)

Qualcomm Neural Processing SDK for AI: Qualcomm's SDK for AI (https://developer.qualcomm.com/software/qualcomm-neural-processing-sdk)

Huawei NPU: A neural-network processing unit (https://developer.huawei.com/consumer/en/service/HiAI.html)

8.2 Neural Networks

A *neural network* (NN), also called an *artificial neural network* (ANN), is a mathematical algorithm for problem-solving. The concept of artificial neural networks was first developed in 1943, by Warren S. McCulloch (neuroscientist) and Walter Pitts (logician) in the United States, inspired by the biological neural networks that constitute the human brain. The biological neural networks are made of a large number of interconnected neurons. The human brain typically has about 100 billion neurons. Each neuron consists of three main parts: the dendrites, a cell body (soma), and an axon. Dendrites are the tree-like structures for receiving input signals from surrounding neurons, the cell body is for processing the input signals, and the axon is for connecting to another neuron's dendrites; the contact is made through a synapse. Synapses allow a neuron to pass an electrical or chemical signal to another neuron, and the strength of a synaptic connection varies. A neuron will sum all the inputs and then fire an output signal via an axon to the next neuron. This signal can be either excitatory or inhibitory, which means increasing or decreasing the firing, depending on certain conditions. Figure 8.4 shows the typical structure of a neuron and different types of neurons (`https://en.wikipedia.org/wiki/Neuron`).

Figure 8.5 shows an interesting neural network tutorial that explains how to use mathematical functions to create an artificial neuron based on real neurons (`https://leonardoaraujosantos.gitbooks.io/artificial-inteligence/content/neural_networks.html`). More details are available in next section.

8.2.1 The Perceptron

Like the biological neural networks, artificial neural networks are also made of an interconnected individual neuron, called *perceptron*. The perceptron is the most fundamental element of the neural networks. The perceptron algorithm was defined by Frank Rosenblatt, an American psychologist, at the Cornell Aeronautical Laboratory in the United States in 1957. Figure 8.6 shows the structure of a perceptron, which has inputs (dendrites), a body, and an output (axon). The weight for each input reflects the synaptic connection strength. The perceptron adds up all the inputs according to their weight and a bias and then feeds the result into an activation function, which will decide the output of the perceptron. A perceptron is a typical feedforward network, where the connections between the nodes do not form a cycle. There is no feedback between layers.

If $x_1, x_2, ..., x_n$ are the inputs of the perceptron, $w_1, w_2, ..., w_n$, are the corresponding weights for the inputs, n is the total number of inputs, and b is the corresponding bias, then the weighted sum of the inputs can be calculated as follows:

$$z = \sum_{i=1}^{n} w_i x_i + b$$

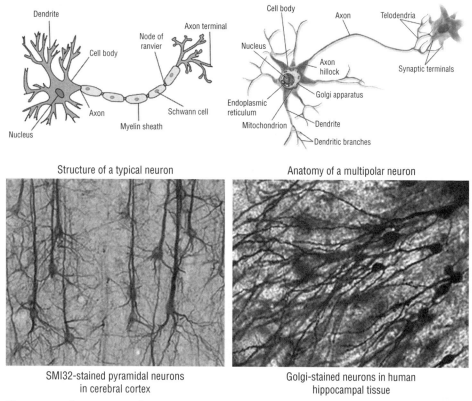

Structure of a typical neuron

Anatomy of a multipolar neuron

SMI32-stained pyramidal neurons
in cerebral cortex

Golgi-stained neurons in human
hippocampal tissue

Figure 8.4: The structure of a typical neuron (top left), a multipolar neuron (top right), SMI32-stained pyramidal neurons in the cerebral cortex (bottom left), and Golgi-stained neurons in human hippocampal tissue (bottom right)

Here, $w_i x_i$ means w_i multiplies x_i, i is the ith term of each set of data, and Σ means to calculate the sum of $w_i x_i$ from term 1 to n. This will then be fed into an activation function to generate the output of the perceptron.

$$y = \delta(z) = \delta\left(\sum_{i=1}^{n} w_i x_i + b\right)$$

There are several popular choices for the activation function. The simplest and most commonly used activation function, $\delta(z)$, is a step function, which gives an output of 0 or 1.

$$\delta(z) = \begin{cases} 1, & if \ z > 0 \\ 0, & else \end{cases}$$

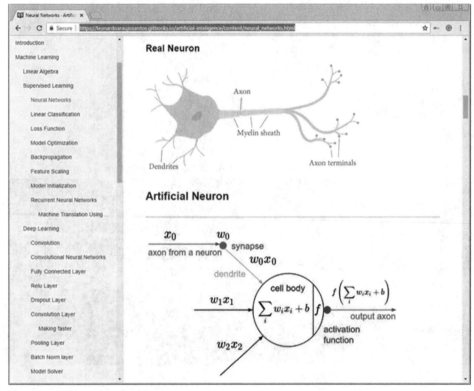

Figure 8.5: Natural and artificial neurons

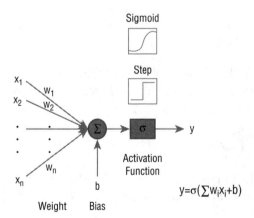

$$y=\sigma(\textstyle\sum w_i x_i + b)$$

Figure 8.6: The structure of a perceptron, which has inputs (dendrites), a body, and output (axon)

Another commonly used activation function is the sigmoid function, which is a smoothed version of the step function. A sigmoid function gives a continuous output between 0 and 1.

$$\delta(z) = \frac{1}{1 - e^{-z}}$$

Similar to the sigmoid function, another common choice for f is the hyperbolic tangent, or **tanh**, function.

$$\delta(z) = \tanh(z) = \frac{e^z - e^{-z}}{e^z + e^{-z}}$$

Next you need to train the perceptron. To do that, you need a set of data samples, with given inputs and desired output. The training is done by continuously adjusting w and b values, until for a given input (x), you can get the desired output (y). This needs to be done over several iterations, called an *epoch*. The following pseudocode shows the logic:

Generate random weights and bias

For each of iteration

  For each set of sample

    //Calculate the output

    $y' = \delta\left(\sum w_i * x_i + b\right)$

    //Calculate the error

    $\varepsilon = y - y'$

    //Calculate the adjustment (gradient)

    delta = learnrate $* x * \varepsilon$

    //Update the weight

    w = w + delta

    //Update the bias

    b = b + delta

    Until sample finished

    if error is small enough or total number of epoch reached

      stop

    Else

      continue.

End of iteration

This is called the *backpropagation* method, and the key is to calculate the gradient for adjusting the weights and bias. Once trained, the perceptron should be able to produce output for any unseen data. Perceptrons have been successfully used in many applications, such as logical operations, AND, OR, NOT, and XOR. However, a single perceptron, or a single layer of perceptrons, is not sophisticated enough to solve complex problems. *Multiple-layer perceptrons* were therefore developed. Section 8.6 contains Java example programs for a single perceptron and multiple-layer perceptrons.

See the following for more information about perceptrons:

```
https://appliedgo.net/perceptron/
http://neuralnetworksanddeeplearning.com/chap1.html
https://github.com/mnielsen/neural-networks-and-deep-learning
https://towardsdatascience.com/what-the-hell-is-perceptron-
626217814f53
https://natureofcode.com/book/chapter-10-neural-networks/
```

8.2.2   MultiLayered Perceptron/Backpropagation/Feedforward

Conventional neural networks are made of multilayered perceptrons (MLPs), which typically have three layers: input layer, hidden layer, and output layer. Each layer can have a number of perceptrons. Figure 8.7 shows an example of a neural network that has four perceptrons in the input layer (that is, four inputs), three perceptrons in the hidden layer, and two perceptrons in the output layer.

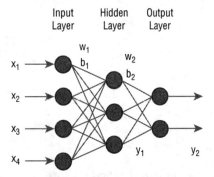

Figure 8.7: Traditional neural network with one input layer, one hidden layer, and one output layer

If x_1, x_2, x_3, x_4, are the inputs of the input layer, $w1_1, w1_2, ..., w1_{12}$ are the corresponding weights of the outputs of the input layer, and $b1_1, b1_2, b1_3$, are the corresponding biases for the hidden layer, then the outputs of the hidden layer $y1_1, y1_2, y1_3$ can be calculated as follows:

$$y1_j = \sum_{i=1}^{4} w1_{((i-1)*3+1)} x_i + b1_j$$

Then, if $w2_1, w2_2, \ldots, w2_6$ are the corresponding weights of the outputs of the hidden layer and $b2_1, b2_2$ are the corresponding biases for the output layer, the outputs of the output layer $y2_1, y2_2$, can be calculated as follows:

$$y2_j = \sum_{i=1}^{3} w2_{((i-1)\cdot 3+1)} y1_i + b2_j$$

By using a sigmoid activation function, you can calculate the final output of the neural network as follows:

$$y = \delta(y2) = \frac{1}{1 - e^{y2}}$$

Again, you can train the network using the backpropagation method, described earlier. You need a set of data samples, with given inputs and desired output. The training is done by continuously adjusting w and b values, until for a given input (x), you can get the desired output (y). This needs to be done over several iterations, called *epochs*. The following pseudocode shows the logic:

Generate random weights and bias

For each of iteration

    For each set of sample

        //Calculate the hidden layer output

        $y1 = \Sigma w1 * x + b1$

        //Calculate the hidden layer output

        $y2 = \delta(\Sigma w2 * y1 + b2)$

        //Calculate the output layer error

        $delta2 = y - y2$

        //Calculate the hidden layer error

        $delta1 = delta2 * w2$

        //Update the hidden layer weights,

        $w1 = w1 + learnrate * x * delta1 * y1 * (1 - y1)$

        //Update the hidden layer weights,

        $w2 = learnrate * x * delta2 * y2 * (1 - y2)$

        //Update the hidden layer bias

        $b1 = b1 + delta1$

        //Update the output layer bias

        $b2 = b2 + delta2$

    Until sample finished

    if error is small enough or total number of epoch reached

      stop

   Else

     continue

  End of iteration

Figure 8.7 shows a traditional neural network with one input layer, one hidden layer, and one output layer. Each individual neuron has the inputs and outputs illustrated in Figure 8.6 earlier.

See the following resources for more information on neural networks:

```
https://www.nnwj.de/
https://www.cse.unsw.edu.au/~cs9417ml/MLP2/
https://kunuk.wordpress.com/2010/10/11/neural-network-backpropagation-
with-java/
https://www.doc.ic.ac.uk/~nd/surprise_96/journal/vol4/cs11/report.html
http://diffsharp.github.io/DiffSharp/0.6.3/examples-neuralnetworks.html
http://www.theprojectspot.com/tutorial-post/introduction-to-artificial-
neural-networks-part-1/7
http://www.theprojectspot.com/tutorial-post/introduction-to-artificial-
neural-networks-part-2-learning/8
https://machinelearningmastery.com/neural-networks-crash-course/
```

8.3   Machine Learning

Machine learning (ML) is a category of mathematical algorithms that allow software to become more accurate in predicting outcomes for a given set of data. The term was coined in 1959 by Arthur Samuel (an American Pioneer in computer and artificial intelligence), while at IBM. ML can be divided into the categories *supervised learning, unsupervised learning, semi-supervised learning,* and *reinforcement learning.*

> **Supervised Learning**   In supervised learning, the algorithms are trained using labeled data. The learning algorithms calculate the output with a given input, compare the calculated output with desired output, and then adjust the algorithms accordingly. A good example is to use a support vector machine to classify the type of iris according to its sepal length, sepal width, petal length, and petal width. Other examples include speech recognition, handwriting recognition, pattern recognition, spam detection, and optical character recognition.

Unsupervised Learning   In unsupervised learning, the algorithms are fed unlabeled data. The learning algorithms will study the structure of the data and divide it into groups with the closest features. *K-mean clustering* is a popular example of a type of unsupervised learning algorithm. Examples of unsupervised learning applications include grouping customers according to their purchasing behavior, associating certain customers with certain types of products, and so on.

Semi-supervised Learning   In semi-supervised learning, both labeled and unlabeled data is used. This approach is particularly suitable when the cost for labeling is too high to allow a fully labeled training process or when not all the data can be labeled. Examples of semi-supervised learning include speech analysis and web content analysis.

Reinforcement Learning   In reinforcement learning, the learning algorithms learn to find, through trial and error, which action can yield the greatest reward. This is normally done in the absence of existing training data. Reinforcement learning is often used in robotics, gaming, and navigation.

The following is a list of commonly used machine learning algorithms:

- Linear regression
- Logistic regression
- Linear discriminant analysis
- Classification and regression trees
- Naive Bayes
- K-mean clustering
- Learning vector quantization
- Support vector machines
- Bagging and random forest
- Boosting and AdaBoost

Figure 8.8 shows the machine learning information web page from SAS (`https://www.sas.com/en_gb/insights/analytics/machine-learning.html`).
See the following resources for more information on machine learning:

`https://www.toptal.com/machine-learning/machine-learning-theory-an-introductory-primer`

`https://www.kaggle.com/kanncaa1/machine-learning-tutorial-for-beginners`

`https://www.digitalocean.com/community/tutorials/an-introduction-to-machine-learning`

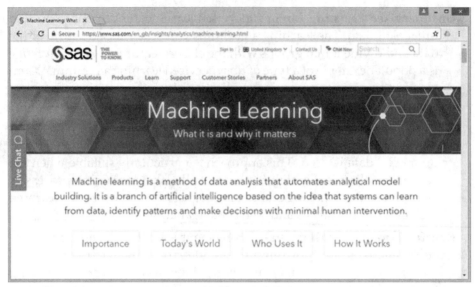

Figure 8.8: The machine learning web page from SAS

8.4   Deep Learning

Conventional neural networks have only three layers: one input layer, one hidden layer, and one output layer. There is only one hidden layer, because the training of neural networks is done using a method known as *gradient descent*. This is an iterative algorithm for finding the minimum of a function. It starts with an initial value and then takes steps proportional to the negative of the gradient of the function at the current point until it reaches the minimum value, where the gradient is close to zero. As the number of hidden layers increases, training also becomes slow and difficult. This is called the *vanishing gradient* problem.

In 2009, a free database—ImageNet—with more than 14 million labeled images was launched by AI professor Fei-Fei Li at Stanford University. The aim was to use big data to improve machine learning. In 2010, the ImageNet Large Scale Visual Recognition Challenge (ILSVRC) was started. In this annual challenge, contestants were encouraged to train their algorithms using ImageNet and submit their predictions. The breakthrough came in 2012, when AlexNet, a convolutional neural network (CNN) developed by Alex Krizhevsky, Ilya Sutskever, and Geoff Hinton (University of Toronto), halved the existing prediction error rate to 15.3 percent, more than 10.8 percentage points ahead of the runner up. AlexNet had several key features. First, AlexNet had eight layers, of which the first five were convolutional layers, and the last three were fully connected layers, as illustrated in Figure 8.9 (http://www.mdpi.com/2072-4292/9/8/848).

Convolutional layers apply a convolution operation to the input, which reduces the number of parameters of the problem, to allow deep layers with fewer parameters. In fully connected layers, every neuron in one layer is connected to every

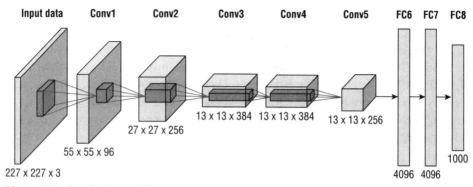

Figure 8.9: The AlexNet architecture

neuron in another layer. As a result of this eight-layer architecture, there are 60 million parameters. Second, AlexNet used graphics processing units (GPUs) to train the model. GPUs are essentially parallel floating-point calculators, which are much faster than conventional central processing units (CPUs). Using GPUs meant they could train larger models, which led to lower error rates. Finally, they used the non-saturating rectified linear activation unit (ReLU) activation function, which had reduced overfitting and improved training performance over other activation functions such as tanh and sigmoid. Today, AlexNet has made a significant impact on deep learning, particularly machine vision. Through 2018, AlexNet has been cited more than 25,000 times. Figure 8.10 shows some examples of the activation functions in neural networks (`https://towardsdatascience.com/activation-functions-neural-networks-1cbd9f8d91d6`).

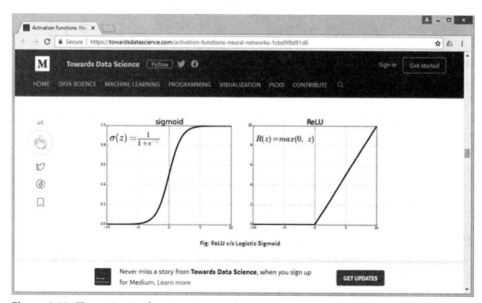

Figure 8.10: The activation functions in neural networks

Another impressive winner of the ILSVRC challenge was GoogLeNet in 2014. GoogLeNet has achieved an amazing error rate of 6.67 percent. This is equivalent to human performance on this dataset. GoogLeNet is a convolutional neural network (CNN) 22 layers deep and has reduced the number of parameters from 60 million (AlexNet) to 4 million. Figure 8.11 shows a colorful explanation of how a convolutional neural network (CNN) works (`https://indoml.com/2018/03/07/ student-notes-convolutional-neural-networks-cnn-introduction/`). CNNs are effective for any type of prediction problem involving image data as an input.

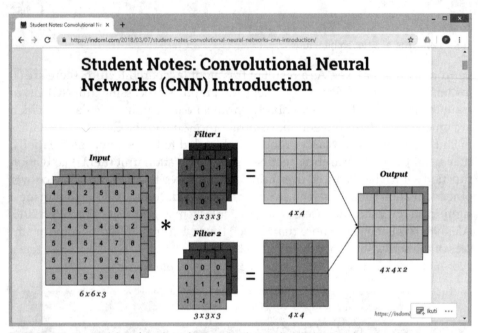

Figure 8.11: A colorful explanation of how convolutional neural networks

Finally, last but not least, is the winner of the ILSVRC challenge in 2015: Residual Neural Network (ResNet) developed by Kaiming He et al. from Microsoft. It achieved an error rate of 3.57 percent, which is better than the human-level performance on this dataset. ResNet used a novel architecture with "skip connections" and features heavy batch normalization, which allowed them to train a neural network with 152 layers while still having lower complexity.

Another type of deep learning network is the *recurrent neural network* (RNN), which was designed to work with sequence prediction problems. Examples of sequence prediction problems include one-to-many, many-to-one, and many-to-many. A one-to-many problem is when an observation as input is mapped to multiple outputs. A many-to-one problem is when a sequence of multiple inputs is mapped to a single output prediction. A many-to-many problem is when a sequence of multiple inputs is mapped to multiple outputs. You can use RNN for text data, speech data, and time-series data.

Figure 8.12 shows the deep learning information web site from SAS (`https://www.sas.com/en_gb/insights/analytics/deep-learning.html`). Figure 8.13 shows the Keras tutorial web site on deep learning in Python (`https://www.datacamp.com/community/tutorials/deep-learning-python`).

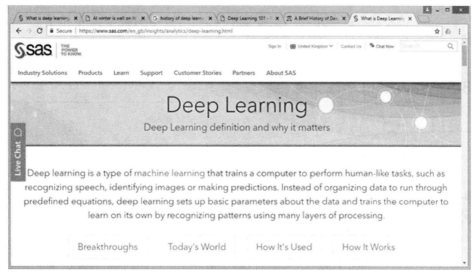

Figure 8.12: The Deep Learning web site from SAS

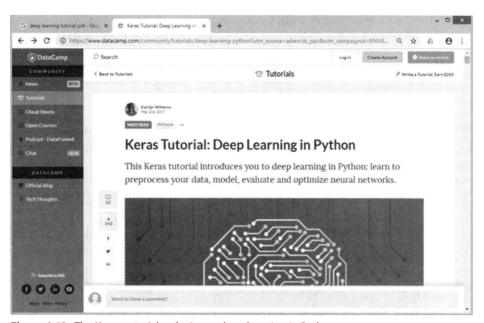

Figure 8.13: The Keras tutorial web site on deep learning in Python

See the following resources for more information about deep learning:

https://papers.nips.cc/paper/4824-imagenet-classification-with-deep-convolutional-neural-networks.pdf

https://machinelearningmastery.com/crash-course-convolutional-neural-networks/

https://machinelearningmastery.com/crash-course-recurrent-neural-networks-deep-learning/

8.5   Java AI Libraries

The following is a list of Java AI libraries.

Expert Systems

Apache Jena, free and open source Semantic Web framework for Java (http://jena.apache.org/)

Neural Networks

Neuroph, a lightweight and flexible Java neural network framework (http://neuroph.sourceforge.net/index.html)

Deeplearning4j, a deep learning programming library with wide support for deep learning algorithms (https://deeplearning4j.org/index.html)

Natural Language Processing

Apache OpenNLP, a machine learning library for processing natural language text (https://opennlp.apache.org/)

Stanford CoreNLP, a set of human language technology tools written in Java (https://stanfordnlp.github.io/CoreNLP/)

Machine Learning

Java-ML, a collection of machine learning algorithms written in Java (http://java-ml.sourceforge.net/)

Weka 3: Data Mining Software in Java, a collection of machine learning algorithms for data mining tasks (https://www.cs.waikato.ac.nz/ml/weka/)

SMILE, a fast and general machine learning engine for big data processing (http://haifengl.github.io/smile/, https://github.com/haifengl/smile)

Computer Vision

JavaCV, a Java interface to OpenCV (https://github.com/bytedeco/javacv)

OpenCV Java, Java applications using OpenCV

https://opencv-java-tutorials.readthedocs.io/en/latest/

https://opencv-java-tutorials.readthedocs.io/en/latest/01-installing-opencv-for-java.html

https://docs.opencv.org/2.4/doc/tutorials/introduction/java _ eclipse/
java _ eclipse.html#java-eclipse
https://opencv.org/opencv-java-api.html
https://www.tutorialspoint.com/java _ dip/introduction _ to _ opencv.htm
https://www.behance.net/gallery/9972461/Java-OpenCV-Webcam

Other Resources
https://www.baeldung.com/java-ai
https://skymind.ai/wiki/java-ai

8.6   Java Examples for Neural Networks

Now let's look at some examples of Java applications for neural networks.

8.6.1   Java Perceptron Example

Example 8.1 shows a simple Java perceptron (single neuron) application. It has two Java files, Neuron1.java and Neuron1Demo.java. The Neuron1.java file is the single neuron class, which defines the input and output. The output is simply the weighted sum of all inputs. Neuron1Demo.java is the example program that uses the Neuron1 class to create a perceptron object. Figure 8.14 shows the compilation, execution, and output of the Neuron1Demo.java program.

Example 8.1A is the code for Neuron1.java.

EXAMPLE 8.1A   JAVA PERCEPTRON (SINGLE NEURON) EXAMPLE

```java
//Example 8.1A Java Perceptron (single neuron) example
public class Neuron1 {
    final double x[], w[];
    Neuron1(double x[], double w[]) {
        this.x = x;
        this.w = w;
    }
    public double Output() {
        double sum = 0.0;
        for(int i=0;i<x.length;i++)
        {
            sum += w[i]*x[i];
        }
        return Math.tanh(sum);
    }
}
```

Example 8.1B is the code for `Neuron1Demo.java`.

EXAMPLE 8.1B   JAVA PERCEPTRON (SINGLE NEURON) DEMO

```java
//Example 8.1B Java Perceptron (single neuron) demo example
import java.util.Random;

public class Neuron1Demo{
    public static void main(String[] args) {
        double x[] = {1.4, -0.33};
        double w[] = {new Random().nextDouble(), new Random().nextDouble()};
        Neuron1 n = new Neuron1(x, w);

        System.out.println(x[0]);
        System.out.println(x[1]);
        System.out.println(n.Output());
    }
}
```

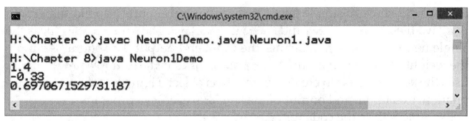

Figure 8.14: The compilation, execution, and output of `Neuron1Demo.java`

Example 8.2 shows another Java perceptron implementation, this time with training. It also consists of two Java files, `Neuron2.java` and `Neuron2Demo.java`. The `Neuron2.java` file is the single neuron class, which has defined the input and output. The output is simply the weighted sum of all inputs. It also has a `Train()` method that can train the perceptron to make it behave as a logical AND function. The `Neuron2Demo.java` file is the example program that uses the `Neuron2` class to create a perceptron object. Figure 8.15 shows the compilation, execution, and output of the `Neuron2Demo.java` program.

Example 8.2A lists the code for `Neuron2.java`.

EXAMPLE 8.2A   JAVA PERCEPTRON (SINGLE NEURON) EXAMPLE 2 WITH TRAINING

```java
//Example 8.2A Java Perceptron (single neuron) example 2 with training
import java.util.Random;
public class Neuron2 {
    double w[];        //weights
    double threshold;  //threshold
```

```java
    public int Output(double x[]) {
        double sum = 0.0;
        for(int i=0;i<x.length;i++)
        {
            sum += w[i]*x[i];
        }
        if(sum>threshold)
            return 1;
        else
            return 0;
    }
    public void Train(double[][] x, int[] y, double threshold, double
learnrate, int epoch)
    {
        this.threshold = threshold;
        int N = x[0].length;
        w = new double[N];
        Random r = new Random();

        //initialize weights
        for(int i=0;i<N;i++)
        {
            w[i] = r.nextDouble();
        }
        //do the training
        for(int i=0;i<epoch;i++)
        {
            int totalError = 0;
            for(int j =0;j<y.length;j++)
            {
                //calculate the output and error
                int output = Output(x[j]);
                int error = y[j] - output;
                totalError +=error;
                //update the weights
                for(int k = 0;k<N;k++)
                {
                    double delta = learnrate * x[j][k] * error;
                    w[k] += delta;
                }
            }
            if(totalError == 0)
                break;
        }
    }
}
```

Example 8.2B lists the code for `Neuron2Demo.java`.

EXAMPLE 8.2B   JAVA PERCEPTRON (SINGLE NEURON) EXAMPLE 2 WITH TRAINING

```
//Example 8.2B Java Perceptron (single neuron) example 2 with training

public class Neuron2Demo{
    public static void main(String[] args) {
        double x[][] = {{0,0},{0,1},{1,0},{1,1}};
        int y[] = {0,1,1,1};                      //Logical AND
        Neuron2 n = new Neuron2();
        n.Train(x, y,0.2, 0.5, 1000);

        System.out.println(n.Output(new double[]{0,0}));
        System.out.println(n.Output(new double[]{0,1}));
        System.out.println(n.Output(new double[]{1,0}));
        System.out.println(n.Output(new double[]{1,1}));
    }
}
```

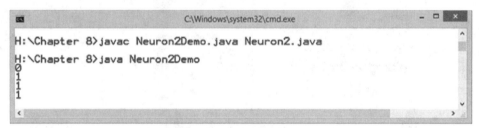

Figure 8.15: The compilation, execution, and output of the `Neuron2Demo.java` program

8.6.2   Java Neural Network Backpropagation Example

Example 8.3 shows a Java backpropagation neural network example. It is adapted from the following code example:

https://supundharmarathne.wordpress.com/2012/11/23/a-simple-backpropagation-example-of-neural-network/

This program creates a simple neural network with one input layer, one hidden layer, and one output layer. The input layer has four neurons, the hidden layer has three neurons, and the output layer has two neurons. Figure 8.16 shows the compilation, execution, and output of the `BackpropagationDemo1.java` program after 10 iterations. Figure 8.17 shows the compilation, execution, and output of `BackpropagationDemo1.java` after 1,000 iterations. Please note that your program's outputs might be different from Figures 8.16 and 8.17, as the parameters initial values are generated randomly.

EXAMPLE 8.3   JAVA BACKPROPAGATION EXAMPLE

```java
//Example 8.3 BackpropagationDemo1.java Java backpropagation example
//Modified from
//https://supundharmarathne.wordpress.
com/2012/11/23/a-simple-backpropagation-example-of-neural-network/

public class BackpropagationDemo1 {

    //Simple NN with 1 input layer, 1 hidden layer, and 1 output layer
    static int nInputs =4, nHidden=3, nOutput=2;

    static double[][] input = {{0,1,1,0}, {1,0,0,1}, {1,1,0,0}};
    static int[][] target = {{0,1}, {1,0}, {1,1}};

    //initialize input layer weights w1 and hidden layer weights w2
    static double [] w1 = new double [nInputs*nHidden];
    static double [] w2 = new double [nHidden*nOutput];

    //initialize hidden layer output y1 and output layer output y2
    static double [] y1 = new double [nHidden];
    static double [] y2 = new double [nOutput];

    //initialize hidden layer errors delta1 and output layer errors
delta2
    static double [] delta1 = new double [nHidden];
    static double [] delta2 = new double [nOutput];

    //initialize hidden layer bias b1 and output layer bias b2
    static double [] b1 = new double [nHidden];
    static double [] b2 = new double [nOutput];

    //learning rate
    static double learningRate=0.4;
    static int count = 0;
    static int maxCount = 1000;
    static boolean loop = true;
    public static void main(String[] args) {

        generateWR() ;
        while(loop){
            for(int i=0;i<input.length;i++){
                calculateY(input[i]);
                calculateDelta(i);
                calculateNewWeights(i);
                calculateNewBias();
                count++;
                System.out.println(y2[0] + ", "+ y2[1]);
            }
            System.out.println("=============================");
```

```
                    if(count>=maxCount){
                        loop = false;
                    }
                }
            }
    static private void generateWR() {
        //Generate random w1 and w2
        for(int i=0; i<nInputs*nHidden; i++) {
            w1[i] = Math.abs(Math.random() - 0.5);
        }
        for(int i=0; i<nHidden*nOutput; i++) {
            w2[i] =  Math.abs(Math.random() - 0.5);
        }
        //Generate random b1 and b2
        for(int i=0; i<nHidden; i++) {
            b1[i] =  Math.abs(Math.random() - 0.5);
        }
        for(int i=0; i<nOutput; i++) {
            b2[i] = Math.abs(Math.random() - 0.5);
        }
    }
    static void calculateY(double x[]){
        //Calculate the hidden layer output y1
        for(int i=0; i<nHidden; i++){
            y1[i]=0;
            for(int j=0; j<nInputs; j++){
                y1[i] += (x[j]*w1[i+j*nHidden]);
            }
            y1[i] = sigmoid(y1[i]+b1[i]);
        }
        //Calculate the output layer output y2
        for(int i=0; i<nOutput; i++) {
            y2[i]=0;
            for(int j=0; j<nHidden; j++){
                y2[i] += (y1[j]*w2[i+j*nOutput]);
            }
            y2[i] = sigmoid(y2[i]+b2[i]);
        }
    }

    static void calculateDelta(int j){
        for(int i=0; i<nOutput; i++) {
            delta2[i] = target[j][i] - y2[i];
        }
        for(int i=0; i<nHidden; i++) {
            delta1[i]=0;
            for(int k=0; k<nOutput; k++){
                delta1[i] += (delta2[k]*w2[i*nOutput+k]);
            }
```

```
                }
            }

    private static void calculateNewWeights(int j){
        for(int i=0; i<nInputs; i++) {
            for(int k=0; k<nHidden; k++){
                int n= i*nHidden+k;
                w1[n] += (learningRate*delta1[k]*input[j]
[i]*y1[k]*(1-y1[k])));
            }
        }

        for(int i=0; i<nHidden; i++) {
            for(int k=0; k<nOutput; k++){
                int n= i*nOutput+k;
                w2[n] += (learningRate*delta2[k]*y1[i]*y2[k]*(1-y2[k]));
            }
        }

    }
    private static void calculateNewBias(){
        for(int i=0; i<nHidden; i++) {
            b1[i] +=delta1[i];
        }
        for(int i=0; i<nOutput; i++) {
            b2[i] += delta2[i];
        }
    }
    static double sigmoid(double exponent){
        return (1.0/(1+Math.pow(Math.E,(-1)*exponent)));
    }
}
```

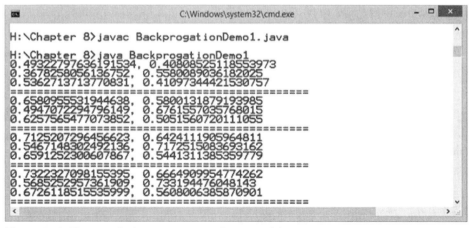

Figure 8.16: The compilation, execution, and output of the `BackpropagationDemo1.java` program after 10 iterations

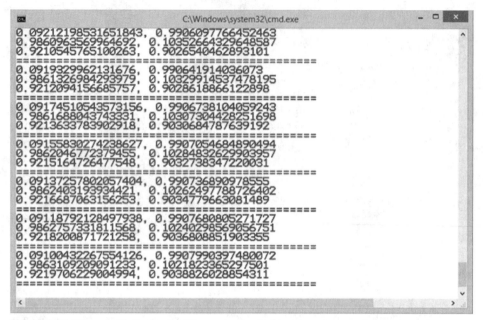

Figure 8.17: The compilation, execution, and output of `BackpropagationDemo1.java` after 1,000 iterations

8.7   Java Examples for Machine Learning

Several Java-based library packages are available for machine learning. One commonly used library is Waikato Environment for Knowledge Analysis (Weka), which is a collection of machine learning algorithms for data mining tasks developed at the University of Waikato in New Zealand. It contains tools for data preparation, classification, regression, clustering, association rules mining, and visualization.

To use Weka, first you will need to download the Weka library.

http://www.cs.waikato.ac.nz/ml/weka/snapshots/weka _ snapshots.html

Download the file `stable-3-8.zip`, and unzip it to a folder. Find the JAR file `weka.jar` and data file `iris.arff`.

Use IntelliJ IDEA to create a new Java project, and add the `weka.jar` and `iris.arff` files to the IntelliJ IDEA project. Create an empty Java class named `WekaTest.java`, and copy the source code in Example 8.4 to the `WekaTest.java` file. This is a simple Weka classification demo modified based on the example code at the following link:

https://www.programcreek.com/2013/01/a-simple-machine-learning-example-in-java/

This example reads the Iris classification data from the file, splits it into a training set and a testing set, runs the J48 decision tree classifier, and prints out the results.

```
//Example 8.4 modified from
//https://www.programcreek.com/2013/01/a-simple-machine-learning-
example-in-java/

import java.io.BufferedReader;
import java.io.FileNotFoundException;
import java.io.FileReader;
import weka.classifiers.Classifier;
import weka.classifiers.Evaluation;
import weka.classifiers.evaluation.NominalPrediction;

import weka.classifiers.trees.J48;
import weka.core.FastVector;
import weka.core.Instances;

public class WekaTest {
    public static BufferedReader readDataFile(String filename) {
        BufferedReader inputReader = null;

        try {
            inputReader = new BufferedReader(new FileReader(filename));
        } catch (FileNotFoundException ex) {
            System.err.println("File not found: " + filename);
        }

        return inputReader;
    }

    public static Evaluation classify(Classifier model,
            Instances trainingSet, Instances testingSet) throws
Exception {
        Evaluation evaluation = new Evaluation(trainingSet);

        model.buildClassifier(trainingSet);
        evaluation.evaluateModel(model, testingSet);

        return evaluation;
    }

    public static double calculateAccuracy(FastVector predictions) {
        double correct = 0;
```

```java
        for (int i = 0; i < predictions.size(); i++) {
            NominalPrediction np = (NominalPrediction) predictions.
elementAt(i);
            if (np.predicted() == np.actual()) {
                correct++;
            }
        }

        return 100 * correct / predictions.size();
    }

    public static Instances[][] crossValidationSplit(Instances data, int
numberOfFolds) {
        Instances[][] split = new Instances[2][numberOfFolds];

        for (int i = 0; i < numberOfFolds; i++) {
            split[0][i] = data.trainCV(numberOfFolds, i);
            split[1][i] = data.testCV(numberOfFolds, i);
        }

        return split;
    }

    public static void main(String[] args) throws Exception {
        BufferedReader datafile = readDataFile("iris.arff");

        Instances data = new Instances(datafile);
        data.setClassIndex(data.numAttributes() - 1);

        // Do 10-split cross validation
        Instances[][] split = crossValidationSplit(data, 10);

        // Separate split into training and testing arrays
        Instances[] trainingSplits = split[0];
        Instances[] testingSplits = split[1];

        // Use a classifier
        Classifier models = new J48(); // a decision tree

        // Collect every group of predictions for current model in a
FastVector
        FastVector predictions = new FastVector();

        // For each training-testing split pair, train and test the
classifier
        for (int i = 0; i < trainingSplits.length; i++) {
            Evaluation validation = classify(models, trainingSplits[i],
testingSplits[i]);
```

```
            predictions.appendElements(validation.predictions());
        }

        // Calculate overall accuracy of current classifier on all
splits
        double accuracy = calculateAccuracy(predictions);

        // Print current classifier's name and accuracy in a
complicated,
        // but nice-looking way.
        System.out.println("Accuracy of " + models.getClass().
getSimpleName()+ ": "
                    + String.format("%.2f%%", accuracy)
                    + "\n-------------------------------");


    }
}
```

Figure 8.18 shows the content of the `iris.arff` file and the Eclipse project WekaTest and its output.

See the following resources for more information about Weka:

`https://www.cs.waikato.ac.nz/ml/weka/`

`http://www.cs.umb.edu/~ding/history/480 _ 697 _ spring _ 2013/homework/ WekaJavaAPITutorial.pdf`

`http://www.cs.ru.nl/P.Lucas/teaching/DM/weka.pdf`

Another popular machine learning library that supports the Java programming language is Library for Support Vector Machines (LIBSVM), illustrated in Figure 8.19 (`https://www.csie.ntu.edu.tw/~cjlin/libsvm/`). LIBSVM supports vector classification and distribution estimation. It also supports multiclass classification. On the web site, there is also a simple Java applet demonstrating SVM classification and regression.

8.8   Java Examples for Deep Learning

Deep learning is another hot research topic at the moment. The best way to do deep learning with Java is to use the Deeplearning4J library; Figure 8.20 shows the download page (`https://deeplearning4j.org/docs/latest/deeplearning4j-quickstart`). You can also download the entire Deeplearning4J library as a zipped file from its GitHub web site.

`https://github.com/deeplearning4j/dl4j-examples`

Then unzip it to a folder. Inside there should be a subfolder named `dl4j-examples`, where you can find many deep learning example applications.

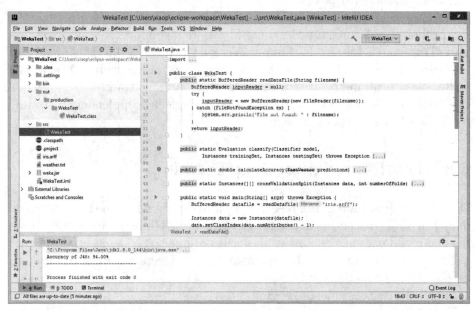

Figure 8.18: The content of the `iris.arff` file (top) and the IntelliJ IDEA project WekaTest and its output (bottom)

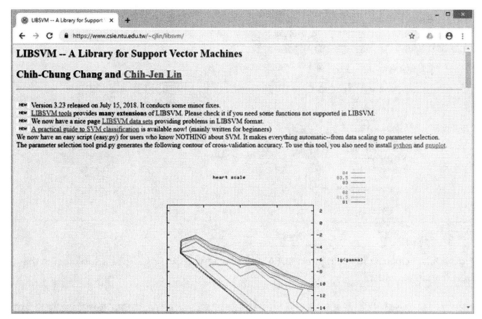

Figure 8.19: The LIBSVM Library for support vector machines

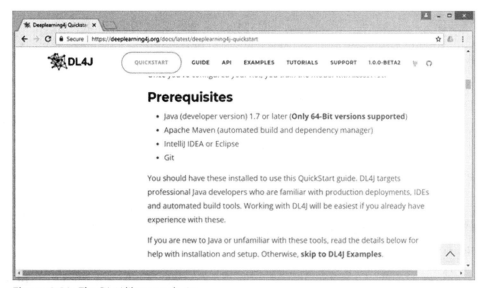

Figure 8.20: The DL4J library web site

To run the DL4J examples, again you will use IntelliJ IDEA for its simplicity and friendliness. From IntelliJ IDEA, open a project, select the dl4j-examples subfolder in the Deeplearning4J folder, and click OK, as shown in Figure 8.21. Once the project is open, it will look like Figure 8.22. There are many different deep learning example programs. From here you can run the existing examples, modify examples, and create your own programs.

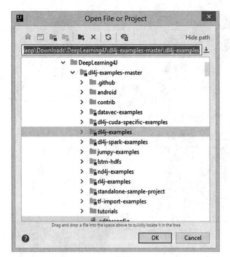

Figure 8.21: Open a project in IntelliJ IDEA, and select the `dl4j-examples` subfolder in the Deeplearning4J folder.

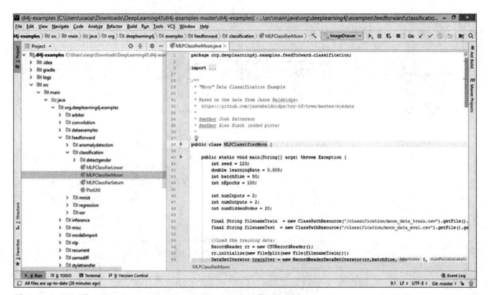

Figure 8.22: The `dl4j-examples` project in IntelliJ IDEA

Figure 8.23 shows the `XorExample.java` program and its running output. `XorExample.java` uses a simple multiple-layer, feedforward neural network to implement an XOR functions; it has two input-neurons, one hidden-layer with four hidden-neurons, and two output-neurons.

Figure 8.24 shows the `MLPClassifierLinear.java` program and its running output. `MLPClassifierLinear.java` uses multiple-layer perceptron neural networks as a linear classifier to separate two groups of the data.

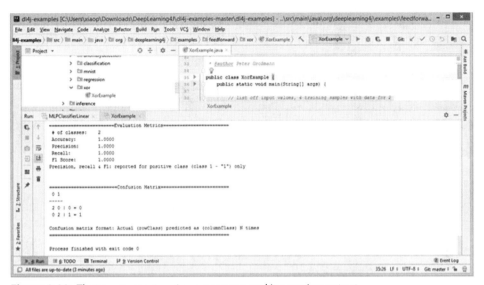

Figure 8.23: The `XorExample.java` program and its running output

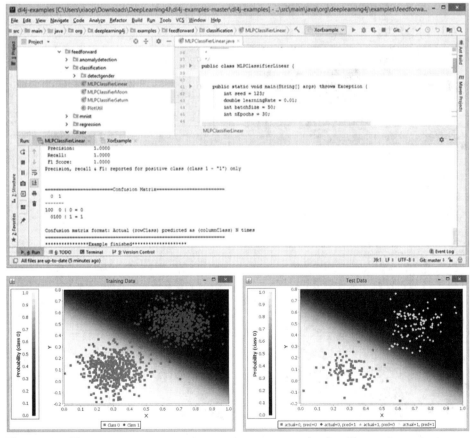

Figure 8.24: The `MLPClassifierLinear.java` program (top) and its running output (bottom). The bottom left shows the training set data results, and the bottom right shows the test set data results.

Figure 8.25 shows the interesting `ImageDrawer.java` program and its running output. `ImageDrawer.java` uses the deep learning neural networks to redraw the image (Mona Lisa) that it is given, pixel by pixel. It will first get a very rough

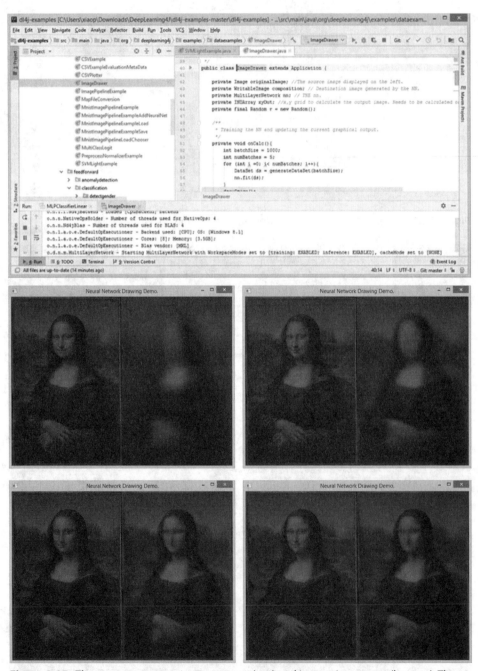

Figure 8.25: The `ImageDrawer.java` program (top) and its running output (bottom). The bottom shows the target image and the redrawn image after about five minutes, 30 minutes, six hours, and seven hours.

representation of the target image and then continue to fine-tune it until it gets the image to appear exactly the same, which normally takes a couple of hours.

The following Google paper explains how to use a recurrent neural network for image generation, that is, drawing the image:

`https://arxiv.org/pdf/1502.04623.pdf`

This is an interesting, free, short course on deep learning, as well as using Deeplearing4J:

`http://www.whatisdeeplearning.com/course/`

You can also use Deeplearning4J to create and train a neural network on an Android device.

`https://deeplearning4j.org/docs/latest/deeplearning4j-android`

8.9   TensorFlow for Java

TensorFlow is an open-source software library developed by Google for the purpose of machine learning. It is one of the most popular machine learning libraries, particularly for deep learning. TensorFlow can work on a range of different operating systems, such as Ubuntu Linux, Windows, macOS, and even Raspbian!

The default TensorFlow programming language is Python. But TensorFlow also provides APIs for Java programs, as shown in Figure 8.26 (`https://www.tensorflow.org/install/install _ java`).

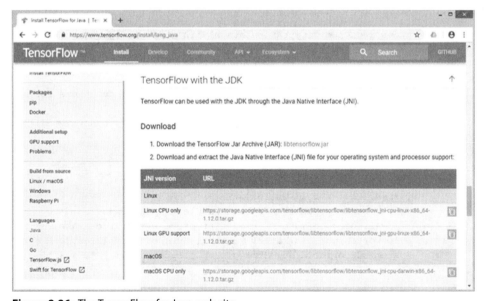

Figure 8.26: The TensorFlow for Java web site

To use TensorFlow for Java, you will need to download two files from the web site.

1. Download the TensorFlow Jar Archive (JAR) called `libtensorflow.jar` from `https://storage.googleapis.com/tensorflow/libtensorflow/libtensorflow-1.12.0.jar`.

2. Download and extract the Java Native Interface (JNI) file for your operating system and processor support. In this example, I downloaded the JNI file for Windows CPU and from the downloaded zipped file extracted a file named `tensorflow _ jni.dll`.

Put both the `libtensorflow.jar` and `tensorflow _ jni.dll` files into your Java program folder (in this example, `H:\Chapter 8`), and create a file named `Hello-TensorFlow.java`. You can get the contents of the file from the TensorFlow for Java web site, as shown next:

```
//Example code from https://www.tensorflow.org/install/lang_java

import org.tensorflow.Graph;
import org.tensorflow.Session;
import org.tensorflow.Tensor;
import org.tensorflow.TensorFlow;

public class HelloTensorFlow {
  public static void main(String[] args) throws Exception {
    try (Graph g = new Graph()) {
      final String value = "Hello from " + TensorFlow.version();

      // Construct the computation graph with a single operation, a
constant
      // named "MyConst" with a value "value".
      try (Tensor t = Tensor.create(value.getBytes("UTF-8"))) {
        // The Java API doesn't yet include convenience functions for
adding operations.
        g.opBuilder("Const", "MyConst").setAttr("dtype", t.dataType()).
setAttr("value", t).build();
      }

      // Execute the "MyConst" operation in a Session.
      try (Session s = new Session(g);
        // Generally, there may be multiple output tensors,
        // all of them must be closed to prevent resource leaks.
        Tensor output = s.runner().fetch("MyConst").run().get(0)) {
        System.out.println(new String(output.bytesValue(), "UTF-8"));
      }
    }
  }
}
```

Example 8.5 is a simplified version of the previous program, which just prints `Hello from xxx`, where xxx is the version of TensorFlow.

EXAMPLE 8.5   TENSORFLOW JAVA EXAMPLE

```
//Example 8.5 TensorFlow Java Example
import org.tensorflow.TensorFlow;

public class TensorFlowExample {
    public static void main(String[] args) {
        final String value = "Hello from " + TensorFlow.version();
        System.out.println(value);
    }
}
```

To compile and execute this program, you will need to run the following commands:

```
javac -cp libtensorflow-1.12.0.jar HelloTensorFlow.java
java -cp libtensorflow-1.12.0.jar;. -Djava.library.path=. HelloTensorFlow
```

The `-cp libtensorflow-1.12.0.jar` command includes the `libtensorflow.jar` file in the classpath, and the `-Djava.library.path=.` command specifies where you can find the `tensorflow_jni.dll` file. In this example, it is "." which means the current folder. Figure 8.27 shows the compilation and execution of the `HelloTensorFlow.java` program. The version of TensorFlow is 1.12.0.

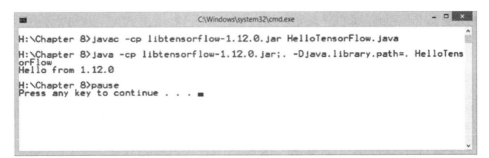

Figure 8.27: The compilation and execution of the `HelloTensorFlow.java` program

There are many tutorials and TensorFlow Java example programs available. Figure 8.28 (`https://sites.google.com/view/tensorflow-example-java-api`) shows the Google TensorFlow Java API example site, which uses the YOLO model (`https://pjreddie.com/darknet/yolo/`) for object detection, for example, to detect cats in a picture.

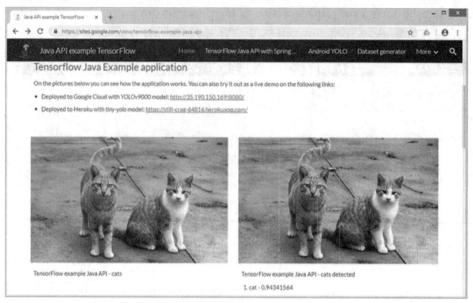

Figure 8.28: The Google TensorFlow Java API example site

The following GitHub site has a simple, illustrative tutorial showing how to get started with TensorFlow with Java. It offers a `Hello TensorFlow` example (the same as in the previous example) and a `LabelImage` example, which uses the `tensorflow_inception_graph.pb` TensorFlow model file for image classification.

```
https://github.com/loretoparisi/tensorflow-java
```

The following is another simple guide to getting started with TensorFlow with Java and JavaScript, that is, within a web browser:

```
https://dzone.com/articles/getting-started-with-tensorflow-
using-java-javascr
```

The following GitHub site has several interesting TensorFlow Java examples, including hello-world, image-classifier, sentiment-analysis, audio-classifier, audio-recommender, and audio-search-engine programs.

```
https://github.com/chen0040/java-tensorflow-samples
```

The following is the TensorFlow Java API documentation web site:

```
https://www.tensorflow.org/api_docs/java/reference/org/tensorflow/
package-summary
```

More TensorFlow Java examples are available from these sites:

```
https://github.com/tensorflow/models/tree/master/samples/languages/
java
```

```
https://github.com/szaza/tensorflow-example-java
```

8.10   AI Resources

This section provides a list of interesting AI resources, including books and tutorials.

The following is a good book about artificial intelligence and deep learning:
`https://leonardoaraujosantos.gitbooks.io/artificial-inteligence/content/`

The following link shows the latest *Machine Learning Yearning* book by Andrew Ng, who is one of the leading scientist and most influential figure in the area of AI:
`https://www.deeplearning.ai/copy-of-machine-learning-yearning`

The Neural Networks and Deep Learning web site offers a free online book:
`http://neuralnetworksanddeeplearning.com/`

The following book uses a hands-on approach, and all the example codes are available from its GitHub web site:
`https://github.com/mnielsen/neural-networks-and-deep-learning`

The following link shows the *Machine Learning and Big Data* book web site. This book teaches you different machine learning algorithms, illustrated with C++, Scala, Java, and Python example programs.
`http://www.kareemalkaseer.com/books/ml`

The following link shows Chapter 10 of the book *The Nature of Code*. Chapter 10 introduces the neural networks, with many short code examples and animated visualizations.
`https://natureofcode.com/book/chapter-10-neural-networks/#`

The following link shows the Deep Learning tutorial from Stanford University, a popular deep learning tutorial web site:
`http://deeplearning.stanford.edu/wiki/index.php/UFLDL _ Tutorial`

The following link shows another popular machine learning course by Andrew Ng from the online course web site Coursera. This is one of the must-learn courses if you want to learn AI.
`https://www.coursera.org/learn/machine-learning`

8.11   Summary

This chapter first introduced the concept of artificial intelligence and then illustrated some Java examples of AI applications. You looked at the types of AI: narrow AI, general AI, and super AI. You also surveyed the stages of the development of AI. You saw that neural networks started in the 1950s, machine learning started in the 1980s, and deep learning started in the 2010s. For neural networks, the chapter introduced the concept of a perceptron—a single neuron—along with multilayer perceptron, backpropagation networks, and feedforward networks. The chapter also introduced the different types of machine learning: supervised learning, unsupervised learning, semi-supervised learning, and reinforcement learning. It introduced a brief history of deep learning and the popular types of deep learning networks, such as AlexNet, GoogLeNet, and ResNet. Finally, you looked at a series of Java examples for neural networks, for machine learning, and for deep learning, and you looked at the TensorFlow machine learning library for Java.

8.12   Chapter Review Questions

Q8.1.   What is artificial intelligence?

Q8.2.   What are the three types of artificial intelligence?

Q8.3.   What are the three stages of development for artificial intelligence?

Q8.4.   What are neural networks?

Q8.5.   What is a perceptron?

Q8.6.   What are multilayer perceptrons (MLPs)?

Q8.7.   What are feedforward networks?

Q8.8.   What is machine learning? What are the different types of machine learning?

Q8.9.   What is deep learning?

Q8.10.   Do some research on convolutional neural networks (CNNs). What are the key features of CNNs?

Q8.11.   Do some research on recurrent neural networks (RNNs). What are the key features of RNNs?

Java Programming for Cybersecurity Applications

"Security depends not so much upon how much you have, as upon how much you can do without."

—Joseph Wood Krutch

9.1 What Is Cybersecurity?

Cybersecurity is about threats from the Internet. As our lives become increasingly dependent on the Internet, cybersecurity is also becoming increasingly important. A recent example is the WannaCry virus attack in 2017, which affected more than 200,000 computers across 150 countries. The WannaCry virus targeted older

Windows operating systems; it locked the affected computers and demanded ransom payments in the Bitcoin cryptocurrency. Hospitals with infected computers had to cancel operations, and factories had to halt production. Another example is the hacking of TalkTalk, a British telecommunication firm, in 2015 by a 15-year-old schoolboy in Northern Ireland. Thousands of customers' online details were stolen. The boy claimed he did this just to show off to friends. TalkTalk said the hack cost the firm £42m and lost 98,000 broadband customers.

In this era of digital technologies, cybersecurity is of paramount importance. This chapter will first introduce the key terms and technologies used in cybersecurity and then show some Java programming examples for cybersecurity applications.

Cybersecurity addresses the following key aspects:

Confidentiality   *Confidentiality* means that the information transmitted between senders and receivers should be accessible only to the corresponding parties.

Authentication   *Authentication* means determining that the information you're getting is from the source it claims to come from.

Integrity   *Integrity* means that the information you have accessed must be original, intact, and complete.

Availability   Availability means that the information you are authorized to access is always accessible.

The commonly used approach to improving cybersecurity is encryption.

9.2   What Is Encryption?

Encryption is one of the oldest security techniques; it dates back at least to the Roman era, when a cipher encryption, now known as the Caesar cipher, was named after the emperor Julius Caesar. In this simple *shift cipher,* letters in the text are shifted a fixed number of places down the alphabet to make them unreadable.

For example, if you shift each letter three places to the left in the alphabet, the following clear text:

```
attack london
```

will become the following:

```
xqqxzh ilkalk
```

The result is initially unreadable, but this kind of encryption is easy to decrypt. Modern encryption uses far more sophisticated and advanced mathematical algorithms that are much more secure. Modern encryption techniques can be classified as either *private key encryption* (also called *symmetric key encryption*) or *public key encryption* (also called *asymmetric key encryption*). The technical field of study underlying encryption and secure communication is known as *cryptography*.

9.2.1 Private Key Encryption

In private key encryption, the sender and the receiver use the same key to encrypt the message and to decrypt the message, as illustrated in Figure 9.1. You can imagine the private key as simply a sequence of random numbers. Because both parties use the same key, this is also called *symmetric key encryption*.

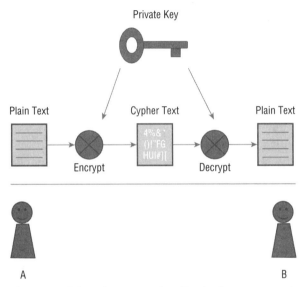

Figure 9.1: Private key encryption. Sender A uses a secret key to encrypt the plain text into cipher text. Receiver B will use the same secret key to decrypt the cipher text back to plain text.

The most popular private key encryption is Advanced Encryption Standard (AES), also known as Rijndael, developed by Belgian cryptographers Vincent Rijmen and Joan Daemen. In AES, plain text is divided into 128-bit blocks. The secret key, which can be 128, 192, or 256 bits, is expanded into several round keys through a key expansion algorithm. The combined plain text and the corresponding round keys are then put through several rounds of mathematical operations, such as adding the round key (AddRoundKey), substituting bytes (SubBytes), shifting rows (ShiftRows), and mixing columns (MixColumns). The number of rounds depends on the key size: 10 rounds for 128-bit keys, 12 rounds for 192-bit keys, and 14 rounds for 256-bit keys. The cipher text will appear at the end. The beauty of this scheme is that encryption and decryption are the same operation but in reverse order, as illustrated in Figure 9.2.

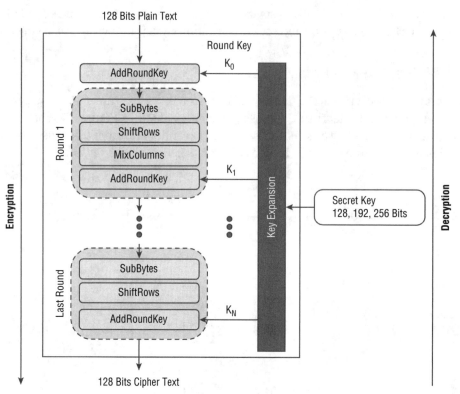

128 Bits Plain Text

Figure 9.2: The operation of AES. The encryption and decryption are the same operation but in reverse order.

To date, AES is more secure and more widely used than any other algorithms, including Data Encryption Standard (DES), Triple DES, Twofish, and so on. Cracking an AES 256-bit encryption by brute force—that is, searching 2^{256} possibilities—would take an estimated 3×10^{51} years even by 50 supercomputers that could check a billion billion (10^{18}) AES keys per second.

The advantage of secret key encryption is that it is secure and can be used for large volumes of text. The disadvantage is that both the sender and the receiver need to use the same key, so key distribution is always an issue.

See the following resources for more information about AES:

https://parsiya.net/blog/2015-01-06-tales-from-the-crypto---leaking-aes-keys/

https://www.tutorialspoint.com/cryptography/advanced_encryption_standard.htm

https://iis-people.ee.ethz.ch/~kgf/acacia/c3.html#tth_sEc3.2

9.2.2   Public Key Encryption

In contrast to private key encryption, with public key encryption the sender and receiver use different keys to encrypt the message and to decrypt the message, as illustrated Figure 9.3. First, everyone needs to generate a pair of their own keys, one private key and one public key. They will keep the private key to themselves and give the public key to everyone else. Then, if A wants to send a secret message to B only, A will use B's public key to encrypt the message, and B will use B's private key to decrypt the message. In this case, only B can decrypt the message. Because senders and receivers use different keys, this is also called *asymmetric key encryption*. The beauty of this encryption method is that there is no key distribution issue; others can never figure out what your private key is from your public key.

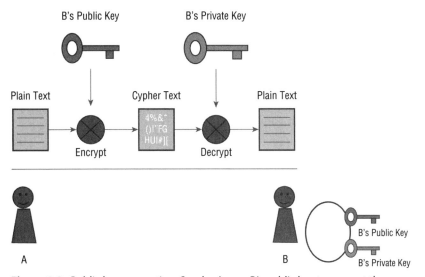

Figure 9.3: Public key encryption. Sender A uses B's public key to encrypt the message, and receiver B uses B's private key to decrypt the message.

Public key encryption can also be used for authentication purposes. For example, to prove that the message is coming from A, sender A can encrypt the message using A's private key, and receiver B will know it is indeed coming from A if B can decrypt the message using A's public key, as shown in Figure 9.4.

The most popular public key encryption is Rivest–Shamir–Adelman (RSA), designed by Ron Rivest, Adi Shamir, and Leonard Adelman in 1977. The RSA algorithm involves three key steps: key generation, encryption, and decryption.

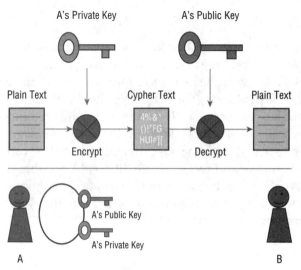

Figure 9.4: Public key encryption for authentication. Sender A uses A's private key to encrypt the message, and receiver B uses A's public key to decrypt the message. This proves the message is coming from A.

Key Generation

Select two distinct prime numbers p and q.

Calculate $n = p \times q$.

Calculate $z = (p - 1) \times (q - 1)$.

Select integer e, where $gcd(z, e) = 1; 1 < e < z;$.

Select integer d, so that $(e \times d - 1)$ is exactly divisible by z.

Public key: (n, e).

Private key: (n, d).

Here **gcd** is the greatest common divisor, and **mod** is the modulus operator, which calculates the remainder of the division of two numbers. The public key is (n, e), and the private key is (n, d).

Encryption

Plain text: $M (< n)$

Cipher text: $C = M^e \, mod \, n$

Decryption

Cipher text: C

Cipher text: $M = C^d \, mod \, n$

Let's use an example to illustrate how RSA work. To create your public and private keys, you need to pick two distinct prime numbers, $p = 11$, and $q = 19$. Then calculate $n = p \times q = 11 \times 19 = 209$, calculate $z = (p - 1) \times (q - 1) = 10 \times 18 = 180$, select $e = 13$ so that the greatest common divisor of z and e is one, and finally select $d = 97$, as $97 \times 13 - 1 = 1260 = 180 \times 7$. Your public key is $(209, 13)$, and your private key is $(209, 97)$.

Imagine you want to send the number 5 (letters can also be treated as numbers) to encrypt the plain-text M ($M = 5$). Using the public key, you can have the cipher text $C = M^e \bmod n = 5^{13} \bmod 209 = 169$. This is the cipher text you send out. To decrypt the cipher message, you have $M = C^d \bmod n = 169^{97} \bmod 209 = 5$.

Ta-da! The original message! It can also work the other way around; that is, you can encrypt the message with the private key and decrypt it using the public key. This is the beauty of mathematics at its best.

The advantage of public key encryption is the ease of key management. Everyone can publish their public keys while keeping the private keys secret. There are no security issues in this process. The disadvantage of public key encryption is that it is computationally expensive, as it needs to calculate the power of the numbers. Public key encryption cannot work on large texts.

So, in reality, public key encryption and private key encryption are often used together. A sender first uses public key encryption to set up the connection and shares a temporary session private key. This temporary session private key is randomly generated and valid only for the current session. Then the two parties will use this shared temporary session private key encryption to encrypt the subsequent messages, as illustrated in Figure 9.5.

Figure 9.6 shows an interesting online RSA key generator (`http://travis-tidwell.com/jsencrypt/demo/`), where you can generate a pair of private and public keys of different size, give a plain-text message, and convert it into a cypher text.

9.3 Hash Functions and Message Digests

A *hash function* is one that can turn a large, long text message into a short, fixed-length message, called a *message digest*, as illustrated in Figure 9.7. Hash functions and message digests are important and are widely used in cryptography. The simplest hash function is a checksum calculation, in which the long message is first cut into many small pieces of the same fixed length, and then all the pieces are added together. A hash function is a many-to-one function; and one important feature is that when the long text message changes, the short message digest will also change. With hash functions and message digests we can introduce the concept of *digital signatures* and *digital certificates*.

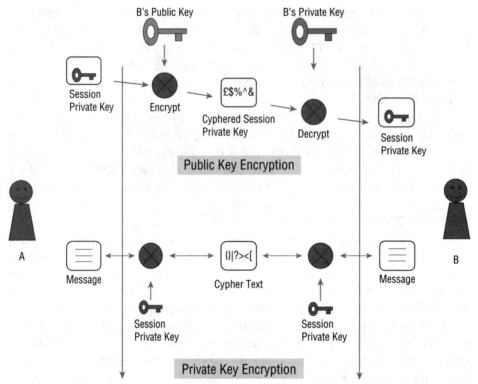

Figure 9.5: Sender A first uses public key encryption to share a temporary session private key with receiver B. Then A and B can use private key encryption to encrypt all their subsequent messages using the shared temporary private key.

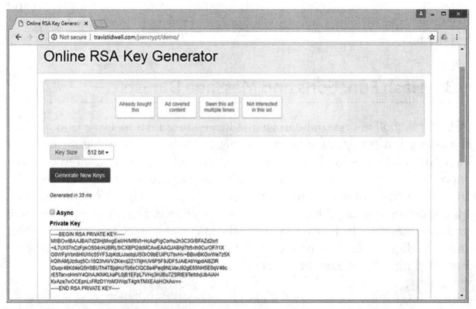

Figure 9.6: An online RSA key generator

Long Text (M)

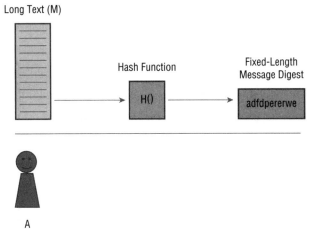

A

Figure 9.7: A long message is turned into a short fixed-length message digest using a hash function.

One of the most commonly used hash functions is Secure Hash Algorithm (SHA), designed by the United States National Security Agency (NSA). There are three versions: SHA-1, the original version; SHA-2, the second version, currently in use; and SHA-3, the planned newest version. SHA-2 supports hash values of 224, 256, 384, or 512 bits in length. The most commonly used are SHA-256 and SHA-512. For example, Bitcoin, the most popular cryptocurrency, uses SHA-256 for verifying transactions and calculating proof of work. More details about cryptocurrency and the use of hash functions can be found in the next chapter.

Figure 9.8 shows an interesting online SHA-256 hash generator, where you can type in the text, and it will generate corresponding hash values (`https://passwordsgenerator.net/sha256-hash-generator/`).

Another widely used hash function is the message-digest algorithm (MD5), version 5. MD5 was initially designed as a cryptographic hash function, but because of its many vulnerabilities, MD5 is commonly used as a checksum to verify data integrity. MD5 produces a 128-bit hash value. When you download files from the Internet, many web sites also provide the corresponding MD5 message digest for you to check the integrity of the downloaded files.

9.4   Digital Signatures

When you write a paper letter, you sign it at the bottom to prove that you have written the letter. So, how do you sign a digital text message? The answer is to use a digital signature, as illustrated in Figure 9.9. When sender A wants to send a long text message to receiver B, sender A uses a hash function to generate a message digest from the long text message, then uses A's private key to encrypt the message digest to create the digital signature. The combined long text and digital signature are then sent to receiver B.

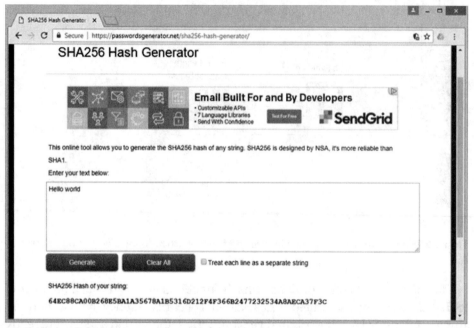

Figure 9.8: An online SHA256 hash generator

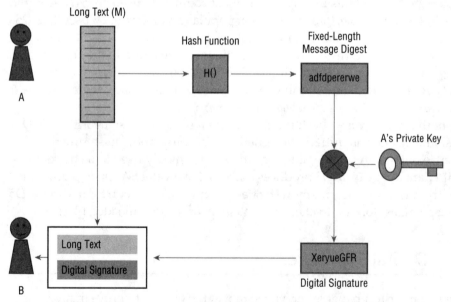

Figure 9.9: When sender A wants to send a long text message, A uses a hash function to generate a message digest and then uses A's private key to encrypt the message digest to create the digital signature. The combined long text and digital signature are then sent to receiver B.

When receiver B receives the combined message, it first separates out the long text message and digital signature and then uses the same hash function to generate a message digest and uses A's public key to decrypt the message digest from the digital signature. Finally, receiver B compares the calculated message digest with the received message digest. If the two match, then you know the message is authentic; otherwise it is fake, as shown in Figure 9.10.

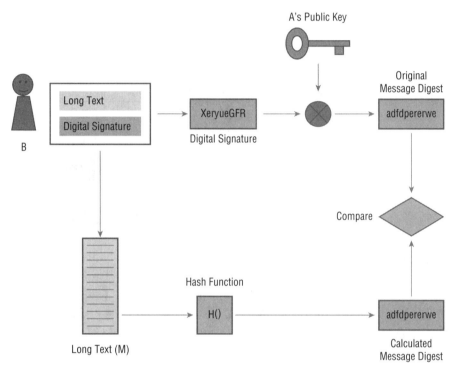

Figure 9.10: When receiver B receives the combined message, it first separates out the long text message and digital signature and then uses the same hash function to generate a message digest and uses A's public key to decrypt the message digest from the digital signature. Finally, receiver B compares the calculated message digest with the received message digest.

9.5 Digital Certificates

When you receive a public key from someone, how do you know it is the true public key from that person? The answer is to use *digital certificates*. ITU X.509, developed by International Telecommunications Union (ITU) in 1988, is the most commonly used digital certificate standard. ITU X.509 certificates are used in many Internet protocols, including Hyper Text Transfer Protocol Secure (HTTPS), which is the secure version of Hypertext Transfer Protocol (HTTP). While HTTP is for standard World Wide Web (WWW) services, HTTPS is for online banking, online shopping, and so on, where secure communications are required.

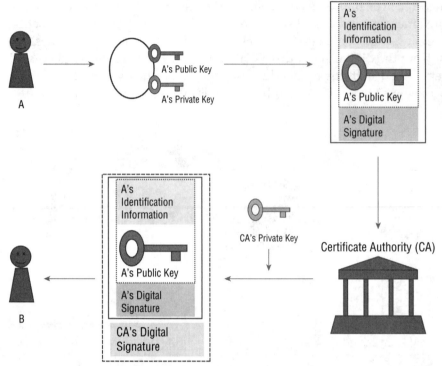

Figure 9.11: The operation of ITU X.509 digital certificate standard

Figure 9.11 shows how ITU X.509 digital certificates work. In this case, you need a third party, called the *certificate authority* (CA), that both A and B can trust.

If sender A wants a signed digital certificate, sender A needs to do this via a certificate signing request (CSR), using the following steps:

1. Sender A generates a pair of keys (a private key and a public key).

2. Sender A sends A's identification information (name, organization, address, and so on) and A's public key to CA. A also signs this message using A's private key.

3. The CA verifies A's information and A's public key and then uses CA's private key to generate a digital signature.

4. The CA combines A's original message with its own signature, creating what is called a *digital certificate*, and sends them to receiver B.

When receiver B receives the digital certificate, receiver B will then be able to get sender A's information and public key with the CA's public key using the steps shown in Figure 9.9 earlier.

Figure 9.12 shows the contents of an ITU X.509 digital certificate.

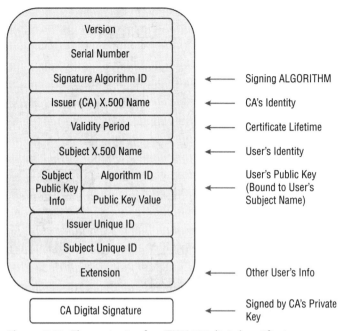

Version		
Serial Number		
Signature Algorithm ID	←	Signing ALGORITHM
Issuer (CA) X.500 Name	←	CA's Identity
Validity Period	←	Certificate Lifetime
Subject X.500 Name	←	User's Identity
Subject Public Key Info	Algorithm ID	← User's Public Key (Bound to User's Subject Name)
	Public Key Value	
Issuer Unique ID		
Subject Unique ID		
Extension	←	Other User's Info
CA Digital Signature	←	Signed by CA's Private Key

Figure 9.12: The contents of an ITU X.509 digital certificate

9.6   Case Study 1: Secure Email

Next, you will look at two case studies demonstrating how to use the encryption technologies in real life. The first example is secure email. Traditional email sends and receives a message as clear, plain text. However, this is not desirable for business communications, where messages need to be sent and received securely. You can secure your emails by using Pretty Good Privacy (PGP), an encryption program that was developed by Phil Zimmermann in 1991. PGP is mainly used for encrypting, decrypting, and signing emails or files. PGP follows the OpenPGP standard (RFC 4880) for encrypting and decrypting data. In PGP, the sender uses a randomly generated key to encrypt the email (or data) and uses receiver's public key and RSA algorithm to encrypt the randomly generated key. The sender then sends both to receiver. The receiver uses its private key and RSA algorithm to decrypt the randomly generated key, and then it uses the randomly generated key to decrypt the email (or data). Figure 9.13 shows how PGP works (`https://en.wikipedia.org/wiki/Pretty _ Good _ Privacy`).

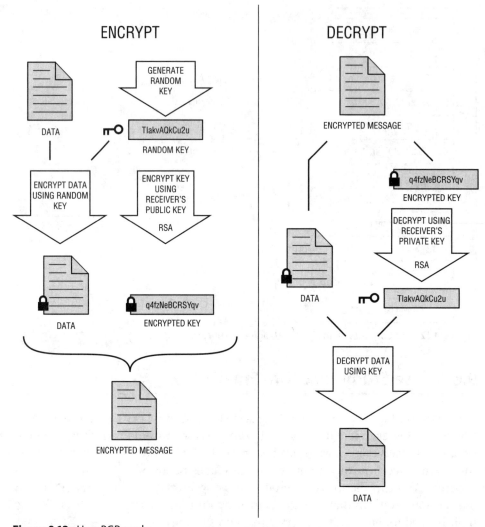

Figure 9.13: How PGP works

9.7 Case Study 2: Secure Web

The second example is secure web. Like email, traditional web services, built on the HTTP, use clear, plain text to send and receive messages. Again, this is not desirable for business applications such as online banking and online shopping. This is where Transport Layer Security (TLS) and its predecessor, Secure Sockets Layer (SSL), are needed. Secure web uses HTTPS based on TLS or SSL to provide secure web communications. The following are the steps.

1. The web client sends a ClientHello message to the web server; the message contents include the highest TLS protocol version the client supports, a random number, and a list of preferred encryption methods.

2. The web server replies with a ServerHello message, which includes the chosen TLS protocol version and the encryption method, all from the choices offered by the client. It also includes a random number and the web server's digital certificate. The digital certificate includes the web server's public key and is certified by a CA.

3. The web server sends a ServerHelloDone message, indicating the conclusion of this initial handshake.

4. The web client has a list of entrusted CAs and a public key for each CA. First, the web client verifies the web server's digital certificate and generates a symmetric session key. Then the web client encrypts the key with the web server's public key and sends the encrypted symmetric session key to the web server.

5. The web server decrypts the symmetric session key using its private key.

6. The web client sends another message to indicate that all subsequent messages will be encrypted with the symmetric session key.

7. The web server replies with a message to confirm that all future messages will be encrypted with the same symmetric session key.

8. The web client and web server can now securely communicate with encrypted messages.

9.8   Java Private Key Encryption Example

Example 9.1 is a Java program demonstrating encryption and decryption using a private key—a symmetric key. It is based on a code example from the following web site:

```
http://jexp.ru/index.php/Java _ Tutorial/Security/Key _ Generator
```

It first generates a private key based on the AES algorithm, and then encrypts and decrypts a clear text message, "Hello World." It also displays the private key information. Figure 9.14 shows the compilation and execution of the program.

EXAMPLE 9.1   JAVA PRIVATE KEY ENCRYPTION

```
//Example 9.1 Private Key Encryption
//Modified from
//http://jexp.ru/index.php/Java_Tutorial/Security/Key_Generator
import java.security.*;
import javax.crypto.*;

public class PrivateKeyDemo1 {
  static String algorithm = "AES";
  static Key key ;
```

```
static Cipher cipher;
public static void main(String[] args) throws Exception {
  key = KeyGenerator.getInstance(algorithm).generateKey();
  cipher = Cipher.getInstance(algorithm);
  String text="Hello World";
  byte[] encryptionBytes = encrypt(text);
  System.out.println("Original Text:   " + text);
  System.out.println("Key: " + key.toString());
  System.out.println("Encrypted Text: " + encrypt(text));
  System.out.println("Decrypted Text: " + decrypt(encryptionBytes));
}
private static byte[] encrypt(String input) throws Exception  {
  cipher.init(Cipher.ENCRYPT_MODE, key);
  byte[] inputBytes = input.getBytes();
  return cipher.doFinal(inputBytes);
}
private static String decrypt(byte[] encryptionBytes) throws Exception
{
  cipher.init(Cipher.DECRYPT_MODE, key);
  byte[] recoveredBytes = cipher.doFinal(encryptionBytes);
  String recovered = new String(recoveredBytes);
  return recovered;
}
}
```

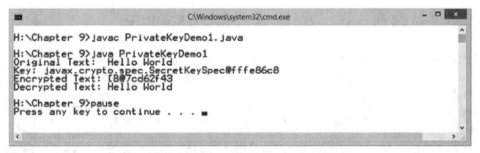

Figure 9.14: The compilation and execution of the `PrivateKeyDemo1.java` program

9.9   Java Public Key Encryption Example

Example 9.2 is a Java program demonstrating encryption and decryption using asymmetric keys. It is based on a code example from the following web site:

http://www.javacirecep.com/java-security/java-rsa-encryption-decryption-example/

It first generates a public/private key pair based on the RSA algorithm and then encrypts a clear text message, "Hello World," using the public key, and then decrypts the message using the private key. It also displays the public/

private key information. Figure 9.15 shows the compilation and execution of the program.

EXAMPLE 9.2   JAVA PUBLIC KEY ENCRYPTION

```
//Example 9.2 Java Public Key Encryption
//Modified from:
//http://www.javacirecep.com/java-security/
java-rsa-encryption-decryption-example/

import java.security.*;
import javax.crypto.*;
import java.util.*;

public class PublicKeyDemo1 {
    private static KeyPair keyPair;
    private static String algorithm = "RSA"; //DSA DH etc
    public static void main(String[] args) throws Exception{
        KeyPairGenerator keyPairGenerator = KeyPairGenerator.
getInstance(algorithm);
        keyPairGenerator.initialize(1024);
        keyPair = keyPairGenerator.generateKeyPair();
         final Cipher cipher = Cipher.getInstance(algorithm);
        final String plaintext = "Hello World";

        System.out.println("Public Key = " + keyPair.getPublic().
toString());
        System.out.println("Private Key = " + keyPair.getPrivate().
toString());

        // ENCRYPT using the PUBLIC key
        cipher.init(Cipher.ENCRYPT_MODE, keyPair.getPublic());
        byte[] encryptedBytes = cipher.doFinal(plaintext.getBytes());
        String ciphertext = new String(Base64.getEncoder().
encode(encryptedBytes));
        System.out.println("encrypted (ciphertext) = " + ciphertext);

        // DECRYPT using the PRIVATE key
        cipher.init(Cipher.DECRYPT_MODE, keyPair.getPrivate());
        byte[] ciphertextBytes = Base64.getDecoder().decode(ciphertext.
getBytes());
        byte[] decryptedBytes = cipher.doFinal(ciphertextBytes);
        String decryptedString = new String(decryptedBytes);
        System.out.println("decrypted (plaintext) = " +
decryptedString);
    }
}
```

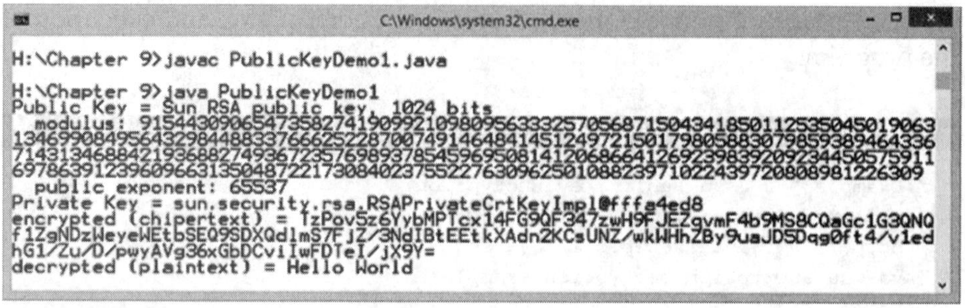

Figure 9.15: The compilation and execution of the `PublicKeyDemo1.java` program

For more examples of using Java for asymmetric cryptography, please visit the following resources:

> https://www.mkyong.com/java/java-asymmetric-cryptography-example/
>
> https://www.devglan.com/java8/rsa-encryption-decryption-java
>
> https://javadigest.wordpress.com/2012/08/26/rsa-encryption-example/

9.10   Java Digital Signature/Message Digest Example

Example 9.3 shows how to create a message digest using the SHA-256 hash function in Java. Figure 9.16 shows the compilation and execution of the program.

EXAMPLE 9.3   JAVA MESSAGE DIGEST

```
//Example 9.3 Java Message Digest

import java.security.MessageDigest;
public class MessageDigestDemo1 {
  public static void main(String[] args) throws Exception {
    String stringToEncrypt="Hello World";
    MessageDigest messageDigest = MessageDigest.getInstance("SHA-256");
    messageDigest.update(stringToEncrypt.getBytes());
    String encryptedString = new String(messageDigest.digest());
    System.out.println("Original Text: " + stringToEncrypt);
    System.out.println("Message Digest: " + encryptedString);
  }
}
```

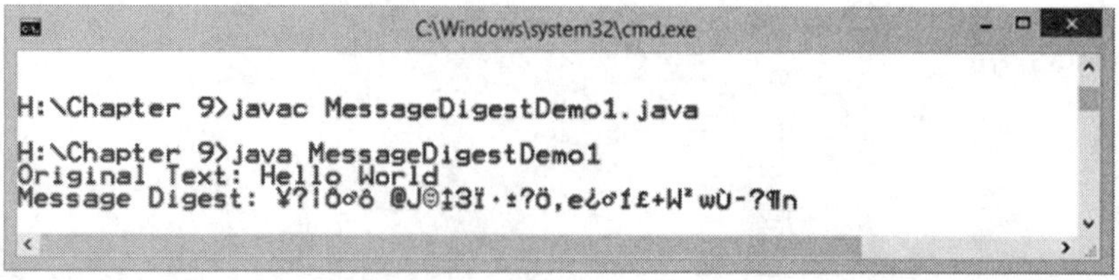

Figure 9.16: The compilation and execution of the `MessageDigestDemo1.java` program

Example 9.4 shows a variation of the previous application. Here a `bytesTo-Hex()` method is used to convert the message digest into hex values. Figure 9.17 shows the compilation and execution of the program.

EXAMPLE 9.4   JAVA MESSAGE DIGEST 2

```
//Example 9.4 Java Message Digest 2

import java.security.MessageDigest;
public class MessageDigestDemo2 {
  public static void main(String[] args) throws Exception {
    String stringToEncrypt="Hello World";
    MessageDigest messageDigest = MessageDigest.getInstance("SHA-256");
    byte[] encodedhash = messageDigest.digest(stringToEncrypt.
getBytes());
    String encryptedString = bytesToHex(encodedhash);
    System.out.println("Original Text: " + stringToEncrypt);
    System.out.println("Message Digest: " + encryptedString);
  }
  private static String bytesToHex(byte[] hash) {
    StringBuffer hexString = new StringBuffer();
    for (int i = 0; i < hash.length; i++) {
    String hex = Integer.toHexString(0xff & hash[i]);
    if(hex.length() == 1) hexString.append('0');
        hexString.append(hex);
    }
    return hexString.toString();
  }
}
```

Figure 9.17: The compilation and execution of the `MessageDigestDemo2.java` program

Example 9.5 is a Java program demonstrating digital signatures. It is based on examples from the following web site:

http://tutorials.jenkov.com/java-cryptography/signature.html

It first generates a public/private key pair and uses the private key to create a digital signature based on the SHA256WithDSA algorithm and then uses the digital signature to sign a clear text message, "Hello World," and finally uses the public key to create another digital signature to validate the original signature. This process is similar to the diagram shown in Figure 9.18 (https://en.wikipedia.org/wiki/Digital_signature).

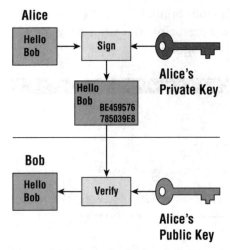

Figure 9.18: Example of using digital signatures to verify a message

EXAMPLE 9.5   JAVA DIGITAL SIGNATURE

```
//Example 9.5 Java Digital Signature
//created based on examples from
//http://tutorials.jenkov.com/java-cryptography/signature.html
import java.security.*;
public class DigitalSignatureDemo1 {
  public static void main(String[] args) throws Exception {
    String m = "Hello World";
    Signature signature = Signature.getInstance("SHA256WithDSA");
    SecureRandom secureRandom = new SecureRandom();
    KeyPairGenerator keyPairGenerator = KeyPairGenerator.
getInstance("DSA");
    KeyPair keyPair = keyPairGenerator.generateKeyPair();

    //initialize the digital signature
    signature.initSign(keyPair.getPrivate(), secureRandom);
    byte[] data = m.getBytes("UTF-8");
    signature.update(data);
    byte[] digitalSignature = signature.sign();
    System.out.println("Create Digital Signature: " + digitalSignature.
toString());

    Signature signature2 = Signature.getInstance("SHA256WithDSA");
    signature2.initVerify(keyPair.getPublic());
    byte[] data2 = m.getBytes("UTF-8");
    signature2.update(data2);
```

```
        boolean verified = signature2.verify(digitalSignature);
        System.out.println("signature verifies: " + verified);
    }
}
```

Figure 9.19 shows the compilation and execution of the program.

Figure 9.19: The compilation and execution of the `DigitalSignatureDemo1.java` program

More examples of digital signatures are available from

`https://www.mkyong.com/java/java-digital-signatures-example/`

Figure 9.20 shows an illustrative online private key encryption demonstration tool from Tools4noobs (`https://www.tools4noobs.com/online_tools/encrypt/`), which has two pages, one for encrypting the message and one for decrypting the message. You can choose your key values, choose the message content, and choose the algorithms for the encryption and decryption.

Figure 9.21 shows a public-key encryption demo from the Computer Science Department of the University of Georgia in the United States (`http://cobweb.cs.uga.edu/~dme/csci6300/Encryption/Crypto.html`).

Figure 9.22 shows an online RSA key generator demo from Travis Tidwell, in which you can specify the key size, 512, 1024, 2048, or 4096 bits (`http://travis-tidwell.com/jsencrypt/demo/`).

Figure 9.23 shows an interesting JavaScript-based online hash function demo, which implements the entire family of SHA hashes as defined in FIPS PUB 180-4 and FIPS PUB 202 (SHA-1, SHA-224, SHA3-224, SHA-256, SHA3-256, SHA-384, SHA3-384, SHA-512, SHA3-512, SHAKE128, and SHAKE256) (`https://caligatio.github.io/jsSHA/`).

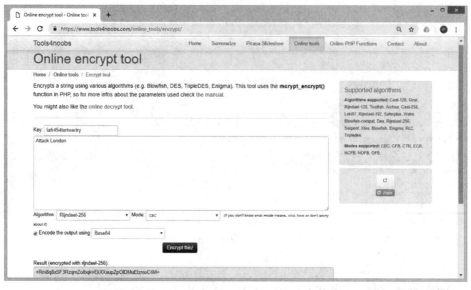

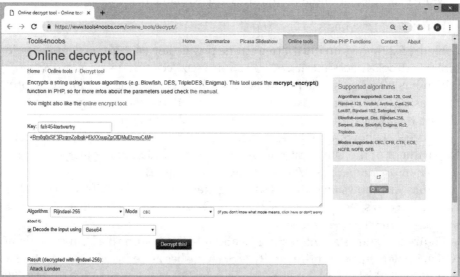

Figure 9.20: The online private key encryption tool from Tools4noobs, which has two pages, one for encrypting the message (top) and one for decrypting the message (bottom)

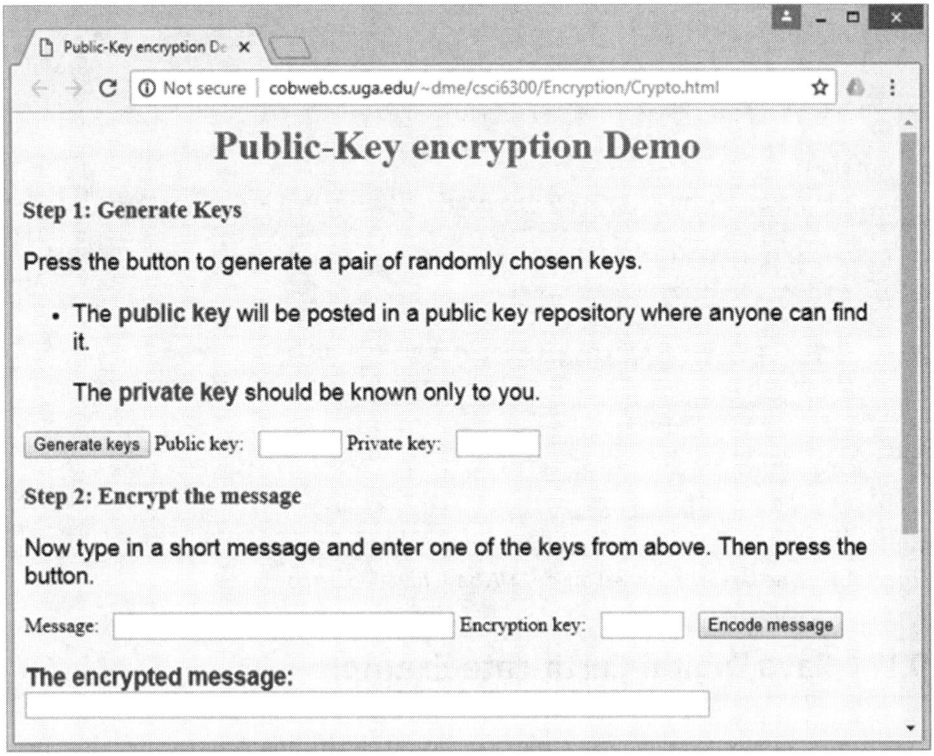

Figure 9.21: The public-key encryption demo

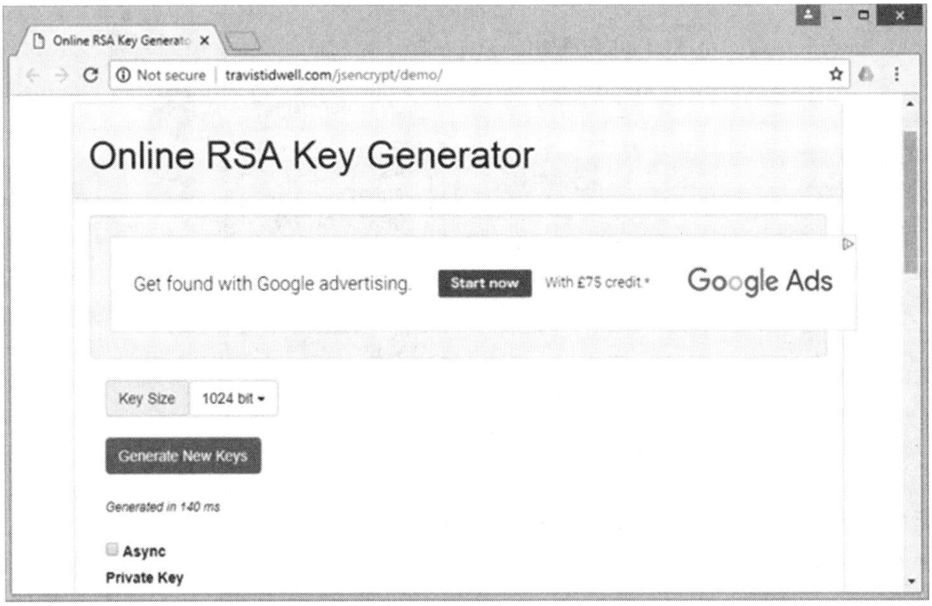

Figure 9.22: The online RSA key generator demo

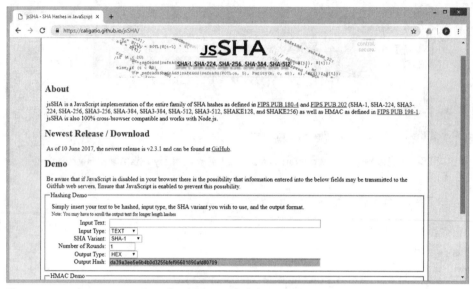

Figure 9.23: The JavaScript-based online SHA hash function demo

9.11   Java Digital Certificate Example

Figure 9.24 shows a typical example of a digital certificate. A user provides their details and the public key to the certificate authority and gets the corresponding certificate.

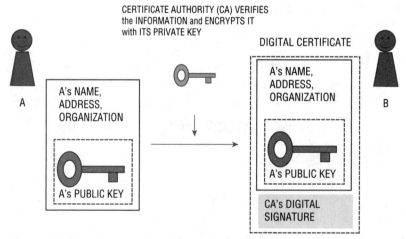

Figure 9.24: The digital certificate for a user and its public key

In Java you can create a digital certificate using the `keytool` command from the SUN certificate authority. Take the following steps to try an example:

1. Create a self-signed server digital certificate by typing the following command all on one line. It uses RSA to generate the public key, the server alias is LSBU, the store password is `storepassword`, the store type is PKCS12, and the Java key store file name is `keystore.pfx`. The filename extension for PKCS12 files is `.pfx` or `.p12`.

   ```
   keytool -genkey -alias LSBU -keyalg RSA -storepass storepassword
   -storetype PKCS12 -keystore keystore.pfx
   ```

   When you press Enter, `keytool` prompts you to enter the server name, organizational unit, organization, locality, state, and country code. You must type the server name in response to `keytool`'s first prompt, in which it asks for first and last names; in this case, it is www.lsbu.ac.uk. See Figure 9.25 for the details.

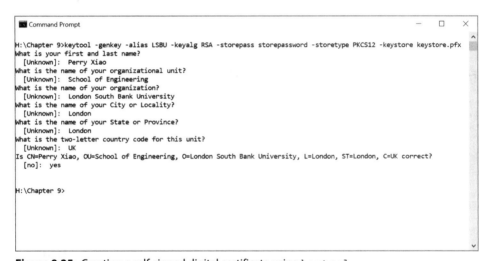

Figure 9.25: Creating a self-signed digital certificate using `keytool`

2. Use the following command to verify the `keystore` file generated. Figure 9.26 shows the output.

   ```
   keytool -list -v -keystore keystore.pfx -storetype pkcs12
   ```

3. Export the generated self-signed server certificate in the `keystore.pfx` file into the `server.cer` file, as shown in Figure 9.27.

   ```
   keytool -export -alias LSBU -storepass storepassword -file server.cer
   -keystore keystore.pfx -storetype pkcs12
   ```

```
H:\Chapter 9>keytool -list -v -keystore keystore.pfx -storetype pkcs12
Enter keystore password:
Keystore type: PKCS12
Keystore provider: SUN

Your keystore contains 1 entry

Alias name: lsbu
Creation date: 9 Apr 2019
Entry type: PrivateKeyEntry
Certificate chain length: 1
Certificate[1]:
Owner: CN=Perry Xiao, OU=School of Engineering, O=London South Bank University, L=London, ST=London, C=UK
Issuer: CN=Perry Xiao, OU=School of Engineering, O=London South Bank University, L=London, ST=London, C=UK
Serial number: 75067fd6
Valid from: Tue Apr 09 08:10:44 CST 2019 until: Mon Jul 08 08:10:44 CST 2019
Certificate fingerprints:
     SHA1: 9F:75:65:87:1D:71:87:49:D3:10:58:88:E7:C0:03:53:BA:37:BD:10
     SHA256: 8D:13:49:5F:F0:2A:82:FA:B2:67:5A:20:7C:F4:CA:C7:DA:E5:E8:AE:72:32:C0:87:DA:38:F9:AD:26:BD:41:0B
Signature algorithm name: SHA256withRSA
Subject Public Key Algorithm: 2048-bit RSA key
Version: 3

Extensions:

#1: ObjectId: 2.5.29.14 Criticality=false
SubjectKeyIdentifier [
KeyIdentifier [
0000: 0D 9A 2B BD A4 11 31 4D   E4 11 9D 6A C6 35 99 2C  ..+...1M...j.5.,
0010: 83 C3 BD 82                                        ....
]
]
```

Figure 9.26: Verifying the digital certificate store file using `keytool`

```
H:\Chapter 9>keytool -export -alias LSBU -storepass storepassword -file server.cer -keystore keystore.pfx -storetype pkc
s12
Certificate stored in file <server.cer>

H:\Chapter 9>
```

Figure 9.27: Exporting the generated self-signed server certificate in the `keystore.pfx` file into the `server.cer` file using `keytool`

4. Add the server certificate to the `truststore` file `cacerts.pfx`. Type **yes** when prompted, and press Enter, as shown in Figure 9.28.

```
keytool -import -v -trustcacerts -alias LSBU -file server.cer
-keystore cacerts.pfx -storepass storepassword -storetype pkcs12
```

Example 9.6 shows the Java program to read information from the `keystore.jks` file. Figure 9.29 shows the beginning and the ending of the output of the program; the full output is too large to display.

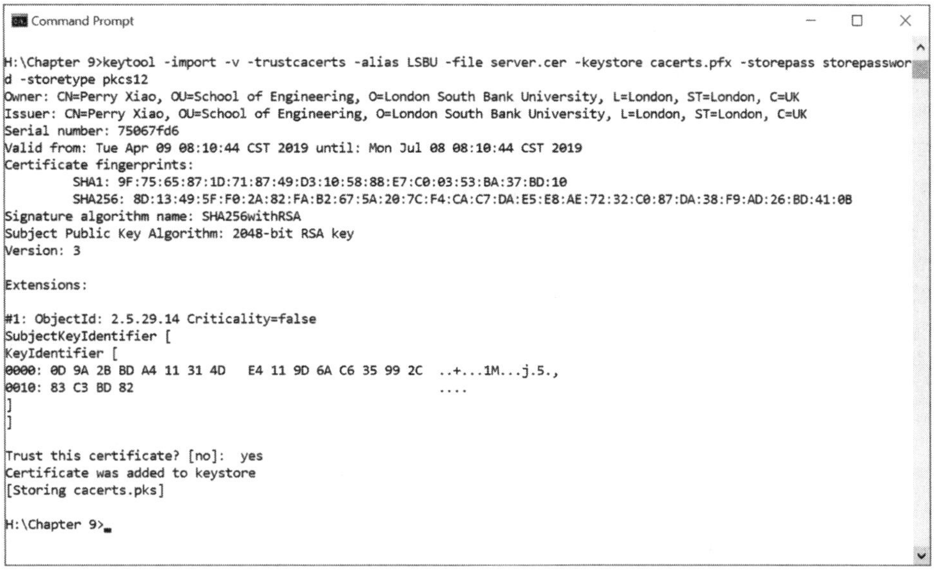

Figure 9.28: Adding the server certificate to the `truststore` file `cacerts.pfx` using `keytool`

EXAMPLE 9.6   JAVA KEY STORE

```java
//Example 9.6 Java Key Store
import java.io.FileInputStream;
import java.security.*;
import java.security.cert.Certificate;

public class PKCS12Example {
  public static void main(String[] argv) throws Exception {
    String storefile ="keystore.pfx";
    String alias = "LSBU";
    String storepass ="storepassword";

    FileInputStream is = new FileInputStream(storefile);
    KeyStore keystore = KeyStore.getInstance("PKCS12");
    keystore.load(is, storepass.toCharArray());

    Key key = keystore.getKey(alias, storepass.toCharArray());
    if (key instanceof PrivateKey) {
      // Get certificate of public key
      Certificate cert = keystore.getCertificate(alias);
```

```
        System.out.println(cert.toString());
        // Get public key
        PublicKey publicKey = cert.getPublicKey();
        System.out.println(publicKey.toString());
        // Return a key pair
        KeyPair kp = new KeyPair(publicKey, (PrivateKey) key);
        System.out.println(kp.toString());
    }
  }
}
```

For more details on digital certificates using `keytool`, see the following Oracle article:

```
https://docs.oracle.com/cd/E19798-01/821-1841/gjrgy/
```

Figure 9.30 shows how to view the certificate of a web site in the Google Chrome browser. Just click the lock icon next to the web site URL, and select Certificate.

Figure 9.31 shows how to view a list of trusted CAs in the Google Chrome browser. From the top-right corner of the browser, select Settings ➪ Advanced ➪ Privacy And Security ➪ Manage Certificates.

9.12   Other Java Examples

Here are some other Java examples:

The following is the web site of the book *Beginning Cryptography with Java*, by David Hook (Wrox, 2005). This book gives an interesting introduction to cryptography, illustrated with simple Java code, and is suitable for beginners.

```
www.wrox.com/WileyCDA/WroxTitle/productCd-0764596330,descCd-DOWNLOAD
.html
```

The following is the corresponding GitHub web site of the book, where you can download all the Java example code:

```
https://github.com/boeboe/be.boeboe.spongycastle
```

The Java example code in *Beginning Cryptography with Java* is developed by using the Legion of the Bouncy Castle Java Cryptography APIs:

```
https://www.bouncycastle.org/java.html
```

The following is a comprehensive Java security tutorial from Java2S:

```
www.java2s.com/Tutorial/Java/0490 _ _ Security/Catalog0490 _ _ Security
.htm
```

```
Command Prompt                                                          —    □    ×

H:\Chapter 9>javac PKCS12Example.java

H:\Chapter 9>java PKCS12Example
[
[
  Version: V3
  Subject: CN=Perry Xiao, OU=School of Engineering, O=London South Bank University, L=London, ST=London, C=UK
  Signature Algorithm: SHA256withRSA, OID = 1.2.840.113549.1.1.11

  Key:  Sun RSA public key, 2048 bits
  modulus: 21784245738210549611025619537078407056017077257886662295959724838066175485107207154428480842915872838460
6151618511527602743584721393054248472250502924686519411311146869285909288018453546217959962252649356064937360195094
5110155462749076161831348454452402730737740563192209773766868108066042678362194900578695768118140100881961928927169
3879328396194423820405092074715740765558418543773920884207923142189080883228911622328821396738487562888576254164602
3078376122139298312612349219871511246775769033158361883167427687735318802536483628655860150152776897351078572972752
47586203734543450031353188858718632819990408687847

  public exponent: 65537
  Validity: [From: Tue Apr 09 08:10:44 CST 2019,
             To: Mon Jul 08 08:10:44 CST 2019]
  Issuer: CN=Perry Xiao, OU=School of Engineering, O=London South Bank University, L=London, ST=London, C=UK
  SerialNumber: [    75067fd6]

Certificate Extensions: 1
[1]: ObjectId: 2.5.29.14 Criticality=false
SubjectKeyIdentifier [
KeyIdentifier [
0000: 0D 9A 2B BD A4 11 31 4D   E4 11 9D 6A C6 35 99 2C  ..+...1M...j.5.,
0010: 83 C3 BD 82                                        ....
]
]

]
  Algorithm: [SHA256withRSA]
  Signature:
0000: 19 7E 91 26 21 33 9C 31   D0 E6 78 A1 B2 A3 CA 85  ...&!3.1..x.....
```

```
Command Prompt                                                          —    □    ×
0010: 83 C3 BD 82                                        ....
]
]

]
  Algorithm: [SHA256withRSA]
  Signature:
0000: 19 7E 91 26 21 33 9C 31   D0 E6 78 A1 B2 A3 CA 85  ...&!3.1..x.....
0010: C6 0E 3B 03 94 30 D6 85   BD 0B 79 E4 54 3F 6D B0  ..;..0....y.T?m.
0020: CF 03 4F 15 C0 15 A0 73   94 06 BA A4 D3 1C 96 7D  ..O....s........
0030: CF 42 1B 29 0E BD CC EB   45 64 2D 44 76 DC FF F0  .B.)....Ed-Dv...
0040: A3 3A BD 47 6A B9 54 4D   3C 88 C2 3F D9 B0 7E A3  .:.Gj.TM<..?....
0050: 29 79 F0 A8 59 AB 27 BB   13 E3 1D 36 DD B1 8E 81  )y..Y.'....6....
0060: B8 8D 69 BC 21 79 96 1D   42 15 F3 CE A4 46 A8 29  ..i.!y..B....F.)
0070: 8E 40 64 C2 B0 70 40 55   D0 96 C8 A9 AF 14 8D CC  .@d..p@U........
0080: 3E 97 60 34 9A FD E5 59   CC 65 E2 22 FF FE 36 B8  >.`4...Y.e.".6.
0090: C9 34 3F CF ED 21 B4 DE   56 4A 39 C5 9E A0 09 B5  .4?..!..VJ9.....
00A0: 69 EB A6 7F ED 61 0E E1   B2 ED 1C BE D3 9C E9 BC  i....a..........
00B0: 94 63 75 93 47 B1 06 CD   3D A2 15 FB F8 D7 69 E9  .cu.G...=.....i.
00C0: 85 20 AB 7F 66 D4 07 8D   DF AE 4C 34 28 EE AE 37  . ..f.....L4(..7
00D0: 3F BA A4 3C 1D 8E AB 0C   62 E2 4A A4 16 DD E2 7B  ?..<....b.J.....
00E0: 56 18 1D A0 6D 19 25 28   20 80 B8 F4 3C 35 90 34  V...m.%( ...<5.4
00F0: 8C 2C D6 D3 C4 55 04 96   DC 1D C7 49 BD 62 32 1D  .,...U.....I.b2.
]
Sun RSA public key, 2048 bits
  modulus: 21784245738210549611025619537078407056017077257886662295959724838066175485107207154428480842915872838460
6151618511527602743584721393054248472250502924686519411311146869285909288018453546217959962252649356064937360195094
5110155462749076161831348454452402730737740563192209773766868108066042678362194900578695768118140100881961928927169
3879328396194423820405092074715740765558418543773920884207923142189080883228911622328821396738487562888576254164602
3078376122139298312612349219871511246775769033158361883167427687735318802536483628655860150152776897351078572972752
47586203734543450031353188858718632819990408687847

  public exponent: 65537
java.security.KeyPair@1f28c152

H:\Chapter 9>
```

Figure 9.29: The output from the `PKCS12Example.java` program

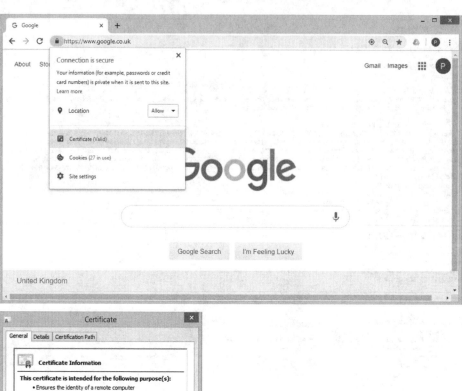

Figure 9.30: Viewing the certificate of a web site in Google Chrome browser

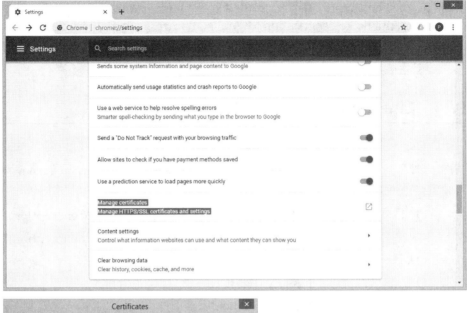

Figure 9.31: Viewing a list of trusted CAs in Google Chrome

9.13   Summary

This chapter introduced the concept of cybersecurity, explaining key concepts such as encryption, hash functions, message digests, digital signatures, and digital certificates. You looked at both private key encryption and public key encryption. The chapter also presented some Java examples for private key encryption, public key encryption, digital signatures, a message digest, and a digital certificate. Finally, you saw some interesting Java security programming resources.

9.14 Chapter Review Questions

Q9.1. What is cybersecurity?

Q9.2. Find two recent examples of cybersecurity breaches in the news.

Q9.3. What is encryption?

Q9.4. What is private key encryption (or symmetric key encryption)?

Q9.5. What is public key encryption (or asymmetric key encryption)?

Q9.6. What is a hash function?

Q9.7. What is a message digest?

Q9.8. What is a digital signature?

Q9.9. What is a digital certificate?

Q9.10. What is PGP?

Q9.11. What is the difference between TTL and SSL?

Q9.12. What is the difference between HTTP and HTTPS?

Java Programming for Blockchain Applications

You can fool all the people some of the time and some of the people all the time, but you cannot fool all the people all the time.

—Abraham Lincoln

10.1   What Is Blockchain?

Blockchain is another one of the hottest buzzwords at the moment. What is blockchain, and what has it to do with Bitcoin? Well, blockchain is a technology that was invented in 2008 by the mysterious Satoshi Nakamoto, whose real identity is still unknown. (It is largely believed to be a person or a group of people living in Japan.) The original purpose of blockchain technology was to serve as the distributed, digital, public transaction ledger of the cryptocurrency Bitcoin to solve the *double-spending* problem. In digital currency, double-spending occurs when the same single digital token can be spent more than once. With a public ledger, when you try to spend the same digital token the second time, the transaction will not be validated. But today, blockchain has shown potential in many other areas, such as smart contracts, smart property, insurance, music, healthcare, manufacture, supply chain, arts, government, the Internet of Things (IoT), and so on. Blockchain is another digital technology that may revolutionize the way we live and work.

In the simplest terms, as illustrated in Figure 10.1, a *blockchain* is basically a chain of blocks, each of which contains some information—data. In the case of digital currency, this can be the amount of money transferred, the identities of the sender and receiver, the date and time, and so on. Each block also contains an index, the previous block's hash, a timestamp, a nonce value, and its own hash. Each block is connected to the previous block through the previous block's hash, so all blocks are connected like a daisy chain, which is where it gets the name blockchain. The first block in the chain, called the *genesis*, does not have a previous block, so the previous block's hash is NULL. The index is a unique number for each block. The index of the first block is 0, the second block is 1, the third block is 2, and so on. The timestamp is the date and time when the block is created, and the nonce is a 32-bit (4-byte) integer whose value controls the outcome of the calculated hash of the block.

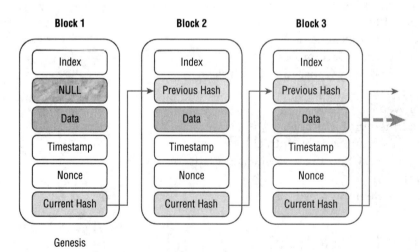

Genesis

Figure 10.1: The schematic diagram of a blockchain

Each block uses its index, the previous block's hash, its data, its timestamp, and its nonce value to feed into a hash function, such as SHA-256, to create its own hash, as shown in Figure 10.2. As described in Chapter 9, a hash function is a mathematical function that can map data of any size to fixed-size data. Unlike encryption, a hash cannot be reversed. If someone gets the hash of the current block, there is no way they can figure out the information in the block that was hashed.

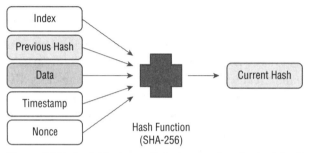

Figure 10.2: Each block uses its index, previous hash, data, timestamp, and nonce to feed into a hash function, such as SHA-256, to calculate the current hash.

10.2   How Do You Validate a Blockchain?

A blockchain is a record of a series of items of information, such as a series of transactions. After a blockchain is formed, it must be validated. To validate a blockchain, you must validate every single block on the chain, starting from the first block, the genesis.

Validating a block is not difficult; it takes just two steps. First, you need to test whether the previous hash is the same as the current hash of the previous block; you can skip this step for the first block. Second, you need to use the block's index, the previous block's hash, and the block's data, timestamp, and nonce to feed into a hash function (such as SHA-256) to calculate its hash, exactly as it was calculated in the first place, as shown in Figure 10.2, to see if the newly calculated hash is the same as the original current hash in the block. If both steps are successful, then this block is valid. If all the blocks on the chain are valid, then it is a valid blockchain.

Now, let us try to alter the data in block 2 of Figure 10.1 after the chain has been created. What will happen? When you alter the data, the block will become invalid, as the new hash will not match the existing hash. You can replace the existing hash with the new hash to make this block valid, but then block 3 will not be valid, as its previous hash no longer matches block 2's new hash. You can of course replace the previous hash in block 3 with block 2's new hash, but then you will need to recalculate block 3's hash to make block 3 valid again. Then you will have to repeat this for blocks 4, 5, 6, . . ., until the end of the chain. This is the beauty of using a hash in the blockchain; once the chain is created, nothing can be changed. The same will happen when you try to remove blocks from the chain or insert new blocks into it.

The only way you can make a change on the chain is to recalculate the hash for all the blocks after the changed block. But blockchain technology has a consensus mechanism to prevent this from happening. It is called *proof of work*, which requires you to mine the blocks.

10.3   How Do You Mine the Blocks?

The proof-of-work system in the blockchain technology means that when you calculate a hash, the hash needs to start with a certain number of zeros, described as its *difficulty*. More zeros means greater difficulty; fewer zeros means less difficulty. Blockchain uses difficulty to control the time of creating one block. If the difficulty value is 5, that means the hash must start with five zeros. Because all other information in the block, such as the index, previous hash, data, and timestamp, is fixed, the only thing you can change is the nonce, which is a 32-bit integer. By trying different nonce values, you repeatedly calculate the hash, until you get the hash starting with the desired number of zeros. This is called *mining* the block. Clearly, the higher the difficulty value, the longer it takes to mine the block. On average, it takes about 10 minutes to mine one block. If you have a long chain of blocks, it will take longer to mine all the blocks; and this is just for one chain. If there are millions of users, you will need to change millions of chains. The proof of work system makes it practically impossible to alter the information on a blockchain. This is what makes blockchain different from other technologies, and it is exactly why it is potentially useful in many applications.

10.4   How Does Blockchain Work?

To see how blockchain works, let's consider the transfer of money as an example. Traditionally, if person A wants to send some money to person B, A will use a bank, as both can trust the bank, see Figure 10.3 (left). This is a centralized approach, in which the bank behaves as a ledger. There are several issues with this approach. First, the bank will charge for the service. Especially for a large sum of money, this could become expensive. Second, transactions take time, especially international transactions. Finally, if the bank has a problem, as happened in the 2008 financial crisis, both person A and person B will suffer.

Blockchain instead uses a distributed approach. In this case, if person A wants to send some money to person B, A will simply add a new block to the existing blockchain, see Figure 10.3 (right). The new block will contain information such as sender name, receiver name, and amount of money sent. The blockchain is then copied to every user on the network, called *peers*. Peers form a peer-to-peer network, and all the peers together behave as a form of distributed ledger.

Therefore, there is no centralized ledger. This brings several benefits: it is free, it is fast, and it is transparent. Also different from the traditional bank-based approach is that person A did not actually send anything to B—there is no account, and there is no balance. There is only a blockchain shared by all the users, which is then used to work out who sent what, who received what, and what is the final balance. There is no currency item per se; digital currency is just the numbers existing in a record of a series of transactions.

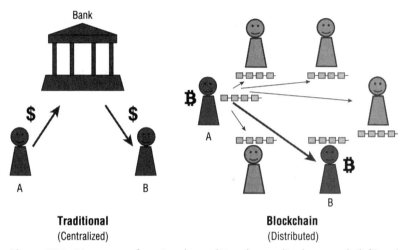

Figure 10.3: Money transfer using the traditional centralized approach (left) and the blockchain distributed approach (right)

If person B wants to commit fraud by altering the information on the chain, not only does he need to alter his own chain, he also needs to alter the majority of the chains among the users on the network, of which there could be millions. With the proof-of-work system, this is practically impossible.

The following are blockchain technology's key features and benefits:

Decentralization   This is the core concept of blockchain technology and also its core benefit. There is no centralized ledger to record and validate transactions; instead, the users on the network collectively act as a distributed ledger. As a result, it is free, and it is fast. There is no central bank to charge for the service, and instead of days, a transaction could take just a few hours.

Immutability   Once the block is created, it cannot be changed. You cannot add or remove blocks from the chain, nor alter any information inside the blocks. The only thing you can do is to add a new block at the end of the chain. This immutability is another key benefit of blockchain, which brings security and reliability.

Transparency   Because the transaction records are shared with all the users in a peer-to-peer network, everything is transparent; there are no black boxes.

High Availability   Also, because the transaction records are shared with all the users in a peer-to-peer network, there is no single point of failure; data is highly available. Figure 10.4 shows an interesting blockchain virtual demo web site (`https://blockchaindemo.io/`), in which you can see the contents of a block, add new blocks to the chain, and add more peers.

Figure 10.4: A virtual blockchain demo

10.5   Uses of Blockchain

Blockchain technology can be used in many applications; here are some examples.

10.5.1   Bitcoin

The first and most important application is digital currency, also called *cryptocurrency*, as it is protected through encryption. There are many digital currencies; the most popular one is Bitcoin (BTC), symbol ₿. Bitcoin was invented by Satoshi Nakamoto and released as open-source software in 2009. Bitcoin can be transferred and exchanged for real currencies, products, and services. There are millions of Bitcoin users in the world, which generate millions of transactions every month. The price of a Bitcoin has been rising from a fraction of a dollar to several thousands of dollars. It reached a peak value of nearly $20,000 in December 2017. When trading, you don't need to buy one whole Bitcoin. The smallest Bitcoin unit you can buy and sell is called a satoshi, which is 100 millionth of a Bitcoin. Unlike real currency, which can be supplied unlimited, Bitcoin has limited supply. Bitcoin is created through a process called Bitcoin mining, as described in section 10.3. Bitcoin mining is basically a process that validates the recent transactions, adds new blocks to the chain, and gets rewards. Through Bitcoin mining new Bitcoins are created, but only a small amount can be created each hour, tightly controlled by its underlying algorithm. The new Bitcoins will be continuously created until they reach the maximum of 21 million. This limited supply makes Bitcoin a potential asset: as the demand increases, the value will also increase.

Figure 10.5 shows the structure inside a Bitcoin block. Each block has a header and a body. The header contains a hash of the previous block header, along with the timestamp, difficulty target, nonce, and Merkle root. Within the body are all the transactions. Each block contains about 500 transactions. Each transaction will have its own hash computed, and from all the hashes together a final hash will be computed. The final hash is stored in the Merkle root, or Tx_Root, as shown in Figure 10.5.

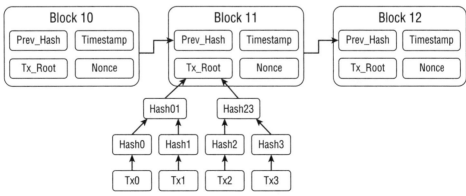

Figure 10.5: The structure of the Bitcoin block

Adapted from https://upload.wikimedia.org/wikipedia/commons/thumb/5/55/
Bitcoin_Block_Data.svg/1200px-Bitcoin_Block_Data.svg.png

Figure 10.6 shows the three layers of the Bitcoin service architecture, adapted from the Luxsci web site. At the bottom is the peer-to-peer network; this is where all the nodes, or users, are connected together. In the middle is the decentralized ledger, where the blockchain technology is implemented. On the top is the applications layer, where application programs such as Bitcoin wallets are implemented.

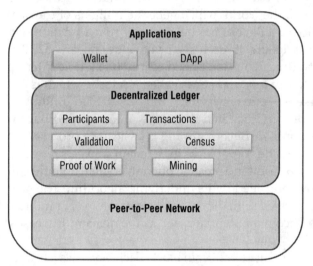

Figure 10.6: The three layers of the Bitcoin architecture

Adapted from `https://luxsci.com/blog/understanding-blockchains-and-bitcoin-technology.html`

Several web sites allow you to look into the structure of a Bitcoin chain. Figure 10.7 shows an example from Block Explorer (`https://www.blockchain .com/explorer`), where you can see that the total number of blocks on the Bitcoin main chain (called its *height*) was at that time 539,602, the latest block was created about 6 minutes earlier (called the chain's *age*), it contains 652 transactions, the number of Bitcoins sent is 1,686.25, and the size of the block is 313.35 KB.

The following is another Bitcoin block explorer web site where you can view the latest transactions and the structure of Bitcoin blocks:

`https://blockexplorer.com/`

Another interesting web site is Learn Me a Bitcoin, at the following URL, where you can learn Bitcoin terminology and also visualize the details of Bitcoin blocks:

`http://learnmeabitcoin.com/guide/`

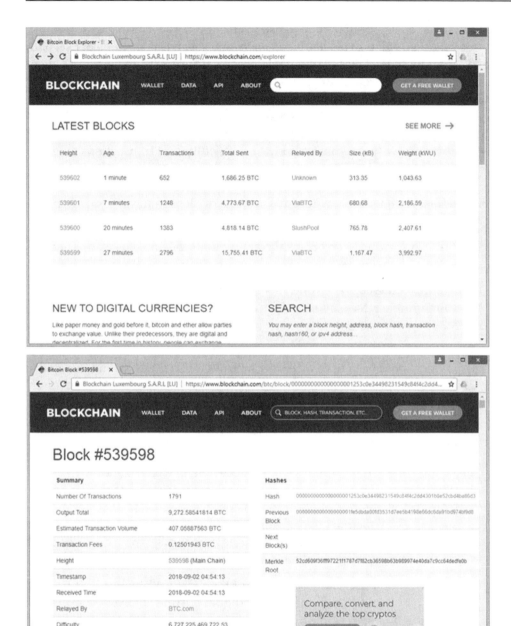

Figure 10.7: Cryptocurrency Bitcoin Block Explorer (top) and the structure of the latest block (bottom)

However, as its popularity increases, Bitcoin has shown several scalability issues: it uses 1 MB size blocks, it can have only seven transactions per second, and each transaction takes 10 minutes to process. This has led to the development of a new cryptocurrency: Bitcoin Cash (BCH), which is a different version of Bitcoin. This illustrates what is called a *fork* in software development, as Bitcoin and Bitcoin Cash are based on the same technology (the main branch), and Bitcoin Cash is forking out as a new subbranch. With Bitcoin Cash, it uses 8 MB size blocks, with an adjustable level of difficulty, and transactions take two minutes to process.

If you are interested in trying Bitcoin or other cryptocurrencies, such as Bitcoin Cash, Ether, Ripple, Litecoin, Peercoin, or Dogecoin, you can download and install one of the following popular cryptocurrency digital wallets:

Bitcoin Core   Created by Satoshi Nakamoto for Bitcoin, it is also called the Satoshi client (`https://bitcoin.org/en/bitcoin-core/`).

Ethereum   Ethereum is an open-source, public, blockchain-based distributed computing platform, which offers a cryptocurrency called Ether (`https://www.ethereum.org/`).

Ripple   Ripple is a real-time payment system, based on a shared public XRP Ledger. It has been used by banks such as UniCredit, UBS, and Santander (`https://ripple.com/`).

Bitcoin Cash   Bitcoin Cash is a hard fork of Bitcoin, only started in 2017. Bitcoin Cash claims to be faster and cheaper to use, with the maximum block size of 8MB (`https://www.bitcoincash.org/`).

Electrum   Electrum is a lightweight Bitcoin client, which comes with both a hardware wallet and a software wallet. Hardware wallets allow users to store the Bitcoin information such as private keys in a hardware device, such as a USB memory stick. Unlike a software wallet, a hardware wallet can be physically secured and is immune from viruses, which are designed to steal from software wallets. (`https://electrum.org/`).

Coinbase   Coinbase claims to be one of the most well-known and trusted apps to buy, sell, and manage your digital currency (`https://www.coinbase.com/`).

Blockchain Luxembourg   This platform has a beautiful user interface that's easy to use and many useful features for cryptocurrency (`https://www.blockchain.com/`).

Figure 10.8 shows more cryptocurrency wallets from the `bitcoin.org` web site (`https://bitcoin.org/en/choose-your-wallet`). Figure 10.9 shows the Live Coin Watch web site, where you can find more details, such as price, market capitalization, volume, and trend, of each cryptocurrency (`https://www.live-coinwatch.com/`). According to Live Coin Watch, the top three most popular cryptocurrencies are BTC (Bitcoin), XRP (Ripple), and ETH (Ethereum), according to their Market Cap (market capitalization; that is, the total dollar market value). BTC is about $70B, XRP is about $15B, and ETH is about $12B, far ahead of the other cryptocurrencies.

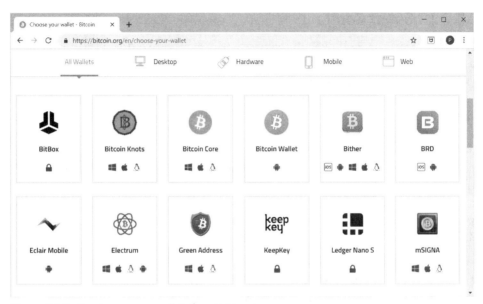

Figure 10.8: Cryptocurrency wallets from `Bitcoin.org`

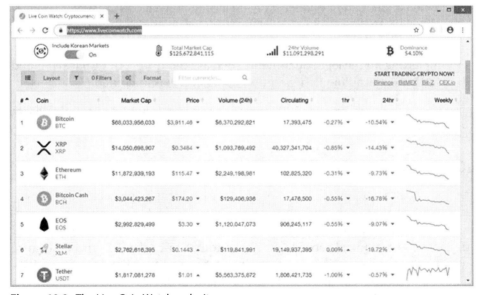

Figure 10.9: The Live Coin Watch web site

For more information, please read Satoshi Nakamoto's white paper, and visit the Bitcoin wiki and the Bitcoin.org pages.

```
https://bitcoin.org/bitcoin.pdf
https://en.bitcoin.it/wiki/Main _ Page
https://bitcoin.org/en/
```

10.5.2   Smart Contracts

Smart contracts are self-executing contracts designed to enforce the terms of an agreement. Smart contracts are used to control the transfer of digital currencies or assets between parties under certain conditions. With smart contracts, you exchange money, property, shares, or anything of value without needing a middleman. Smart contracts not only define all the rules and all the penalties but also automatically enforce these obligations.

Buying a house, for example, usually involves buyer, seller, and multiple third parties such as real estate agents and lawyers. With a smart contract and digital currency, this can be done just between the buyer and the seller. Once all the conditions are met, the smart contract, which is essentially a software program, will automatically complete the transaction using digital currency. The process consists of the following steps:

1. Buyer and seller agree on the house price in digital currency, and write the contract into the blockchain. The contract includes all the buyer's and seller's information and terms and conditions. Because the contract is in the public ledger, it therefore cannot be changed.

2. When all the conditions are met and a trigger event occurs, such as expiration date, the contract will execute itself according to agreed terms.

3. Seller gets the payment in digital currency and buyer gets the house, including all the legal documents such as land deed. All the clearing and settlement is automated, and the ownership is undisputed.

Figure 10.10 shows the operation of a smart contract, adapted from the Block-Geeks site.

10.5.3   Healthcare

Personal health data can also be stored in the blockchain, protected by encryption, to allow access only by specific users, such as doctors and insurance providers. Doctors will have the full patient history and hence can provide better diagnosis. The medical records will be automatically shared with insurance providers to support claims. Blockchain can be used to verify the authenticity of drugs, to prevent counterfeit drugs and medical devices, and to improve the quality and reliability of clinical trials data.

How Smart Contracts Works

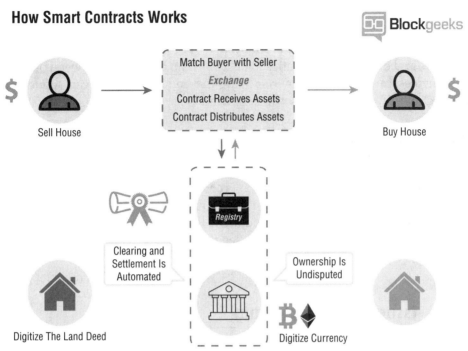

Figure 10.10: The operation of a smart contract

Adapted from `https://blockgeeks.com/guides/smart-contracts/`.

10.5.4 Manufacture and Supply Chains

Blockchain technology can also be used in manufacturing and supply chains to record any exchange, agreements/contracts, tracking, and payment. Because every transaction is recorded on a block and across multiple copies of the ledger that are distributed among users, this recording method is highly transparent. It's also highly secure. It will be extremely efficient and scalable. You will be able to see the whole record of a product or a component, including where it comes from and where it has been. This is called *traceability*. Blockchain technology can increase the efficiency and transparency of supply chains. For example, multinational retailer Walmart has partnered with IBM to track food staples from supplier to shelf using its Hyperledger Fabric blockchain. The technology has also been used to track art works, antiques, jewelry, and other valuables for authentication and proof of ownership and to combat counterfeiting.

10.5.5 Internet of Things

With the Internet of Things (IoT), billions of devices will be interconnected. Securely storing the enormous amounts of data generated by the IoT systems presents a huge challenge. With blockchain technology's distributed ledger, IoT data can be stored distributed in a trustless fashion, and it can be better organized and analyzed to produce valuable insights. Blockchain is perfectly suited for both public- and private-sector IoT systems, because of its identification, verification, and data transfer abilities. Blockchain can build trust between parties and devices, can reduce cost by removing the middlemen, and can accelerate transactions by reducing the settlement time.

10.5.6　Government

Voting is one of the most important democratic processes for a government. With blockchain, voting can be more open, less costly, and less prone to fraud. Many kinds of government information and data can also be stored in blockchain, which will make it easier to access and make the government more transparent and reduce corruption. To learn more, see this site:

```
https://blockgeeks.com/guides/blockchain-applications/
```

10.6　Issues with Blockchain

Just like any other technology, blockchain also has some limitations.

Security　Because blockchain relies on the users to store the record, if a majority of the users decide to alter a record, then that change of the record will be accepted. This is called a *51 percent attack*. Satoshi Nakamoto highlighted this security flaw when bitcoin was launched. To minimize the possibility of this 51 percent attack, the network will need to be larger than a certain size so that no one or no one group can have more than 51 percent of the control. Hacking is also a common threat to digital currencies.

Complexity　Blockchain is based on huge, complex technologies that involve sophisticated mathematics and huge amounts of software programming. The complexity of blockchain will make it difficult for anyone to understand how it works and what benefits it brings and therefore hinder its application.

Lack of Regulation　Because blockchain technology is so new, there is little regulation. The lack of regulation creates a risky environment, where fraud, scams, and market manipulation are commonplace.

Quantum Readiness　Blockchain is built on encryption, which is safe for today's computers. But with the emergence of technology such as quantum computing, computers could run 100 million times faster than they currently do, which will pose a significant threat to all the forms of encryption you are using today. To face this challenge, a quantum-resistant cryptographic system needs to be developed.

Scalability   As the network grows, the processing of transaction on the block-chain can be slow and cumbersome because of the complexity, encrypted, and distributed nature. For example, popular blockchain platforms like Bitcoin and Ethereum can process around 7 to 15 transactions per second on average, while Visa currently processes around 5,000 to 8,000 transactions per second on average. More research is needed to improve scalability.

10.7   Java Blockchain Examples

Let us look at some examples of Java blockchain applications. Example 10.1 shows a simple Java blockchain demonstration program. It consists of two Java files, `Block.java` and `BlockChainMain.java`. The first, `Block.java` (Example 10.1A), has the task of creating a single block. In each block there are six attributes and three methods. The attributes are the same as explained earlier: `index`, `timestamp`, `currentHash`, `previousHash`, `data`, and `nonce`. The three methods are `calculateHash()`, `mineBlock()` and `toString()`. The `calculateHash()` method is for calculating the current hash of the block, `mineBlock()` is for mining the block according to the specified difficulty (the number of leading zeros), and `toString()` is for display the information of the block. To create a block you will need to provide information about `index`, `previousHash`, and `data`.

EXAMPLE 10.1A   THE BLOCK.JAVA **PROGRAM**

```java
//Example 10.1A Block.java
import java.security.*;
import java.util.*;

public class Block {
    public int index;
    public long timestamp;
    public String currentHash;
    public String previousHash;
    public String data;
    public int nonce;

    public Block(int index, String previousHash, String data) {
        this.index = index;
        this.timestamp = System.currentTimeMillis();
        this.previousHash = previousHash;
        this.data = data;
        nonce = 0;
        currentHash = calculateHash();
    }
```

```
    public String calculateHash(){
        try {
            String input = index + timestamp + previousHash + data +
nonce;
            MessageDigest digest = MessageDigest.getInstance("SHA-256");
            byte[] hash = digest.digest(input.getBytes("UTF-8"));

            StringBuffer hexString = new StringBuffer();
            for (int i = 0; i < hash.length; i++) {
                String hex = Integer.toHexString(0xff & hash[i]);
                if(hex.length() == 1) hexString.append('0');
                hexString.append(hex);
            }
            return hexString.toString();
        }
        catch(Exception e) {
            throw new RuntimeException(e);
        }
    }
    public void mineBlock(int difficulty) {
        nonce = 0;
        String target = new String(new char[difficulty]).replace('\0',
'0');
        while (!currentHash.substring(0,  difficulty).equals(target)) {
            nonce++;
            currentHash = calculateHash();
        }
    }
    public String toString() {
        String s = "Block #       :  " + index + "\r\n";
        s = s +    "PreviousHash :  " + previousHash + "\r\n";
        s = s +    "Timestamp    :  " + timestamp + "\r\n";
        s = s +    "Data         :  " + data + "\r\n";
        s = s +    "Nonce        :  " + nonce + "\r\n";
        s = s +    "CurrentHash  :  " +currentHash + "\r\n";
    return s;
    }
}
```

BlockChainMain.java (Example 10.1B) is the main program, which creates a blockchain and adds two blocks to the chain. Figure 10.11 shows the compilation and execution of BlockChainMain.java.

EXAMPLE 10.1B   THE BLOCKCHAINMAIN.JAVA **PROGRAM**

```
//Example 10.1B BlockChainMain.java
import java.util.*;

public class BlockChainMain {
```

```
        public static ArrayList<Block> blockchain = new ArrayList<Block>();
        public static int difficulty = 5;

        public static void main(String[] args) {
            Block b = new Block(0, null, "My First Block");  //The genesis
block
            b.mineBlock(difficulty);
            blockchain.add(b);
            System.out.println(b.toString());

            Block b2 = new Block(1, b.currentHash, "My Second Block");
            b2.mineBlock(difficulty);
            blockchain.add(b2);
            System.out.println(b2.toString());
        }
}
```

Figure 10.11: The compilation and execution of `BlockChainMain.java`

You can modify the `BlockChainMain.java` program to also validate the blocks, as shown in Example 10.1C, the `BlockChainMain2.java` program. It uses a new function named `ValidateBlock()`, which can validate a block based on its index, the previous hash, and the current hash. Figure 10.12 (top) shows the compilation and execution of `BlockChainMain2.java`. As you can see, both blocks added are valid.

EXAMPLE 10.1C THE BLOCKCHAINMAIN2.JAVA **PROGRAM**

```
//Example 10.1C BlockChainMain2.java
import java.util.*;

public class BlockChainMain2 {

    public static ArrayList<Block> blockchain = new ArrayList<Block>();
    public static int difficulty = 5;
```

```java
    public static void main(String[] args) {
        Block b = new Block(0, null, "My First Block");
        b.mineBlock(difficulty);
        blockchain.add(b);
        System.out.println(b.toString());
        System.out.println("Current Block Valid: " + validateBlock(b,
null));

        Block b2 = new Block(1, b.currentHash, "My Second Block");
        b2.mineBlock(difficulty);
        blockchain.add(b2);
        //b2.data="My Third Block";
        System.out.println(b2.toString());
        System.out.println("Current Block Valid: " + validateBlock(b2,
b));
    }
    public static boolean validateBlock(Block newBlock, Block
previousBlock) {

        if (previousBlock == null){   //The first block
            if (newBlock.index != 0) {
              return false;
            }

            if (newBlock.previousHash != null) {
              return false;
            }

            if (newBlock.currentHash == null ||
                    !newBlock.calculateHash().equals(newBlock.
currentHash)) {
                return false;
            }

            return true;

        } else{                      //The rest blocks
            if (newBlock != null ) {
                if (previousBlock.index + 1 != newBlock.index) {
                  return false;
                }

                if (newBlock.previousHash == null  ||
                    !newBlock.previousHash.equals(previousBlock.
currentHash)) {
                    return false;
                }

                if (newBlock.currentHash == null  ||
                    !newBlock.calculateHash().equals(newBlock.currentHash))
{
                    return false;
```

```
            }

          return true;
        }
        return false;


    }
  }
}
```

Now if you uncomment the following line in the program, the effect is equivalent to manually modifying the block after it is created:

```
//b2.data="My Third Block";
```

When you recompile and run the program, it will show that the second block is not valid, as shown in Figure 10.12 (bottom).

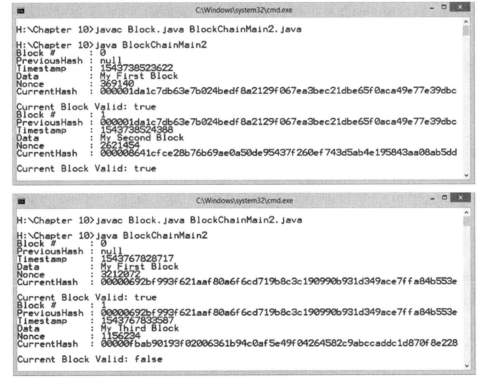

Figure 10.12: The compilation and execution of `BlockChainMain2.java`, with both blocks valid (top) and the second block not valid (bottom)

Example 10.1D (`BlockChainMain3.java`) shows how to validate the whole block-chain. To do that, you will need to validate all the blocks in the blockchain. The new `ValidateChain()` method uses a loop to go through all blocks on the chain and validate each block using the previous `ValidateBlock()` method. Figure 10.13 shows the compilation and execution of the `BlockChainMain3.java` program.

EXAMPLE 10.1D   THE BLOCKCHAINMAIN3.JAVA **PROGRAM**

```java
//Example 10.1D BlockChainMain3.java
import java.util.*;

public class BlockChainMain3 {

    public static ArrayList<Block> blockchain = new ArrayList<Block>();
    public static int difficulty = 5;

    public static void main(String[] args) {
        Block b = new Block(0, null, "My First Block");
        b.mineBlock(difficulty);
        blockchain.add(b);
        System.out.println(b.toString());

        Block b2 = new Block(1, b.currentHash, "My Second Block");
        b2.mineBlock(difficulty);
        blockchain.add(b2);
        System.out.println(b2.toString());
        System.out.println("Current Chain Valid: "
+validateChain(blockchain));
    }
    public static boolean validateChain(ArrayList<Block> blockchain) {
        if (!validateBlock(blockchain.get(0), null)) {
          return false;
        }

        for (int i = 1; i < blockchain.size(); i++) {
          Block currentBlock = blockchain.get(i);
          Block previousBlock = blockchain.get(i - 1);

          if (!validateBlock(currentBlock, previousBlock)) {
            return false;
          }
        }

        return true;
    }
    public static boolean validateBlock(Block newBlock, Block
previousBlock) {
        //The same code as before
        ... ...
    }
}
```

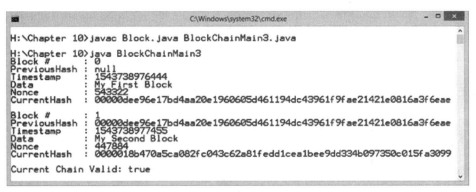

Figure 10.13: The compilation and execution of `BlockChainMain3.java`

10.8   Java Blockchain Transaction Examples

Now you are ready to start doing something interesting with the blockchain. Example 10.2 shows how to use a blockchain record transaction. It contains four Java classes, `Block2.java`, `Transaction.java`, `Wallet.java`, and `BlockChainMain4.java`. The `Block2.java` program (Example 10.2A) is similar to the previous `Block.java`, but instead of using `String` data, it uses `ArrayList<Transaction>` transactions inside each block. The `ArrayList` is used to store several transactions.

EXAMPLE 10.2A   THE `BLOCK2.JAVA` PROGRAM

```java
//Example 10.2A Block2.java
public class Block2 {
    public int index;
    public long timestamp;
    public String currentHash;
    public String previousHash;
    public String data;
    public ArrayList<Transaction> transactions = new
ArrayList<Transaction>(); //our data will be a simple message.
    public int nonce;

    public Block2(int index, String previousHash, ArrayList<Transaction>
transactions) {
        this.index = index;
        this.timestamp = System.currentTimeMillis();
        this.previousHash = previousHash;
        this.transactions = transactions;
        nonce = 0;
        currentHash = calculateHash();
    }

    public String calculateHash(){
        try {
```

```
            data="";
            for (int j=0; j<transactions.size();j++){
                Transaction tr = transactions.get(j);
                data = data + tr.sender+tr.recipient+tr.value;
            }
            String input = index + timestamp + previousHash + data +
    nonce;

            MessageDigest digest = MessageDigest.getInstance("SHA-256");
            byte[] hash = digest.digest(input.getBytes("UTF-8"));

            StringBuffer hexString = new StringBuffer();
            for (int i = 0; i < hash.length; i++) {
                String hex = Integer.toHexString(0xff & hash[i]);
                if(hex.length() == 1) hexString.append('0');
                hexString.append(hex);
            }
            return hexString.toString();
        }       catch(Exception e) {
            throw new RuntimeException(e);
        }
    }

    public void mineBlock(int difficulty) {
        nonce = 0;
        String target = new String(new char[difficulty]).replace('\0',
    '0');
        while (!currentHash.substring(0,  difficulty).equals(target)) {
            nonce++;
            currentHash = calculateHash();
        }
    }

    public String toString() {
        String s = "Block #        : " + index + "\r\n";
        s = s +    "PreviousHash : " + previousHash + "\r\n";
        s = s +    "Timestamp    : " + timestamp + "\r\n";
        s = s +    "Transactions  : " + data + "\r\n";
        s = s +    "Nonce        : " + nonce + "\r\n";
        s = s +    "CurrentHash  : " +currentHash + "\r\n";
        return s;
    }
}
```

Transaction.java (Example 10.2B) simply records a transaction, which includes information such as sender, recipient, and value.

EXAMPLE 10.2B   THE TRANSACTION.JAVA **PROGRAM**

```
Transaction.java
import java.util.*;

public class Transaction {
    public String sender;
    public String recipient;
    public float value;

    public Transaction(String from, String to, float value) {
        this.sender = from;
        this.recipient = to;
        this.value = value;
    }
}
```

Wallet.java (Example 10.2C) creates a digital wallet for a user. It uses generateKeyPair() to generate a public/private key pair for the user, getBalance() to get the user's balance, and send() to send some digital coins to another user using the public keys of the sender and recipient. The getBalance() method basically goes through the entire blockchain searching for transactions for the user. If a transaction is sending, the method deducts the transaction value from the balance; if receiving, it adds the value to the balance. For the sake of simplicity, each digital wallet contains 100 digital coins.

EXAMPLE 10.2C   THE WALLET.JAVA **PROGRAM**

```
//Example 10.2C Wallet.java
import java.security.*;
import java.util.*;

public class Wallet {

    public String privateKey;
    public String publicKey;
    private float balance=100.0f;
    private ArrayList<Block2> blockchain = new ArrayList<Block2>();

    public Wallet(ArrayList<Block2> blockchain) {
        generateKeyPair();
        this.blockchain = blockchain;
    }

    public void generateKeyPair() {
```

```
        try {
            KeyPair keyPair;
            String algorithm = "RSA"; //DSA DH etc
            keyPair = KeyPairGenerator.getInstance(algorithm).
generateKeyPair();
            privateKey = keyPair.getPrivate().toString();
            publicKey = keyPair.getPublic().toString();

        }catch(Exception e) {
            throw new RuntimeException(e);
        }
    }


    public float getBalance() {
        float total = balance;
        for (int i=0; i<blockchain.size();i++){
            Block2 currentBlock = blockchain.get(i);
            for (int j=0; j<currentBlock.transactions.size();j++){
                Transaction tr = currentBlock.transactions.get(j);
                if (tr.recipient.equals(publicKey)){
                    total += tr.value;
                }
                if (tr.sender.equals(publicKey)){
                    total -= tr.value;
                }
            }
        }
        return total;
    }


    public Transaction send(String recipient,float value ) {
        if(getBalance() < value) {
            System.out.println("!!!Not Enough funds. Transaction
Discarded.");
            return null;
        }

        Transaction newTransaction = new Transaction(publicKey,
recipient , value);
        return newTransaction;
    }


}
```

BlockChainMain4.java is the main program that uses Wallet.java for blockchain transactions. It simply creates two digital wallets and displays their balance, as illustrated in Figure 10.14.

EXAMPLE 10.2D   THE BLOCKCHAINMAIN4.JAVA **PROGRAM**

```java
//Example 10.2D BlockChainMain4.java
import java.util.*;

public class BlockChainMain4 {

    public static ArrayList<Block2> blockchain = new
ArrayList<Block2>();
    public static ArrayList<Transaction> transactions = new
ArrayList<Transaction>();
    public static int difficulty = 5;

    public static void main(String[] args) {
        Wallet A = new Wallet(blockchain);
        Wallet B = new Wallet(blockchain);
        System.out.println("Wallet A Balance: " + A.getBalance());
        System.out.println("Wallet B Balance: " + B.getBalance());


    }
}
```

```
Command Prompt - BlockChainMain4Run.bat                    _ □ ×

H:\Chapter 10>javac Block2.java Wallet.java Transaction.java BlockChainMain4.jav
a
H:\Chapter 10>java BlockChainMain4
Wallet A Balance: 100.0
Wallet B Balance: 100.0
```

Figure 10.14: The compilation and execution of BlockChainMain4.java

Next, you can add some transactions. In Example 10.2E, two transactions were added: A sends 10 coins to B, and A sends 20 coins to B. You can also use the previous ValidateChain() to validate the whole blockchain. Figure 10.15 shows the output of the program. As you can see, both transactions went through, and the whole blockchain is valid.

EXAMPLE 10.2E   THE BLOCKCHAINMAIN5.JAVA **PROGRAM**

```java
//Example 10.2E BlockChainMain5.java
import java.util.*;

public class BlockChainMain5 {

    public static ArrayList<Block2> blockchain = new
ArrayList<Block2>();
    public static ArrayList<Transaction> transactions = new
ArrayList<Transaction>();
```

```java
    public static int difficulty = 5;

    public static void main(String[] args) {
        Wallet A = new Wallet(blockchain);
        Wallet B = new Wallet(blockchain);
        System.out.println("Wallet A Balance: " + A.getBalance());
        System.out.println("Wallet B Balance: " + B.getBalance());

        System.out.println("Add two transactions... ");
        Transaction tran1 = A.send(B.publicKey, 10);
        if (tran1!=null){
            transactions.add(tran1);
        }
        Transaction tran2 = A.send(B.publicKey, 20);
        if (tran2!=null){
            transactions.add(tran2);
        }

        Block2 b = new Block2(0, null, transactions);
        b.mineBlock(difficulty);
        blockchain.add(b);

        System.out.println("Wallet A Balance: " + A.getBalance());
        System.out.println("Wallet B Balance: " + B.getBalance());
        System.out.println("Blockchain Valid : " +
validateChain(blockchain));

    }
    public static boolean validateChain(ArrayList<Block2> blockchain) {
        if (!validateBlock(blockchain.get(0), null)) {
          return false;
        }

        for (int i = 1; i < blockchain.size(); i++) {
          Block2 currentBlock = blockchain.get(i);
          Block2 previousBlock = blockchain.get(i - 1);

          if (!validateBlock(currentBlock, previousBlock)) {
            return false;
          }
        }

        return true;
    }
    public static boolean validateBlock(Block2 newBlock, Block2
previousBlock) {
            //The same as before
    }
}
```

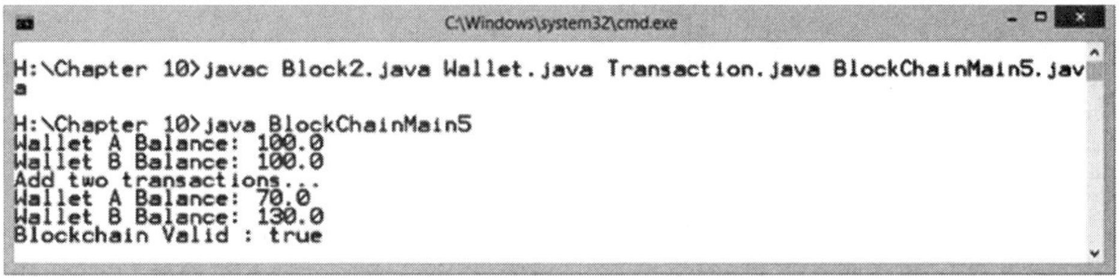

Figure 10.15: The compilation and execution of `BlockChainMain5.java`

If you change the second transaction to 200 (that is, A sends 200 coins to B), this exceeds the total balance of wallet A; therefore, the transaction is discarded, as shown in Figure 10.16.

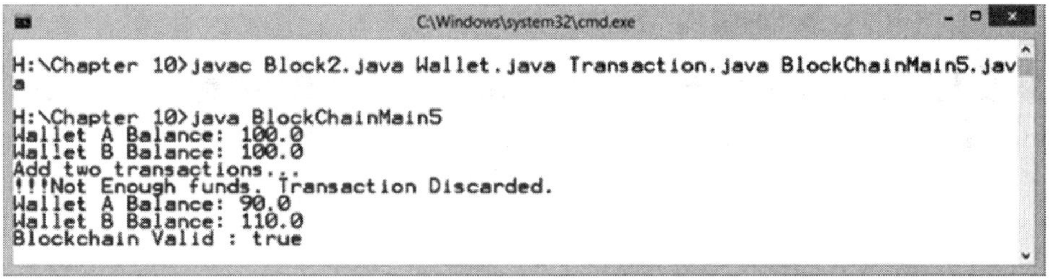

Figure 10.16: The compilation and execution of `BlockChainMain5.java`

The most popular Blockchain libraries for Java developers are these:

BitcoinJ: `https://github.com/bitcoinj/bitcoinj`

Web3j: `https://github.com/web3j/web3j`

EthereumJ: `https://github.com/ethereum/ethereumj`

HyperLedger Fabric: `https://github.com/hyperledger/fabric-sdk-java`

10.9   Java BitcoinJ Example

BitcoinJ is an open source library for developing Java Bitcoin applications. BitcoinJ allows you to maintain a wallet and to send and receive transactions without needing a local copy of Bitcoin Core. To use BitcoinJ, first you will need to download the BitcoinJ JAR file `bitcoinj-core-0.14.4-bundled.jar` from its web site.

`https://bitcoinj.github.io/getting-started-java`

Alternatively, you can just directly download the JAR file from the following links:

`https://search.maven.org/remotecontent?filepath=org/bitcoinj/bitcoinj-core/0.14.4/bitcoinj-core-0.14.4-bundled.jar` https://jar-download.com/artifacts/org.bitcoinj

Second, you will also need to download the Simple Logging Facade for Java (SLF4J) library from this site:

https://www.slf4j.org/download.html

Extract the downloaded file to a folder, and get a file named something like slf4j-simple-1.7.25.jar. Again, don't worry if your version number is slightly different.

Example 10.3 is a simple demonstration program, modified from the BitcoinJ example DumpWallet.java at this site:

https://github.com/bitcoinj/bitcoinj/blob/master/examples/src/main/java/org/bitcoinj/examples/DumpWallet.java

EXAMPLE 10.3   THE DUMPWALLET1.JAVA PROGRAM

```
//Example 10.3 DumpWallet1.java
//Modified from https://github.com/bitcoinj/bitcoinj/blob/master/
examples/src/main/java/org/bitcoinj/examples/DumpWallet.java
import java.io.File;
import org.bitcoinj.wallet.Wallet;
/**
 * DumpWallet loads a serialized wallet and prints information about
what it contains.
 */
public class DumpWallet1 {
    public static void main(String[] args) throws Exception {
        String walletfile="/path/to/your/walletfile";
        File f=new File(walletfile);
        Wallet wallet - Wallet.loadFromFile(f);
        System.out.println(wallet.toString());
    }
}
```

Put the DumpWallet1.java file, bitcoinj-core-0.14.4-bundled.jar, and slf4j-simple-1.7.25.jar all into one folder. Then you can compile and run the Dump-Wallet1.java program by typing the following commands:

```
javac -classpath ".;bitcoinj-core-0.14.4-bundled.jar;slf4j-
simple-1.7.25.jar" DumpWallet1.java
java -classpath ".;bitcoinj-core-0.14.4-bundled.jar;slf4j-simple-1.7.25.
jar" DumpWallet1
```

You will need a wallet file to make this program work. See section 10.10 to learn how to create a digital wallet file. For more BitcoinJ examples, you can download the entire source code from its Github web site here:

https://github.com/bitcoinj/bitcoinj

This site offers a simple tutorial on how to build a simple GUI wallet using BitcoinJ library:

```
https://bitcoinj.github.io/simple-gui-wallet
```

10.9.1   The Testnet

Before you run your program on real Bitcoin, it is always a good idea to test it in a simulated environment. The Bitcoin community provides a simulated Bitcoin network called the *testnet*. With the testnet, you can send and receive coins. The coins on the testnet have no value and can be obtained for free from testnet faucet sites like these:

```
https://testnet-faucet.mempool.co/
http://tpfaucet.appspot.com/.
```

For more information about the BitcoinJ library, see the following:

```
https://bitcoinj.github.io/
https://github.com/bitcoinj/bitcoinj
```

10.10   Java Web3j Examples

Web3j is a lightweight Java library for integration with Ethereum clients. With Web3j you can create a digital wallet, manage the wallet, send Ether, the Ethereum digital cryptocurrency, and create a smart contract. The easiest way to use the Web3j library is to download its command line tools from the following GitHub site:

```
https://github.com/web3j/web3j/releases/tag/v4.0.1
```

There, look for a zip file named web3j-4.0.1.zip. More information about the Web3j command-line tools can be found here:

```
https://docs.web3j.io/command _ line.html
```

Unzip the web3j-4.0.1.zip file to a folder, in this case E:\web3j-4.0.1\. The main command-line tool program is named web3j.bat in the E:\web3j-4.0.1\bin\ folder. Open an MS-DOS terminal, go to the E:\ folder, and type in the following command to create a digital wallet, as shown in Figure 10.17:

```
.\web3j-4.0.1\bin\web3j wallet create
```

You will need to provide a password to your digital wallet; once you've done that, a wallet file with a filename like the following will be created:

```
UTC--2018-11-26T13-18-32.250132200Z--ccded263b9310c875d615bf66ba678e
121c26362.json
```

The default location for the digital wallet is shown next, where `%USERPROFILE%` is your user folder. For example, on my computer it is `C:\Users\xiaop`.

`%USERPROFILE%\AppData\Roaming\Ethereum\testnet\keystore`

But you can change it to another folder.

You can use the Windows `type` command (or any text editor) to display the content of the wallet file, as shown in the following output. The address in the wallet is your unique address, which can be used to send Ether or create a smart contract. The crypto in the wallet specifies the encryption algorithm you are using and your private key.

```
{
"address":"168d8513597cc0958f635a679a5b60ccd13d6ef1",
"id":"721b533c-c552-4f94-9860-5b70cb45497a",
"version":3,
"crypto":{"cipher":"aes-128-ctr",
"ciphertext":"1924aaf30e9b6ea7360caeeab7f1afac196aa9455fea022186642a6dc3
5c7cd7",
"cipherparams":{"iv":"70c135529198af334f952192f577f2b6"},
"kdf":"scrypt",
"kdfparams":{"dklen":32,"n":262144,"p":1,"r":8,"salt":"68a357b71dc0f3a
92726a761125f9cabee2ed4a1d6d0ea183ee6c37d608c97e9"},
"mac":"6dab6ec9ee482c10556e26264c13047a6d9386f2c1ae4cea1c26e0bc5d662bab"}
}
```

Figure 10.17: The Web3j command to create a digital wallet (top) and using the type command to display the content of the wallet (bottom)

You can use the Etherscan web site to display the transactions at your address; the URL is as follows:

```
https://etherscan.io/address/<your address>
```

Figure 10.18 shows the Etherscan web site of the address specified in the digital wallet (`https://etherscan.io/address/0x168d8513597cc0958f635a679a5b60ccd1 3d6ef1`). Because you have just started, there are no transactions at the moment.

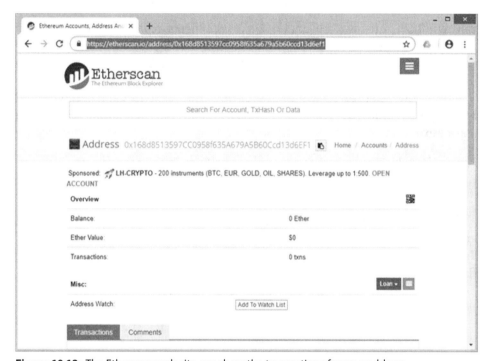

Figure 10.18: The Etherscan web site can show the transactions for your address.

Before you can send anybody any Ether, you will need to get some Ether. You can get Ether either by mining it or by obtaining it from someone else. Once you have some Ether, you can use the following command to send it to someone:

```
.\web3j-4.0.1\bin\web3j wallet send <walletfile> 0x<address>|<ensName>
```

It will ask you to enter the wallet password, confirm the receiver address, specify the amount of Ether you want to send, and specify the Ether unit (such as ether or wei).

For more details on smart contracts and Web3j examples, see the following web sites:

```
https://docs.web3j.io/smart_contracts.html
https://github.com/web3j/sample-project-gradle
https://github.com/web3j/examples
```

The following are Web3j official web sites:

```
https://web3j.io/
https://github.com/web3j/web3j
https://docs.web3j.io/
```

10.11 Java EthereumJ Examples

EthereumJ is a pure-Java implementation of the Ethereum protocol. The EthereumJ library allows you to interact with the Ethereum blockchain using Java. The easiest way to obtain and use EthereumJ is by using Git; see Appendix C for more details on how to download, install, and use Git.

In Windows, just run the Git Bash program, and from the Git Bash command line, type the following command to download and run a simple EthereumJ starter example:

```
git clone https://github.com/ether-camp/ethereumj.starter
cd ethereumj.starter
./gradlew run
```

Please note that the `./gradlew run` command will download quite a few files and may take several minutes. It will also configure and run a local REST server. To check the results, type the following command at the Git Bash command line, to view the information for the local blockchain:

```
curl -w "\n" -X GET http://localhost:8080/bestBlock
```

The following command will download, or clone, the entire EthereumJ project source:

```
git clone https://github.com/ethereum/ethereumj
```

After the download, you can change to the `ethereumj` subfolder and run an example program named TestNetSample, which is an example for Testnet (see section 10.9.1). Also shown here are the truncated results (the full results are too long):

```
cd ethereumj
./gradlew run -PmainClass=org.ethereum.samples.TestNetSample

Starting a Gradle Daemon, 1 incompatible Daemon could not be reused, use
--status for details
Building version: 1.13.0-SNAPSHOT (from branch develop)
publishing if master || develop current branch: null
[buildinfo] Properties file path was not found! (Relevant only for
builds running on a CI Server)

:ethereumj-core:processResources
```

```
This will be printed after the build task even if something else calls
the build task
:ethereumj-core:classes
:ethereumj-core:run
20:09:17.397 INFO [sample]  Starting EthereumJ!
20:09:17.444 INFO [general]  Starting EthereumJ...
20:09:26.092 INFO [general]  External address identified: 59.72.70.14
20:09:26.170 INFO [discover]  Pinging discovery nodes...

20:09:26.339 INFO [general]  EthereumJ node started:
enode://23b940843d8adf1fb0ccfe4a781e9e35850be7f3aaf6dd5e3b1f2371c1361
cc2baaac2d8c95882c34b7ae5ff18bf8a504d50e99f22ad4ee60963fa4930d0c9e
8@59.72.70.14:30303
20:09:26.355 INFO [general]  DB is empty - adding Genesis
20:09:26.424 INFO [general]  Genesis block loaded
20:09:26.439 INFO [ethash]  Kept caches: cnt: 1 epochs: 0...0
20:09:26.471 INFO [general]  Bind address wasn't set, Punching to
identify it...
20:09:47.519 WARN [general]  Can't get bind IP. Fall back to 0.0.0.0:
java.net.ConnectException: Connection timed out: connect
20:09:47.519 INFO [discover]  Discovery UDPListener started
20:09:47.688 INFO [net]  Listening for incoming connections, port:
[30303]
20:09:47.688 INFO [net]  NodeId:
[23b940843d8adf1fb0ccfe4a781e9e35850be7f3aaf6dd5e3b1f2371c1361
cc2baaac2d8c95882c34b7ae5ff18bf8a504d50e99f22ad4ee60963fa4930d0c9e8]
20:09:47.741 INFO [discover]  Reading Node statistics from DB: 0 nodes.
20:09:48.085 INFO [discover]  Received response.
20:09:49.001 INFO [discover]  New peers discovered.
20:09:57.570 INFO [net]  TCP: Speed in/out 3Kb / 3Kb(sec), packets in/
out 91/150, total in/out: 31Kb / 37Kb
20:09:57.570 INFO [net]  UDP: Speed in/out 8Kb / 6Kb(sec), packets in/
out 438/465, total in/out: 81Kb / 63Kb
20:10:07.575 INFO [net]  TCP: Speed in/out 3Kb / 4Kb(sec), packets in/
out 98/162, total in/out: 66Kb / 78Kb
20:10:07.575 INFO [net]  UDP: Speed in/out 4Kb / 2Kb(sec), packets in/
out 178/192, total in/out: 123Kb / 89Kb
20:10:48.541 INFO [discover]  Write Node statistics to DB: 829 nodes.
```

You can also run other example programs, such as these:

```
./gradlew run -PmainClass=org.ethereum.samples.BasicSample
./gradlew run -PmainClass=org.ethereum.samples.FollowAccount
./gradlew run -PmainClass=org.ethereum.samples.PendingStateSample
./gradlew run -PmainClass=org.ethereum.samples.PriceFeedSample
./gradlew run -PmainClass=org.ethereum.samples.PrivateMinerSample
./gradlew run -PmainClass=org.ethereum.samples.TransactionBomb
```

For more details about EthereumJ, see this page:

```
https://github.com/ethereum/ethereumj
```

10.12   Java Ethereum Smart Contract Example

In the chapter's final Java example, you'll learn how to create an Ethereum Smart Contract. To that, you will need to use Solidity, the designated programming language for Ethereum Smart Contracts, which can be downloaded from the following web site:

```
https://github.com/ethereum/solidity/releases
```

(In this book, the Solidity downloaded is version 0.5.7.) For Windows, just look for an archive named `solidity-windows.zip`. Download it and unzip it to a local folder; in this example, you use `E:\solidity-windows\`. The `solc.exe` file in the folder is what you need to compile Solidity programs.

For other operating systems, just follow their instructions accordingly.

You will also need Web3j. Please see section 10.10 for download details. Again, you assume it is downloaded and unzipped into a local folder named `E:\web3j-4.0.1\`.

Create a folder named `E:\contracts\solidity\`. Use a text editor to create a file named `Greeter.sol` in this folder, and save the content in Example 10.4 into the file. This is a simple Smart Contract application, which essentially has just one function, `greet()`, which just returns the value in a `String` variable named `greeting`.

EXAMPLE 10.4   THE SOLIDITY SMART CONTRACT PROGRAM

```
pragma solidity >0.4.17;
contract mortal {
    address owner;
    function mortal() public { owner = msg.sender; }
    function kill() public { if (msg.sender == owner)
selfdestruct(owner); }
}
contract greeter is mortal {
    string greeting;
    // constructor
    function greeter(string _greeting) public {
        greeting = _greeting;
    }
    // getter
    function greet() public constant returns (string memory) {
        return greeting;
    }
}
```

From a Windows terminal, go to the `E:\contracts\solidity\` folder, and type in the following command to compile the Solidity program:

```
E:\solidity-windows\solc Greeter.sol --bin --abi --optimize -o ../build
```

This will create the following two `.bin` files and two `.abi` files in `E:\con-tracts\build\` folder:

```
E:\contracts\build\Greeter.bin
E:\contracts\build\Greeter.abi
E:\contracts\build\Mortal.bin
E:\contracts\build\Mortal.abi
```

For more information about Solidity programming, see the following site:

```
https://solidity.readthedocs.io/
```

Then, from the `E:\contracts\build\` folder, type in the following command to create a Java project for the Ethereum Smart Contract:

```
E:\web3j-4.0.1\bin\web3j solidity generate ./greeter.bin ./greeter.abi
-o ../../src/main/java
```

This will create the Java project in the `E:\src\` folder, which has the following structure and contains a Java program called `Greeter.java`:

```
E:\
   \src
      \main
          \java
              \Greeter.java
```

Example 10.5 is the generated `Greeter.java` program.

EXAMPLE 10.5   THE WEB3J-GENERATED GREETER.JAVA **PROGRAM**

```java
import java.math.BigInteger;
import java.util.Arrays;
import java.util.Collections;
import org.web3j.abi.FunctionEncoder;
import org.web3j.abi.TypeReference;
import org.web3j.abi.datatypes.Function;
import org.web3j.abi.datatypes.Type;
import org.web3j.abi.datatypes.Utf8String;
import org.web3j.crypto.Credentials;
import org.web3j.protocol.Web3j;
import org.web3j.protocol.core.RemoteCall;
import org.web3j.protocol.core.methods.response.TransactionReceipt;
import org.web3j.tx.Contract;
import org.web3j.tx.TransactionManager;
import org.web3j.tx.gas.ContractGasProvider;

/**
 * <p>Auto generated code.
 * <p><strong>Do not modify!</strong>
```

```
  * <p>Please use the <a href="https://docs.web3j.io/command_line.
html">web3j command line tools</a>,
  * or the org.web3j.codegen.SolidityFunctionWrapperGenerator in the
  * <a href="https://github.com/web3j/web3j/tree/master/
codegen">codegen module</a> to update.
  *
  * <p>Generated with web3j version 4.0.1.
  */
public class Greeter extends Contract {
    private static final String BINARY = "608060405234801561001057600080
fd5b506040516102f03803806102f0833981018060405260208110156100335760080fd
5b810190808051640100000000811115610004b57600080fd5b82016020810184811115
61005e57600080fd5b815164010000000081118282018710171561007857600080fd5b5050
6000805460016001600a01b031916331790558051909350610a492506001915060208401
906100ab565b5050610146565b828054600181600116156101000203166002900490600
0526020600020906010602090481019282601f106100ec57805160ff19168380011785
55610119565b828001600101855582156101019579182015b828111156101195782518255
9160200191906001019061006fe565b5061012592915061012956b5090565b6101439190
5b8082111561012557600081556001016101012f565b90565b61019b806101556000396000
f3fe60806040523480156100105760080fd5b506004361061003657600035600e01c8063
41c0e1b51461003b578063cfae321714610045575b600080fd5b6100436100c2565b005b
61004d6100da565b604080516020808252835181830152835191928392908301918501901
80838360005b838110156100875781810151838201526020016100f565b5050505090500
90810190601f1680156100b4578082038051600183602003610100a0319168152602001
91505b50925050506040518091039f35b6000546001600160a01b03163314156100d857
33ff5b565b6001805460408051602060601f600260001961010087891615020190951694901
94049384018190048102820181019092528281526060093909290918301828280156101651
5780601f1061013a5761010080835404028352916020019161610165565b82019190600052
6020600020905b815481529060010190602001808311610148578290036001f168201915b
505050505090509056fea165627a7a72305820855e7ee1fb28333dc0c79be44c87e61ad0
a03ed6e471852ff59c26020f966aa30029";

    public static final String FUNC_KILL = "kill";

    public static final String FUNC_GREET = "greet";

    @Deprecated
    protected Greeter(String contractAddress, Web3j web3j, Credentials
credentials, BigInteger gasPrice, BigInteger gasLimit) {
        super(BINARY, contractAddress, web3j, credentials, gasPrice,
gasLimit);
    }

    protected Greeter(String contractAddress, Web3j web3j, Credentials
credentials, ContractGasProvider contractGasProvider) {
        super(BINARY, contractAddress, web3j, credentials,
contractGasProvider);
    }

    @Deprecated
```

```java
    protected Greeter(String contractAddress, Web3j web3j,
TransactionManager transactionManager, BigInteger gasPrice, BigInteger
gasLimit) {
        super(BINARY, contractAddress, web3j, transactionManager,
gasPrice, gasLimit);
    }

    protected Greeter(String contractAddress, Web3j web3j,
TransactionManager transactionManager, ContractGasProvider
contractGasProvider) {
        super(BINARY, contractAddress, web3j, transactionManager,
contractGasProvider);
    }

    public RemoteCall<TransactionReceipt> kill() {
        final Function function = new Function(
                FUNC_KILL,
                Arrays.<Type>asList(),
                Collections.<TypeReference<?>>emptyList());
        return executeRemoteCallTransaction(function);
    }

    public RemoteCall<String> greet() {
        final Function function = new Function(FUNC_GREET,
                Arrays.<Type>asList(),
                Arrays.<TypeReference<?>>asList(new
TypeReference<Utf8String>() {}));
        return executeRemoteCallSingleValueReturn(function, String.
class);
    }

    @Deprecated
    public static Greeter load(String contractAddress, Web3j web3j,
Credentials credentials, BigInteger gasPrice, BigInteger gasLimit) {
        return new Greeter(contractAddress, web3j, credentials,
gasPrice, gasLimit);
    }

    @Deprecated
    public static Greeter load(String contractAddress, Web3j web3j,
TransactionManager transactionManager, BigInteger gasPrice, BigInteger
gasLimit) {
        return new Greeter(contractAddress, web3j, transactionManager,
gasPrice, gasLimit);
    }

    public static Greeter load(String contractAddress, Web3j web3j,
Credentials credentials, ContractGasProvider contractGasProvider) {
        return new Greeter(contractAddress, web3j, credentials,
contractGasProvider);
    }
```

```
        public static Greeter load(String contractAddress, Web3j
web3j, TransactionManager transactionManager, ContractGasProvider
contractGasProvider) {
        return new Greeter(contractAddress, web3j, transactionManager,
contractGasProvider);
    }

        public static RemoteCall<Greeter> deploy(Web3j web3j, Credentials
credentials, ContractGasProvider contractGasProvider, String _greeting)
{
        String encodedConstructor = FunctionEncoder.encodeConstructor(Ar
rays.<Type>asList(new org.web3j.abi.datatypes.Utf8String(_greeting)));
        return deployRemoteCall(Greeter.class, web3j, credentials,
contractGasProvider, BINARY, encodedConstructor);
    }

        public static RemoteCall<Greeter> deploy(Web3j web3j,
TransactionManager transactionManager, ContractGasProvider
contractGasProvider, String _greeting) {
        String encodedConstructor = FunctionEncoder.encodeConstructor(Ar
rays.<Type>asList(new org.web3j.abi.datatypes.Utf8String(_greeting)));
        return deployRemoteCall(Greeter.class, web3j,
transactionManager, contractGasProvider, BINARY, encodedConstructor);
    }

    @Deprecated
        public static RemoteCall<Greeter> deploy(Web3j web3j, Credentials
credentials, BigInteger gasPrice, BigInteger gasLimit, String _greeting)
{
        String encodedConstructor = FunctionEncoder.encodeConstructor(Ar
rays.<Type>asList(new org.web3j.abi.datatypes.Utf8String(_greeting)));
        return deployRemoteCall(Greeter.class, web3j, credentials,
gasPrice, gasLimit, BINARY, encodedConstructor);
    }

    @Deprecated
        public static RemoteCall<Greeter> deploy(Web3j web3j,
TransactionManager transactionManager, BigInteger gasPrice, BigInteger
gasLimit, String _greeting) {
        String encodedConstructor = FunctionEncoder.encodeConstructor(Ar
rays.<Type>asList(new org.web3j.abi.datatypes.Utf8String(_greeting)));
        return deployRemoteCall(Greeter.class, web3j,
transactionManager, gasPrice, gasLimit, BINARY, encodedConstructor);
    }
}
```

Next, use Web3j to create a digital wallet. The procedure is the same as illustrated in section 10.10. Enter the password when prompted, and save the wallet in a folder on your E:\ drive.

```
E:\web3j-4.0.1\bin\web3j wallet create
```

The digital wallet will be something like the following, where d517e874a888b58d-02dad75c26f2a7ddec14f07b is the wallet ID.

```
E:\UTC--2019-04-12T03-47-43.931058900Z--d517e874a888b58d02dad75c26f2a7dd
ec14f07b.json
```

You will need this wallet password and ID later. Next go to the Infura (https://infura.io/) web site to register an account, create a new project, and copy out the secret key. Infura is an online platform that provides a wide variety of tools to connect your applications to Ethereum. For more information about using Infura with Web3j, see the following site:

```
https://docs.web3j.io/infura.html
```

Example 10.6 shows a Java program that can use the `Greeter.java` program to deploy the Smart Contract and execute the Smart Contract. In this program, the `rinkebyKey` is the project ID or token ID you got from Infura, and the `walletFilePassword` and `walletId` are what you have created using Web3j. Please update them with your own values.

EXAMPLE 10.6   THE GREETING.JAVA **SMART CONTRACT PROGRAM**

```java
import java.io.IOException;
import java.util.concurrent.ExecutionException;
import org.web3j.crypto.CipherException;
import org.web3j.crypto.Credentials;
import org.web3j.crypto.WalletUtils;
import org.web3j.protocol.Web3j;
import org.web3j.protocol.http.HttpService;
import org.web3j.tx.Contract;

public class Greeting {
  public static void main(String[] args) throws IOException,
CipherException, ExecutionException, InterruptedException {

        String rinkebyKey = "498d65b077ea40ae9aeb2bbb014947cc";
        String rinkebyUrl = "https://rinkeby.infura.io/" + rinkebyKey;
        Web3j web3j = Web3j.build(new HttpService(rinkebyUrl));

        String walletFilePassword = "0000000000";
        String walletId = "d517e874a888b58d02dad75c26f2a7ddec14f07b";
        String walletSource = "E:\\UTC--2019-04-12T03-47-43.931058900Z--"
+ walletId + ".json";
        Credentials credentials = WalletUtils.loadCredentials(walletFilePa
ssword, walletSource);

        try {
            //Deploy Smart Contract with a Hello Smart Contract message
            Greeter greeter = Greeter.deploy(web3j, credentials, Contract.
GAS_PRICE, Contract.GAS_LIMIT, "Hello Smart Contract!!!").send();
```

```
        //Display Smart Contract address
        System.out.println(greeter.getContractAddress());
        //Execute Smart Contract's greet() function
        System.out.println(greeter.greet().send());
    }catch(Exception e){
        System.out.println(e.toString());
    }
  }
}
```

You can compile and run the `Greeting.java` and `Greeter.java` programs by typing the following commands:

```
javac -classpath ".;E:\\web3j-4.0.1\\lib\\*" Greeter.java Greeting.java
java -classpath ".;E:\\web3j-4.0.1\\lib\\*" Greeting
```

If everything is correct, you should see a "Hello Smart Contract" message on the screen; otherwise, it will display an error message to explain what is going wrong. A common error is "insufficient funds for gas * price + value." This is simply because you have not got enough Ether coin in your account. You can either get real Ether:

```
https://github.com/ethereum/wiki/wiki/Getting-Ether
https://www.ethereum.org/ether
```

or get Ether for testing:

```
https://faucet.rinkeby.io/
```

10.13   Go Further: Choosing a Blockchain Platform

If you want to go further with blockchain, whatever your applications might be—cryptocurrency, healthcare, manufacturing, supply chains, or the IoT—the next and most important step is to choose a suitable blockchain platform and then develop your own decentralized applications, known as *DApps*. Decentralized applications are different from traditional centralized applications, such as Google, Facebook, or Amazon, where the contents are owned by a central entity. For decentralized applications, the contents are owned by the users. The following is a list of popular blockchain platforms:

Bitcoin   (`https://bitcoin.org/en/`) This is the first blockchain platform, where it all started. This platform is solely designed for one purpose only, which is for the crypocurrency Bitcoin (BTC). The software implementation of Bitcoin is called Bitcoin Core (`https://bitcoincore.org/`), also called Bitcoin client. Bitcoin Core is written in C++. Today, Bitcoin is the most successful digital currency, with billions of dollars invested in it around the world.

Ethereum (https://www.ethereum.org/) Ethereum was founded in November 2013, by Vitalik Buterin, a Russian-Canadian programmer, when he was only 19 years old! Unlike the Bitcoin platform, the Ethereum platform can do more than just cryptocurrency. Ethereum is written in a Turing-complete language, which includes seven different programming languages. Featuring smart contract functionality, Ethereum is an open source software platform that enables developers to build and deploy decentralized applications based on blockchain technology. Ethereum has its own cryptocurrency, Ether (ETH), and its own programming language, Solidity, a contract-oriented programming language for writing smart contracts.

Eris (https://monax.io/platform/) Built on the Ethereum blockchain, Eris is another free, open platform for building, testing, maintaining, and operating decentralized applications. Eris makes it easy and simple to implement smart contracts.

IBM Blockchain (https://www.ibm.com/blockchain) IBM Blockchain, which is based on the open source Hyperledger Fabric, is a public cloud service that aims for business customers to build secure blockchain networks. Hyperledger Fabric is different from traditional blockchain networks, which can't support private transactions or confidential contracts, which are key for businesses. Hyperledger Fabric addresses this issue by keeping private transactions private and keeping the specific data to be accessible only to who needs to know.

NEO (https://neo.org/) NEO is a nonprofit community-driven blockchain platform. It aims to create a "smart economy," by utilizing digitize assets, digital identity, and smart contracts. Using a distributed network, Neo uses an interesting consensus mechanism that can improve its scalability.

10.14   Summary

This chapter introduced the concept of blockchains, as well as how to validate a blockchain and how to mine the blocks. Then you learned how blockchains work and what they can be used for. You also saw variations of a simple Java blockchain example, using the BitcoinJ, Web3j, and EthereumJ open source libraries. Finally, you looked at the platforms you'll need to choose from when you decide to go further and use blockchain in your own business. Blockchain is a fascinating technology. Although it still has some issues, it is nevertheless amazing and has the potential to fundamentally change the world.

10.15   Chapter Review Questions

Q10.1.   When was blockchain invented, and who invented blockchain?

Q10.2.   Use a suitable diagram to illustrate what is inside a block and what is the relationship between two adjacent blocks.

Q10.3.   How do you validate a blockchain?

Q10.4.   What is a blockchain consensus?

Q10.5.   What does it mean to mine a blockchain? What is proof of work?

Q10.6.   What can blockchains be used for?

Q10.7.   What are the issues with blockchain technology?

Q10.8.   What are Bitcoin and Bitcoin Cash? What is a fork in software development?

Q10.9.   What is a smart contract?

Q10.10.   What are the differences between the Bitcoin blockchain platform, the Ethereum platform, and the Hyperledger Fabric platform?

Java Programming for Big Data Applications

Data is the new oil.

—Clive Humby

11.1   What Is Big Data?

Data is important for our lives, and we are using data all the time. For example, experimental data saved in a file, student record or employee record saved in a database, sales figures saved in a spreadsheet, as well as common Word, Excel, PowerPoint files, sound files, and movie files, are all traditional data files, which can be stored, analyzed, and displayed using a standard personal computer. The sizes of traditional data files range from kilobytes (KB, 2^{10} bytes), megabytes (MB, 2^{20} bytes) to gigabytes (GB, 2^{30} bytes), and sometimes to terabytes (TB, 2^{40} bytes). However, with the rapid expansion of the Internet and the increase in mobile users, data can be measured with sizes larger than petabytes, 2^{50} bytes. These data stores are called *big data*. Big data is too large and too complicated to be stored and analyzed using traditional computer hardware and software.

According to Wikipedia, the world's technological per-capita data capacity has doubled roughly every 40 months since the 1980s. As of 2012, about 2.5 exabytes (2.5×10^{18} bytes) of data were generated every day. According to an International Data Corporation (IDC) report prediction, the volume of global data will grow exponentially from 4.4 zettabytes (4.4×10^{21} bytes) to 44 zettabytes between 2013 and 2020. There will be 163 zettabytes of data by 2025, as illustrated in Figure 11.1.

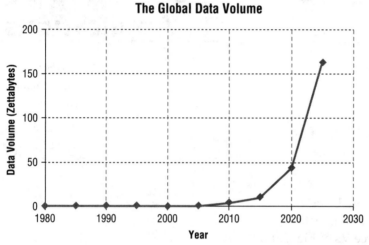

Figure 11.1: The global data volume in zettabytes according to an IDC report prediction

Plotted according to the data from `https://www.seagate.com/files/www-content/our-story/trends/files/idc-seagate-dataage-whitepaper.pdf`

Java, as a modern high-level programming language, is well suited for big data applications. Java is the language of Hadoop, the most popular big data software framework. Many Hadoop key modules, such as MapReduce, are run on Java Virtual Machines (JVMs). Java can be run on many devices and platforms. Java models and implements stack data structure, which can re-establish the statistics quickly. Java can automate trash gathering and memory distribution. Java has rich networking functionalities. Java has a great security compliance and is a secure programming language.

11.2   Sources of Big Data

Several sources are generating big data today.

Social Media Web Sites   Web sites such as Facebook, Twitter, Snapchat, WhatsApp, YouTube, Google, Yahoo, and others generate massive amounts of data each day, from their billions of users around the world.

E-commerce Web Sites   Online shopping web sites such as Amazon, eBay, Alibaba, and the like also generate tons of data, which can be analyzed to understand consumer shopping habits and sales predictions.

Telecommunication Companies   Telecommunication giants such as Verizon, AT&T, China Mobile, Nippon, EE, Vodafone, and Telefonica also generate huge amounts of data by storing communication records and customer information.

Stock Market   Stock markets around the world generate huge amounts of data by storing daily transactions.

Internet of Things (IoT)   With billions and billions of devices connected to the IoT, the IoT also generate an enormous amount of data every day from sensor-enabled devices.

Hospitals   Hospitals generate massive amounts of data from patient records.

Banks   Banks generate massive amounts of data from the transactions of their customers.

Weather Stations   Weather stations generate a massive amount of data from satellite images for weather forecasting.

Government Departments   Government departments also hold personal information of millions and millions citizens.

11.3   The Three Vs of Big Data

The three defining characteristics of Big Data are its volume, velocity, and variety, sometimes described as "the three Vs of Big Data." Here's a quick look at each:

Volume   The volume of big data is massive, typically ranging from tens of terabytes to hundreds of petabytes. For example, Facebook has 2 billion users, WeChat has 1 billion users, YouTube has 1 billion users, WhatsApp has 1 billion users, Instagram has 1 billion users, Alibaba has 600 million users, Twitter has 300 million users, and Snapchat has 180 million users. These users generate billions of images, posts, videos, tweets, and so on, every single day.

Velocity   The speed at which big data is generated is also breathtaking. Facebook, for example, has 317,000 status updates, 400 new users, 147,000 photos uploaded, and 54,000 shared links every 60 seconds. Big data is also growing at an increasing speed. According to the IDC report mentioned earlier, it is estimated that the amount of data will double every two years.

Variety   Big data can consist of many available data types. They include structured data types such as texts, pictures, and videos; semistructured data types such as XML data; and unstructured data types such as handwritten text, drawings, voice records, and measurement data. All of these forms of data will require additional preprocessing to derive meaning and support metadata.

11.4   Benefits of Big Data

Big data is really one of the most important emerging digital technologies in the modern world. Big data analysis can have many benefits. For example, by analyzing the information kept in a social network like Facebook, you can better understand users' responses to product advertisements and to social, economic, and political issues. By analyzing the information on e-commerce web sites, product companies and retail organizations can better plan their production according to the preferences and product perceptions of their consumers. By analyzing the previous medical history of millions of patients, doctors can make easier and earlier diagnoses, and hospitals can provide better and quicker service.

11.5   What Is Hadoop?

Hadoop is an open-source software framework developed by the Apache Software Foundation in the mid-2000s for the purpose of working with big data. Hadoop allows users to store and process large datasets in a distributed environment across clusters of computers using simple programming models. Hadoop is designed to scale up from a single computer to thousands of computers, each having its own local computation and storage. A Hadoop cluster consists of a master node and a number of slave nodes. Hadoop can handle various forms of structured and unstructured data, which makes big data analysis more flexible. Hadoop uses a namesake distributed file system that's designed to provide rapid data access across the nodes in a cluster. Hadoop also has fault-tolerant capabilities so that applications can continue to run even if individual nodes fail. Thanks to these advantages, Hadoop has become a key data management platform for big data analytics, such as predictive analytics, data mining, and machine learning applications. Hadoop is mostly written in Java, with some native code in C and command-line utilities written as shell scripts.

To date, financial companies have used Hadoop to build applications for assessing risk, building investment models, and creating trading algorithms. Retailers use Hadoop for analyzing structured and unstructured data to better understand and serve their customers. Telecommunications companies use Hadoop-powered analytics for predictive maintenance on their infrastructure, as well as for supporting customer-facing operations. By analyzing customer behavior and billing statements, they can offer new services to existing customers. Hadoop has been used extensively in many other applications and is a de facto standard in big data.

11.6   Key Components of Hadoop

Hadoop consists of several key components: Hadoop Distributed File System (HDFS), MapReduce, Hadoop Common, and Hadoop Yet Another Resource Negotiator (YARN).

11.6.1   HDFS

Hadoop Distributed File System (HDFS) provides data storage. It is designed to run on low-cost hardware with high fault tolerance. In HDFS, files are split up into blocks that are replicated to the DataNodes. By default, each block is 64 MB in size and is replicated to three DataNodes in the cluster. HDFS uses TCP/IP sockets for communication. Clients in the cluster use remote procedure calls (RPC) to communicate with each other.

HDFS has five services.

- NameNode (master service)
- Secondary NameNode (master service)
- JobTracker (master service)
- DataNode (slave service)
- TaskTracker (slave service)

The first three services are master services, and the last two are slave services. Master services run on the master node, and slave services run on both the master node and the slave nodes.

The NameNode is the master, and the DataNodes are its corresponding slaves. A Hadoop cluster has a single NameNode and a cluster of DataNodes. The NameNode can track the files and manage the file system. The NameNode contains detailed information including the total number of blocks, the locations of specific blocks (to determine what parts of the data are stored in which node), where the replications are stored, and the like.

DataNodes store data as blocks for the clients to read and write. DataNodes are slave daemons. DataNodes send a heartbeat message to the NameNode every three seconds to show they are alive. If the NameNode does not receive a heartbeat from a DataNode for two minutes, it will assume that DataNode is dead.

The Secondary NameNode, also known as the checkpoint node, is a helper node for the NameNode. It periodically updates the file system metadata by fetching relevant files (such as edits and fsimage) from the NameNode and merges them.

JobTracker receives the requests for MapReduce execution from the client. JobTracker communicates with the NameNode to know about the location of the data. The NameNode provides the metadata to the JobTracker.

The TaskTracker takes the task and the code from the JobTracker. The Task-Tracker will apply the code to the file, a process known as *mapping*.

11.6.2   MapReduce

MapReduce provides data processing. It is a software framework written in Java that can be used to create applications for processing large amounts of data. Similar to HDFS, MapReduce is also built to be fault tolerant and to be able to work in large-scale cluster environments. MapReduce splits up input data into smaller tasks (the process of *mapping* tasks) that can be executed in parallel processes. The output from the map tasks is then reduced, and the results are saved to HDFS. For example, suppose you want to create a word count or concordance; that is, to count the number of times each word is used across a set of documents, MapReduce will divide this job into two phases: the map phase and the reduce phase. The map phase counts the words in each document, and then the reduce phase aggregates the counts in each document into word counts spanning the entire collection.

MapReduce is Hadoop's native batch processing engine, which involves the following basic steps:

1. Reading data from HDFS.
2. Dividing data into small chunks and distributed among nodes.
3. Applying the computation on each node.
4. Saving the intermediate results to HDFS.
5. Redistributing the intermediate results to group by key.
6. Reducing the value of each key by summarizing and combining the results from each node.
7. Saving the final results to HDFS.

11.6.3   Hadoop Common

Hadoop Common is a set of shared Java utilities and libraries, which are required by other Hadoop modules. These Java libraries provide file system and OS-level abstractions and contain the necessary Java files and scripts required to start Hadoop.

11.6.4   Hadoop YARN

Hadoop YARN is a framework for job scheduling and cluster resource management. YARN makes it possible to run much more diverse workloads on a Hadoop cluster.

11.6.5   Overview of a Hadoop Cluster

Figure 11.2 shows the schematic diagram of a multinode Hadoop cluster. A typical small Hadoop cluster includes a single master node and multiple slave (worker) nodes. The master node consists of a JobTracker, TaskTracker, Name Node, and DataNode. A slave or worker node consists of both a DataNode and a TaskTracker.

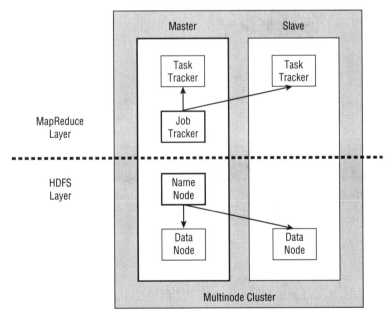

Figure 11.2: A multinode Hadoop cluster

Adapted from `https://en.wikipedia.org/wiki/Apache_Hadoop`

11.7 Implementing Hadoop on a Raspberry Pi Cluster

Hadoop can run only in a Linux-like operating system, and it requires Java Runtime Environment (JRE) 1.6 or higher. It also requires that Secure Shell (SSH) be set up between nodes in the cluster for the standard Hadoop startup and shutdown scripts. In this chapter's hands-on example, we are going to set up Hadoop on a two-node Raspberry Pi 3 cluster, as illustrated in Figure 11.3 and summarized in Table 11.1. Raspberry Pi provides an excellent cheap solution for building your own Hadoop data cluster for learning and practicing purposes. Even though the data this system will handle won't be very "big," it will demonstrate the structure of a cluster.

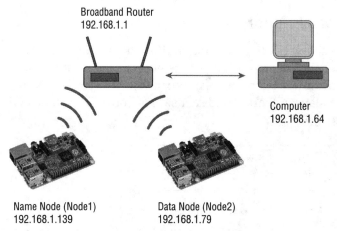

Figure 11.3: Hadoop on a two-node Raspberry Pi cluster

Table 11.1: The Hadoop Configuration on the Two Raspberry Pi Nodes

NAME	IP ADDRESS	HADOOP SERVICES
Node1	192.168.1.139	NameNode
		Secondary NameNode
		JobTracker
		DataNode
		TaskTracker
Node2	192.168.1.79	DataNode
		TaskTracker

11.7.1   Raspberry Pi Installation and Configuration

Please refer to Chapter 7 section 7.6 for Raspberry Pi installation and configuration.

Once the Raspberry Pi is up and running, open a Raspberry Pi terminal window; the rest of the procedure will be done through the terminal window.

Type `sudo nano /etc/hostname` in the terminal window, and change its content to the following:

```
node1
```

This will change the hostname of Raspberry Pi to `node1`. Here, `nano` is a Linux text editor, and `sudo` instructs the system to modify the file as a superuser. You can also use other Linux text editors, such as `vi`, `vim`, `pico`, `emacs`, or `sublime`.

Type `sudo nano /etc/hosts` in the terminal window, and append the following to its content. This will set the IP address of node1.

```
192.168.1.139          node1
```

Java should be preinstalled with Raspbian; you can double-check this by typing `java -version` from Raspberry Pi terminal window.

```
java -version

java version "1.8.0_65"
Java(TM) SE Runtime Environment (build 1.8.0_65-b17)
Java HotSpot(TM) Client VM (build 25.65-b01, mixed mode)
```

Now restart Raspberry Pi by typing the following command:

```
sudo reboot
```

11.7.2   Hadoop Installation and Configuration

In this section, you'll take the following steps to install and configure Hadoop on your cluster:

1. Prepare the Hadoop user account and group.
2. Configure SSH.
3. Download and install Hadoop.
4. Configure the environment variables.
5. Configure Hadoop.
6. Start and stop Hadoop services.
7. Test Hadoop.
8. Hadoop on a Web Browser.

Prepare the Hadoop User Account and Group

To install Hadoop, you will need to prepare a Hadoop user account and a Hadoop group. From a Raspberry Pi terminal window, type the following commands to create a Hadoop group called hadoop, add a user called hduser to the group, and make hduser a superuser or administrator. The second command will prompt you for your password and other information for hduser, provide a password, and use default values for all the rest of the information.

```
$sudo addgroup hadoop
$sudo adduser --ingroup hadoop hduser
$sudo adduser hduser sudo
```

Configure SSH

Type the following commands to create a pair of SSH RSA keys with a blank password so that Hadoop nodes will be able to talk with each other without prompting for a password:

```
$su hduser
$mkdir ~/.ssh
$ssh-keygen -t rsa -P ""
$cat ~/.ssh/id_rsa.pub > ~/.ssh/authorized_keys
$exit
```

Type the following commands to verify that hduser can log in to SSH:

```
$su hduser
$ssh localhost
$exit
```

Download and Install Hadoop

Type the following commands to download and install Hadoop version 2.9.2:

```
$cd ~/
$wget http://mirror.vorboss.net/apache/hadoop/common/hadoop-2.9.2/
hadoop-2.9.2.tar.gz
$sudo mkdir /opt
$sudo tar -xvzf hadoop-2.9.2.tar.gz -C /opt/
$cd /opt
$sudo mv hadoop-2.9.2 hadoop
$sudo chown -R hduser:hadoop hadoop
```

Configure Environment Variables

Type **sudo nano /etc/bash.bashrc** to add the following lines at the end of the bashrc file:

```
export JAVA_HOME=$(readlink -f /usr/bin/java | sed "s:bin/java::")
export HADOOP_HOME=/opt/hadoop
export HADOOP_INSTALL=$HADOOP_HOME
export YARN_HOME=$HADOOP_HOME
export PATH=$PATH:$HADOOP_INSTALL/bin
```

Then type **source ~/.bashrc** to apply the changes. Now switch to hduser to verify that the Hadoop executable is accessible outside the /opt/hadoop/bin folder:

```
$su hduser
$hadoop version

hduser@node1 /home/hduser $ hadoop version
Hadoop 2.9.2
Subversion https://git-wip-us.apache.org/repos/asf/hadoop.git -r
826afbeae31ca687bc2f8471dc841b66ed2c6704
Compiled by ajisaka on 2018-11-13T12:42Z
Compiled with protoc 2.5.0
From source with checksum 3a9939967262218aa556c684d107985
This command was run using /opt/hadoop/share/hadoop/common/
hadoop-common-2.9.2.jar
```

Type **sudo nano /opt/hadoop/etc/hadoop/hadoop-env.sh**, and then append the following lines:

```
export JAVA_HOME=$(readlink -f /usr/bin/java | sed "s:bin/java::")
export HADOOP_HEAPSIZE=250
```

Configure Hadoop

Now move to the /opt/hadoop/etc/hadoop/ directory and use a text editor to edit the following configuration files as a superuser:

core-site.xml

```
<configuration>
  <property>
    <name>fs.default.name</name>
    <value>hdfs://node1:9000</value>
  </property>
</configuration>
```

mapred-site.xml

```
<configuration>
  <property>
    <name>mapreduce.framework.name</name>
    <value>yarn</value>
  </property>
</configuration>
```

hdfs-site.xml

```
<configuration>
  <property>
    <name>dfs.replication</name>
    <value>1</value>
  </property>
  <property>
    <name>dfs.namenode.name.dir</name>
    <value>file:/opt/hadoop/hadoop_data/hdfs/namenode</value>
  </property>
  <property>
    <name>dfs.datanode.name.dir</name>
    <value>file:/opt/hadoop/hadoop_data/hdfs/datanode</value>
  </property>
</configuration>
```

yarn-site.xml

```
<configuration>
  <property>
    <name>yarn.nodemanager.aux-services</name>
    <value>mapreduce_shuffle</value>
  </property>
  <property>
    <name>yarn.nodemanager.aux-services.mapreduce.shuffle.class</name>
    <value>org.apache.hadoop.mapred.ShuffleHandler</value>
  </property>
</configuration>
```

Type the following commands to create and format an HDFS file system:

```
$sudo mkdir -p /opt/hadoop/hadoop_data/hdfs/namenode
$sudo mkdir -p /opt/hadoop/hadoop_data/hdfs/datanode
$sudo chown hduser:hadoop /opt/hadoop/hadoop_data/hdfs -R
$sudo chmod 750 /opt/hadoop/hadoop_data/hdfs

$cd $HADOOP_INSTALL
$hdfs namenode -format
```

Start and Stop Hadoop Services

Type the following commands to switch to `hduser` and start Hadoop services. The command `jps` will display all the services running:

```
$su hduser
$cd $HADOOP_HOME/sbin
$./start-dfs.sh
$./start-yarn.sh
$jps
2082 NameNode
2578 ResourceManager
2724 Jps
2344 SecondaryNameNode
2683 NodeManager
2189 DataNode

$./stop-dfs.sh
$./stop-yarn.sh
```

Test Hadoop

Type in the following commands to run an example file provided with Hadoop, named `pi`, which calculates the value of pi:

```
$cd $HADOOP_INSTALL/bin
$./hadoop jar /opt/hadoop/share/hadoop/mapreduce/hadoop-mapreduce-
examples-2.9.2.jar pi 16 1000
```

Let's run another example provided with Hadoop, named `wordCount`.

Enter the following commands to copy the `LICENSE.txt` file from the local file system in the `/opt/hadoop/` folder to Hadoop's distributed file system as `license.txt` in the root folder; that is, the `/` folder.

```
$hdfs dfs -copyFromLocal /opt/hadoop/LICENSE.txt /license.txt
```

Enter the following commands to list the content of Hadoop distributed file system in the `/` folder.

```
$hdfs dfs -ls /
```

Enter the following commands to run the `wordCount` example and save the result into a folder called `license-out.txt`.

```
$cd /opt/hadoop/bin
$./hadoop jar /opt/hadoop/share/hadoop/mapreduce/hadoop-mapreduce-
examples-2.9.2.jar wordcount /license.txt /license-out.txt
```

Figure 11.4 shows the output from running `wordCount` on the file `license.txt`. Because the output is long, only the beginning (top) and end of the output (bottom) are shown.

Figure 11.4: The output from running the `wordCount` example on the file `license.txt`

Type in the following command to copy the `license-out.txt` file from the Hadoop distributed file system to local file system, and open `license-out.txt/part-r-00000` with nano.

```
$hdfs dfs -copyToLocal /license-out.txt ~/
$nano ~/license-out.txt/part-r-00000
```

Figure 11.5 shows the previous commands and all the word count results with `nano`.

Figure 11.5: The commands to copy the `license-out.txt` file to local file system and to open `license-out.txt/part-r-00000` with nano (top) and result of opening the license-out.txt/part-r-00000 file with the nano text editor (bottom)

If you don't want to open the `license-out.txt/part-r-00000` file, you can also use the following command just to display the content.

```
$cat ~/license-out.txt/part-r-00000
```

The following command shows how to delete a directory with nonempty files in it:

```
$hdfs dfs -rm -r /license-out.txt
```

Hadoop on a Web Browser

You can view Hadoop and its application cluster with a web browser, as shown in Figure 11.6.

```
http://node1:50070
http://node1:8088
```

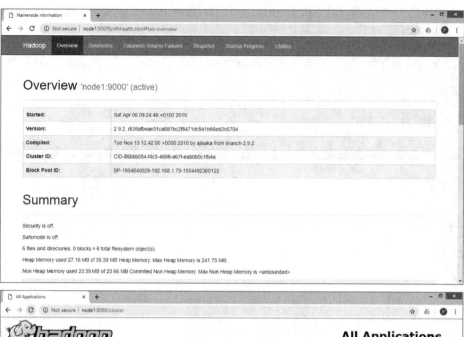

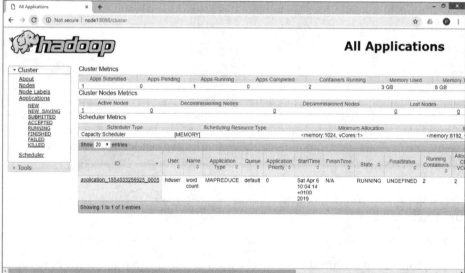

Figure 11.6: The web view of Hadoop software (top) and the application cluster (bottom) with a web browser

To add the second node to the Hadoop cluster, node2, just get another Raspberry Pi, ideally an identical one. Then you can simply clone the node1's Raspberry Pi SD Card for node2, by using Win32 Disk Imager, as shown in Figure 11.7.

```
https://sourceforge.net/projects/win32diskimager/files/latest/
download
```

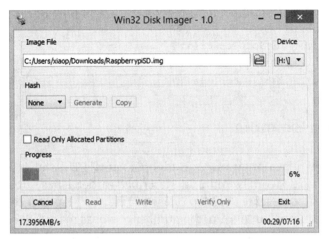

Figure 11.7: Cloning the Raspberry Pi SD Card using Win32 Disk Imager

Once the node2 is up and running, remember to edit the /etc/hosts file to include the IP address of node2, as shown next. Please change the IP addresses to yours accordingly. You will also need to reconfigure SSH for node2.

```
$sudo nano /etc/hosts
192.168.1.139 node1
192.168.1.76 node2
```

Finally, type in the following commands to delete HDFS storage and add permissions on node1:

```
$sudo rm -rf /opt/hadoop/hadoop_data
$sudo mkdir -p /opt/hadoop/hadoop_data/hdfs/namenode
$sudo mkdir -p /opt/hadoop/hadoop_data/hdfs/datanode
$sudo chown hduser:hadoop /opt/hadoop/hadoop_data/hdfs -R
$sudo chmod 750 /opt/hadoop/hadoop_data/hdfs
```

Type in the similar commands on node2:

```
$sudo rm -rf /opt/hadoop/hadoop_data
$sudo mkdir -p /opt/hadoop/hadoop_data/hdfs/datanode
$sudo chown hduser:hadoop /opt/hadoop/hadoop_data/hdfs -R
$sudo chmod 750 /opt/hadoop/hadoop_data/hdfs
```

See the following resources for more information about Hadoop:

http://hadoop.apache.org/docs/stable/

https://hadoop.apache.org/docs/stable/hadoop-project-dist/hadoop-common/SingleCluster.html

https://hadoop.apache.org/docs/stable/hadoop-project-dist/hadoop-common/ClusterSetup.html

https://www.javatpoint.com/hadoop-tutorial

https://howtodoinjava.com/hadoop/hadoop-big-data-tutorial/

https://www.guru99.com/bigdata-tutorials.html

11.8 Java Hadoop Example

You can also write your own Java program for Hadoop. Example 11.1 shows a simple Java program that can do word counting, as described earlier. It has three classes: The MyMapper class represents the Map phase of Hadoop MapReduce, which implements the map() method to count the number of words in each document. The MyReducer class represents the Reduce phase of Hadoop MapReduce, which implements the reducer() method to aggregate the counts in each document into word counts of all the documents. The main class calls the MyMapper class and the MyReducer class and displays the final results.

EXAMPLE 11.1 JAVA HADOOP WORD COUNT PROGRAM

```java
import java.util.*;
import java.io.IOException;
import org.apache.hadoop.conf.*;
import org.apache.hadoop.io.*;
import org.apache.hadoop.mapreduce.*;
import org.apache.hadoop.fs.Path;
import org.apache.hadoop.mapreduce.lib.input.FileInputFormat;
import org.apache.hadoop.mapreduce.lib.output.FileOutputFormat;
import org.apache.hadoop.util.GenericOptionsParser;

//The MyMapper class - MapReduce's Map Phase
class MyMapper extends Mapper<Object, Text, Text, IntWritable>{

    private final static IntWritable one = new IntWritable(1);
    private Text word = new Text();

    public void map(Object key, Text value, Context context) throws
IOException, InterruptedException {
        StringTokenizer itr = new StringTokenizer(value.toString());
        while (itr.hasMoreTokens()) {
          word.set(itr.nextToken());
          context.write(word, one);
        }
    }
}
//The MyReducer class -- MapReduce's Reduce Phase
class MyReducer extends Reducer<Text,IntWritable,Text,IntWritable> {
    private IntWritable result = new IntWritable();
```

```
    public void reduce(Text key, Iterable<IntWritable> values, Context
context) throws IOException, InterruptedException {
      int sum = 0;
      for (IntWritable val : values) {
        sum += val.get();
      }
      result.set(sum);
      context.write(key, result);
    }
  }

//The main class
public class MyWordCounter {

  public static void main(String[] args) throws Exception {
    Configuration conf = new Configuration();
    String[] otherArgs = new GenericOptionsParser(conf, args).
getRemainingArgs();
    if (otherArgs.length != 2) {
      System.err.println("Usage: MyWordCounter <in> <out>");
      System.exit(2);
    }

    //For the latest Hadoop versions 3.x.y
    Job job = new Job.getInstance(conf, "word count");
    //For Hadoop version 2.9.2 or earlier
    //Job job = new Job(conf, "word count");

    job.setJarByClass(MyWordCounter.class);
    job.setMapperClass(MyMapper.class);
    job.setCombinerClass(MyReducer.class);
    job.setReducerClass(MyReducer.class);
    job.setOutputKeyClass(Text.class);
    job.setOutputValueClass(IntWritable.class);
    FileInputFormat.addInputPath(job, new Path(otherArgs[0]));
    FileOutputFormat.setOutputPath(job, new Path(otherArgs[1]));
    System.exit(job.waitForCompletion(true) ? 0 : 1);
  }
}
```

To compile the previous Java Hadoop program, you need to include the Hadoop class path into the compilation class path. From the Raspberry Pi Terminal window, type in the following command to display the content of the Hadoop class path:

```
$hadoop classpath
```

```
/opt/hadoop/etc/hadoop:/opt/hadoop/share/hadoop/common/lib/*:/opt/
hadoop/share/hadoop/common/*:/opt/hadoop/share/hadoop/hdfs:/opt/hadoop/
share/hadoop/hdfs/lib/*:/opt/hadoop/share/hadoop/hdfs/*:/opt/hadoop/
```

```
share/hadoop/yarn:/opt/hadoop/share/hadoop/yarn/lib/*:/opt/hadoop/
share/hadoop/yarn/*:/opt/hadoop/share/hadoop/mapreduce/lib/*:/opt/
hadoop/share/hadoop/mapreduce/*:/usr/lib/jvm/jdk-8-oracle-arm32-vfp-
hflt/jre//lib/tools.jar:/opt/hadoop/contrib/capacity-scheduler/*.jar
```

Type in the following command to compile the Java program, which includes the Hadoop class path:

```
$javac -cp $(hadoop classpath) MyWordCounter.java
```

Enter the following command to list all the class files that have been generated:

```
$ls -la My*.class
-rw-r--r-- 1 hduser hadoop 1682 Apr 10 04:45  MyMapper.class
-rw-r--r-- 1 hduser hadoop 1690 Apr 10 04:45  MyReducer.class
-rw-r--r-- 1 hduser hadoop 1728 Apr 10 04:45  MyWordCounter.class
-rw-r--r-- 1 hduser hadoop 1734 Apr 10 04:41  'MyWordCounter$MyMapper.
class'
-rw-r--r-- 1 hduser hadoop 1743 Apr 10 04:41  'MyWordCounter$MyReducer.
class'
```

Then use the following command to include all the class files into a JAR file called Test.jar:

```
$jar -cvf Test.jar My*.class
```

Now enter the following command to run the Test.jar file on the /license.txt file and save the result in a folder named /licentse-out.txt, exactly as we did previously.

```
$hadoop jar Test.jar MyWordCounter /license.txt /license-out.txt
```

Similarly, type in the following command to copy the license-out.txt file from the Hadoop distributed file system to the local file system, and open license-out.txt/part-r-00000 with nano:

```
$hdfs dfs -copyToLocal /license-out.txt ~/
$nano ~/license-out.txt/part-r-00000
```

Finally, type in the following command to delete the /licentse-out.txt directory:

```
$hdfs dfs -rm -r /license-out.txt
```

Example 11.2 shows a variation of the previous Java program. It counts the number of characters in documents. The main difference is in the MyMapper class, where it counts the characters rather than the words. The MyReducer class and the main class are quite similar. Also different from the previous example, both the MyMapper class and the MyReducer class extend from the MapReduceBase class, which is common for earlier versions of Hadoop. You can compile and run this program exactly the same as the previous program.

EXAMPLE 11.2   JAVA HADOOP CHARACTER COUNT PROGRAM

```java
import java.io.IOException;
import java.util.Iterator;
import org.apache.hadoop.io.IntWritable;
import org.apache.hadoop.io.Text;
import org.apache.hadoop.mapred.MapReduceBase;
import org.apache.hadoop.mapred.OutputCollector;
import org.apache.hadoop.mapred.Mapper;
import org.apache.hadoop.mapred.Reducer;
import org.apache.hadoop.mapred.Reporter;
import org.apache.hadoop.io.LongWritable;
import org.apache.hadoop.fs.Path;
import org.apache.hadoop.mapred.FileInputFormat;
import org.apache.hadoop.mapred.FileOutputFormat;
import org.apache.hadoop.mapred.JobClient;
import org.apache.hadoop.mapred.JobConf;
import org.apache.hadoop.mapred.TextInputFormat;
import org.apache.hadoop.mapred.TextOutputFormat;

//The MyMapper class - MapReduce's Map Phase
class MyMapper extends MapReduceBase implements
Mapper<LongWritable,Text,Text, IntWritable>{
    public void map(LongWritable key, Text value,OutputCollector<Text,
IntWritable> output, Reporter reporter) throws IOException{
        String line = value.toString();
        String  tokenizer[] = line.split("");
        for(String SingleChar : tokenizer)
        {
            Text charKey = new Text(SingleChar);
            IntWritable One = new IntWritable(1);
            output.collect(charKey, One);
        }
    }

}
//The MyReducer class - MapReduce's Reduce Phase
class MyReducer  extends MapReduceBase implements
Reducer<Text,IntWritable, Text,IntWritable> {
    public void reduce(Text key, Iterator<IntWritable> values, OutputCol
lector<Text,IntWritable> output, Reporter reporter) throws IOException {
        int sum=0;
        while (values.hasNext()) {
            sum+=values.next().get();
        }
        output.collect(key,new IntWritable(sum));
    }
}
public class MyCharCounter {
    public static void main(String[] args) throws IOException{
```

```
        JobConf conf = new JobConf(MyCharCounter.class);
        conf.setJobName("Character Count");
        conf.setOutputKeyClass(Text.class);
        conf.setOutputValueClass(IntWritable.class);
        conf.setMapperClass(MyMapper.class);
        conf.setCombinerClass(MyReducer.class);
        conf.setReducerClass(MyReducer.class);
        conf.setInputFormat(TextInputFormat.class);
        conf.setOutputFormat(TextOutputFormat.class);
        FileInputFormat.setInputPaths(conf,new Path(args[0]));
        FileOutputFormat.setOutputPath(conf,new Path(args[1]));
        JobClient.runJob(conf);
    }
}
```

Let's look at another Java Hadoop program. Assume for the purpose of a simple example that a text file named `grades.txt` contains the student marks for four different subjects as shown in the following excerpt. In each line, data are tab-separated. The first item is the student's given name, and the second to fifth are the student's marks in the respective subjects.

```
Tony        56   76   83   42
William     33   91   82   73
Alan        76   39   65   89
Tom         51   68   77   52
John        88   54   94   98
```

Example 11.3 shows another Java Hadoop program, which reads the student marks from a file and counts the total marks for each student. Again, there are three classes. The `MyMapper` class counts the characters rather than the words. The `MyReducer` class and the main class are quite similar.

EXAMPLE 11.3   JAVA HADOOP TOTAL MARKS PROGRAM

```
import java.util.*;
import java.io.IOException;
import org.apache.hadoop.fs.Path;
import org.apache.hadoop.conf.*;
import org.apache.hadoop.io.*;
import org.apache.hadoop.mapred.*;
import org.apache.hadoop.util.*;

//Mapper class
class MyMapper extends MapReduceBase implements
    Mapper<LongWritable, Text, Text, IntWritable>
    {
        //Map function
        public void map(LongWritable key, Text value,
        OutputCollector<Text, IntWritable> output,
```

```
    Reporter reporter) throws IOException {
        String line = value.toString();    //read each line
        String lasttoken = null;
        //separate items in each line
        StringTokenizer s = new StringTokenizer(line,"\t");
        String name = s.nextToken();       //get the student name

        while(s.hasMoreTokens()) {
            lasttoken = s.nextToken();     //get all the subject marks
        }
        int mark = Integer.parseInt(lasttoken);
        output.collect(new Text(name), new IntWritable(mark));
    }
}
//Reducer class
class MyReduce extends MapReduceBase implements Reducer< Text,
IntWritable, Text, IntWritable > {

    //Reduce function
    public void reduce( Text key, Iterator <IntWritable> values,
    OutputCollector<Text, IntWritable> output, Reporter reporter)
throws IOException {
        int sum=0;
        while (values.hasNext()) {
            sum+=values.next().get();      //add all the subject marks
for each student
        }
        //return the total marks of each student
        output.collect(key, new IntWritable(sum));
    }
}

//The main class
public class MyMarker {


    //Main function
    public static void main(String args[])throws Exception {
        JobConf conf = new JobConf(MyMarker.class);

        conf.setJobName("max_eletricityunits");
        conf.setOutputKeyClass(Text.class);
        conf.setOutputValueClass(IntWritable.class);
        conf.setMapperClass(MyMapper.class);
        conf.setCombinerClass(MyReduce.class);
        conf.setReducerClass(MyReduce.class);
        conf.setInputFormat(TextInputFormat.class);
        conf.setOutputFormat(TextOutputFormat.class);
```

```
        FileInputFormat.setInputPaths(conf, new Path(args[0]));
        FileOutputFormat.setOutputPath(conf, new Path(args[1]));

        JobClient.runJob(conf);
    }
}
```

Type in the following commands to compile and to run the Java program:

```
$javac -cp $(hadoop classpath) MyMarker.java
$jar -cvf Test.jar My*.class
$hdfs dfs -copyFromLocal ~/marks.txt /marks.txt
$hadoop jar Test.jar MyMarker /marks.txt /marks-out.txt
$hdfs dfs -copyToLocal /marks-out.txt ~/
$cat ~/marks-out.txt/part-r-00000
```

Finally, type in the following command to delete the /marks-out.txt directory:

```
$hdfs dfs -rm -r /marks-out.txt
```

11.9 Summary

This chapter introduced the concept of big data, the sources of big data, the three Vs of big data, and the benefits of big data. It also introduced Hadoop, the open source software for big data, and showed how to download, set up, and use Hadoop software on Raspberry Pi.

11.10 Chapter Review Questions

Q11.1.   What is big data?

Q11.2.   Explain terms of kilobyte, megabyte, gigabyte, terabyte, petabyte, exabyte, and zettabyte.

Q11.3.   What are the sources of big data?

Q11.4.   What are the three Vs of big data?

Q11.5.   What is Hadoop?

Q11.6.   What are the key components of Hadoop?

Q11.7.   What are HDFS, MapReduce, Hadoop Common, and Hadoop YARN?

Q11.8.   What are the Hadoop five services?

Q11.9.   How do you set up SSH for Hadoop?

Q11.10. How do you start and stop Hadoop?

Java Documentation and Archiving Tools and Online Resources

This appendix shows how to use the tools that Java provides for self-documenting and archiving your code, and it lists the most important online resources for learning about Java.

Javadoc Tutorial

Documentation is important in many science and engineering disciplines, so maintaining it becomes a familiar habit. For software, the situation is slightly different, as the software may be changing constantly. Creating documents after the software has been created and then modifying them every time the software is changed is inefficient and cumbersome. To solve this problem, the Java JDK provides a tool called `javadoc`, which allows users to generate Java code documentation in HTML format from Java source code using a predefined comment format.

Recall that in Java, you use `//` to create a single-line comment and `/* */` for multiple-line comments.

```
//This is a single line comment

/*
This is a multiple
line comment
*/
```

Once you've invoked the `javadoc` command, you can then use /**   */ to create a Java document. In the following example, the comment placed at the beginning of the code creates a document for the Java program. The `@author` tag specifies the author of the program, the `@version` tag specifies the version, the `@since` tag specifies the date of the software, and the `@see` tag specifies the URL of the program.

```
/**
 * The HelloWorld program implements an application that
 * simply displays "Hello World!" to the standard output.
 *
 * @author   Dr Perry Xiao
 * @version 1.0
 * @since    2018-12-08
 * @see <a href="http://www.yourcompany.com/yourApp/">Hello World</a>
 */
public class HelloWorld {
    public static void main(String[] args) {
        System.out.println("Hello World!");
    }
}
```

If you have a method in the program, you can also use `javadoc` to create documentation for the method, as illustrated next. The `@param` tag specifies the input parameters of the method, and `@return` tag specifies its output.

```
/**
 * This method is used to print title and name on screen
 *
 * @param title  This is the title
 * @param name   This is the name
 */
 public void printName (String title, String name)
 {
     System.out.println("Hello " + title + " " +name);
 }
```

You can put these two pieces of the code together to create a full Java program. Here is the full program with `javadoc` comments.

```
/**
 * The HelloWorld program implements an application that
```

```
 * simply displays "Hello World!" to the standard output.
 *
 * @author  Dr Perry Xiao
 * @version 1.0
 * @since   2018-12-08
 * @see <a href="http://www.yourcompany.com/yourApp/">Hello World</a>
 */
public class HelloWorld {
    /**
     * This method is used to print title and name on screen
     *
     * @param title  This is the title
     * @param name   This is the name
     *         */
    public void printName (String title, String name)
    {
        System.out.println("Hello " + title + " " +name);
    }
    /**
     * This is the main method of the program
     *
     * @param args  This is the command line parameter,
     *                 where args[0] is title, and args[1] is name
     */
    public static void main(String[] args) {
        HelloWorld hw = new HelloWorld();
        hw.printName(args[0],args[1]);
    }
}
```

To create the Java document of this program, just type the following command in a Windows terminal:

```
javadoc HelloWorld.java
```

Figure A.1 shows the result of executing this command to create Java documents and the corresponding HTML files and the `resources` subdirectory created. The Java documentation is in HTML format, as web pages. The main page is named `index.html`.

Figure A.2 shows the `index.html` file in a browser. It is divided into sections: the header and the class information, the constructor summary and method summary, the constructor detail and method detail, and the footer.

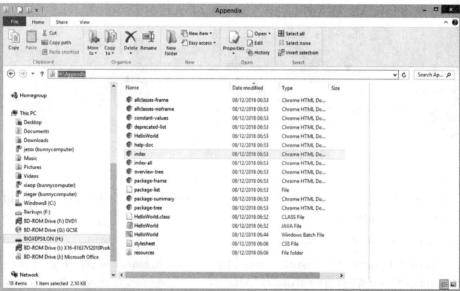

Figure A.1: The command to create Java documents (top) and the corresponding HTML files and the resources subdirectory created (bottom)

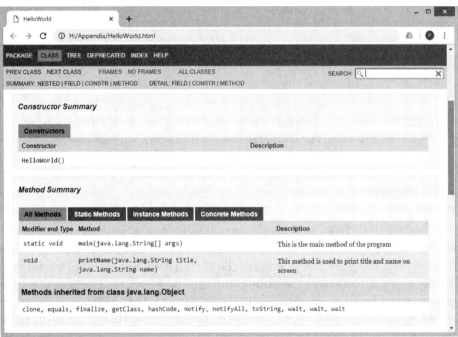

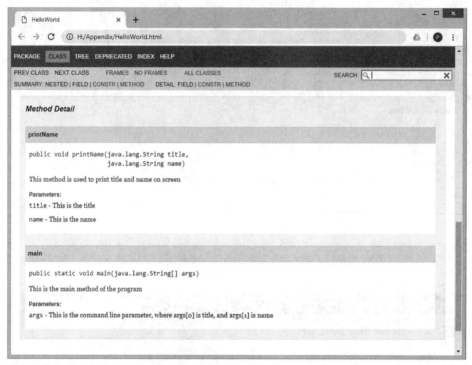

Figure A.2: The index.html file in a web browser. From top to bottom are the header and the class information, constructor summary and method summary, and method detail.

JAR Tutorial

The Java Archive (JAR) format allows you to compress and bundle multiple files into a single JAR file. JAR is a platform-independent file format, based on the popular ZIP algorithm. It mimics the Unix TAR (tape archive) file format. The jar and tar tools have the same command-line options. The Java Runtime (JRE) can run Java programs directly from the JAR file, without the need to decompress the file. JAR files can also be opened directly by the WinZIP or WinRAR program.

There are several benefits of using JAR files in your projects.

Compression: By compressing the files, you will achieve a smaller project size.

Ease of deployment: A single JAR file is much easier to deploy and distribute.

Authentication: By digitally signing the JAR file, you can provide users with authentication through the digital signature and the digital certificate.

You can use the `jar` tool to create a JAR file from multiple Java files or from multiple directories. For example, the following command creates a JAR file named `hello.jar` from two Java classes, `HelloWorld.class` and `HelloWorld2.class`:

```
jar cvf hello.jar HelloWorld.class HelloWorld2.class
```

where the options are as follows (note that the dash prefix shown in JAR documentation is optional):

-c	Creates a new archive
-v	Instructs the system to generate verbose output on standard output
-f	Specifies the archive file name, in this case `hello.jar`

To find out more about JAR options, just type **jar** alone on the command line.

```
jar
```

The following command creates a JAR file named `hello.jar` from all the Java classes (`*.class`):

```
jar cvf hello.jar *.class
```

The following command creates a JAR file named `hello.jar` from all the Java classes (`*.class`) and the subdirectory `images`:

```
jar cvf hello.jar *.class images
```

The following command creates a JAR file named `hello.jar` from all the Java classes (`*.class`) in the subdirectory `ProjectA`:

```
jar cvf hello.jar ProjectA/*.class
```

The following command creates a JAR file named `hello.jar` from three subdirectories named `DIR1`, `DIR2`, and `DIR3`. Unlike the previous example, which added only class files, this example adds all the files to the JAR file:

```
jar cvf hello.jar DIR1 DIR2 DIR3
```

One of the most important usages of the JAR tool is to create executable JAR files. This way, you can run your Java program just by double-clicking the executable JAR file.

To create an executable JAR file, you will first need to create a manifest file, which specifies the main Java class you want to run. For example, the following manifest file specifies that the main Java class is `HelloWorld.class` and the class path is `hello.jar`:

```
Main-Class: HelloWorld
Class-Path: hello.jar
```

Save this content in a text file named `hello.mf`. The following command combines the manifest file and all of the Java (`*.class`) files to create an executable JAR file named `hello.jar`:

```
jar cmf hello.mf hello.jar *.class
```

where the option `-m` instructs JAR to include manifest information from a specified manifest file.

To run this JAR file, just double-click it in the File Explorer or type the following command in a Windows terminal:

```
java -jar hello.jar
```

Useful Java Resources

The following is a list of useful resources for Java, including documentation and download web sites, as well as sites recommending online Java books:

The Java official web site:

```
https://www.java.com/
https://www.oracle.com/java/
```

The Java SE JDK download web site:

```
https://www.oracle.com/technetwork/java/javase/downloads/index.html
```

The Java SE Documentation web site:

```
https://www.oracle.com/technetwork/java/javase/documentation/api-jsp-136079.html
```

The Java JDK version 10 API web site:

```
https://docs.oracle.com/javase/10/docs/api/overview-summary.html
```

The Javadoc web site:

```
https://www.oracle.com/technetwork/java/javase/tech/index-137868.html
https://www.tutorialspoint.com/java/java _ documentation.htm
```

The command-line `jar` tool: `jar.exe`:

```
http://docs.oracle.com/javase/7/docs/technotes/tools/windows/jar.html
```

Java books:

```
https://whatpixel.com/best-java-books/
https://dzone.com/articles/10-all-time-great-books-for-java-programrs-
best
https://www.journaldev.com/6162/5-best-core-java-books-for-beginners
https://www.javacodegeeks.com/2011/10/top-10-java-books-you-dont-want-
to-miss.html
```

Apache Maven Tutorial

When you are developing a Java software project, there are many tasks to take care of: downloading dependencies, putting JAR files on a classpath, compiling source code into binary bytecode, running tests, packaging bytecode into deployable JAR files, deploying JAR files to a remote repository server, and so on. Apache Maven, a software project management and comprehension tool that is based on the concept of a project object model (POM), can automate all of these tasks. Maven is intended primarily as a tool for managing Java-based projects, but it can also be used for projects using other programming languages such as C# and Ruby. As alternatives to Maven, Ant and Gradle are also popular software project management tools.

For more information about Ant, see `http://ant.apache.org/`.

For more information about Gradle, see `https://gradle.org/guides/#getting-started`.

For a comparison between Ant, Maven, and Gradle, see `https://www.baeldung.com/ant-maven-gradle`.

Downloading Maven

You can download Apache Maven as a zipped file, `apache-maven-3.6.0-bin.zip`, from the following address:

```
https://maven.apache.org/download.cgi
```

After downloading it, just unzip the file to a directory, for example, `c:\apache-maven-3.6.0\`. Once it is unzipped, you will find the Maven program, `mvn.jar`, in the `bin` subdirectory. To test your Maven, just run the following command:

```
mvn --version
```

But you need to add `c:\apache-maven-3.6.0\bin\` to your system PATH first, or simply run the Maven program with its full path. Either way, the result should show the version of Maven, the version of Java, and the information about your operating system, as shown in Figure B.1.

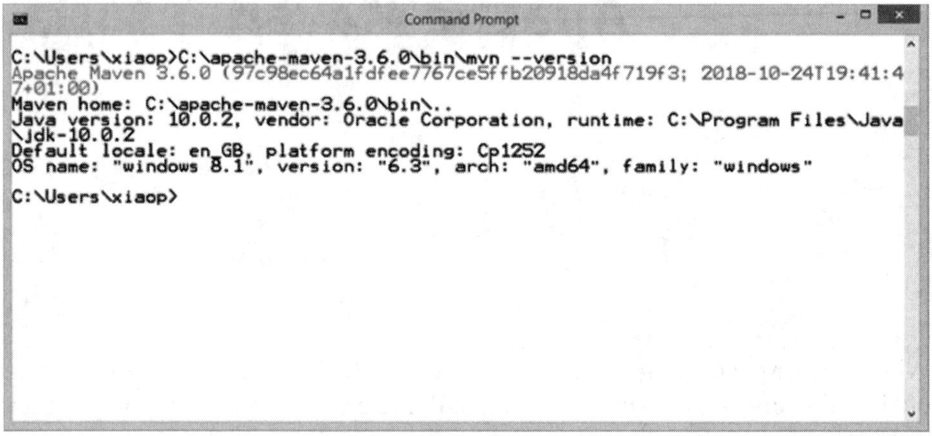

Figure B.1: Displaying the version of Apache Maven

Creating a Maven Project

The following command creates a Maven project, called `my-app`, with a group ID of `com.mycompany.app`, as shown in Figure B.2.

```
mvn archetype:generate -DgroupId=com.mycompany.app -DartifactId=my-app
-DarchetypeArtifactId=maven-archetype-quickstart -DinteractiveMode=false
```

Once the project is successfully created, a project directory called `my-app` will be created, and Figure B.3 shows the structure of the project directory, which will basically include a `pom.xml` file, an `App.java` file, and an `AppTest` `.java` file.

The `pom.xml` file, as shown next, is the core of the Maven project, which describes the project details, manages dependencies, and configures plugins for building the software. Please make sure you insert the `<Properties>` section as shown in the listing.

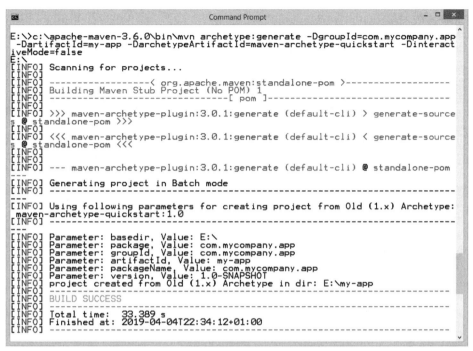

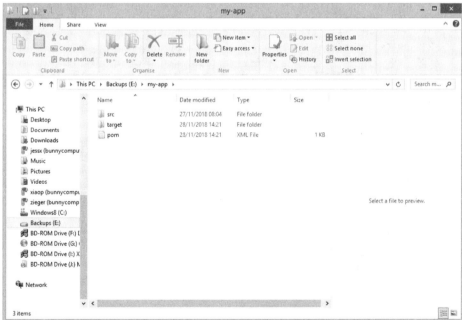

Figure B.2: The command to create a Maven project, messages to show the project is created successfully (top), and project directory and content (bottom)

```
my-app
|--pom.xml
`-- target
`-- src
   |-- main
   |  `-- java
   |     `-- com
   |        `-- mycompany
   |           `-- app
   |              `-- App.java
   `-- test
      `-- java
         `-- com
            `-- mycompany
               `-- app
                  `-- AppTest.java
```

Figure B.3: The structure of a Maven project directory

```
<project xmlns="http://maven.apache.org/POM/4.0.0"
xmlns:xsi="http://www.w3.org/2001/XMLSchema-instance"
  xsi:schemaLocation="http://maven.apache.org/POM/4.0.0 http://maven.
apache.org/maven-v4_0_0.xsd">
  <modelVersion>4.0.0</modelVersion>
  <groupId>com.mycompany.app</groupId>
  <artifactId>my-app</artifactId>
  <packaging>jar</packaging>
  <version>1.0-SNAPSHOT</version>
  <name>my-app</name>
  <url>http://maven.apache.org</url>
  <properties>
    <maven.compiler.source>1.8</maven.compiler.source>
    <maven.compiler.target>1.8</maven.compiler.target>
  </properties>

  <dependencies>
    <dependency>
      <groupId>junit</groupId>
      <artifactId>junit</artifactId>
      <version>3.8.1</version>
      <scope>test</scope>
    </dependency>
  </dependencies>
</project>
```

The App.java file, shown next, is the main Java program of the project, which specifies what your project will do. In this example, it just displays "Hello world!"

on the screen. The `AppTest.java` file, also shown, is the app program that calls the `App.java` program to run.

This is the code for the `App.java` file:

```
package com.mycompany.app;

/**
 * Hello world!
 *
 */
public class App
{
    public static void main( String[] args )
    {
        System.out.println( "Hello World!" );
    }
}
```

This is the code for the `AppTest.java` file:

```
package com.mycompany.app;

import junit.framework.Test;
import junit.framework.TestCase;
import junit.framework.TestSuite;

/**
 * Unit test for simple App.
 */
public class AppTest
    extends TestCase
{
    /**
     * Create the test case
     *
     * @param testName name of the test case
     */
    public AppTest( String testName )
    {
        super( testName );
    }

    /**
     * @return the suite of tests being tested
     */
    public static Test suite()
    {
        return new TestSuite( AppTest.class );
    }
```

```
    /**
     * Rigourous Test :-)
     */
    public void testApp()
    {
        assertTrue( true );
    }
}
```

Compiling and Building the Maven Project

Type the following command to compile and build the project, as shown in Figure B.4. This will compile the project and package the binary bytecode into a deployable JAR file called `my-app-1.0-SNAPSHOT.jar` in the `/my-app/target/` subdirectory.

```
mvn package
```

Running the Maven Project

Type the following command to run the project, which should display "Hello world!" as shown in Figure B.5.

```
java -cp target/my-app-1.0-SNAPSHOT.jar com.mycompany.app.App
```

For more information about Maven, see the following resources:

https://maven.apache.org/guides/getting-started/maven-in-five-minutes.html

https://www.javatpoint.com/maven-tutorial

http://tutorials.jenkov.com/maven/maven-tutorial.html

https://www.guru99.com/maven-tutorial.html

https://examples.javacodegeeks.com/enterprise-java/maven/create-java-project-with-maven-example/

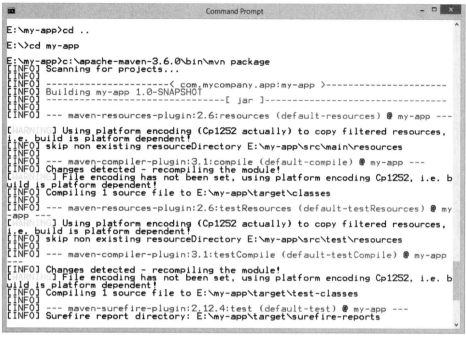

Figure B.4: The command to compile and build the Maven project (top) and the messages to show the project has been successfully built (bottom)

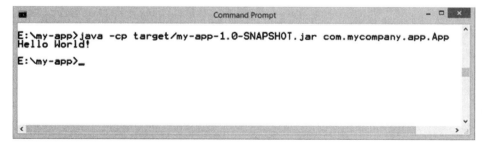

Figure B.5: The result of the command to run the Maven project

Git and GitHub Tutorial

Git is one of the most widely used distributed/decentralized version control systems. To use Git, you first need to download and install it on your computer. For Windows, you can download the Git installer (at the time of writing, a file named `Git-2.20.1-64-bit.exe`) from the following web site:

```
https://gitforwindows.org/
```

For other operating systems, check the following web site for details:

```
https://www.atlassian.com/git/tutorials/install-git
```

Double-click the installer file `Git-2.20.1-64-bit.exe` to install Git, and accept all the default settings during the installation. After successful installation, run the program named Git GUI, shown in Figure C.1A. Select Create New Repository, and a new window will pop up, as shown in Figure C.1B. Select the directory where your project will be located, in this case, `E:\MyProject`, and then click the Create button. The Git GUI program's main interface will appear, as shown in Figure C.1C. From the Repository menu, select Git Bash, which is a terminal program, as shown in Figure C.1D. This is where you are mainly going to use Git. You can use standard commands, such as **pwd** to display the current project directory and **dir** or **ls** to list its content, as shown in Figure C.1D.

For more details about Git, check this free online *Pro Git* book:

```
https://git-scm.com/book/en/v2
```

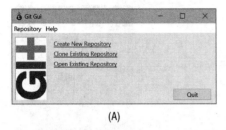

(A)

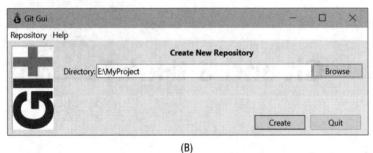

(B)

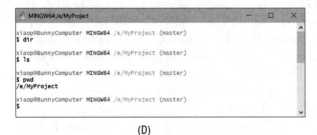

(C)

(D)

Figure C.1: The Git GUI program and Git Bash program

To start with version control using Git, first you will need to use the `git config --global` command to configure your name and your email address in the Git Bash program, as shown in Figure C.2 (top). You can also use the `git config --list` command to list all your configurations.

Then type `git init` to initialize the version control. This will generate a hidden directory named .git, which will contain all the details about your project version control. You can also type `git status` to get the status of the project version control, as shown in Figure C.2 (bottom). Each Git project is called a *repository*.

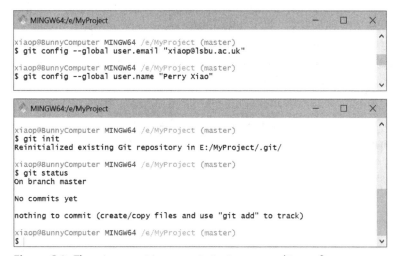

Figure C.2: The `git config -- global` command to configure your name and email (top) and the `git init` and `git status` commands (bottom) in the Git Bash program

Now you can add your Java programs to your project, an operation called *staging*. Let's use the `HelloWorld.java` program shown in Example 2.1 in Chapter 2 as an example. Use Windows Explorer to add the `HelloWorld.java` program into your project directory at E:\MyProject. It is always useful to have a README file in your project to explain what your project is about. You can either use a text editor to create a text file named README.md (*not* README.md.txt) in your project directory or simply type the following command in the Git Bash window:

```
echo "# MyProject" >> README.md
```

To add files to Git version control, type the following command in the Git Bash program:

```
git add .
```

This will add all your files in the current directory into the Git version control; see Figure C.3 (top). The `git add .` command does not add subdirectories; so, to add everything, including files and subdirectories, type

```
git add --all
```

or

```
git add -A
```

You can also use the `git rm <file name>` or `git reset <file name>` command to remove any files from the version control. When you are happy with your project, you can commit your project, which will save the changes in Git, as shown in Figure C.3 (bottom). You can commit as many times as you like. You can also use `git log` to trace all the changes, and you can use the `git reset --soft HEAD~1` command to revert the commit.

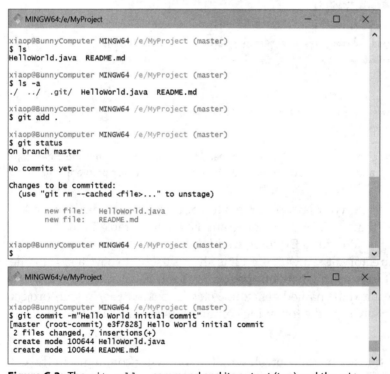

Figure C.3: The `git add .` command and its output (top) and the `git commit` command and output (bottom) in the Git Bash program

To share the project with others, you will need a remote version control server; the obvious choice is GitHub, one of the most popular web-based version control hosting servers. To use GitHub, just go to its website (`https://github.com/`) and create an account on GitHub (Figure C.4A). After you sign up and log in, click the Start A Project button and create a new repository for your project (Figure C.4B). Give your project a name, and use all the default settings to create the repository (Figure C.4C). A new Quick setup page will appear, from which you can find the HTTPS link address to your new repository. In this example, it is as follows:

```
https://github.com/PerryXiao2015/MyProject.git
```

If you want to use an SSH link, it will be as follows:

```
git@github.com:PerryXiao2015/MyProject.git
```

> **NOTE**   Secure Shell (SSH) is a communication protocol that provides secure remote login, with authentication and encryption. It is designed to replace the traditional unsecure remote login protocols such as Telnet and rlogin. Hypertext Transfer Protocol Secure (HTTPS) is a secure version of web protocol HTTP. See Chapter 9 for more details about security.

You can set your GitHub link to your local Git origin and upload, or push, your local repository to the GitHub remote repository, using the following commands:

```
git remote add origin https://github.com/PerryXiao2015/MyProject.git
git push -u origin master
```

or

```
git remote add origin git@github.com:PerryXiao2015/MyProject.git
git push -u origin master
```

Before you can push your local repository to the GitHub remote repository, you need to make sure the contents will be encrypted, by generating a public/private key pair. Figure C.5 (top) shows how to generate an RSA key pair. (The algorithm is named after its creators Rivest Shamir Adleman.) RSA is a public-key encryption algorithm that is widely used for secure data transmission. You can also use different algorithms to generate a public/private key pair. More details about encryption, RSA, and public/private key pairs are available in Chapter 9. The key pair generated is stored in the `.ssh` hidden directory. By default, the private key is stored in a file named `id_rsa`, and the public key is stored in a file named `id_rsa.pub`. Figure C.5 (bottom) shows how to display the `.ssh` hidden directory and the public key. The content of the public key should start with `ssh-rsa`.

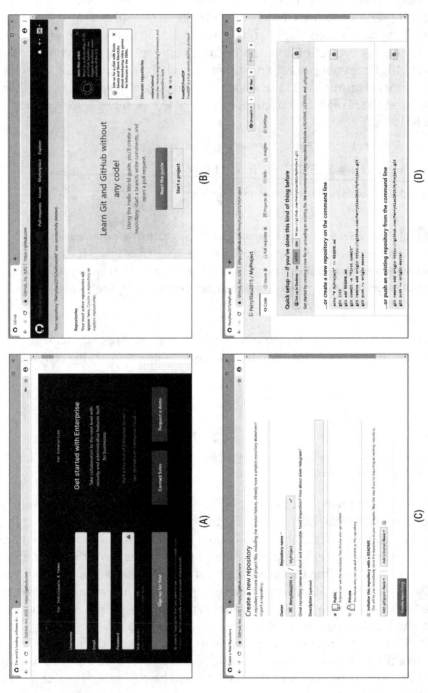

Figure C.4: The GitHub web site for signing up (A), starting a project (B), creating a new repository (C), and quick setup (D)

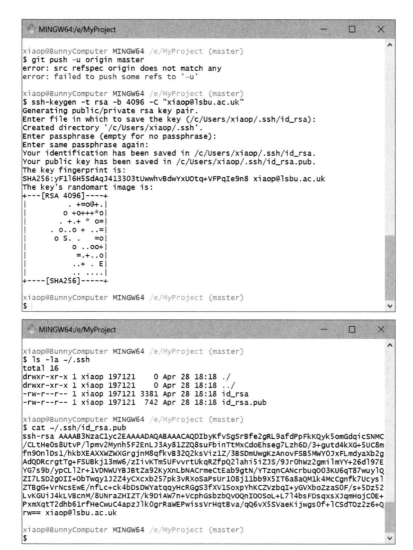

Figure C.5: The Git command to generate an RSA public/private key pair (top) and the Git commands to display the `.ssh` hidden directory, create the Hub remote repository to your Git project, and push your project to the remote repository (bottom)

Copy the public key, and then go to the GitHub website, select Deploy Keys from the project settings, and add a new key. Give it a name, paste the public key into the key content, and click the green Add Key button, as shown in Figure C.6.

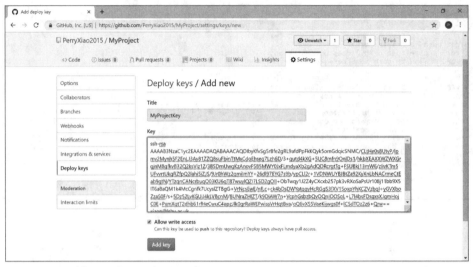

Figure C.6: Add a new key in the GitHub project site.

Figure C.7A shows how to add your GitHub project site and how to push the local Git repository to the remote GitHub repository. A GitHub login window will appear, as shown in Figure C.7B. Type in your GitHub login username and password, and your GitHub project site will be updated with your files, as shown in Figure C.7C.

Now, let's modify the `HelloWorld.java` program to make it like Example 2.2, with `args[0]` used. If you run the **git status** command, it will show that the `HelloWorld.java` program has been modified by displaying it in red (Figure C.8). The red color markup here indicates that the changes have not been staged to commit. You need to use the **git add .** or **git add -A** command to add changed files to the local repository. If you run **git status** again, it will show that the `HelloWorld.java` program has been modified by displaying it in green. The green color markup here indicates the changes are ready to commit.

You can commit the program again and push it to the GitHub master repository. In Figure C.9, you can see that the files in the GitHub site have been updated accordingly. The GitHub web site also shows how many commits have been made, along with details and corresponding files of each commit. Each commit represents a different version of your project code.

You can also use the **git log --online** command to show the history of commits from the Git Bash window, as shown in Figure C.10 (top). Each commit has a unique number, presented in hexadecimal format. If a disastrous event happens, you can always revert to the previous version of a program by using the **git checkout <unique number>** command, as shown in Figure C.10 (bottom). Now your local repository files will revert to the previous version.

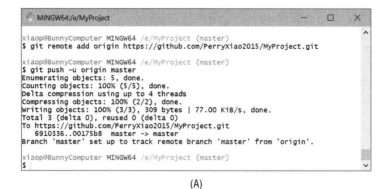

(A)

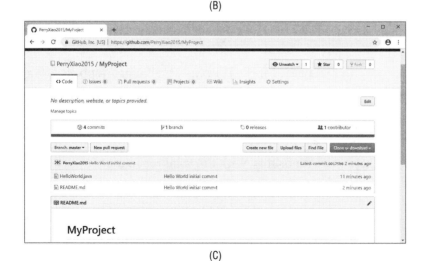

(C)

Figure C.7: Git commands to add GitHub site (A), GitHub login window (B), and updated GitHub project site (C)

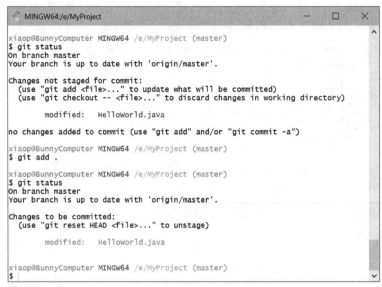

Figure C.8: Git commands to update the changes

Terms and Definitions

The following is a list of Git terms.

Repository (or Repo)   The directory that stores all the files and all the sub-directories of your project

Stage   To add files and subdirectories to your repository

Commit   To save the changes to your repository

Branch   A version of the repository that diverges from the main working project

Master   The primary branch of all repositories

Origin   The conventional name for the primary version of a repository

Head   The most current commit of your repository

Clone   To make a copy of a repository

Fork   To create a copy of a repository

Push   To update a remote repository with the local repository

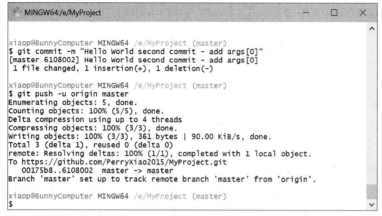

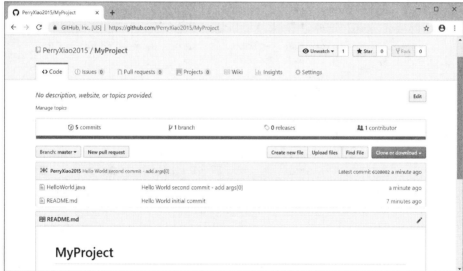

Figure C.9: Git commands to commit the changes and push the local repository to the GitHub remote repository (top) and the result in the updated GitHub project site (bottom)

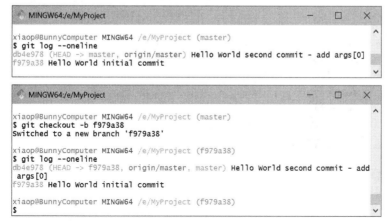

Figure C.10: Git commands to display the history of commits through the online log file (top) and check out different versions of a program (bottom)

Pull To fetch and download content from a remote repository and immediately update the local repository to match that content

CheckOut To switch to different versions of the repository

Cheat Sheet

Table C.1 is a cheat sheet summarizing the Git commands.

Table C.1: Git Command Cheat Sheet

COMMAND CATEGORY	COMMAND	WHAT IT DOES
Configuration	`git config --global user.name "Your _ Name"`	Sets up your name in Git
	`git config --global user.email "YourEmail@ wherever.com"`	Sets up your email address in Git
	`git config --list`	Lists your Git configuration
Starting a Repository	`git init`	Initializes Git
	`git status`	Gets the status of Git
Staging Files	`git add <filename> <filename> ...`	Adds files to the local repository
	`git add .`	Adds all files in the current directory (subdirectories not included) to the local repository
	`git add –all`	Adds all files in the current directory and subdirectories to the local repository
	`git add –A`	Adds all files in the current directory and subdirectories to the local repository
	`git rm <filename>`	Removes a file from the local repository
	`git reset <filename>`	Removes a file from the local repository
Generating an SSH Public/ Private Key Pair	`ssh-keygen -t rsa -b 4096 -C "your _ email@example.com"`	Generates an RSA key pair

COMMAND CATEGORY	COMMAND	WHAT IT DOES
	`ls -la ~/.ssh`	Lists the content of the `.ssh` hidden directory
	`cat ~/.ssh/id_rsa.pub`	Displays the content of the RSA public key
Committing to a Repository	`git commit -m "Your message here"`	Saves changes to the local repository
	`git commit --amend -m "Your amend message here"`	Modifies the commit
	`git reset --soft HEAD~1`	Reverts the commit
	`git log`	Displays the history of commits
Pushing and Pulling from GitHub	`git remote add origin <your GitHut link>`	Sets your GitHub link to the local Git origin
	`git push -u origin master`	Uploads the local repository to the GitHub remote repository
	`git clone <project name>`	Gets a copy of an existing Git repository
	`git pull`	Fetches and downloads content from a remote repository and immediately updates the local repository to match that content
	`git log --oneline`	Displays the history of the remote repository commits
	`git remote rm origin`	Removes the remote origin
Branching	`git branch`	Creates a version of the repository that diverges from the main working project
	`git branch <branch name>`	Creates a version of the repository with a given name
	`git checkout <branch name>`	Sets the current branch as the main working project
	`git merge <branch name>`	Merges changes from one branch into another

Index